# MACE STUTZMAN

## Jeff Lombardo

ISBN 978-1-63784-060-3 (paperback)
ISBN 978-1-63784-061-0 (digital)

Hawes & Jenkins Publishing
16427 N Scottsdale Road Suite 410
Scottsdale, AZ 85254
www.hawesjenkins.com

Printed in the United States of America

For Bill Viera, whose intelligence became part of the soul of Mace Stutzman. For my brother Chris Lombardo who has always been there for me in the most loving, strong, and pragmatic ways.

# CHAPTER 1

His mother was the real killer. She was the ruthless assassin of dreams, the destroyer of hope, the murderess of joy, the saboteur of laughter. No one could be around her and not be deflated by her relentless pedantic preaching about how the New Testament should be interpreted. In her personal sermons, there was no love to be found anywhere within the biblical text. She twisted everything to suit her abject pursuit of coldness. Sadly, she was not responsible for her horrendous emotional and intellectual structure.

Once, she was an innocent little girl. She had a loving mother and father and no siblings. She had no religion then. Neither did her parents. The family did not go to church. In fact, her mother and father were extremely quiet individuals who kept to themselves so much so that the few people they did know, thought of them as somewhat of a mystery. The reality was, however, that they were not at all mysterious. They were merely extremely quiet souls. One could say that they were so, not only with their neighbors and acquaintances but with each other.

One night, her father tiptoed into the little girl's bedroom and sat on his daughter's bed. He pulled back the covers and began gently rubbing the girl as if she were a lover and not a helpless child. She did not wake from her usual deep sleep, even when her father barely penetrated her tiny body. She felt everything that was happening to her, but it was all as if it was a dream and not an unpleasant one. Her father tried to be gentle with the unconscious virgin. He did not wish to hurt her physically, though he had no clue as to the unfathomable devastation of his actions of this night would begin to cause.

When he finished, he lingered for several minutes, reverting to the gentle rubbing of his daughter before he kissed her flush on her pretty lips before slinking soundlessly back to his marital bed. Never waking during her father's daring exploit, the entire incident had been indelibly imprinted upon the deepest parts of her. The physical feeling had hit her brain, and her brain transferred it to memory. Even though she did not yet consciously understand what had happened to her, the events slipped immediately into her subconscious mind where the first seeds of devastation were sowed.

His mother was the real killer, but she had mitigating circumstances. Add twelve years and over two thousand more nocturnal visits by her father into his daughter's bedroom, and one could easily understand how her spirit became irreversibly crooked.

But perhaps I am wrong. Maybe the innocent little girl's father was the real killer. After all, for over a decade, he had gotten away with a crime that many believe is worse than taking someone's life. But can we truly place the blame on a selfish, ignorant simpleton who preceded the actual killer by two generations? Perhaps I am wrong to place so much responsibility upon the killer's mother. I am simply surmising, as I try to recreate for you how the story unfolds. Unfortunately, this is the tale of how life can truly develop. It is unbalanced, lopsided, and unmerciful, especially where mercy is needed the most. Could his mother be held accountable? Could her father? No one knows how far back you can trace the origin of a murderous heart. I want to stay focused on the mother who started life as does every other little girl, formative, helpless. As time slowly passed and her father's nightly visits continued, the little girl began to wake up and see, not only feel what was happening. Only six and not even enrolled in school yet, she began to analyze what her father was doing. First, he was coming into her room.

Second, he was being affectionate when he rubbed her. Third, it hurt her when he put that big part of his body inside her. Fourth, his kisses were different from the ones he gave her in front of Mommy, but they were not unpleasant. In fact, when she was a little girl, her father's kisses were always gentle.

Fifth, when he was finished, her father would always tell her, "Remember, these nighttimes we spend together are yours and my secret, okay, sweetheart?"

She would answer, "Okay, Daddy," and mean it.

But unknown to her for many years by agreeing to keep the secret, she in effect gave up her voice in these situations.

But she was always thinking, always analyzing, as best she could. As the years went by and she took a school bus seventeen miles from the farm to her small public school, she never heard anyone talk about father-daughter relationships. Not only was she voiceless about her sexual abuse, but she also did not know she was being abused. There was no TV on the farm, no radio, no newspaper delivery, and no telephone. Whatever the great outside world was, it was an infinity away from this relatively isolated child.

She grew to believe her father's visits were normal, and if he was absent for more than a couple of nights, she missed him. She almost yearned for him, and the attention she had come to believe was special.

In her life, there were no toys ever. There were just chores, school, homework, and learning to cook, sew, knit, and crochet, which she learned from her mother. Of course, there were her father's regular late-night visits. Her mother was weak-willed and often ill, hosting a variety of ailments from chronic fatigue syndrome before it was a recognized illness, to leukemia, which finally claimed her life when her daughter was only fifteen. It was no wonder she would sleep through the night. Her husband would spend extended periods with his daughter. Elise's mother was always exhausted from each of the typical workdays on the farm. There were few women who needed extended sleep more than she did. Though a frail and barely educated woman, she bore her physical sorrows elegantly, only speaking about them to her husband on rare occasions. Her death left her husband alone with his daughter.

It was another year after her mother died before the daughter first heard about the sinfulness of father-daughter relationships. An extremely quiet and shy teenager, she had very few even casual friendships. She did have one friend, a girl not unlike herself. She, too, was quiet and shy and had been abused by her father for many years. The real killer in the story was attracted to her friend's quiet and shyness. She had no way of knowing about the abuse she was experiencing, but not long after beginning her third year of high school in the tiny school of eighty-three, about 250 feet from the three-room grade school she had attended, the girls began to talk about the Bible. The conversation was predicated by a friend who lived eleven miles from their school in the exact opposite direction from where the future murderess of joy lived. She attended a church thirteen miles farther away from her home in that same exact opposite direction. The girls who got to school by bus did not have the ability to see each other after school, except when the school buses were made aware of the approximate ending time of an event. The result was that the girls talked only at school and almost exclusively to one another.

One day, the little friend started talking. "Do you read the Bible?"

Her much taller friend answered, "No. My father and I don't even own one. Why?"

"I've been talking with a couple of women at the church lately about something that's really beginning to bother me."

"What is it?"

"Can you keep a huge secret, please?"

"I've never kept a secret before, but I think I can."

"I really need you to swear not to tell anyone because if anyone, but you knew this, I'll be mortified."

"I promise I'll keep the secret. Besides, I hardly ever talk to anybody but you anyway."

"Okay, I'll tell you."

Little Edna was in a tangled bundle of knotted nerves but was excited to share with her friend. "My father's been abusing me for a long time, and it's really beginning to hurt me."

"How does he abuse you? Does he hit you?"

"He does that too, but what's really bothering me is that he's abusing me sexually."

"What do you mean sexually?"

"He comes into my room night after night and has intercourse with me."

Elise plummeted into a deeper state of shock.

"How did you find out it was wrong?"

"Don't you know that it's wrong?"

Edna's taller friend shuddered when asked the question.

"I've never thought about it," she answered. And she was telling the truth. She had always thought about her father's and her interactions as normal life, certainly not as a sin of which she knew nothing.

"A couple of nice old ladies at the church were talking one day while I was sitting in their midst, and the subject just came up. I don't remember where from. Then suddenly, one of the old ladies says that she was sexually abused by her father on their farm from the time she was twelve till she ran away from home when she was sixteen. Then she talked about how her father's behavior almost ruined her whole life and destroyed her first marriage before she ran away with saved grocery money to Chicago. She got help there from the priest, who also had a degree in psychology. Together, they talked about all the ways her father had hurt her both psychologically and physically."

Little Edna's only true friend listened intently while attempting to do her best to hide the fact that she was absolutely stunned.

"One night, recently while I was asleep, my father came into my bedroom and crawled into my bed like he often does, and when he began to touch me, I let out a bloodcurdling scream that shook the house and woke up my brother, sister, and my mom. My father jumped out of the bed and ran out of the room. I wonder what he said to my mom. He hasn't been back to my room since then."

Little Edna's beautiful friend remained silent, though her mind was working like an express train, trying to sort things out.

"What do you think about all that I just told you?"

Not only was the tall beauty taken aback by the question, but she was also frightened about saying something terribly wrong and embarrassing herself in front of her friend. Her swiftly moving mind decided to put the question back on Edna. That would be the safest path to take right now, coaxing Edna to open up and talk more about herself.

"I would think right now that the most important question is, what do you think about everything you told me?"

Edna jumped at the opportunity to continue talking about something that was shredding her soul apart.

"I'm angry more than any other feeling. I'm hurt too, but the anger and disgust are far outweighing any hurts. I want to run away right now. I want to hurt my father like he has hurt me. But nothing I could ever do to him could cause as much destruction to him as it has to me. I know where he hides his money, and I'm thinking about stealing it and running away to Chicago soon. But can you imagine how afraid I am?"

Edna had no clue how deeply she was planting the seeds of her friend's future character. "Yes, but what do you think you'll really do?"

"Steal my father's money and run away to Chicago at the end of the school year."

The buds of an early Illinois spring were decorating trees everywhere around the schoolyard and as far as the eye could see. It was too early in the season to see tall green stalks filled with fresh unshucked corn. But the fields were moist with the ultrarich soil in anticipation of the crops it would birth.

Edna's friend's only safety was in complete silence, but Edna was still bubbling over.

"I knew that what I said is a lot to take in, but I've wanted to talk with you about it for a couple of weeks."

Edna's friend wanted only to be a receptacle of information not a purveyor of it. She chose her words carefully, worrying that she would expose herself if she made a single mistake.

"I totally support whatever you choose to do. Your plan sounds very bold and brave."

In an instant, Edna leaped toward her friend and hugged her affectionately around her neck as she joyfully spoke her next words.

"You're my first and only friend that I've told about this. If you had not understood and accepted me, it would have broken my heart."

As Edna spoke, her friend stiffened like an old wooden ironing board, not knowing how to respond, believing that this was the first time she had ever been touched by anyone other than her mother and father. Her arms, which could have responded lovingly by returning the hug, remained motionless at her side, pinned there by the abject, unknowing of how to return genuine affection.

Edna hardly noticed, still effervescent that her friend had not scolded her for her plan. "Thank you for not hating me," Edna said.

"Why would I hate you?"

"Because I hate my father, and I hate myself. If anyone else knew about this, they would hate me too."

"That's not true. The ladies in school don't hate you." She was making certain that she spoke each word carefully.

"They're different," Edna blurted. "The old churchwomen, they are a different breed. They'll never say anything to anyone about my business."

The two young ladies continued talking till the school bell rang. About fourscore children quickly ceased their schoolyard playing and talking, and returned to their individual classrooms for their afternoon education. Edna and her friend were the last to enter the school building.

Each young woman was imbued with different thoughts that second half of the school day. Edna was pondering her plan to run away. She was pondering whether in her family there was someone she could trust with keeping her runaway story a secret while she was able to live with them. She was wondering where she would work and whether she would be able to finish her senior year of high school while she was working and living more than a hundred miles from home.

Edna's friend was still in shock, unable to understand any of the afternoon lessons. She was contemplating for the first time the concept of sin and that her father was responsible for it. She was remembering her recent years interacting with her father, as she had passed from childhood to young womanhood. He had been kind to her, always away from the bedroom. Inside the bedroom, he had been everything a male could be with a female. He was gentle, tender, and affectionate at times. And on countless occasions, he had been passionate, paying attention to every female part of her, which would bring her intense pleasure.

Long ago, she had learned to enjoy her father's nocturnal visits. Now she had been told by a trusted friend those visits were not only sins but sins of a heinous nature. What was she to think now? What was she to do? But think she did. She wondered whether she was a bad girl because she looked forward to her father's visits. She enjoyed sex and having orgasm even though she had experienced them but had never heard the word *orgasm.*

Her teacher was speaking countless words, but she heard none of them. Her youthful mind was contemplating her next move. In a couple of hours, she would be home. What would she say to her father, who was the father she loved, as well as the man she loved? She needed more proof from Edna that father-daughter intimate relationships were wrong. She decided that she needed to see in the Bible the exact passage that would prove her father and she were longtime sinners. Even though she knew little about the Bible and certainly did not believe in it, it was the only thing she could rely on to support Edna's frightening claims.

# CHAPTER 2

Five days later, Elise owned her first Bible. She had asked Edna Wickersham to try to get her one as soon as possible. Edna, who only had one Bible, asked her lady friends if they had an extra one. She asked them when she first saw them walking up the church steps before the Sunday services began. By the time the congregation was leaving the building after the service, Matilde, the old lady who was abused by her father over fifty years ago, handed Edna a small Bible almost immediately after Edna walked outside through the front door.

"Thank you, Matty," Edna said, as she looked at the title, Holy Bible.

"You're welcome, sweety," Matilda said softly. "I have several more at home if you need them."

The next day, Edna gave a very curious and appreciative Elise the Holy Bible.

"Thank you, Edna," Elise said matter-of-factly. "I promise to read every single word."

Her previous weekend with her father had been the same as every other weekend for a long time. They worked together on the farm, then slept together at night. Elise's father was a minimalist, so was her mother. Their family home was modestly furnished. There was not even a radio. To relax, the father would read Louie Lamour novels. He would dream, Walter Mitty style, of being a cowboy who became a sheriff. He fantasized himself as a good guy who protected women, children, and entire towns from ruthless bandits and killers. He was a hero in his daydreams and had no idea how terribly wrong he was doing to his daughter. A diminutive man, several inches shorter than Elise, he was a beautiful lover. Therein lay the quandary Elise faced as she began to read the Bible.

The first night Elise possessed her new Bible, she began to read. Ahead of her were thousands of words and ideas she would have to interpret alone. She had no minister to interpret passages for her, to guide her. In fact, she barely knew anything about God. He had always been an unspoken subject around Elise and her father's home. She knew him through the Pledge of Allegiance and through occasional references to Him in textbooks. Elise went to public schools. Her teachers followed the strict rule of keeping God out of the classroom as much as possible. Elise had no idea at all about the width and breadth of God or the Bible when she began reading it. While her mentally stunted father was fantasizing about being a sheriff in Dodge City, one night after dinner, Elise opened the Bible to Genesis.

*What am I getting into?* she thought as she opened the book, which she hoped would bring some answers. Before she read the first word, she thought, *Why am I even reading this? I don't believe in this stuff. It's not my religion. I don't have any religion. My father never hurt me. He's always been kind to me. Just because Edna says my relationship with my father is wrong doesn't make it so.*

Her curiosity was propelling her, as if a tornado were behind it, to read. She began with Genesis. She read about God's creations. She thought there was a whole bunch of "let there be." When she came to the words, "Where God created man in his image," she immediately thought of God as a handsome man of about forty-five and Adam and Eve as beautiful young adults of about twenty years old. At first, she thought she was reading a simple story that would continue that way. It was sort of a love story, and it was rather pleasant reading, all the way to Genesis 3, the temptation and fall of man. Suddenly, the story turned ugly.

A talking snake told Eve if she ate some fruit from this special tree, she would be like God. So she did. A moment later, she gave some fruit to Adam. Suddenly, they both felt naked, and the next time God came to visit and found out what happened, he got angry with the snake and Adam and Eve. He told the snake to crawl on its belly forever and eat dust. He told Eve that she would suffer during childbirth and that her husband would be her boss. And he cursed the ground for Adam and told him that when he farmed the land, thorns and thistles would come up. Then he kicked Adam and Eve out of the garden of Eden and put angels with flaming swords at the east end of Eden to make sure they couldn't get back in.

Here is where Elise had her first of many problems with the Bible. She closed her new book for several minutes and lay on her bed, thinking why couldn't God have forgiven them, given them a second chance. They were obviously sorry and ashamed. This was their first mistake. God suddenly seemed cruel, especially since he created all these beautiful things. Eve thought that if a talking snake said the same things to her, a brand-new person, that she would be like God if she ate some fruit, why wouldn't she? She liked God, admired him, maybe even loved him. Of course, she would want to be like God. And God suddenly seemed hypersensitive to her and prone to extreme anger, even in an easily understandable and forgivable situation. After all, he was God, the top dog, who had just proven he could make anything.

As Elise kept reading, things became worse. She read about Cain and Abel next and about jealousy and the first murder. Again, God's reaction was strange. He said that if anyone killed Cain, vengeance would be taken on them sevenfold. Where would all these people come from who might want to kill Cain? So far in the story, it was just Adam and Eve. Cain and Abel who was now dead. If anyone would want to kill Cain, it would have to be a much younger brother or sister or Eve or Adam. Then a moment after she read where Cain moved to, the Bible said that Cain knew his wife. Where did she come from?

Elise's logic told her that his wife had to be his sister.

She continued to read. Next was the genealogy of Adam. She could not understand 930 years, 840 years, 962 years, 365 years. It did not make sense. And Methuselah lived 969 years. Elise was beginning to become angry. Even though she had lived an extremely isolated home life she had at least gone to school. She had taken science several times. Here intelligent brain asked her, "How did these uneducated people know even what a year was? Were they Cro-

Magnon people? Were they Neanderthal people?" Elise was trapped between her ability to accept what she was reading as fact and the logical questions she was suddenly having to ask after nearly every sentence.

She had developed a headache. She decided to get up, go to the bathroom, get a couple of Anacin, and go into the kitchen and take them with a glass of ice-cold water. On her way to the kitchen, she noticed her father snoozing in his favorite chair with his current Louis Lamour open on his lap. She hoped he would sleep a couple of hours so she could continue reading the Bible uninterruptedly. She took the Anacin and went back to reading. Tonight, her other homework, though minimal, would have to wait.

By the time her father came stumbling into her room three hours later, Elise had read about the great flood. She again became bewildered that God wanted to destroy every person in the world because they were sinful, except for one family. She had read about Lot's two daughters, how they slept with their father, each having a son by him to preserve the father's lineage. Their sons became great leaders of tribes.

What she had been specifically looking for, that it was a sin for fathers and daughters to sleep together, was more difficult to find. What she did read in Genesis were several instances of incest. There were stories of a man sleeping with his father's concubine, a man unwittingly sleeping with his daughters-in-law. There was Jacob sleeping with two sisters, Leah and Rachel. The story she found particularly interesting was when Abraham admitted to Abimelech that his wife was his sister—the daughter of his father but not of his mother, a half sister.

As her father crawled into bed with her, all Elise could think about were the facts that she had finished reading in Genesis. Nowhere had it said it was a sin for his father to sleep with his daughter. There had been brief discussions about incest that made her feel uneasy, but as her father affectionately put his arm around her chest, she readied herself for what might happen next. Thankfully, her father was tired and made no further moves toward her. She was fatigued too. Pondering Genesis had drained her. After the creation of the earth and Adam and Eve, Cain and Abel, etc., she did not like the story. She did not like God. She would read the rest of the Bible because she felt like a detective looking for a clue that might be buried in tens of thousands of words.

Tonight, Elise lay silently beneath her father's unmoving arm. She was deeper in thought than she had ever been. She was nearly seventeen years old, and she was wondering who she was. What was she to her father? Who did she want to become? She had never read anything like Genesis. Even though she had nearly hated what she read, she had no clue how much this book would impact the rest of her life.

# CHAPTER 3

By the time Elise was finished reading the Bible about two months later, the early corn was growing on her farm and countless others like hers. School was out, and Edna had already run away to stay with a sympathetic aunt. Edna had met her only once, many years before, but they had developed a good rapport. Before Edna left Central Illinois for Chicago, she and Elise had talked about the Bible and their fathers at least fifty more times. By the thirty-fifth conversation between them, Elise was almost begging Edna to point her to a specific verse that confirmed that father-daughter sexual relations were a sin. But Edna could not do so.

"Could you ask the old ladies to help you?" Elise asked Edna one late spring day.

"I will," Edna answered. But when she came back, she did not return with the answer Elise wanted to hear.

"None of us could find a specific passage," Edna said.

"That makes two of us," Elise answered.

When Edna left for Chicago with $953 of her father's money, she left $250 under the floor by the window. Elise had no one to bounce her questions and criticisms off. She was on her own again to figure things out for herself, to arrive through her own pondering, at her own conclusions. As she began to feel completely alone in her interpretations of myriad Bible passages, she felt a couple of facts for certain. She did not like God. The New Testament had not changed her negative opinions from the Old Testament. In her mind, there was no real love in the Bible at all. Her opinions had been severely tainted by Edna's revelations that what she and her father were doing was terribly wrong.

Elise thought throughout the summer that little Edna ran away, that most fathers slept with their daughters, that type of nocturnal goings-on was happening in all the farmhouses that seemed to spring up from the Illinois soil like corn. She wondered how something that felt so right could be so wrong. All that summer of agonizing thinking, she pondered the concept of sin. She did not like the concept of sin even though the mention and effect of it were almost everywhere in the Bible, the book to which she had become addicted.

Being alone with all these chapters, contributed much to Elise's polluted interpretations. There was simply no one to guide her through her summer of tumultuous change. Therefore, she read through the Bible as if it were a forest that was always dark, incessantly dangerous. She morphed into a young woman who believed that almost everything people did was a sin. She evolved to believe that God was evil and sinful because he had created humanity in His image, then destroyed them in bunches. It was logical to Elise that if he had truly created man in his image, then he must be intrinsically sinful. She never let go of the fact that God could not forgive Adam and Eve for eating some fruit that a conniving snake had seduced them to eat. The snake was the only bad thing in the garden of Eden. They were not used to anything bad. They had no experience. Why couldn't God forgive them? Why did humanity have to fall so hard and so fast downhill almost from the beginning of their existence? If God had approached Adam and Eve's mistake with compassion, then the history of the world would be totally different.

She grew to hate sin. She grew to believe that man's basic behavior was sinful, especially sleeping with her father. Still, she loved him. When she was not thinking of what she was reading in the Bible, she was thinking of him. Boys at school meant nothing to her. Her father was her man.

Elise thought about her homelife all summer long. Hers was such a simple existence. It was quiet. Her father, though he always maintained his tenderness toward her, he had also retained a shyness toward her. And she toward him. Spoken words were rare in their home. Each of them did what they had to do to accomplish their myriad daily chores. Her father was an extremely quiet man. At this point in her adolescence, she was still a quiet teenager. There was no cruelty in the house, but there was no laughter either.

Then came the nighttimes and both tenderness and the over-whelming passion to which Elise had become accustomed. Sometimes during that long friendless, except for her father, summer, she began not to be able to reconcile the sin of her father with her attraction for him. The battle for peace when thinking about her father raged silently within her week after week, day after eternally long summer day. Because she could never resolve her knowledge of her silent sin with her need to be with her father, that summer in one key part of her psyche, Elise became irrevocably insane.

# CHAPTER 4

Senior year was next for Elise. Many of her fellow classmates were buzzing about applying to colleges. But she had never considered it. College was a subject that Elise and her father had never discussed. When she thought about it, she knew she could never go. Her father was poor. The farm was small. There was no saved money for higher education. There was no hidden stash under attic floorboards. In fact, Elise had never seen where her father hid his money. She assumed it was in his bedroom, which he had maintained the exact way it was the day his wife died. He threw away nothing that belonged to her. He was sentimental. He missed her.

Elise was not sad about not going to college. She did not have a car. Her father had an old Ford pickup truck that was not far from being a piece of junk. But her father, with his adequate knowledge of automotive mechanics, kept it running and functional. But even if it had been prudent to have received permission to use the truck, it would never have made it day after day to even the nearest college.

Life continued with almost the same normalcy to which she had become accustomed. With little Edna gone, Elise did not have a single friend. At seventeen, she was a hardworking five-foot-eleven-inch tall farm girl with the face of American beauty. Her hair was light brown. It had never been cut. Her legs were long and lean and perfectly shaped. Her feet were long and narrow, very pretty. Her breasts were the perfect size for her height and weight. They were firm and youthful and unusually equal in size and form. Her shoulders were strong and muscular, the result of having used a variety of farm implements for several years. But she had no sophistication and was lacking in social skills. Even her speech was a little hickish.

Although her school was rather small, there were a couple of cool kid cliques to which both boys and girls belonged. She did not. The result was that she had no one to talk to. She was a simple farm girl. She was easy for at least the girls to ignore. Besides, most of them were envious of her good looks. The girls also knew that the boys would never stop trying to woo her. But to her, boys were like rain falling on a windshield. She simply splashed them away with her wipers. Elise learned to live more and more within her own head in that chamber that was already incurably insane.

On February 18 of her senior year, a huge winter snowstorm hit the entire state of Illinois, bringing with it eight inches of heavy wet snow. At 2:13 a.m., on February 19, an enormous piece of snow-swollen roof crashed downward to the barn below. Long enduring planks that had protected the contents of the building for decades had splintered into myriad chips upon the implements below. The sound of the disaster rivaled the terror of a vicious thunderclap that exploded right above Elise and her father's head.

Elise and her father were jolted from their sleep. As Elise sat straight-up in bed, her father was already pulling on his coveralls over his thermal underwear. Elise followed, quickly dressing in something warm in case they had to go outside. Had the crash occurred inside the house? Had a huge tree branch snapped and smashed into the house, sounding like a bomb? That had happened before. The curious tandem checked each room of the upstairs first, peering out every window to see whether a huge piece of a once-vibrant tree had hit the outside of their home. They looked at the siding, then down to the ground to see any sign of damage or a broken tree. They saw nothing.

When they quickly found that the roof to their precious home had not been damaged, they ran downstairs and began checking everywhere to see if there was any damage. Again, Elise looked out every window to see if she had missed any fractures of trees while looking out the upstairs windows. She saw no problem. That was a good sign. Her father scurried around each room downstairs. He found nothing out of the ordinary. That meant they had to go outside into the cold.

Ironically, they both finished their surveying of the house at the same instant. Without speaking a word, they headed for the front door, reaching it simultaneously. Elise allowed her much smaller father to pass through the front door first, showing him the respect she always had for him. Her father sprinted to the left, surveying the house as quickly as he could. Elise went to the right, looking at the house the same way her father was doing. Again, they met almost directly in the middle of the old house. The good news was they had found no damage.

The bad news was that damage must have occurred somewhere else. An enormous sound of thunder meant there had been significant damage to another structure. After checking the chicken coop and a couple of small sheds that held shovels, rakes buckets, scythes, lawn mowers, and a few other nonmotorized, handheld work tools, they looked worried at each other and sprinted toward the barn. The barn, thirty years old, was about two hundred fifty feet from the northwest corner of the house.

It only took a few seconds of swift running through deep moist snow before Elise and her father stopped abruptly upon seeing the devastation. The hole in the roof measured eighty feet, and now water and snow were pouring atop the aged wooden planks that littered the earthen floor. The planks had also smashed against the motorized farm implements that were vital to the successful operation of the farm.

"Jesus," the little father said. He rarely used words like that, not being a believer, but he had heard other people use this expletive when they were extremely frustrated. Elise was as shocked at her father's use of Jesus as she was at the destruction she saw with the barn. She had never heard her father use that word before, and she had never seen so much damage done by nature to any building or property.

Her father's shoulders slumped before her eyes as if a ton of wet snow had fallen upon them and pushed them toward the ground. His face showed consternation, thinking this cleanup and repair job will be more than Elise and he will be able to handle by themselves. Elise had an identical look on her young and beautiful face.

"What are we going to do, Daddy?"

"First thing in the morning, I'll drive over to Watson's farm and ask them if they know anyone reasonable who can help us. I have insurance on the barn and the vehicles inside, but this looks like a monster job, and I'm not sure if my insurance will cover everything. I know you and I can't do all the work by ourselves. We need to get work started right away, and it's the middle of winter. We are going to have to clear the remaining snow off the roof, then check the rest of the wood to see how hard it is."

The strength that Elise's father had was being expressed now as he talked about one of the two elements of life that were his most beloved. One was the farm. The other was Elise.

"Daddy, can we go back inside the house? I'm freezing."

"I want to check out the inside of the barn first. Will you come with me?"

"No, Daddy. I think it will be foolish to go in there now. We won't be able to see much, and there is litter all over the place. We could get really hurt in there, especially if more of the roof caves in."

She was adamant, taking charge of her father for the first time in her life. Then she softened her tone when she spoke again. She was skillfully and tactfully logical to get what she wanted.

"Don't you agree that we'll be able to see things and assess the damage better in the light of day after a good night's sleep?"

Her father had heard both statements and tones from her and found them curious. Prior to this moment, most of the time, he would dictate something for her to do and Elise would silently comply. But in the icy cold and wet snow, something was different about his daughter. Maybe it was a sign of growing up. He looked at her standing a full seven inches taller and outweighing him by twenty-six pounds. He wasn't thinking she could kick his ass if she wanted to do so. He looked at her as a goddess, not a make believe character from a Greek tale but a real-life goddess. She was statuesque and beautiful in every way. In this unplanned moment in the freezing barnyard, he noticed not only her strength but her elegance for the first time.

"How can I deny you, Elise? You are right, of course. Let's go back inside."

Elise took a couple of slippery steps and threw her right arm around her father's shoulders while he put his left arm around her waist. Then they trudged together the couple of hundred steps to the heat of the house. Both hung their coats on an old rack near the front door, brushed their teeth, and headed to bed in Elise's room. Her father never slept again in his marital bed after his wife died. What he did was suck every ounce of sympathy he could from his young daughter. She did not start out like a cold bitch, but she started to become one when she began to feel resentment for her father. She began to realize how dependent he was on her for everything in his life. There was cooking three meals a day seven days a week. There was cleaning almost continually. There was the mending of her and her father's clothes. The outdoor chores were endless and growing as she became physically stronger and more capable. At seventeen, Elise had finally begun to think of her future and freedom. She did not know what she would do if she had freedom, but she began to think about it.

That night in her return to bed, Elise was asleep in two minutes. Her father crawled in behind her he wrapped his right arm around her waist and pressed his face snuggly into her back. He felt needy. Thank God, his daughter was beside him. That night, he did not fall asleep for over an hour. His mind held a variety of swirling worries that bounced off one another like goldfish in an overcrowded aquarium. Each concern had its own degree of dismay. The one that troubled him the most was the torturous pondering of what life would be without his daughter by his side.

The next morning, Elise woke well-rested, a full thirty minutes before her father. This was the norm for their small family. Elise's body clock had been adjusted this way when she was a little girl, so she could assume the key morning chore of making breakfast for her father. Forty minutes later, her father arrived in the dining room, fully ready to eat and assess the barn after breakfast. Elise had made a special meal for her father that morning, knowing that he was going to have a long busy, and stressful day. She made pancakes, link sausage, three eggs over easy, four pieces of toast, and real butter. Strawberries decorated the outer rim of the plate. Her father dug in. There was no thank you. That was his pattern, only a "Mornin', Elise" when she joined him at the table, bringing her full plate with her from the kitchen.

It was not that her father was not appreciative of his daughter's cooking. Indeed, he was. He simply did not express it—he never had. In fact, he loved Elise dearly, even passionately. But he never expressed it in words. That was how Elise was raised. Even during sex, he was wordless. Because of that, Elise was also wordless, her voice being unwittingly robbed from her in another key area of her life. This is also how Elise had been raised. Not only did an overwhelming silence exist between them, but it had also created an impenetrable wall around her psyche, which would never be destroyed.

"You comin' with me to check the barn?" her father asked after finishing his breakfast.

"I will. If you don't mind that, I have the breakfast dishes in the sink."

"I don't mind at all, Elise. I'd rather have the company than a clean sink. Besides, I'd want you to see the damages."

"Let's hurry up then, Daddy. I don't want to miss the school bus."

It was 6:23 a.m. Elise's big yellow ride to school was scheduled to arrive at 6:55 a.m.—moments before the first-morning sun would crack through the nighttime blackness. That meant Elise would have about thirty minutes to survey the damages with her father.

The damage to the barn and the equipment inside was almost unfathomable for Elise and her father to witness. The only real sight that could be viewed without almost complete obstruction was the enormous hole in the roof. During the night as the temperature kept falling, the snow became even heavier. The result was that everything beneath the open wound of the roof was covered with seven inches of ghostly-looking snow. Elise and her father were using flashlights as their only illumination. A true assessment would have to be done after the sun rose. By that time Elise would be long gone from home, her father would have to do the initial cleanup and inspection on his own.

Elise saw the despair in her father's face and was still young enough and sensitive enough that she broke down and cried. She took three long strides to her father and threw her arms around his neck.

"It'll be all right, Daddy," she said as she snuggled her face against his chin.

He could feel her warm breath against his frigid skin. Oddly, her breath was more comforting to him than her hug. A moment later, Elise separated from her father. She walked to the back door, opened it, peered inside the warm house, grabbed her schoolbooks, closed the door, then walked around to the front of the house out to the driveway. She walked from there to the driveway, not knowing that school had been canceled for that day. This had happened to her several times over the years. Still, her father refused to buy a radio or phone. Perhaps it was because he was content to read and fantasize about his westerns in the days of old, and he simply did not realize what might be missing. Possibly, it could have been that his own simpleton parents never had a radio or phone, and he was copying them.

Elise's father walked slowly through the barn time after time, seeing more specifics each trip as the sun broke through the deep morning blue. Meanwhile, unknown to her "daddy," Elise waited in front of the house in the freezing cold in ankle-deep snow for the school bus that never came.

Eventually, Elise shared the surveying of the barn with her father. A couple of walks through and her father was ready to drive to Watson's farm.

"I'll be back in a couple of hours, Elise," he said, realizing that her presence at school had probably been canceled. Unexpectedly, in the same powerful voice, as she exhibited in the wee hours of the morning, Elise asked, "Can I come with you, Daddy?"

Momentarily stunned, but not angry, after a brief moment's thought, he answered, "I don't see any reason why not."

This was an absolute departure for him. Prior to the last few hours, he had always been in control of everything, especially keeping Elise at home as much as possible, except for school. But today, he gave in to his daughter's request. He wasn't sure whether he gave into her because of kindness or because she was almost eighteen and was growing up. Maybe it was because he was afraid of her. *Goodness,* he thought, *she is so tall.*

On the way to the Watson farm, Elise dropped the biggest bombshell of her seventeen years on her father.

"Daddy, can you start teaching me how to drive sometime soon?"

Stunned did not begin to describe the depth of shock the little father felt upon hearing this new request. Again, there was no anger in his being at her request. He felt bewilderment mostly and did not begin to know what to say in those few moments after the question was asked. Daddy waited several moments before speaking while myriad possibilities of how to answer rustled around his brain like leaves in a whirlwind. Ultimately, his answer emerged, surprising both himself and Elise.

"I think we should wait a couple of months till all the snow and ice melts away. How about we start in early spring?"

Elise answered immediately, "That would be really great and something I'll look forward to."

For the rest of the ride to the Watson farm, about three miles, neither Elise nor her father spoke another word. There was a joyful feeling inside the truck as both father and daughter sensed that the other was happy. When the Watson farm came into view all Elise's father could focus on was Earl Watson's two-year-old barn. Even though the enormous roof was covered in a thick blanket of clean snow, the side and front opening still reflected the bright red of relative newness. Daddy was envious of its beauty and functionality compared to the barn that he and his father had built nearly thirty years ago. He did not care much about modernness in most cases, but in the case of his barn, he did. The barn was one of the many great problems and sources of life for himself and Elise. He just wished he had a newer one—that's all. But he dismissed that thought almost as quickly as he had it before he reached the Watson farm. Earl was his friend since second grade. There was no reason for jealously of any kind.

Elise's father parked his old Ford truck in front of the Watson's farmhouse. The house was about the same size as Elise's, maybe a hundred square feet larger, two stories, like most of the farmhouses in this part of Illinois. Elise and her father hopped off the truck into several inches of fresh snow and headed straight for the front door.

Mrs. Watson greeted them. She was a gracious woman, almost five feet, seven inches with a genteel demeanor, warm smile, ample breasts, and a solid girth that reflected a long diet of corn, potatoes, green beans, and steak. She was thick but inviting and attractive. Elise's father thought about just how attractive she was after she greeted him and stopped inside her warm and inviting home.

"What brings you out to these parts after that formidable storm we had last night?"

"Part of my barn roof collapsed last night, Claire. The wood was incredibly old and rotten. The weight of the snow brought it to the ground with a terrible thud. The falling wood hit some of my machinery. I really can't figure out how much damage there is yet because there is too much wood and snow on top of everything. I can't see what might be broken beneath all that debris and nature. I came to see if Earl might know someone who could go up on the roof. See if there is any more really bad wood and, if so, replace it and repair that gaping hole before I lose livestock and much more."

"Earl is probably in the barn right now," Mrs. Watson said. "You are welcome to go out there and see him. I'm sure he will appreciate the company. And while you are out there talking, I could use the company of your daughter."

"Okay," Elise's father said.

He had wanted his daughter to come with him to the barn, but since he was trouble avoidant, he allowed Elise to accept Mrs. Watson's offer.

When Elise's father stepped back outside into the midwestern deep freeze, Mrs. Watson immediately asked Elise if she would like some hot chocolate and good conversation. Elise said yes with a smile, but underneath her facade, she was afraid to talk to the kindhearted lady who was walking toward the kitchen. She wondered what she would talk about because she really did not have anything to talk about except her father, who was practically her entire life. Still, she was young enough and open enough to spend the next thirty minutes with a woman who was genuinely loving and affectionate—two traits that she was not used to at this time of day.

Meanwhile, Elise's father had caught up with Earl Watson in Earl's relatively clean barn with no hole in the roof. Upon seeing Elise's father, Earl strode immediately toward him and clamped him with a bear hug. This was his custom. The little father stiffened. This was his custom. Earl knew his friend was never affectionate. He did not mind. He had known his friend since they were little boys. He thought he knew his friend implicitly. Earl was a six-foot-two-tall and 225-pound hardworking farmer. His buddy was five feet four and 113 pounds. They were quite a contrasting pair.

"What brings you to my barn this glorious morning?" Earl asked.

"The wet snow last night collapsed a huge portion of my barn roof. I've got to fix that hole right away. I need to clear the rest of the snow off the roof, check the rest of the planks for rot, and start rebuilding from there. I am afraid to do all that by myself. I couldn't forgive myself if Elise got hurt, especially if I was watching. I came to see if you knew someone who could help me right away. They would have to be good, affordable, and brave. That's a high roof, and it looks higher to me every year."

Elise's father was fifty-two years old, and fixing barn roofs was not something he looked forward to doing.

Earl answered immediately, "There's a fella in Toluca who's been making quite a name for himself around these parts, a carpenter of the highest caliber. His name is Willie Stutzman. He is twenty-two, muscles all over the place, and a real likable kid. I've heard he is fearless."

"Have you ever seen any of his work?"

"Indeed, I have. I've seen it in Toluca, Wenona, Minonk, Washburn, Metamora, lots of little towns around here.

"Is he affordable? I don't know how much of those repairs my insurance will cover."

Earl was elated to be sharing this information.

"I've heard that he is fair."

"I wonder if he is available now and willing to work in this weather?"

"There is a simple way to find out," Earl answered. He ceased what chores he had been doing and gave his little friend his undivided attention. "Let's go inside, have my wife make us a cup of hot chocolate, and I'll give Willie a phone call."

"Okay," Elise's father said, feeling anxious being around Mrs. Watson, worrying that he might get caught staring at her breasts rather than looking at her eyes. He had always been that way around her.

The Watson home was warm and inviting, the smell of it already permeating the antique-filled dormitory. Mr. Watson removed his stinky boots at the door and placed them on a large throw rug that served that very purpose. Elise's father followed suit. Elise and Mr. Watson were chatting in the tiny room with Claire Watson doing most of the talking. Earl Watson bounded across the house, put his hands on his wife's shoulders, and kissed her gently on the lips.

"Claire, could you make two more cups of hot chocolate, please? I have an especially important phone call to make."

"Of course, honey," she said, then excused herself from Elise as she invited Elise's father to sit in the dining room while Mrs. Watson left for the kitchen.

Mr. Watson headed for his old telephone about fifteen feet away on the other side of the dining room.

"How is the hot chocolate, honey?" Elise's father asked his daughter softly.

"Really good, Daddy!"

Somewhat worried, he asked her very casually, "What have you two been talking about?"

"A lot of stuff," Elise answered, "school, her kids, their farm. Mrs. Watson is entering a quilting contest in Streator in the spring."

Mr. Watson could be heard speaking her quiet tones to someone. A moment later, he said, "I think it would be best for you to talk with him personally. Would you like to do that?"

A single second passed, and they all turned directly to Elise's father, who had his eyes trained on Earl. Earl waved him over. A moment later, the two men, who would change the other's life within the next four months, began speaking.

After three minutes of politeness and questions, with no words wasted, it was agreed that Willie Stutzman and Elise's father would meet in two hours at the hole in the roof barn. There was still time for that cup of hot chocolate and some pleasant conversation, but nothing of substance. That was pretty much what it was wherever Elise's father went. For a fleeting moment, right before he and Elise stepped back outdoors, the two Watson children rushed downstairs. Elise's father felt the pain of the remembrance of his schoolmates taunting him because he was a step lower and twenty IQ points beneath where they were.

It took twenty-four minutes to drive home, each person in the old Ford truck wondering what kind of person Willie Stutzman would be. As they wondered, they did not speak. All the way home, the only sounds that could be heard were the heater, the sound of snow crushing beneath the tires. The truck's old radio was silent. It had been broken and unfixed for the past nine years.

When they reached their own homestead, the clock indicated there were seventy minutes before Willie Stutzman arrived. Elise hopped wordlessly from the truck and headed straight for the kitchen sink and the breakfast dishes. Elise's father stepped very slowly from his old worn seat to the snow. He groaned as the arthritis pain throbbed in both knees. It was not that he was old or that he hated Illinois winters, but it was simply that he no longer loved them like he had when he was a kid, and he and Earl would go rabbit hunting with Earl's .22.

He elected to go to the barn. It was now 8:00 a.m. The sun was rising as the only object in a clear blue sky. The dirty moisture-laden storm clouds of the night before had emptied themselves and evaporated into ethereal nothingness. This morning, the earth's carpet was a wondrous sparkling mirror, making everything in sight—including houses and barns, dead, and dormant trees—seem illuminated in endless brightness.

Right on the dot at the agreed-upon time, Willie Stutzman pulled into the driveway of his soon-to-be new friends. A moment before he stopped his shiny black-and-red year-old Chevy truck, he did something no one had ever done while pulling into that driveway. He beeped the horn. *Toot! Toot!*

Elise's and her father's ears perked up instantly. Elise, who was relaxing on the sofa, reading the Bible, raised her eyes immediately to the open 1940 blinds in the living room. There was Willie Stutzman's beautiful well-cared-for truck directly in her line of sight. She watched him bounce out of the front seat after a little scoot to the left, slam the door with a smile on his face, and started bounding to the front door. He stood five feet seven tall with hair cut short to the perfect gentlemanly length, the kind of lay that would make a good impression on a boss if he were going to a job interview. But extremely oddly to Elise's way of looking at life, in the 125 feet between the Chevy and the farmhouse, Willie Stutzman began whistling. It made her realize that never had she whistled, never.

In a moment, she was up off the couch, doing something else she had never done before. With her two hands, she smoothed both sides of her hair so it would rest more beautifully on her head. She did not want any wild brown hairs sticking up or out at some awkward angle. For some not understood but excited reason, she wanted to make a good impression. Then Willie knocked on the door, and Elise opened it. Willie's sparkling blue eyes met Elise's sea-green eyes four inches above hers.

"I'm Willie Stutzman," he said proudly.

"I'm Elise," she said, analyzing every visible aspect of him as quickly as any of today's computers could.

Even though he stood a full four inches shorter than she, he seemed taller than that. He stood erect with military posture. She noticed his mesomorphic chest muscles beneath his half-unzipped coat. They were rock hard like the biceps she noticed beneath his outer sleeves. He was twenty-two, more mature than the boys at school, and he had a splendid spark of personality the likes of which she had never seen. She liked him immediately.

He, on the other hand, had never seen a young woman like her. He had seen tall girls before, but they had been gangly and unproportioned. They were homely and had poor posture. But Elise was striking, pretty, extremely well-proportioned, and movie star gorgeous. He felt his hormones leap for joy. He was smitten by her instantly.

Before Willie stepped into the warm house and closed the door behind him, he surprised Elise. He reached out and shook Elise's hand with both of his cold hands. Daddy was right behind him on the doorstep. He had trotted about as fast as he could from the barn to meet the young man before he met Elise. But he had missed his chance, and the two young adults had already had the opportunity to stare unabashedly into each other's eyes with curiosity, delight, and desire. Though Elise's father found Willie extremely likable, he was jealous immediately of Willie's good looks, youth, and flamboyant personality.

But right now, there were more serious jobs to be done. There was no time for socializing now. That hole in the barn roof needed to be at least temporarily covered. The barn roof needed to be cleared off, and the wood beneath the snow needed to be inspected for rot. The man of Elise's house also thought that it would be wise to clean the snow off the roof of the main house in hope that Willie would be willing to do that chore. Then there was the task of clearing the snow and wood from the inside the barn, then assessing the degree of damage that had been done to the machinery beneath.

In the next twenty minutes, Elise's father talked with Willie about all of it while Elise sat at the far end of the table opposite her father, almost demurely, only two feet from the handsome stranger. Salary, work hours, workdays, how long would the job take, it was discussed and agreed upon. In thirty minutes, Willie and Elise's father began to work after Elise made both men a tasty hot chocolate with a heaping dose of whipped cream.

When the clock hit twelve noon exactly, Elise threw her coat, socks, and shoes on, walked out to the barn, and told the men it was time for dinner. That was always how Elise and her family referred to what most people called lunch. In her household, it was always breakfast, dinner, and supper. Elise's father was somewhat shocked at the prospect of sharing the midday meal with Willie. He had not thought about it until the moment Elise asked the two of them to come into the house. But he asked her about it with a hint of negativity in his vocal tone.

"You've set a table for three, Elise?"

Elise, instantly zoning in on the minuscule touch of negativity, stood more erect on the spot, towering over the man of the house while strongly answering, "It's the right thing to do, don't you think, Father?"

She had never called him father. Suddenly, Daddy felt an uncomfortable trio of feelings. First, he felt his lack of physical stature. Elise seemed like a giant to him now. She was also stronger than he was emotionally at this moment. Willie had him by three inches too. Now Daddy, or was it Father now, was the little guy in the trio. He also felt he lacked the basic hospitality he should have had toward Willie. Dinner was not at all too much to offer this hardworking kid. But Elise's father once again experienced his more often occurring loneliness.

It had already begun, that slow slide of Elise from the sinful relationship with her father to the spotless one with Willie Stutzman. Elise imagined what it must have been like to be Adam and Eve in the garden of Eden. Even though this rude Illinois winter with its muscle-numbing frigidity and its frozen whiteness covering the ground was the antithesis of the warm, plush garden of Eden, this little farm seemed transformed because Willie had entered it.

The working relationship between Willie and Elise's father became a good one. By the end of the first day, Willie had cleared the snow off the entire barn roof and had carefully crawled on his belly to inspect the rest of the wood. It was bad. Though only 25 percent of the roof had collapsed, about 60 percent of it would have to be rebuilt. It would be expensive and take time, much more than a simple repair. It was only February 11, and bad weather could cause both short delays and complete stoppage of work. By the end of the first day of working together, Elise's father had grown to admire how Willie Stutzman worked. He was fast and smart and brave. Willie told Elise's father that he did not mind working on the roof while

Daddy worked in the unheated barn, removing snow and fallen wood, checking to see what damage had been done to farm machinery. Oddly, what impressed Elise's father the most was that Willie whistled nearly constantly while he worked. One song after another poured forth from his lips, some of which Daddy knew, most that he did not. After all, Elise's father did not even have a radio.

He listened to Willie change the speed of his songs from frisky to slow, from happy to haunting, from classical to popular. He figured that some of the shorter, friskier songs were popular songs from present or recent times. He liked listening to Willie's whistling. It had been a long time since he had heard and enjoyed music of any kind. And today, from down in the wind-chilled barn, he was enjoying quite a variety coming from Willie on the rickety roof.

Elise's father began to develop some complex inner dynamics in relation to Willie during their first few hours of knowing one another. He liked Willie because he was easygoing, hardworking, skilled, and a friendly young gentleman. On the other hand, he was afraid that Willie would be attracted to Elise and that Elise might respond to his attention in a favorable way.

Unfortunately for Elise's father, he was right. There would be a move made that would lead to the couple's bonding. But one truth would never be known to the tiny father with the below-average IQ. Elise would make the first move and many greater ones after that and finally the ultimate move that would change all three peoples' lives forever.

# CHAPTER 5

The next thirty days moved interminably slow in the slice of Illinois in which Elise, her father, and Willie lived. The earth had turned unmercifully into a frozen wasteland that the locals would talk about for decades. Though the cold felt artic outside Willie worked as much as he possibly could on the barn roof, he did so as much to see and get to know Elise as to move along with improvement of the roof.

Seeing Elise was easy. Getting to know her was an entirely different matter. Though Elise was away at school Monday through Friday from about 7:00 a.m. to 4:00 p.m., Willie learned her bus schedule quickly so he could arrive at her house slightly before 7:00 a.m. to be able to say hello to her before she left for school.

Several hours later, he would make sure he worked till he was able to see and speak to her after she arrived home from school.

When it was a Saturday or Sunday, being near her was much easier. Each of those days, she would prepare dinner for Willie and her father. During every meal, she would sit quietly and demurely. Willie fell into the same trap as many of Elise's and her father's acquaintances did. He began to think of Elise as mysterious when what she was, was quiet and shy and afraid to make any move toward Willie.

When her father was around, she was more cautious to talk with Willie. She was afraid that through a giggle, a smile, or a revealing glance that she was interested in Willie in a way that far exceeded an employer and employee relationship.

Beneath her demure facade, she thought constantly about how she could create time to talk to Willie without hurting her father or worse, making him angry. She could not ever remember her father being angry, a little frustrated yes. There was that recent "Jesus" he had said, but most of the time, when he was upset, he'd say, "Oh crap" or an extremely rare, "Oh shit." He was not a vulgar man, and for that, Elise respected him. Elise had never even been spanked, not for any of her childish actions. What she was feeling and hoping to share with Willie was much naughtier and potentially harmful to her father than all her previous grievances combined. Elise knew enough about human nature to understand how devastated her father would be by her potential behavior. This slightly less than eighteen-year-old girl was a tangled mess of emotions. She had thought for a year since little Edna had first suggested that something might be terribly wrong with her relationship with her father. She was still wracking her brain, trying to find absolute truth in the Bible that father-daughter relationships were wrong. But she laughed quietly to herself, thinking that Cain either slept with his mother or his sister to produce a family.

She did not wish to hurt her father who for so long had been the center of her universe. She finally decided to see Willie on those rare occasions when her father was not home. Maybe she would sneak in a few poignant sentences at dinner when her father was in the bathroom or upstairs in the bedroom changing clothes. It would not give her much time, but it would give her some. Then suddenly, one freezing February Friday, Elise came up with her best idea ever. She would face two of her greatest fears, heights and falling off a roof. She would ask Willie if she could help him with his work. This would give them hours to talk about everything that was important in their lives.

As soon as Elise conceived this idea, she made the strong commitment not to tell Willie that her father had been sleeping with her for twelve years. She made a promise never to tell Willie about that aspect of her and her father's lives. It was too dangerous. It might be overwhelmingly toxic and unacceptable to Willie. It might pollute and destroy every good thing the two new friends could create.

One day, after Elise conceived her idea to help Willie with the roof, she posed her concept to him confidently before one dinner while her father was in the upstairs bathroom, changing into dry clothes and scrubbing his filthy hands and face. There was no romance in her soft voice as she matter-of-factly described her plan to Willie. He listened to it merely as a friendly suggestion to help him with a difficult task. There was no debating with himself that fixing the roof would be easier with a partner.

A moment after he considered her helping him, Willie Stutzman's thought pattern changed completely. He realized that he would be working with probably the most beautiful girl he had ever seen. Though he could have interpreted her demure behavior as disinterest, he did not. He sensed that she was shy, but that somewhere within her reserved demeanor, there was a part of her that was strongly attracted to him. It was pure instinct—nothing more. He hoped he was not wrong. In his next fantasy of Elise, he allowed himself to dream about what it would be like to lose his virginity and playfully take her to a fancy hotel room on their honeymoon. He did not have to ask Elise if she was a virgin. He was certain she was. She did not have a flashy bone in her body. *My goodness*, he thought. *She never laughs, and she barely ever cracks a smile. There is no way this isolated young farm girl could be anything but a virgin. Besides, her father, who also never laughs, must be very protective of her. I know I would be. I wonder if he has ever let her out on a real date. She sure looks that innocent.*

It did not take Willie more than a second, including his fanciful thoughts to answer Elise. "Of course, you can, if you are not too afraid of the height of the roof and possibly sliding off it because it's slippery."

"I'm a little afraid, but maybe I'll be able to overcome my fears if you will help me."

"Absolutely," Willie answered.

Again, Elise had spoken matter-of-factly. But at that moment, Willie felt he would be willing to help Elise with anything and forever. No girl or young woman had impacted him this way. And in that fleeting moment of young wonder, he allowed himself to believe that one day he would have Elise exclusively to himself.

When Elise told her father about wanting to help Willie on the roof, he was not at all pleased. He immediately both feared and sensed that she had an ulterior motive for wanting to do so, especially since she had frequently expressed her fear of heights. When he initially told her that there was no way she could help Willie, Elise stood up to him once again. This time, she seemed taller than before. Elise, who had slipped back into her old ways of calling her father Daddy, spoke one sentence to him in a voice from a statuesque being that could not be denied. "Father, my decision has been made, and there is simply no talking me out of it." She told him this as she stood strongly above him as he sat in his comfortable lounge chair. He was once again taken aback. He was speechless as he experienced his recurring loneliness.

How strangely this new relationship between Willie and Elise began to unfold. Elise, though almost always a young woman of few but powerful words, knew that she was up against the clock. The roof repair would not last forever. She assessed correctly that Willie's job on her farm would take about three weeks, maybe a month. It could possibly be slightly longer than that depending on the weather.

Willie was always upbeat, consistently whistling tune after tune when he was not talking positively or optimistically. Willie seemed to love everything. These aspects of his nature made Elise question what might be behind his delightful demeanor.

One blustery morning after several minutes of silence had passed between them while they each carefully stripped pieces of rotting wood from the top of the barn, Elise asked Willie a question.

"Willie, do you believe in God?"

"I do," he answered, feeling warmer when asked the question, "Do you have a religion?"

Elise's curiosity was prompting her to go deep with Willie on their third day of working together.

"I do," Willie answered simply.

"What is it?" Elise asked, her eyes projecting a beauty Willie had not seen to this degree.

They were filled with true wonder, and unknown to Elise, they were glistening. "I'm Catholic." He acknowledged, "May I ask why you are curious?"

Willie stopped his work, unwilling to remove his gaze from Elise's enticing sea-green eyes. Suddenly, Elise became somewhat guarded. "I've been reading the Bible for several months now," she said, "trying to figure something out that's been bothering me."

Suddenly, Elise felt colder and embarrassed.

"Maybe I can help you figure it out," Willie said genuinely.

"No, you can't," Elise snapped, the glistening in her eyes momentarily disappearing, replaced by the flames of a furnace.

As quickly as she angrily whipped out her words, she softened her expression and looked lovely again as she said apologetically, "I am sorry, Willie. It's just that what I am working on is very personal. I don't know if I can discuss it with anyone, much less a man."

Willie was not at all miffed by Elise's abrupt switch of temperament. If Willie was not responsible for hurting someone, he did not let that person's mood change bother him. He never hurt anybody intentionally and hardly ever hurt anyone unintentionally. Consequently, Willie was rarely put off by anyone's moods. He had long ago learned to accept people for who they were and how they behaved. He had learned that from his Catholic faith. Little did he know how valuable this belief would aid him in his relationship with Elise.

"That's perfectly okay, Elise," Willie said with a smile, as he carefully broke off pieces of broken wood. "If something is personal, it's sacred to a person, I'd never pry."

Elise reflected for a moment that she had never heard the word *sacred* before in a conversation; then she thought that Willie was saying and doing the right things to make her feel comfortable at times.

As frigid February turned to a more ravaging March, Willie's relationship was improving. Their friendship, oddly, had few words that passed between them, though strong feelings grew without words. Each day, Willie's desire to make love to her increased. And each day, while Elise analyzed whether Willie was the young man she would run away with, she also wondered what it would be like to be passionately enveloped by him.

The problem continued to be her father, though the youngsters continued to do a good job of hiding any budding romance between them. Elise's father felt the more than subtle undercurrent of something special happening between them. His style was not to get angry. Instead, he tried every way he could to help keep Willie and Elise apart. When these tactics failed, he resorted to the only activity he believed might save his relationship with his daughter. That activity was to put more into his lovemaking with Elise.

From the fourth day of Willie's employment, Elise noticed a significant change in the attentiveness her father was showing in every aspect of what he considered lovemaking. At first, she had no idea why the sudden increase in attention. But over time, she began to figure it out. He was fighting for her in the only way he now knew how. Elise hated him in one compartment of her being since little Edna had explained what her father was doing to her. But there was another compartment inside her that thrilled at her father's new vigor and attentiveness. For Elise, though not yet eighteen years old, was a full-grown woman sexually. Now her torment and joy collided nightly.

Elise was smart and clever. She was a mistress of biding her time and her feelings for her father. She was an expert at stuffing her feelings in general as well. But somewhere in the process of hiding and stuffing, Elise unknowingly began expressing a need for real love. She had never had much love except from her weak and sickly mother. But that was a long time ago, and the memories were now submerged in inaccessible crevices deep within her psyche. Now there was only the desire to escape her scruffy farm and set out on a new life with Willie. She did not know or care what it would be. It would happen with Willie, who laughed, was a good carpenter, and was always pleasant and whistled. That would be enough.

With Willie, there was no conniving. He simply allowed Elise to take the lead because all he wanted was to see her, to be near her, and to eventually touch her. Willie was also intelligent. He wanted to rescue Elise from her rather-pitiful homestead and build a life for her on his nearly three times as large ranch and well-kept estate. His parents had died some years back and left him everything. There was no doubt in Willie's mind that he could provide Elise a splendid life. He was a strong and striking young man, twenty-two years of age.

On the tenth day of stripping wood from what Willie now realized was a horribly damaged roof, at dinnertime, Willie began speaking to Elise's father as they ate baloney sandwiches they each made for themselves.

"Sir," Willie began respectfully, "it looks like we're going to need a whole lot of lumber for that barn roof. I'm going to estimate that the old roof is about 80 percent shot. Will you be able to handle that kid of cost?"

"Yes, I will, son. It looks like my insurance will cover almost all my supplies and your salary too. I'll need you to figure out exactly how much wood we'll need. After that, I'll have to take a ride to Streator one day. There's a big lumberyard there where I can get a good deal."

Elise's father was not intelligent. With an IQ hovering around eighty-five, he barely knew enough to get by. But he knew how to run his farm. His mother and father had helped him, teaching him everything they knew from the time he was a little boy. During school when the little sheriff struggled learning farming concepts, the school found special tutors to help him. When his mother and father were young, strong, and healthy, the farm ran smoothly. Then one night, the high school in Metamora held a dance. Elise's father met Elise's mother, Ellie. She was pretty, shy, and a petite young lady, a little slow, like him. They fell in love almost at first sight but more definitely after the first few sentences that interchanged between them and their first dance, a slow one to Ray Charles's "Ramblin' Rose."

When it was the three of them, Elise's father, Ellie when she still had her health, and Elise was a little girl, running the farm was vastly easier. More hands meant more chores were achieved. Ellie's and Elise's ability to handle mundane tasks left Daddy free to perform the stronger tasks, plowing the fields, caring for the animals doing major repairs, planting, and harvesting corn. If a task was too difficult for them to handle, Daddy would be quick to ask Ellie first, then Elise if they needed help. It was a cute little farm for several years until Ellie would collapse into her bed early each evening, asking if it was God's will to allow her to awaken in the early morning rested and strong to take on the new day with vigor.

Ellie's prayers were not answered. Her increasing weakness and exhaustion prompted her to finally, after three months of suffering in silence, ask her husband to take her to a big town doctor in Peoria.

"I don't want to see a small-town doctor, honey," she said to her husband one cold winter day. "Something is seriously wrong with me. I think I need to go to a big hospital where there are lots of trained people to help me."

Her simpleminded spouse was horrified. A shotgun's blast of loneliness hit his stomach for the first time in his life. Even when his simpleminded grandparents and parents died, he did not feel what he felt now. His heart raced, and his stomach ached unmercifully as his mind contemplated what life would be like without Ellie. He knew that he was way ahead of himself. He was at least that bright. Ellie had not died. She had not ever been told what was wrong with her.

He took Ellie to the doctor immediately in big town Peoria. A few days later, they had to drive back from Peoria to find out the test results. Ellie had leukemia, a virulent form that would ultimately kill her.

Her diagnosis of ill health was the beginning of the deterioration of the once-thriving farm. Flower gardens died, dried up, and appeared unbecoming. Branches of trees that grew too long became brittle and drooped dangerously low. Dirty work clothes sat in unemptied hampers, smelly and unwashed.

Everything inside and outside the house had a sense of decay and forgottenness. Ellie's weight began to decline, and so did her husband's out of fret and worry. His stomach was often upset that he could not eat. And even though he was simple and slow-minded, he often pondered how deeply he loved his precious little Ellie.

Ellie's illness obliterated her husband's motivation to maintain a cute little farm. He became prone to making mistakes that hindered the stability of his farm and family. His nerves were stressed from long drives to Peoria twice a week for Ellie's health treatments. Many man-hours of his work time were lost. Within five months after Ellie became ill, passersby on the road would stare at the tall uncut grass, fallen branches, and the general buildup of clutter. They wondered what was going on with the people who lived there. But the general public and the few friends Elise's family had would not find out what was going on with the people on Ellie's farm until Ellie passed away. Neither petite Ellie nor the little man of the house told anyone of Ellie's condition. They toughed it out together in the quiet way they related to one another. And even though these timid farmers loved each other, they never spoke those words to one another.

When Ellie died, the farm deteriorated quicker than ever. Ellie's husband deteriorated faster. His weight loss continued, and he moved around the house, barn, and fields—a lost and broken-bodied and brokenhearted man. He did as little as possible to keep his farm surviving. His emotional loss he shared with Elise. He never said anything about his emotions to Elise during sex or any other time. Elise could feel her father's loneliness and longing for Ellie in the subtle, different ways he touched her. He also shed tears in the most intimate moments between them, a sure sign of brokenness.

Elise missed Ellie too. For many months after Ellie died, Elise showed definite signs of being damaged, if not broken. Her school-work suffered. Her housekeeping skills declined. Even her cooking was not as good. Like her father, for a significant amount of time, she did as little as she could to survive while a series of unknown inner demons attacked her daily. Even before little Edna had told her that a daughter sleeping with her father was a sin, Elise had questioned what was happening with her own father. Elise heard the girls at school talking about boys and boyfriends for years. But Elise never engaged in those conversations with her friends because she thought they were ridiculous and immature compared to what she had already experienced in life. And she knew that those kinds of relationships in her world would never be allowed.

As time passed, there was a great deal of healing for Elise and her father. They never got back to where they were when Ellie was alive, but they at least got back to branch trimming, weekly clothes washing, and clean windows around the house. But now there was a real threat to the emotional security of Elise's father. And it came in the form of a happy-go-lucky twenty-two-year-old man boy.

After working for Elise's father for one week, Willie approached him with an idea he believed would help their family as well as his pursuit of Elise. They were inside the house, having a hot chocolate while waiting for Elise to bring their midday meal.

Willie led into his suggestion with as much gentility as he could.

"Sir," he said respectfully, "I have an idea that I hope I am not too forward in sharing with you."

"What is it, Willie?"

"I think you two should have a telephone."

"Oh no," Elise's father quickly interrupted. "We've gone this long without one."

"I'm thinking first and foremost that it would be a way for you and me to communicate if there is a problem."

"What do you mean?"

"Say it's a really bad day and I couldn't work that day. I could give you a quick call and tell you that I can't make it. Or you could call me and tell me not to come. You could also call the lumberyard with specs and order what you need instead of driving all the way there, ordering your wood, then having to drive all the way back home, wait a day or two for your order to be ready, then driving all the way back to Streator to pick up the order, then having to drive home again. You could almost pay for the phone with the money you save on gas for useless trips."

Elise came into the dining room and put their food down on her mother's antique white-lace tablecloth.

"What are specs?" Elise's father asked Willie.

"Specs is short for specifications," Willie answered in stride. "It means the exact measurement for things."

"I don't know, Willie," Elise's father said meekly.

"Say there's an emergency and you break a leg or have a heart attack and you can't drive. If Elise can't drive, then you might die out here one day."

Elise jumped in. "What are you two talking about?"

"Whether your dad should get a telephone," Wille answered.

"I've never thought about something like that happening to me and Elise."

"Then there is also the fact that you can talk to your friends anytime you want."

"I don't really have any friends," Elise's father said with a touch of sadness.

"I think it's a great idea," Elise interjected, hiding her hope that a phone would help her connect to the world outside her tiny, lonely farmhouse.

"Elise, this is a big decision. I don't think you realize how expensive a phone is."

"It really isn't, sir, especially when you consider that a phone can save your life and, in general, make it easier," Willie added.

"What if we ever had a fire, Daddy? If it is big enough it could leap from the house to the trees to the barn. We could lose everything."

It was beginning to become evident that Elise not only stood head and shoulders above her father in physical height but in basic intelligence as well.

Still, her father was resistant, "I don't know. I'm not convinced. Do you mind if I think about it for a while?" He was stalling for privacy for as long as he could have it.

Willie was frustrated because he was not able to convince his current employer to get a phone. He had not told him that the main reason he was advocating for one was so that he could talk to Elise whenever possible. Elise, though frustrated, decided to dig in and nag her father until he gave in. If he was going to think about it, she was going to be the constant. She would initially pester him, then nag him incessantly, if need be. She was fighting for her life, battling to get off her little island around the end of senior year. Willie would take her away from the sin in which she had willingly participated for so long. He would save her. He was the perfect candidate.

Elise's father wanted no part of a phone. He wanted to keep himself and Elise isolated for as long as possible. But he was losing control. In the pauses between sentences, he felt what was becoming his greatest enemy—loneliness. He could hardly concentrate on conversations anymore. The nerves in his stomach made the thought of eating this meal before him disgusting.

Both men would soon find out what developed in the new phone controversy. Every day, every chance she could create, she pestered her poor little father about getting a phone. After a few days, he began to wear down, not just about the phone but about life. He understood that Elise was becoming relentless in the pursuit of things she wanted. She was too big, powerful, and smart to argue with. He did not think Elise would strike him, but in recent weeks, he noticed her arm and leg muscles were developing. As the load of her farmwork increased as she aged, so did the size and definition of her muscles. Elise's looks were beautiful. As she grew, however, her father felt a palpable fear of her. She was now an intellectual and physical force to be reckoned with, and it made the little sheriff extremely uncomfortable.

Ten days after Willie interjected his phone concept into their isolated lives, Elise's father broke down and consented to bring a phone into his home. Little did he know that this concession signaled the beginning of the end of his daughter's life. The phone arrived on March 15. Outside the house, the weather continued to be brutal. Intolerable conditions caused Willie to miss several days of work. His job was only 20 percent completed by the Ides of March. His work would probably take him into early May. Elise realized that would not be much time to develop a relationship.

The first night the phone rested on a small table in the living room, Elise called information to find Willie's phone number. She certainly could not ask her father for it. That would hurt him, and she had made up her mind to hurt him only once. That would be the day she left the farm forever. She knew that action would devastate her father, but he deserved it.

Elise felt devastated every day of her life. She was ashamed of her sin and ashamed now of her father. Each day, she told herself, "Stuff your feelings. Stuff them hard and deep, where no one can ever see them. Hang on, hang on, you can make it here until graduation in June. Survive, Elise, survive. Willie will save you. Be quieter than ever around your father. Be smiley. You can escape this place. You can escape. You can escape."

For the next three months, the key word for Elise's life was *sur-reptitious*. It is not a world she would use, but that is the reality of what her situation was. Every chance she had to be near Willie when he was working, she made sure she was by his side. When she helped him, she was always slow and methodical. Willie questioned her about it one day, but she could not tell him she was nervous and cautious of Daddy. Really, she was trying the only way she knew now, to stretch time and spend more precious minutes with Willie. It is not as if she was sharing more of herself with Willie. She was not. Her task was to get Willie to share more of himself with her. The loquacious young man was happy to oblige. He had no idea how many feelings Elise was stuffing or that she already had so many in mind.

June 15 was when he would save her from being surreptitious.

Every chance she got, Elise called Wille. If her father was outside doing chores on a Saturday or Sunday, she called Willie. When her father fell asleep in the living room with his Louis Lamour Western on his lap, Elise would call Willie. There were even a few times when Elise was bold enough to leave her late-night bed with her father in it and tiptoe down the stairs to call Willie. Their conversations were not much in the beginning. Elise was reticent, always directing Willie to talk about himself. She encouraged him to share stories of his boyhood, his high school days, what sports he played, how he learned carpentry, and did he care about what she felt. Any questions she could think of, she posed to Willie.

Within a couple of weeks, Elise knew more intimate details about Willie's life than she did about any other human being except for herself. She began to see her father in a worse light than she had ever seen him in the past. She realized that her father had shared no details with her about his youth. The only events she knew about him were what Ellie had told her about how she and her father had met and fallen in love in Metamora then married three years later.

The more Willie talked, the more Elise listened and wanted to spend more time alone with him away from her father. Concurrently, Elise did not want to waste days as time was so short between the Ides and her magical date of June 15. In effect, she wanted the same thing as Willie, both for different reasons. Elise had a timetable, a hidden agenda. Willie was falling head over heels for Elise while Elise was in survival mode. Love had nothing to do with her feelings for Willie. What she felt for him was a basal animal attraction.

Eventually, they found ways to be together. Willie even found the time to teach Elise how to drive. It was two weeks after he had finished his work on the barn. He was already becoming a distant memory for Elise's father, as Elise never once gave her father a clue she was interacting with Willie. One of the ways she protected their plot was to have Willie promise never to call her house unless it was a dire emergency, in which case Willie would be on his honor to hang up before her father answered. Willie never called, though he was often dying to do so.

Both young people were perfect examples of self-control. Willie restrained because Elise's especially kind powers were so strong when she asked for something, he willingly complied. Deep within Elise, she was not at all strong. She was afraid her plot would fall apart. She was afraid that Willie might dump her for another girl, who was willing to give him what he wanted. She was tormented by her myriad mixed feelings for her father. She cared about him and was oddly connected to him. She had years of memories of the pleasures he had given to her. There would also be more between today and when she ran away. She knew she did not love him, and she did not even know what love was. To her, love was something magical that people in books experienced. She did not feel that she would ever experience that kind of love. She was also afraid that God would smite her at any moment for all her sins. That is why Willie had to keep his distance.

Though there were only two people Elise could influence, she became a masterful manipulator of each man. When Elise wanted something, she instinctively knew how to behave to achieve it. She was not evil. Survival had its dictates, and she was ruled by them.

After Willie finished his job, sex between father and daughter reverted to what it was before Willie had appeared. Daddy was not as intense, not as giving. His memory of Willie quickly faded. So did his fear of Elise leaving him. Willie was gone. In the little sheriff's childish mind, he believed that absolutely nothing had happened between Willie and Elise.

Elise became more disenchanted with her father the closer it came to graduation, June 8. All around her at school, boys and girls were buzzing about where they were going to college. At first, the buzzing did not bother her. When it went on for weeks, she began thinking about her own life. In her house, there had not been a single discussion about college. Nothing! There had been no savings plan, no dreaming, no searching through brochures. Her father figured she would stay with him on the farm. During her junior year in chemistry class, she wished that she could learn more about the subject.

However, in late May, she began to realize that her formal learning would end in a few days. She would miss school terribly, not only because learning was pleasurable but because it got her away from home for a few hours. She began to resent her father for not helping her plan for college. Elise never initiated a conversation with her father about college either. She knew he was slow. She also knew that the farm was poor, according to her father. Still, she blamed him. It was easier that way, not taking any responsibility. That gave her another huge reason to leave the farm.

# CHAPTER 6

As graduation grew closer, so did Willie and Elise. Elise's plan was working. She gave Willie just enough to increase his interest in her and secure his promise to help her leave the farm. Then they would live together in Toluca until they were married. Willie reluctantly agreed. Elise had lied and told Willie that she wanted to wait to lose her virginity until after they were married. She also hurt him deeply when she told him he could not attend her graduation on June 8 or have any contact with her on her eighteenth birthday on June 11. This was part of her plan to keep Willie from her father's consciousness.

Still, they grew together even though the time and minutes they shared were sparse. The most exciting night Elise and Willie shared was the night before her graduation week. It was 9:15 p.m., almost time for bed. Elise was wearing a simple white full-length nightgown with a pattern of little red roses. It was her favorite evening dress, and she wore it well, her goddess-like figure wonderfully outlined beneath it. Her father left the house to retrieve a special wrench so he could perform some minor repairs under the kitchen sink. A few feet from the small outbuilding where he stored various tools, he stepped on a nail that was attached to a small piece of wood. It had blown off the barn roof. The nail went all the way through his foot and up through the top of his foot. The pain was excruciating, and he fell to the hard ground. Instinctively, he pulled the board and nail backward through his foot. He screamed for the second time in less than a minute. He forced himself upright and hoped in the house. A steady stream of blood flowed through his slippers.

"Elise! Elise!" he cried.

Elise was reading Mark in her King James Bible, lying on the living room couch. She heard her father's desperation immediately and jumped up instantly. She ran to the dining room, where her exhausted father had fallen onto the floor.

"Daddy, what happened?" she asked genuinely.

"I stepped on a nail," he said as the blood continued to flow. "It went clear through my foot."

"Daddy, this doesn't look good." She wrapped the wound in a towel. "Daddy, you need to get to an emergency room quickly. You're going to need antibiotics. If you don't get them, you could lose your foot."

"Where should I go?" her father pleaded.

"I think Peoria, Daddy, to the same hospital Mommy went."

"I feel really bad now that I didn't teach you how to drive. You could take me. Will you come with me?"

"I can't, Daddy. I'm in my nightgown, and I've still got to iron my gown and do some other things before I go to bed. I've got to be rested for tomorrow. It's my graduation day. You do remember, don't you, Daddy?"

"I remember," he lied.

In a minute, Elise secured the towel with twine and assisted her father to his truck. He sped out of the driveway into the darkness. The last words he heard from Elise were "Wake me up when you get home and let me know what happened."

Elise waited a full two minutes after her father's taillights disappeared before bounding straight for the phone. She dialed Willie's number. He answered on the second ring.

"Hello."

"Willie, I know it's late, but can you come over for a while? My father just stepped on a nail and is on his way to the hospital in Peoria. I'm sure we'll have an hour, maybe more."

"I'll leave right now, Elise."

"Wait. Make sure that when you get here, you park off to the side of that little dirt road two blocks from here, okay? And make sure that you check for Daddy's truck in the driveway, in case, God forbid, he changed his mind and turns around."

"I will, Elise. Now let me go."

Elise was desperate to see Willie. She was in an odd survival mode, clinging to the first dream she had ever nurtured. If Willie did not save her, she would have nothing. Her once-good feelings for her little father had been souring for months. Now she wanted a younger, talkative, stronger man. She had no idea of how she would handle all of Willie's talking, whistling, and general happiness, but she would try. Elise did not know what happiness was. The day Willie taught Elise how to drive his gorgeous truck while the little sheriff was buying seeds in Streator, Willie was having a blast. Elise was not. She was entrenched in her pitiable survival mode. She did not smile twice that day. Willie chalked it up to beginner's nerves. He was wrong. Elise's smiles would forever be limited.

While Elise was reflecting on her times with Willie, he was speeding toward her. On the dark and deserted miles between Toluca and Elise's farm, Willie reached 102 miles per hour. He felt like a wild mustang galloping toward his mate. Thus far, he had been a perfect gentleman. For over three months, he had felt Elise pushing him away while using her feminine wiles to draw him closer. Tonight, he would throw her a pitch she would not expect. He would express himself boldly. He was determined.

Willie made the thirty-minute trip in twenty-one minutes. He parked the truck and raced under the star-filled sky to Elise's house. When Elise opened the front door to Willie, he picked her entire body off the ground, stretched his neck, and kissed her full on the lips. It was not a peck. It lingered, as pent-up passion and true love. Elise was stunned. Four seconds into the kiss, Elise began to push Willie away. But he did not relent. His arms tightened around her. She could not overcome his strength. Her arms suddenly wrapped around his mesomorph body. Then she rubbed her hands over his well-defined biceps.

Willie could have taken her right there. Instead, he put her down and backed off, feeling he had accomplished his mission without compromising his integrity.

"I missed you terribly, Elise."

"I missed you too, Willie."

She was not lying exactly, but she was mimicking him.

"Are you packed and ready to leave with me a week from tomorrow?"

"I am, Willie. My suitcases are hidden under my mother's bed. My father never goes into that room anymore. It's exactly like it was the day she died. Only I go in there once or twice a month to dust and sweep."

"I wish we could leave right now," Willie said boldly.

"I wish we could too," Elise said with utter sincerity. "But this time next week, I'll be eighteen, and there's nothing my father can do legally to bring me back home."

"I wish I could make love to you right now, Elise," Willie uttered while looking at her beautiful body beneath her favorite well-worn nighties.

"This time in just a handful of days, you'll be able to, Willie." She was flattered that he wanted her.

"Can we finalize the place for our departure, Elise?" Willie asked lovingly.

"Of course, we can, but can we keep our eyes on the front window to see if Daddy comes home?"

They positioned themselves perfectly to see any headlights that may be heading in the direction of the farmhouse from the north. And they talked, bantering out the details of their upcoming escape. It would not be complicated. Elise had recently established that she had been sleepwalking. When her father asked her why she was sleeping on the living room couch after finding her sleeping there several mornings in a row, she had told him she was sleepwalking because of stress from her upcoming final exams before graduation. She was testing him, to see if he woke when she left the bed and at what time he would find her on the couch. Her father proved to be a remarkably deep and consistent sleeper. He never woke when she left the bed. And he always found her sleeping on the couch either a few minutes before or after five or five o'clock exactly. She never really sleepwalked. Her actions were all part of her surreptitious plan to leave her father.

Elise and Willie confirmed the plan that at one thirty in the morning of June 15, she would leave the bed that she had shared with her father for so long, retrieve her two suitcases from a seldom-used downstairs' closet, walk quietly out the front door, and meet Willie who would be parked on the highway headed south of her father's farmhouse toward the beginning of her new life.

When Willie asked her again for the tenth time if she was sure if this was what she wanted, she simply said yes. Why she wanted this, she answered in the same way always, "My father is a control freak."

"Is that all there is, Elise?"

"He won't let me date. He doesn't want my friends to come to our house. He rarely talks to me and won't let me buy any store-bought clothes. I have to make all my own clothes. And when it comes to shopping, he rarely buys anything I want. It's always what he wants or what he thinks we'll both eat. On birthdays, he never gives me a present, and I never give him one. He has said many times that birthdays are worthless days just like any other day. He's told me many times that he just does not want to celebrate birthdays. They just make him think about getting older, and he doesn't want to think about it. Would you like to live like that?"

"No, I would not," Willie answered.

Everything Elise had said had been the absolute truth, including the continual sadness with which she lived her life.

Feeling her sadness, Willie said, "We'll have lots of fun, Elise. I promise."

Fun! That was another word Elise did not fully comprehend. Elise rarely saw fun. She saw it on the playground at school and on the bus. She saw it at the rare school events she forced her father to take her to. At home, there was rarely a smile, much less laughter. What made everything worse was that wherever she went, she was the wallflower, never participating by choice. Elise became more curious about fun as her gangly body was replaced with a supermodel who had filled out perfectly in all the right places. For the last year and a half, she tried to hide from people pressing herself against a wall. She was still the center of attention. The boys could not keep their eyes from her. Continual longing glances came her way from them: the janitor, the male teachers, even the principal. The older girls hated her, as did some of the female teachers and the ladies who worked in the cafeteria. Elise had no idea how beautiful she was.

The future lovers talked for nearly an hour more. The conversation was intense, as they nervously finalized the plans for their daring escape. Elise began to worry about a myriad of things she knew nothing about. She had never seen Willie's house. What did it look like? Was it warm and cozy, or was it cold and uninviting? Was it drastically lacking a woman's touch? What was Willie's bed like? Was it firm like hers, or was it soft and spongy? Was it well-stocked with cooking utensils? Did the bathrooms work well? How big was the farm in comparison to hers? Was it successful? How could Willie be a carpenter and run a farm at the same time? He was only one young man. Suddenly, she was wild with anxiety. As soon as she had the feeling, she stuffed it, not revealing a single truth about her feelings to Willie. Only God knew how much she wanted to escape her farm.

About halfway through their special hour, Willie took both of Elise's hands and held them in his. She flinched. Nobody had ever held her hands this way. In her day-to-day life, there was no affection. There was sex at night in her bed, but that was it. Her father never held her hands or rubbed her back or brushed her hair. To her father, there was no such thing as genuine affection. Willie had tons of it he could wait no longer to bestow on his beloved. Elise had flinched, but she did not pull back. The feel of Willie's hands on hers was not unpleasant, but it was unnerving. It was physical contact in a different part of the house. Looking up from Willie's hands, Elise noticed his passionate eyes. Elise was willing to keep her hands still while her mind wrestled with how she felt about it.

The two lovers were dealing with quite different emotions. Elise was filled with fear, hope, remorse, doubt, resolve, and curiosity. Willie was all external. He wanted to hold Elise's hands, kiss her, take her right now dramatically. He yearned to express his love for this shy girl. He wanted to prove himself with actions, though he had already done that by his willingness to help plan her escape.

Now it was time to leave. Daddy had been gone long enough. He could arrive at any moment. Willie stood up. His body was aching to spend every bit of himself inside Elise. Once again, as he had many times, Willie headed for the front door, without being able to take Elise with him. Slowly, she followed behind him, filled with a type of foreign sadness. A cool breeze kissed Willie almost like a friend as he walked outside. When he felt Elise behind him, he quickly turned, took her by the waist, and kissed her fervently. He loved the puffy fullness of her lips. He had kissed a few girls before, but nobody had lip architecture like Elise. A moment later, he thought the same thing about her perfect breasts that he could feel in every detail under her braless nightgown.

For the first time ever, with anyone but her father, Elise leaned in. For a moment, she kissed Willie. She was trying to show him genuine affection.

"I love you, Elise. I wouldn't be doing this if I didn't."

"I know, Willie," Elise expressed with a heart that she knew only for him. "If it weren't for you, I would have nothing."

It was the most genuine words she had ever spoken to anyone. Once more, Elise leaned into Willie and kissed him tenderly. She was not an evil soul. She was, however, a severely damaged human being. She was physically beautiful but irrevocably wounded. Everlastingly mired in a gut-wrenching, survival mode, her ability to give any kindness to anyone was limited. As her attention to her father waned, her attraction for Willie increased. One thing that Elise knew well was sex. For most of her life, she was ignorant of her sin. This allowed her the comfort to experiment with receiving and giving physical pleasure. Now she wanted to share this one joy in her life with Willie. She dreaded the last upcoming nights with her father even though she had never found a specific passage in the Bible that stated that sex with her father was wrong.

To make matters worse, in the past few days, while reading the Bible, she began to wonder about Noah and his family. God had just completed his worst mass murder. After the arc landed on hard ground, didn't it make sense that Noah's family had to have sex with one another to keep humanity going? What about Noah's grandchildren? Who would they procreate with? Elise was not stupid. She knew the facts of life. No one would ever change her interpretations of the Bible. She was willing to learn Willie's beliefs, but if she disagreed with something, she would simply go her own way. A few days before her eighteenth birthday, she had made up her mind that she would never be a follower and that never again would she allow anyone to manipulate her physically or intellectually. She believed she was smart to judge what was true and false in life. If it did not make sense to her or if it was ridiculously illogical, that is what it was, simply rubbish.

Willie responded to Elise's leaning in by kissing her luscious lips gently, then her left cheek and each of her closed eyelids. Then he gave her a circle kiss, taught to him by his maternal grandmother. Slowly, the kiss covered her entire face. He finished by kissing her lips with such love that Elise's body shuddered.

The experience was the most sensual of her lifetime. Willie's tenderness was an incredible gift her father could never give her. She did not want to let Willie go. She wanted to cling to Willie and her wonderful feeling. The fleeting moment could not last. Her father might drive up at any moment. Deep inside herself, Elise feared she would never feel love again as perfectly as she was in this moment. Still, that survival mode was stronger than any other emotion. She did not want her father to be devastated tonight if he saw Willie at the farm. She had to push Willie away.

"It's time for you to leave, Willie."

Willie wanted to maintain her trust in him, so he turned and left without saying another word. He did not look at the stars. His head hung sadly to the ground his entire walk to his truck. He barely raised it to look over the dash to the road. When he turned south toward Toluca, he did not look back at the farm or his sweetheart. When Elise saw this, she dropped her head and left it down all the way up the stairs to her bedroom. She did not raise her pretty head the entire time she brushed her teeth. She walked that way to bed and tucked herself under the covers. She and Willie would not see each other until the night of their escape. They had planned it that way. They would take no more chances to bring Willie anywhere near Elise's father. Underneath the covers, which she hoped would hide her that night, she suffered immense longing for Willie. Unfortunately, the thin white sheets that she suffered beneath protected her from nothing.

# CHAPTER 7

The next few days for Elise were a blur. Within her was an emptiness that should have been filled with happiness, but it was dotted with episodes of extreme anxiety. Putting on her cap and gown, receiving her diploma, passing her eighteenth birthday, it was all joyless. The little pretend sheriff was his usual uncongratulatory self. The only thing that made him happy on Elise's graduation day was their getting into his old truck and driving her away from the annoying throng. On her eighteenth birthday, he said nothing. He was still trying to teach Elise that a birthday was just another workday on the farm. Sleep that had averaged seven and a half hours of tranquility a night diminished to four hours. Those hours were punctuated by nightmarish dreams and abrupt awakenings. She endured the interminably slow passing days, exhausted and afraid that some minute clue might be dropped to her father about her escape.

Would her father find her packed suitcase? Would Willie call in a panic and ask Elise about their escape within her father's earshot? Would the rapture occur before then and drag Daddy, Elise, and Willie straight to hell? Her endlessly ruminating mind dredged up every possible negative scenario she could feel from her tormented subconscious.

Three days before her scheduled departure, Elise contemplated suicide while peeing in the upstairs toilet. She would go downstairs, cut the phone cord, then slit her wrists in the bathroom. The next night, while they were eating supper, Elise thought she might get her father's gun and blow her brains out that night. The night before her escape, she fantasized about hanging herself from an ancient oak tree.

Each night, Willie saved her. His physical presence did not. It was his spirit. That presence could be summoned by thinking, "Willie, Willie, Willie." Then there he would be, bounding into her crevice of pain, whistling, his broad smile promising a better life for her.

Elise barely made it to her imagined magical day. Her heart was a distorted mass of jumbled data. What saved her was a minute ray of light in the dark cave within which her spirit lived. Hope was the illuminating presence amid her multitude of lightless demons.

That night, Elise had another problem. At 11:45 p.m., her father woke from a pleasant but unfulfilling sexual dream. He decided to continue his dream with Elise. This time, he intended to fulfill himself. He pulled back the spotless sheets and began rubbing his daughter the exact way he did that first night when she was six. Now though, her breasts were more than ample, firm with youth, and ever so sensitive to his touch. Elise, who had fallen asleep twenty minutes earlier, began to feel a sense of warmth flow into her beautiful body. Her father's hands kept moving, lower and lower, till he touched her where it mattered most. Elise woke with a start and a yelp. She sat up in bed. The little sheriff quickly moved his left arm to the back of her head to keep it still. Then he moved his right arm intrusively over her mouth.

"Be quiet, Elise. It's only me."

*Only you?* she thought. *You're not supposed to be here, and why should I be quiet?*

But she was. Lately, she was both unwilling and quiet during sex. Her father wanted it that way. It made him nervous when Elise moved or vocalized in any way. He was easily distracted, and when that happened, his body betrayed him. He liked her better when she would just be quiet and limp, so he could manipulate her any way he wanted for his own pleasure.

What was she going to do tonight, start a fight? Of course not. Once again, she relinquished the rights to her real self and became the dutiful slave her father wanted. Despite all these facts, she still felt pleasure. That was the bewildering irony. Her body often thrived while her mind was an unassembled thousand-piece puzzle strewn all over her inner house.

This night, her body was as limp as her spirit. She had to give in. Nature would have her most ruthless way with Elise slightly past midnight, June 15. In the final wee morning hours that her father would ever release himself inside her, the pretend sheriff impregnated his very real and incurably wounded daughter.

# CHAPTER 8

After her father relieved his stress, his body went limp as he turned his back to Elise and fell asleep. That is what Elise hoped he would do the next night, turn over and fall asleep as soon as he came to bed. On the big night she went to bed at 10:00 p.m., about a half hour before her father, she shivered with anxiety. She did not want him to touch her. Her eyes were shut when her father crawled into bed. Thank God, tonight he did not want sex. He did not throw his arm over her, as he usually did, not as a sign of affection but of absolute ownership.

When her father's snoring began, Elise's shivering ceased. Still, she feared she might fall asleep and ruin everything she and her savior had planned. Fifteen minutes after her now nemesis but long-ago beloved father had fallen asleep, Elise slipped silently from her bed and tiptoed to the curtains that faced the Vander Wal's farm. That farm began across the same road Willie would be driving on in a few hours. Elise pulled back a single curtain so she could get a better look at the road. She wondered how many cars she would see before Willie's truck pulled up beneath the bright June moon. She wished Willie could come earlier, but she trusted he would stick to the plan perfectly.

Soon, Elise would quietly walk out the front door, then sprint down the road to Willie's waiting truck. She would be wearing her slippers and nightgown and carrying two large heavy suitcases she had never used. Everything had been carefully choreographed. Elise would not change clothes. That way, if her father woke up and found her in her nightgown, she could say she was restless, and he would believe her. He would grab a sip of something from the fridge and go right back to bed. She had three pairs of shoes packed and plenty of homemade clothes. She felt that would be sufficient. They agreed upon no coats in the suitcases because they would take up too much room. Willie assured Elise he would buy her any kind of clothing she asked for.

Willie meant it too. He had saved 35 percent of his earnings and 50 percent of his allowance since he was twelve. Everything Willie told Elise about himself and the farm, she believed almost implicitly. Willie could have been the greatest con man in Illinois. He could have been setting her up for complete disappointment. All Elise had to go on was Willie's outgoing personality, his superb work on the barn, and his beautiful new Chevy truck. Elise worried that Willie was a "man of the world" and that she was merely a hick farmer. What chance to succeed with him did she possibly have?

She looked at her old Elgin watch, a rare gift from her mother. It was 11:50 p.m., eighty-five more minutes. She looked outside. All she could see was the epitome of tranquility. She thought of the many times she had sat in this rocking chair and looked out at the same scene during the various seasons. She was nostalgic. After tonight, she would never again have the modest pleasure of this view.

Without her knowing, her head slipped slowly to her chest. The gentle June breeze through the many trees that dotted her property had lulled her to sleep. She dreamed of a wedding cake four feet high, made of ice cream, with a foot-high bride and groom on top. Then she saw herself in a ten-foot white gazebo, kissing Willie. She was happy. She felt romantic. Suddenly, her survival instinct bounded to the forefront of her subconscious. Lightning struck from unknown reaches of the clear blue sky. Killer clouds rushed in, dropping copious amounts of rain on the serene scene. Everything started to melt, even the gazebo and Willie and Elise. Something was miserably wrong. This could not be happening. This is not real. *Wake up, Elise. Wake up*. She did, her entire body quivering with dread the likes of which she had never known. She looked fearfully at her watch. It was 12:37 a.m. Her catnap had lasted less than an hour. She had not ruined her plans. Still, she was terrified. Elise made up her mind to keep moving until she saw Willie's truck. She felt heartache as she feigned sleep-walking around the downstairs. There were so many special things here that she would never see again. Right beside her heartache over leaving her things was heartbreak for her father. She was leaving him, and she knew how he would suffer on the farm without her. She eradicated her sympathy for him almost immediately when she realized what he had taken from her. How many times had he told her, "Remember, Elise, this is our own little secret?"

When she went to check whether her luggage was still where she had hidden it, her watch said 12:40 a.m. She walked from the closet to the front door. She looked outside. Willie's truck was already parked where it was supposed to be. Her heart leaped with joy as she ran back to the closet and grabbed her suitcases. She was shaking as she opened the front door and sprung outdoors with her luggage. She sprinted toward Willie's truck, her heart beating tumultuously. The bright moon lit her way. When she reached the truck, she placed the suitcases quietly into the bed. Willie had the passenger door wide open for her. Elise hopped into the cab, slid all the way across the front seat, thrust her arms around her young man, and kissed him fervently. It lasted a full thirty seconds. Then Willie pushed Elise away and said, "Let's get out of here."

He sped off toward his farm, two miles north of Toluca.

Elise did not leave Willie's side; instead, she rested her head on his shoulder while placing her left hand on his right leg. She looked at the road that was quickly being gobbled up by Willie's speed of seventy-five. It only took twenty-five seconds to hypnotize her into a long-awaited peaceful sleep. She dreamed of her father's name and how she grew to hate him. In her safe harbor dreamworld, she swore she would never say it again. She never wanted to think of it again. She did not even want to be around when someone else spoke his name. Her times with this selfish little man were over, and from within this dream forward, so was any consideration of him.

The Stutzman farm appeared twenty-three minutes after Willie turned over the Chevy. It took only thirty more seconds to park the Chevy as close to the front door as possible. Tomorrow would be the day Elise checked her digs. She was still soundly sleeping. Willie flexed his carpenter's muscles after he turned off the truck. He gently nudged Elise's head from his right shoulder and rested it on the seat. Ultimately, he picked her up in a fireman's carry. It may not have seemed like a romantic action, but it was far more practical than carrying a five-foot-eleven 137-pound woman in front of him. Once over his shoulder, she did not weigh much. Once inside the farmhouse, Willie walked quickly to the first of two downstairs bedrooms. The door was open, and the room was waiting for them. The covers were turned down, and the smell of roses permeated Willie's nose. Earlier in the day, Willie had driven to Toluca's only florist. He tried to purchase every rose they had. Mrs. Schumacher, a retired schoolteacher who had always loved flowers, chuckled. She agreed to sell him six dozen but explained that she needed to keep two dozen in case anyone else in town might want to buy some later in the day.

Willie bent his knees and moved the thorny rose from Elise's new pillow. Then he gently placed his sleeping maiden upon the pillow. When he removed her slippers, revealed were very pretty narrow feet for such a tall girl. He pulled down the sheets and blankets from beneath her legs then pulled them up again and covered her tenderly. He kissed her beautiful lips and exited the bedroom, leaving a floorboard light on next to the bathroom.

He walked to the kitchen and pulled out a Coke from the old Kelvinator. He bounded up the stairs without hardly feeling them. Willie's room was the biggest bedroom in the house. It was enormous. Willie's father, who was a master carpenter, designed and built it for the complete comfort of his beloved thirty years earlier.

Willie brushed his teeth and crawled into bed clad, only in his underwear. His brain and body were exhausted. It was already after 1:00 a.m., and he had a full day planned. First, there would be making breakfast for himself and Elise, early morning chores, then a full workday in Toluca, building a house with several of his friends. Even though Willie was dead tired, he would have easily drawn the strength to make love to Elise, had the opportunity presented itself. Since it had not, Willie had merely tucked her into bed and respected her privacy. Elise had become the great love of Willie Stutzman's life, and she would be till the day he drew his final breath. Willie would see things in Elise that no one else would ever see. He had compassion for her. Falling asleep without Elise this night was difficult for Willie. He could not stop thinking about the first thing he saw in her eyes the day they met. It was sadness.

# CHAPTER 9

Willie Stutzman was smart, but he was not a mind reader. He attributed his perceived sadness in Elise's eyes to the fact she was probably a lonely only child. Her mother had died young, she had no friends, and was being controlled by a bossy father. The idea that she was a sexually abused child and woman never crossed his mind. It never would. Elise would never give him a verbal clue. She was a mistress of concealment. She was utterly successful in any surreptitious behavior.

Determined to bring happiness onto Elise's forlorn facade, Willie was up and making breakfast for himself and Elise at 5:00 a.m. He was tired but going on adrenaline. He could catch up with sleep tonight, depending on what Elise wanted to do.

By 5:25 a.m., Willie had finished preparing breakfast: an almost-buffet of sausage, toast, butter, honey, cheese, and strawberries in the omelet. He also served a large cup of multiple fruits. He placed all the food on beautiful antique serving trays that his maternal grandmother had used. Willie had planned all this, organizing everything neatly in the refrigerator. He got the two serving trays from a kitchen closet. Elise was still in a deep state of unconsciousness when Willie brought her breakfast tray into his guest bedroom and placed it on the bed next to her. That gave him time to go back to the kitchen, pick up his tray, and set it next to Elise's a moment later. Elise was sleeping on her stomach. Willie walked behind the bed, sat next to Elise, and began rubbing her back affectionately.

Elise felt Willie's touch immediately. Instead of jumping up, she lay there and absorbed this unusual type of affection. After less than a brief indulgent minute without moving, she almost whispered, "Good morning, Willie."

"Good morning, Elise."

She began to smell her surprise, slowly turned, and sat up. She put her pillow behind her as Willie grabbed the old tray and placed it over her lower half. Elise saw her breakfast and was overcome with emotion. When she noticed the rose on the serving tray, the petals on the bed, and roses all over the room, tears began falling uncontrollably from her eyes. They were tears of joy, the likes of which she had never experienced. Willie quietly watched them fall. Finally, he said, "You'd better eat up, baby doll, before it gets cold." When she heard his endearing term, her tears streamed strongly for another full minute. All this was so new to her, marvelously joyful.

"Willie, this is all so beautiful. I don't know what to say."

"You just said it, Elise. Now eat."

She did heartily. There were no negative thoughts in her brain. For the first time in her life, Elise was absorbed in a wildly wonderful experience. Never had this kind of attention been bestowed on her. She and Willie both ate their breakfasts quickly, a way of life when there was so much work to do on a farm. Willie, also carrying a full-time job, really needed to do the morning hustle.

"When you finish your breakfast, go back to sleep, Elise. When you're rested, check out the house. It's old and interesting. Take a shower or bath. You'll find everything you need easily. Take a *walk* outside and check out the barn and the outbuildings. There's lots of neat old stuff out there that goes all the way back to my great-grandparents."

"Thanks, Willie. I'm overwhelmed."

That is what she said. The darkest room in her subconscious was whispering, "I'm healing. Remarkably, the pain of my lifetime is regressing." From that moment, they ate in silence, Elise indulging in what she considered a bedroom overgrown with reds, as she thought of them.

When Willie was finished eating, he kissed Elise on the forehead. She felt it in her loins.

"I've got to get working on the farm for an hour or so before I leave for the house I'm building. I'll kiss you goodbye before I leave."

A couple of minutes later, Willie had washed his dishes and started his morning chores. An hour later, he kissed the sleeping Elise and drove to his day job in Toluca. The workday sped by. The thought of returning to Elise dominated his brain. At five o'clock, Willie said goodbye to his buddies and raced home to true love. Elise was in the kitchen cutting carrots. Willie said hello and walked behind her. He spun her around and kissed her confidently on her lips. That moment was the real start of it. Following that kiss were six weeks of bliss with the whistling carpenter and the farm girl. For the first time in months, she felt like she was not in survival mode.

Three hours later after Willie finished his chores, he joined Elise in a sumptuous meal she had prepared. It included baked chicken, sautéed veggies, and homemade apple pie. When Willie asked Elise to come upstairs after dinner, she knew exactly where else they were going. As they walked upstairs hand in hand, Willie complimented her on his wonderful dinner. It was the first homecooked meal anyone had made for him since his mother passed away. Willie led her to his bed and gave her a tender shove that caused her to fall backward. She fell atop a burgundy blanket. A moment later, Willie gently lowered himself onto her. He noticed that her eyes were like a wild animal, ready for the kill. When he felt her breathing increase, he asked, "Are you sure you want to do this, Elise?"

"More than anything, Willie."

"I love you, baby doll."

There it was again, that endearing term. Elise did not know what love was, but when she heard that term, she felt something.

"I know, Willie" was her response.

That was good enough for him. He would help Elise to love him through consistent kindness and abundant passion. He had plenty of those qualities and all the time in the world to display them.

While Willie believed that this would be Elise's first time, Elise was thrilled by the fact that this would be her first time with Willie. From their first touching, there was a profound fusion of tenderness, smiles, and unbridled passion. Willie was thicker than her father and longer. She liked it. Willie kissed places her father never did. He kissed her closed eyelids, her shoulders, her elbows, hands, kneecaps, toes, and the tops and bottoms of her feet. She imagined Willie as an explorer and her body was the land he was discovering.

Three hours passed, and the young lovers were still engaged. Sex was electric between them, like lightning bolts sent from above. Willie turned Elise's body every way he could, believing he was teaching her something brand new. Elise delighted in the way Willie moved her because it was all new with him. Her physical feelings were indescribable. She wondered how much pleasure her body could withstand. At this inception stage of the pairing, Elise was more than willing to let Willie lead. She would never, however, give Willie an overt clue as to how experienced she already was.

Elise felt her body completely surrendering to this dynamic duality of tenderness and passion. Her first three naked hours with Willie Stutzman were the pouring of an uncrackable foundation between them. She did not know it during this brief essential time, but Elise would never sleep with another man.

*****

Thirty minutes away, on a godforsaken piece of Illinois farmland, a small man who fashioned himself a tall western sheriff was suffering excruciating emotional pain. He did not know how to acquire help to find his daughter. He could not call the police. Elise was eighteen, a woman by law. And he knew what he was doing to his daughter for twelve long years was wrong. These horrible facts would come out in any investigation. He would be shamed, arrested, and jailed. He would become the laughingstock of the county. He would lose his precious farm even though it was an eyesore compared to the myriad farms around it.

The little sheriff wondered who stole his daughter. Willie was absent from his consciousness, so it had to be one of those punk boys from her school. Maybe it was a teacher. The little man who loved to live selfishly and, in his fantasies, resigned himself to suffer alone in silence. While Willie and Elise were playing with each other sexually for the first time, the aging farmer sat with his only friend, Louis Lamour. It was 1857, and there was an arsonist loose in a small Kansas town. He was the sheriff, and he had to lead looking for the culprit before the whole town burned to the ground. Maybe Elise would return home. The little sheriff would stay up reading and hoping deep into the night. The house was shut up like a tomb. There was no airflow. He had closed every window. If there was a job to do in the pages of his book, he would suffer less. After the story ended, his emotions would feel like a wounded body bleeding out. He kept reading till he fell asleep in his favorite chair, beside a five-foot-tall antique floor lamp with the faded yellow butterfly shade.

# CHAPTER 10

Six weeks! Heaven sent. These were the happiest days Elise had ever experienced. No longer was she in survival mode. Her transition to being Willie's live-in girlfriend was made smoothly by his easygoing lifestyle. Willie treated Elise to movies in Streator and Peoria. He took her to a good restaurant. He gave her back rubs, foot massages, and even read some short stories to her. A shy and quiet girl because of her upbringing, or lack of it, Elise began to talk with Willie. The conversations were just enough to talk about daily chores or how much or little she enjoyed the stories he read to her. Of course, she would also tell him how much she liked a restaurant or a movie.

At night, however, Elise sparked to life. Before they fell asleep, their bed was a living action-adventure. Anything goes! Never know what to expect next. Neither partner was embarrassed by anything. Let the passion explode. Now is time also to be tender, kisses like hummingbird wings on closed eyelids.

Elise's sexual voice began to grow these swift-moving weeks. She began to ask Willie for what she needed and Willie happily obliged. She smiled during sex and laughed. These were behaviors she rarely displayed outside their house. In public, Elise was demure, almost withdrawn for a farm girl with only a high school education and twelve years of sexual abuse. However, she often exhibited an almost-regal bearing.

Where this came from, who can say? Willie loved everything about Elise's public and private personas. On the streets of the cities and towns that they visited, Elise held Willie's arm, never took the lead in conversation, and was always attentive to her man. It was easy to understand why Willie adored the statuesque beauty who traveled beside him. At the end of the day, in their bedroom, inner sanctum, playground, Willie's rewards were uncountable, and his opportunities to give pleasure to Elise, endless.

On the Sunday of their fifth week together, Willie and Elise were married in St. Anne's Church in Toluca, Illinois, by Father Ben Brubaker. Brubaker was a happy-go-lucky chubby cherub that people called either Father Ben or Father BB, for obvious reasons. The ceremony was extremely simple and short. The church was sparsely dotted with thirty-seven of Willie's friends and a few cousins, who years before had moved to Normal to attend school and had remained there after graduation.

After they said their vows, which were vitally important to both youngsters, everyone in the church, including Father BB, went to Mona's restaurant for raviolis mostly. Willie did let everyone know they could have anything they wanted from the menu. Each person knew that Mona's and her sister restaurant, Caponi's, were famous for their raviolis. Almost everyone had been to each several times. Both Willie and Elise had steak and ravioli. This was a wonderful treat for Elise, who had never eaten at either restaurant.

When dinner and dessert were over, the three-piece band that Willie had hired took over. This was the first and one of the few times that Elise would ever dance in her lifetime. She was nervous and tentative, but Willie guided her gently and taught her smoothly. It all worked out fine because Willie had asked the band to play mostly slow songs so people could dance closer and romantically. He did not think Elise would have handled rock and roll well, and he was correct. Though she did not hear rock and roll music at home, she heard some at school when friends brought their radios and later in life in scores of places, but she never gravitated to it. She also never liked fast, loud music where she could not understand the words. She hated that. Willie was more liberal in his musical tastes, but out of respect for Elise's fragile feelings, once he found out what she did not like, he simply did not play it around the house.

Elise grew to enjoy a great deal of music that Willie liked, including big bands and a broad variety of classical music. During the wedding after-party, whenever any of Willie's friends asked Elise to dance, she was much too shy for that. But when Father BB, who was a genuinely nice man, asked her to dance, she reluctantly gave in. It was her attempt to be polite in an extremely uncomfortable situation. Father BB was five feet five and a half inches tall, a bit shorter than Willie. Unfortunately, he was just short enough to remind her of her father. Though they danced to the lively tune "Return to Sender," she cringed the whole time even though her partner was a perfect congratulatory and encouraging gentleman.

An hour into the dance party, Elise wanted to escape with Willie. It had been a long day. She was up early. No one helped her with her hair or clothes. She was exhausted, physically and mentally. She began to feel claustrophobic, wanting to be alone with her man. Of course, Willie jumped at the idea when she told him what she wanted. Within five minutes, they were being ushered out of Mona's by Willie's friends. Earlier, while the couple was eating, some of his friends had decorated Willie's truck with the customary just married signs and tin cans. A moment later, Willie was speeding away and waving goodbye to everyone.

They were on their way to Chicago, their bags already packed for a week. They were headed to a big city and a big hotel. That was all that Elise wanted to experience. Willie was planning to share quite a bit more with her. His parents had left him everything, including everything their parents and their parents before them farmed a lifetime to attain. Willie, on his wedding day, had $732,000 deposited in the Bank of Toluca. He was sitting pretty for a man of his age. Though he was well-off, Willie desperately missed his family, all who had died in their forties and fifties.

Willie did not share a single fact about his finances with Elise. She knew he owned his farm, which was three times the size of her father's, but as far as cash monies, it was like manna falling from heaven. She asked no question but trusted that Willie would take care of her without complaint.

It was in Chicago that Elise learned much more about Willie's hobbies than she had paid attention to while on the farm. It was interesting learning about them. He loved bird-watching, fishing, hunting, and sailing. He loved guns and had quite a collection in a locked room off the kitchen that Elise had never entered. They were stored in three large cabinets built by Willie's father. There were thirty-six in all. Some of them dated back to the Civil War. Some had been bought at auctions. A few had been purchased at estate sales in Central Illinois. A couple had been handed down to Willie by his great-grandfather on his dad's side of the family. Willie told Elise that it was a cool collection and that he would show it to her when they got home.

"I can teach you when we get back to the farm, Elise. I'll teach you about birds too. And I'll teach you how to sail while we're here in Chicago. What do you think about that? We can go hunting in the winter. It'll all be fun. You'll see."

Elise did not know what she would or would not like once she got back home, but she was curious about everything, especially about sailing this week.

Willie showed Elise everything he could while they were in Chicago. He took her to the Shedd Aquarium, the Adler Planetarium, and the Buckingham fountain at night when the water was dancing with colors. He showed her the wonders of the Museum of Science and Industry, the Art Institute, and the Historical Society. Elise enjoyed the Art Institute the best. On her honeymoon, she began to understand that Willie was a young man of his word. Whatever he promised her, he followed through. The day he taught Elise how to sail was the happiest day of her life. Willie wanted to keep things simple, so he rented a sixteen-foot cherry red catamaran with an identically colored sail. Ironically, Willie had no clue this color was Elise's favorite color.

The day they sailed. Willie was ecstatic to see the unleashed joy on Elise's face. They brought their few supplies on board and headed out. The boat was rented for the entire day. Unknown to Willie, he rarely made better decisions than that. Elise was enthralled from the moment she stepped aboard. The water was crowded with boats of all kinds, and it took a high degree of skill for Willie to navigate through the frenzy. Consistent with her dislike of crowds, Elise asked Willie if he could break away from the hoard and find a spot all to themselves.

"That might be a bit of a challenge, Elise, but I'll try."

He succeeded. It took about a half hour, but Willie found a spot where there was not a boat within a half mile of them. They were three miles from shore, and it was in this peaceful area that Willie taught Elise the simple method of operating a catamaran. She took to it and excelled. Willie was amazed at how strong Elise was, especially when strong winds came up from nowhere and made the cat hard to control. Willie could not take his eyes off Elise, the natural-born sailor. Looking at her was better than watching a movie with a beautiful female lead. Her muscles rippled as she maneuvered the cat farther out on the lake. She was a stunning beauty. He wondered if the joy in their marriage could ever exceed what they were experiencing at this moment on Lake Michigan. He loved Elise abundantly.

Five days later, on August 2, back home on the farm, Elise was still reveling in her honeymoon in Chicago. She woke up feeling extremely nauseated. She stood up next to the bed, feeling so dizzy that she fell back onto it. A moment later, a sharp pain hit the lower part of her stomach. It shot like a stinging dart, all the way to her throat. She felt like vomiting. This was a different feeling for her. She was never sick. She headed straight to the bathroom. She threw up and felt better although she was worried. She brushed her hair and teeth, washed her face, and walked downstairs to tell Willie what happened.

"It's probably a bug you picked up in Chicago, all those people you know."

"You're probably right," Elise responded. "What else could it be?" She hoped, as she spoke, that the incident with the toilet was the first and last of it.

"If you feel weird during the day, let me know and I'll pick up the slack." Willie stepped up.

Elise was fine the rest of the day. By its end, she had almost forgotten its beginning.

The next morning, she woke before Willie, and a half hour later, she was almost finished making his breakfast. Suddenly, she felt nauseated, like yesterday. This time, it was stronger. She nearly dropped her pan with the scrambled eggs in it. She took the pan off the flames and raced to the downstairs bathroom. She vomited profusely and frightenedly in the toilet. Willie heard her on his way downstairs. He hustled straight to the bathroom. Elise was bent over the toilet, not finished yet. Willie noticed tears streaming down her cheeks. She looked, to him, worse than she ever had.

"Honey, are you okay?"

"Not really, Willie," she said, making sure she kept her head turned away from her husband.

"That's some flu you've got, girl. Why don't you do what you have to in here and I'll finish cooking breakfast? Or would you rather I stay in here with you?"

"I'll be okay," she said, bravely.

"I'll see you in a few minutes then."

Before Willie got to the kitchen, he heard Elise vomit again, a horrendously painful sounding upchuck. In the kitchen a few minutes later, Elise was quiet, visibly shaken. Willie was sensitive to her plight.

"Are you feeling better, honey?"

"I am, Willie, but I've never felt this way two days in a row."

"How about you rest, and we'll see how you feel tomorrow?" Willie said nervously. "If this happens again tomorrow, we'll go to the doctor, okay?"

"Okay, Willie."

When the same thing happened to Elise the next morning, it was quickly decided that they would show up at Dr. Warner's office at 10:00 a.m. when it opened. Elise decided not to have breakfast, but Willie convinced her to at least have a piece of dry toast to help settle her stomach. Willie ate toast too but buttered.

Willie moved quickly through his morning chores and some of Elise's. At ten minutes to 10:00 a.m., Willie and Elise were in the parking lot of Dr. Warner's home, which was also where he had his practice, in rooms in the back of the house. They got out of the truck at two minutes till 10:00 a.m. At exactly ten o'clock, the receptionist unlocked the front door and said, "Good morning."

The hellos from Willie and Elise were subdued. They were both worried, and Elise was still woozy. In a few minutes, Dr. Warner showed up with his usual morning grump. Willie had known him for many years and was familiar with his ways. Elise, who was terrified of even a doctor looking at and touching her, was almost in tears.

Dr. Warner could not contain his lustful thoughts when he looked at Elise's perfect body. His nurse noticed it and was not pleased.

"I can't tell you today what I'm thinking until the results of your bloodwork come back in a few days," the handsome young doctor said.

"It's Wednesday. Can you come back Monday?"

Suddenly, time crashed in on itself, as Elise panicked at the thought of how many hours it would be until then.

"Do you think there's something terribly wrong with me, Doctor?" Elise asked plaintively.

"Oh no, honey," Dr. Warner confidently assured. "You're the healthiest specimen of a woman I've ever seen. I think something is going on with you that I think you will be able to handle. Be patient until Monday, and I'm sure we will get to the bottom of this. Meanwhile, I'll give you something for nausea."

Doctor Warner had his suspicions as to what was going on with Elise, but he did not want to tip his hand in case he was wrong.

The next four days were dark for Elise. Time had reversed itself to a mind-numbing snail's pace. She still had nausea in the morning but less as the medicine was working. She threw up only on Saturday morning. Elise was quiet and shy, to begin with, but pain and worry pushed her further into herself, and both she and Willie suffered for it. They made love Saturday night. At least that is what Willie thought it was. It really happened because they were frustrated. Elise's illness had contributed to them, not knowing what to say to each other. The sex was a direly needed pressure release that narrowed the void that had developed between them.

As far off as Monday seemed, it arrived with a spiritual black cloud hanging over it. That cloud threatened to burst the moment of revelation if that something was terribly wrong with Elise. If that cloud burst, it could drown the couple on the spot. Willie was almost as worried as Elise. The young wife was accustomed to emotional fear and pain. She was not structured to think anything, but the worst would happen.

At Dr. Warner's office, Willie asked the receptionist if he could go into the exam room with Elise.

"I'll ask the nurse in a moment, okay?"

There were no other patients in the waiting room, and Elise thought it felt like a morgue. The receptionist finished a piece of paperwork, then left the office. She returned a moment later.

"Mr. Stutzman, the nurse said it will be fine if you accompany your wife."

"Thank you, Rose."

Willie took Elise's left hand into his right. She was still not used to his genuine affection, especially in public, but it was comforting in this anxious moment. The couple looked exhausted as they walked into the doctor's office. Still holding hands, they sat side by side while waiting for what they thought might be terrible news.

Dr. Warner came into his examining room with all smiles.

"Elise, I have very good news for you."

The next sentence was the pin that burst that black cloud. It released its metaphysical deluge, but only on Elise.

"Elise, you're pregnant. I'd say about seven weeks along," Dr. Warner said.

"Oh my god!" Willie and Elise said at the same time but with totally different effects.

Willie was ecstatic. Elise was like a caged animal. Willie was about to witness the first of countless embarrassments he would experience living with Elise.

"Willie, I don't want this," Elise cried out. "It's too soon. We're just beginning to know each other."

"But, honey, this is a blessing, a miracle."

Willie was bubbling over with joy. Elise was filled with fear, the worst of which was that the baby might have been created by her father. She would never know for sure, but she was still gripped with fear.

"Honey, please don't worry. I'll be with you the whole way. Whatever happens, we will handle it together."

Willie's voice and logic were as comforting as his hand was a moment earlier. Because of it, Elise did not become completely unglued in the doctor's office. She was on the precipice of doing so, the first of innumerable such episodes she would have in the years to come. During most of them, she would become completely undone. For the next several days, Elise was so angry that it impaired her ability to eat solid food.

"I don't want this, Willie. It's too soon," she said at least a hundred times. Sometimes she would add, "We were having so much fun."

Willie tried scores of ways to help her.

"We can still have fun, Elise, and in a few short years, we will have a beautiful son to share our adventures."

He was talking to an impenetrable emotional wall, as her reachable humanity was dissipating under the enormity of her pain. Life had slid unmercifully back into the comfortability she had lived in most of her life. Elise knew nothing of how to raise a child. Within minutes of hearing her diagnosis, she decided she would learn how to take care of the baby not because she wanted to but because she did not want to destroy her marriage. She knew how much Willie would want a son. The real Elise was a mother who disliked her unborn child from the instant she knew it existed within her womb. If that secret dimension of Elise that was irrevocably insane could get worse, it did upon the diagnosis of her pregnancy.

Unbelievably, sex between them remained spectacular. No matter what else was happening with Elise or Willie, this was something to look forward to almost every night.

In October, the cold and windy nights gave significant hints of how cold the Illinois winter would be. By all indications, including what the Farmer's Almanac said, it looked like it was going to be back-to-back brutal winters. By December's first snow, a light brushing of the brown grass, the leafless branches, and the top of the mailbox, Elise was hardly showing she was several months pregnant. Her not eating and her extensive working around the farm contributed to her tiny tummy. The few people who knew her thought she looked better than ever.

None of that mattered to Elise. She evaluated her beauty from the inside out. Inside Elise, it was dark and foreboding. She would never let anyone near her mind. Better to keep the darkness, stay on guard, and never let a light go on that may reveal anything too personal. If that happened, what would people think of her then? Her looks would mean nothing. They would hate her. Willie would hate her. She would not let that happen. Willie was her everything. Without him, she would have nothing, be nothing.

The night after the first snow, it poured an almost freezing rain. A couple of hours later, it was sleet. A couple of hours after that, it was snow. It was another light brushing that covered the sleet that had preceded it. The time was 4:35 a.m.

By 6:15 a.m., Elise had finished cooking breakfast, with Willie only wanting two pieces of bacon and a glass of orange juice. In her haste to get to the barn to perform her next chores, she slipped off the top step of the stoop outside the back door. She hit the back of her head forcefully on the hard ground. She knocked herself into a frigid and dreamless state of unconsciousness. Blood poured from a two-inch crack in her skull. Moments later, the blood began to coagulate and then freeze in the twenty-degree air.

Willie found her fourteen minutes later as he walked out the back door. She looked dead. Willie's heart sank to a level it had not reached since his father died. He instinctively whisked Elise up from the ground and ran with her to the truck. He sped at top speed toward Toluca. Even though it was predawn, Willie drove to and stopped at the back of Dr. Warner's house. His horn was beeping loud enough to wake the whole town. Dr. Warner was up in a flash. He had heard those frenzied beeping horns many times before. In forty seconds, he was opening Elise's door and giving her bloody head a cursory check. His instincts had taken over, and he was not wrong.

"Let's get her to an examining table, Willie."

Once inside the house, the doctor asked, "How long has she been like this, Willie?"

"About a half hour, I guess," Willie answered.

The bleeding had stopped. That was good. She had not awakened, however. That was ominous. Dr. Warner removed a sterilized electric razor from a nearby drawer and trimmed a four-inch square of Elise's hair down to the scalp. He carefully cleaned and dressed the wound, checking to see if that part of her skull was still intact.

"I'll give her an IV antibiotic to keep any infection from beginning. We need to keep her warm under some blankets and as comfortable as possible. I checked her neck but did not feel any breaks. It appears that her head took the brunt of the impact. The damage was not quite enough to break the lower bones. She may wake up in a few minutes. That would be good news. If she needs much more time than an hour, I think we should call an ambulance and get her to the hospital. They could check to see if I missed something subtle. Either Streator or Peoria, your choice."

Dr. Warner spoke in dulcet, caring tones. If the speaking voice could have been a song, his was a melody. It was something like a tune you might keep singing to a baby after it falls asleep to continue to soothe but not wake.

Three days later, Elise awoke in her bed at St. Francis Hospital in Peoria. Willie was at her side. He had been adamant about staying with her. On the first night, when a hefty nurse tried to get him to leave long after visiting hours, he was as solid as a rock.

"You'll have to arrest me to get me out of here," he told her.

"Willie!" was Elise's first word when she woke from her long sleep.

Willie stood up and cradled Elise in his arms and kissed her. "Where am I?" she asked somewhat afraid.

"You're in the hospital in Peoria," he answered. "You've been here three days. Do you remember anything?"

"I remember slipping and hitting my head. After that, it's a black hole."

"I'm glad you're back, baby doll."

There it was again, that tender phrase that she so appreciated.

"Willie, you smell ripe," she said in a moment of levity.

"It's because I've been here the whole time, in the same grubby work clothes, without taking a shower."

"That's okay, Willie," she said, thinking about how dear the saying of his words was to her. "Now kiss me again."

Eventually, a nurse came into the room, left in a hurry, and brought back two doctors. They told the young couple that it would not be prudent to allow Elise to return home for another two or three days because they wanted to observe her.

When the doctors and the nurse left the room, Willie told Elise he needed to go home, shower, sleep in his own bed, check the farm, and return the next day. He spent the next thirty minutes giving constant tenderness and encouragement to Elise before he kissed her goodbye and left for home.

The moment Willie left, Elise began shaking with unusual and overwhelming loneliness. It was something she had never felt before. Even though she knew Willie loved her and would always be there for her, his leaving had triggered an uncontrollable emotion. Fear merged with loneliness, followed by shame. Suddenly, she felt as if she was a shell of a woman with nothing of her own. For the first time, a slew of hatred barged into her brain. She hated ice and that God damned little back stoop with no railings. She hated farm life with all its backbreaking chores. She hated Illinois because it had almost killed her. She hated this hospital and being forced to stay here, like a child. The wild mustang within her was raging. She felt like a prisoner. She wanted to be at home with Willie, where she belonged. Though she hated the farm, she longed to be with Willie. After a few minutes of intense hurting, Elise felt bored. She rang the call button. A moment later, a plump, friendly nurse named Dunham appeared.

"What can I do for you, Mrs. Stutzman?" Ms. Dunham asked earnestly.

"I'm bored to death. I need something to do."

"Do you mean a puzzle or some ice cream?" Dunham was being playful.

Elise picked up on it and chuckled.

"No thank you, Nurse. I think I'd like to have a book."

"Would you like a murder mystery, a love story, a book of crosswords?"

"No thank you, Nurse. Do you think you could find me a Bible?"

# CHAPTER 11

Young, strong, and determined to be that way for the rest of her life, Elise healed quickly. Once home, she was without complaint. Being with Willie was her dream come true, as it always would be. She determined to be more careful and protect her unborn child. Ironic, since she did not like the creature inside her. Filled with ironies, she began to think that she would make it an incredible being, unhurtable. In her fractured mind, she wanted to develop him into one of the strongest little boys that ever walked the earth. No one would ever bother him. He would have a different childhood than she had experienced. If the creature were a girl, she also would be made to be strong. Elise promised herself. She would teach her the facts of life early. She would teach her a myriad of self-defense techniques. She could not begin to imagine that Willie would ever molest her. The girl would be able to defend herself against anyone. Unfortunately, because of her fractured psyche, she still worried that Willie might molest his daughter.

By the seventh month of her pregnancy, Elise realized that she had become a much crabbier woman. She had not forgotten her slip and fall, but that was not what was occupying her mind. She began taking her fear and anger out on Willie. She nitpicked and nagged him about everything from forgetting to lock the front door to putting the cap on the toothpaste too tightly. She would engage him in petty little arguments, for which he would always walk away, shaking his head. Willie had long ago determined that someone else's poor mood would not bring him down. Though Elise could be constantly difficult, she was not nearly mean enough to drag Willie beneath himself. Willie Stutzman was a good and patient man. He was a practicing Catholic who believed in love and sacrifice. These qualities he would desperately need in the future to sustain his relationship with Elise. For now, Willie chalked up Elise's crankiness to being seven months pregnant, only eighteen, and carrying a child for the first time. He believed she was afraid of the unknown and angry with the changes her body was experiencing. Willie cut her slack because he figured that he would be cranky too if those changes were happening to his muscular, mesomorphic body.

There was one alteration to Elise's body that pleased both partners. Elise's already ample breasts grew larger and filled with sweet milk that tasted better than any Willie ever drank fresh from a cow or a goat. Willie delighted in their size and sucked that nectar out with extreme gentility and sometimes passion.

If things were not bad enough, something was about to happen to Elise that would change hers and Willie's lives together. It happened on a cold February day. The life changer was a tiny pebble no larger than a marble. The sky was filled with feathering cirrus clouds. The last remnants of the sun were dispersing light in all the colors of the rainbow. Streams of light streaked across the panorama. It appeared that a giant fan was lingering and expanding in the sky. The front of Willie's house faced west, the road. Unknown to Elise, several other farmers were watching the spectacular air show. This kind of beauty was rare anywhere, especially in Illinois, she thought. She wanted to relax and enjoy the show. She walked to the front yard, where Willie had put in a concrete sidewalk the year before near his driveway. The snow was two inches thick along the walkway. It was the crinkly kind, not the wet, good snow you could use to make a snowman or a snowball. Elise walked out of the front door. She was walking toward the mailbox and the road. A silent, subtle piece of treachery lay beneath the snow. Elise stepped on it, as she was looking heavenward. Her ankle turned abruptly. She fell to the concrete the moment she was wishing that Willie were there with her to witness the splendor. Willie, the human dynamo, was finishing his workday. He was planning to go grocery shopping and buy a bouquet of flowers for his beloved.

Elise hit the concrete with brutal impact. Her pregnant body twisted on the way down and the left side of her face and head struck the unforgiving walkway. Her head split open widely, only three inches from her prior wound. Her nose and lips cracked open and spewed blood onto the snow. Her belly took the brunt of the impact and bruised immediately an ugly red and burgundy. She was now in the deepest sleep of her life, a forced passage into blackness. As the brilliance of the sky show played itself out above her, Elise's life was oozing from her. Her body curled itself into a fetal position as her body began to bleed internally.

Two miles away, Willie was deciding which flowers to buy. After he chose and paid for everything, he headed for home, whistling "Rhapsody in Blue." He drove home slowly, taking in the last glistening sparkles of the light show. Not paying attention to anything but God's lovely sunset, he grabbed his grocery bags and flowers and hopped out of the truck, still whistling.

When he saw Elise on the ground, looking dead, the flowers and the groceries fell to the ground. The rhapsody ceased, and Willie let out a plaintiff wail. "This can't be happening again." He bent to the concrete and placed his lips against Elise's to see if she was still breathing. A light wisp of air seeped through them. Willie noticed her bloody head and her nose was an inch off center to her right. Blood had coagulated beneath her left nostril.

Willie instinctively cradled her in his arms and carried Elise to his truck. She seemed weightless as he placed her in the same fetal position as he found her. He whipped off his coat and wrapped it around Elise's bloody skull. He ran around the front end of the truck, jumped in, turned it on, and began speeding toward Peoria like a madman. He made the thirty-seven-minute trip in twenty-nine and pulled directly into ambulance parking. He was off the truck in a split second, racing into the ER. He grabbed the first doctor he saw, a young fella, last name of Jameison. The doctor could see the frenzy in Willie's eyes as he was dragged toward the truck. The doctor knew that in a moment he would have a big job to do.

Sadly, when the doctor saw Elise, he thought she was a victim of spouse abuse and that Willie was the perpetrator.

"My wife slipped and fell on the sidewalk."

"I see that," Jameison said, knowing he would report Willie to the police if Elise woke up and had a different story.

Within seconds, there were several staff helping to get Elise to the ER's center stage. One of the doctors remembered the Stutzman family and spoke to Willie.

"She fell again, Willie?" he said, softly. "She did, Dr. Henry."

When Dr. Jameison heard the exchange between Dr. Henry and Willie, he changed his thinking about spouse abuse. Willie watched what was happening from behind a huge glass window. He watched one nurse quickly start an IV while another cleaned Elise's skull. A third nurse began cutting off Elise's pretty, crème-colored dress from the bottom to the top. When the dress came off, Willie noticed the sickening bruises on her belly. The bruises were an enormous conglomeration of dark and grotesqueness that made Elise appear to have been savagely beaten.

Willie almost vomited. His tender heart ached for what was happening to Elise's body and what might be happening to her unborn child. He became woozy and almost collapsed. Instead, the young man found a nearby chair and brought it to the window, where he could see everything. He plopped down in it and fixed his eyes on the myriad movements occurring before him. A little over an hour later, Willie's body and mind, mutilated by worry and grief, sent him to another realm. His head fell forward to his chest, and he traveled to a peaceful dimension of rest and restoration.

Four hours later, a tired Dr. Henry placed his healing right hand comfortingly on Willie's shoulder.

"Is she okay, Doc? Is she awake?"

Trying to be as tender verbally as his hand was on Willie's shoulder, Dr. Henry responded softly, "I'm afraid the answers are no on both counts, Willie. We have no idea when she will awake. She hit her head hard. Until the swelling subsides, we will not know if there has been any brain damage.

"What about the baby?"

His ruggedly handsome face was filled with compassion.

"We don't know about that either. It will take time to see how strongly the baby's heart continues to beat. X-rays will show how much damage, if any, the baby's body sustained. What I'm most worried about is how long Elise was on the cold ground."

"Concrete," Willie interrupted.

"She is in definite jeopardy of developing pneumonia."

Willie was close to tears, but he suppressed them.

"I guess I'll be staying with her again till she wakes up, huh, Doc?"

"You can try, Willie, but this time might be much longer than last time. She hurt herself pretty badly, not to mention that she's fractured her skull for the second time in two months."

"Thank you, Doctor. I guess I'll just wait till she gets settled into a room, okay."

"I'm afraid not, Willie. The next room Elise will be moved to is intensive care. We need to keep an eye on her, especially if she has a brain injury. It probably would behoove you if you drove home tonight and come back when you are rested. I promise you that we will take good care of her and keep her safe."

Willie took Dr. Henry's advice, drove home, and went to bed, feeling lonely and lost. He woke up the next morning and made several phone calls. He called buddies to work the farm for him so he could spend as much time as possible with Elise. When he arrived at the hospital, Elise was in a deep coma in intensive care. He spent hours with her, watching her breathing. This same process continued for the next eight days until Dr. Henry approached Willie with news of his unborn child.

"Willie, after doing several tests on Elise's belly, we've come to a conclusion about your baby. I'm afraid that its skull took the brunt of the fall. The amount of impact the child sustained was tantamount to being struck by the swing of a baseball bat."

"Will the baby be all right?" Willie asked, a sickening feeling in his gut.

"First of all, that baby is lucky to be alive. Imagine being so tiny and incurring two horrific falls in two months. You've got one really strong unborn there, Willie."

Willie felt a little better for a moment.

"Second, we will not really know until the baby is born, how much, if any, damage to the brain has occurred. There are myriad tests we can do at that time, including the Apgar tests one minute and five minutes after the baby is born. I don't want you to worry, Willie. I have an instinctive feeling that you have got one heck of a fighter in your wife's tummy."

"I can pray about it," Willie said somberly.

"That is a good idea, Willie. Try not to worry. I have a feeling Elise and the baby will be fine. I've got to go now. Till next time."

Willie was alone again, except for his precious snow-white wife and unborn child only a few feet from him. He bent his head and prayed and cried.

More days passed, painfully slowly. On the eleventh day after the fall, the six doctors assigned to Elise decided to move her to a regular room. No system in her body had become worse. In fact, her head was healing nicely, and the doctors had pushed her nose almost to its exact position before the fall. The swelling had subsided on her belly and face. Elise healed in an eerie silence. So did Willie, but he was awake, hour after hour, suffering emotionally.

He had never wished to be Prince Charming, but he wished he could kiss Elise once and she would wake. At least in her regular room, he could kiss her often, whether she woke or not. The Groundhog Day life of Willie Stutzman continued till the seventeenth day. Then at 3:17 p.m., Elise startlingly awoke. She spoke a frightened rattle that shook Willie to his core.

"I've got to get out of here!" she shouted while her curious eyes darted quickly around the room.

"You can't leave, honey. You are in the hospital. You've just awakened from a long coma."

"I don't care about that, Willie. I feel claustrophobic. I can't take this. I've got to get off the farm, away from Toluca, the ice and snow, Illinois. I've been dreaming about it for what seems like an eternity. Dream after dream, with countless variations, but each one ends the same, Illinois is trying to kill me."

"No, it's not, Elise. You have had a couple of bad falls, that's all. Illinois is your home."

"Willie, let me speak. I believe in these dreams. They say that I'm going to fall a third time, and that fall will kill me."

"Baby, they're only dreams."

"Willie, I'm telling you, the very ground and stones of Illinois want to kill me. If they don't get me, then a tree branch will fall on me, like Cyrano. Or a barn roof will fall on me and take me out."

"Honey," he elongated the word.

"There is no honey, Willie. Ice and snow are real, and they want to kill me."

Willie began to think, "If this is what brain damage looks like, then Elise surely has it."

"Ancient Illinois gods are telling me to get out before it's too late. They told me they would kill a baby of mine. Did I have my baby yet?" She had no idea. She woke with a full-blown rant from her first words.

"No, Elise. You've got a little way to go before the baby comes."

"The dreams told me that we have to sell the farm, Willie. They told me that we have to move south, where it's warm and the ground will not rise up and snatch my life away. You don't need to be a farmer, Willie. You are a great carpenter. You can get a job anywhere. You can leave your legacy in a faraway place we have never considered."

Elise was crying desperate tears. It was as if some enormous force was pushing the words out from deep inside her belly. Her anxious husband began to wonder if there would ever be an end to her requests.

"I'm not kidding, Willie. The dreams helped me to think this mess through. They have convinced me that I am vulnerable to ice and snow. They convinced me that leaving Illinois was the most logical thought I could have. If we move to Florida, it would be like moving to Paradise. You can get a pretty penny for the farm. It's so beautiful compared to so many others I've seen. You have done an amazing job maintaining it. I'm sure there is somebody who will fall in love with it. That will free us to go on the adventure of a lifetime.

We could get a fresh start and fall in love with a new place. Maybe we could find a house on a beach. Wouldn't that be wonderful, Willie?"

Elise had used the word *love*. He had never heard her use the word. That is what Willie was thinking. He had told her he loved her hundreds of times. She had never said "I love you" to him.

"Do you love me, Elise?" Willie asked.

Elise paused a moment. "I adore you, Willie Stutzman. You are my hero. I don't know where I'd be without you."

That was all that Willie needed. Those were the kindest words Elise had ever spoken to him. Willie was quiet while thinking. He was contemplating the powerful loquaciousness of his shy wife and the joy he felt that she adored him.

"Willie?"

He was still in the throes of a deep reverie.

"Yes, honey."

"Willie, what do you think about all the things I said?"

"I honestly don't know yet, baby doll. You said quite a bit from your deep heart. You have given me a great deal to think about."

"I didn't mean to overwhelm you, Willie. The dreams just made so much sense."

"I can't make any major decisions right now, Elise. You've just come out of a seventeen-day nap. You have every reason to be afraid after falling a second time, but now that you're awake, you may rethink things. You may not feel tomorrow what you feel today."

"Watch me," she said, rather detached. Then she leaned back, put her head on the pillow, and fell asleep.

Willie was overwhelmed. Sell the farm? Sell the machinery, the animals? Move to a state he had never seen? Start a life as a carpenter somewhere he knew no one? His parents were buried on the farm, two hundred feet from the back door. He would have to leave them too. And what if Elise fell again soon? He could lose his beautiful wife and his unborn child.

The next day, when Will saw Elise, she had not changed a single iota. Day after day, Elise talked about selling the farm. She was relentless. The day she returned home, she spewed more of the same. The shy girl had become a strong proponent of "Let's get out of here." When Willie drove the truck near where Elise had fallen twice, a look of complete terror took over her face. For once, she did not look pretty.

Willie was beside himself with anxieties he had never experienced. However, his love for Elise forced him to begin to consider her demands, though it was terribly difficult. After ten days of Elise's constant nagging, Willie began to be titillated by the idea of moving his family to Florida.

On her eleventh day at home after her coma, Elise asked Willie to meet her in the upstairs bathroom after supper.

"Willie, I've got two terrible problems I want to show you."

"What are they, Elise?"

"Look at my right eye. It's wandering to the left. It makes me look cross-eyed."

Willie looked. "I can't see anything, Elise."

"Look closely."

Willie moved in. "I still can't see anything but two beautiful eyes."

"You must be blind, Willie Stutzman," she said, sounding old and mean.

Neither of them knew it, but they were remarkably close to their first argument.

"Then will you look closely at my nose? It's not coming out straight on my face anymore."

Willie almost laughed but stuffed it. Upon his close observation, there was something barely noticeable. Her nose was not perfectly straight, as he had become used to over the months. It was leaning ever so slightly to the right. Willie remembered seeing her nose in the hospital when she first got there. It was grotesque, cracked more than an inch to the right colored with hideous dark bruises. How the doctors got it back this close to normal, he considered a minor miracle. Now to be supportive and tactful, whatever had happened to her face, Elise was still a babe, and her flaws did not affect Willie negatively.

"You're right, Elise. When I really focus my eyes on your nose, I see a teeny tiny bit of off-centeredness, but when I look at your whole face, I still see the same beautiful Elise I've always seen."

"You are blind, Willie. I am not beautiful. Can't you see how these flaws make me look ugly?"

Willie had nailed it. Elise observed her new imperfections from a place so deep within her fractured self that no other person would be able to measure the depth. When ugliness fills your inner being, it is easier to see it on your surface.

"How can I go through life like this, Willie?"

Willie was compassionate.

"I love you, Elise, no matter how you see yourself. And I will always be there for you. We'll go through life and have fun."

"I don't believe in fun, Willie. I don't think I ever did."

"It doesn't matter, Elise."

It did not to Willie Stutzman. It was sex that held them together. No matter what words were spoken between them during the day, when night fell, sex brought them together. The fact that Elise was pregnant did not dissipate the passions between them. Willie's Catholic faith and Elise's dependency on Willie created another odd bond between them, but it was sex that held them together with a nominal degree of happiness. This fact was true despite how much Elise complained about her fears and imagined bad looks.

*****

On March 14, 1965, Elise birthed a baby boy. Willie was standing at the bedside when a nurse handed Elise the baby. Willie was shocked at what he heard and saw next.

"Oh my god, he is ugly, and fat."

The nurse cracked up and left the room and the couple to their own devices.

"No, he's not, Elise."

"Yes, he is, Willie. Look at his puffy face. It's all red."

"That's how babies are supposed to look. Have you ever seen a newborn before?"

"No."

"That I could have guessed."

"Don't make fun of me, Willie," she said meanly.

"I'm not, Elise," Willie chuckled. He was not going to become upset for any reason, during the second greatest moment of his life. The greatest was the first time he made love to Elise.

"I just think he looks odd, that's all."

"One of the nurses told me a while ago that we need to think of a name quickly. I apologize for not talking with you before now. Your falls and injuries to you and the baby made me forget about a name."

"That's okay, Willie, but it has to be a strong name, a really strong name."

"What about Michael?"

"Too common. People will be calling him Mickey. I don't want that. I want something fresh and new."

In the next few minutes, the couple went through a litany of possible names, none to their satisfaction. During their discussion, a nurse came into the room and explained to Elise that this was the perfect time to put the baby on her breast and allow it to get some nourishment. She explained every detail. Elise looked shocked.

"I'm not going to do that!" Elise almost shouted.

"Why not?" asked the nurse and Willie at the same time.

"It seems too weird."

"That's what most mothers do, Mrs. Stutzman," the nurse quickly countered.

"I'm not most mothers!" Elise quickly snapped.

Willie was silent and miffed, not knowing what to say.

"Most babies develop better when they suckle at their mother's breast," the nurse suggested.

"He'll develop fine, thank you. He will have a great father, and he will have me. He will have everything he needs."

"I'm simply saying he'll have a little quicker and more nurturing start is all."

"Just do for him what you for a mother who died in childbirth. I'm sure you have a backup plan."

"We do, but..."

The baby chose that moment to let out a loud wail.

"Oh my god," Elise said. "That's piercing!"

"All babies sound like that, Mrs. Stutzman," the nurse said, trying to be kind. She knew that this was Elise's first child, and she felt sorry for her nervousness.

Wherever Elise's fears were coming from, they were turning her speech into angry tones.

"Would you please take that little thing outa here for a while?" Elise forcefully requested, as if Willie were not even in the room.

"Whatever you would like, Mrs. Stutzman."

The nurse was professional. No reason to upset a young mother further.

As the nurse began to pick up Elise's baby boy, Elise looked at Willie and said, "I don't think I want another one of these things. They are so strange."

Willie was floored. The birth had been the start of a beautiful moment, but Elise had ruined it.

Thus, it began, the life of Elise and Willie Stutzman and their yet unnamed child, who would grow up to kill over thirty human beings. As soon as the nurse was out of the room with the baby, Elise's effect changed 100 percent. She was smiling before Willie had a chance to talk about why she did not want to breastfeed and have more children.

"Can we get back to picking a name for the baby?" she said with a perky nature.

"Sure, Elise, if that's what you want to do."

"Let's go to the beginning of the alphabet."

"Okay, Willie," she said jovially, not noticing the look of bewilderment on his face.

"Arthur."

"No," Elise said. "Andrew?"

"No, she said again.

"Ace," Willie said confidently. "No."

They were quiet for several seconds. Willie was reaching for an A name. Elise was going in a different direction.

"Mace," said Elise in a voice tone that Willie had never heard from her.

"I like it!" Willie said, the mention of it completely breaking through the ruminations of his wife.

"It's powerful, isn't it?" Elise said confidently again.

"Mace Stutzman. It has a nice ring to it."

"It does," Elise spoke. "It's exactly what we need for this kid. Do you agree?"

"I agree 100 percent," Willie said.

"Now let's pick a middle name."

Elise was a completely different woman than she was only a moment ago when the infant and the nurse were in the room.

At the same time, Willie was wishing he could have held his son. An odd thought came to his now-preoccupied mind. A father cannot hold a son to his chest and nurture him the way a mother can. He was saddened. He worried about Elise's methods of raising Mace, but he knew his own loving nature would contribute much to his son's development.

A few minutes later, they settled on Madison as Mace's middle name. Willie had a favorite actor when he was a little boy. It was Guy Madison, who played Wild Bill Hickok. Hickok was Willie's favorite western character. Elise eventually agreed, though she lobbied a few minutes for Hickok. Mace Madison Stutzman. Baby death had a name.

*****

Three weeks after Mace was home from the hospital, Willie returned to his carpenter's job. It was April 1965, and spring building and repair jobs had just begun all over small towns around and in Toluca. In the early afternoon of the first day Willie was gone, Elise decided to give Mace his first bath. It was not that she wanted to but because she had to—a maternal chore. There was no filter to the bloodcurdling scream she emitted when she saw the red slithery snakelike birthmark behind Mace's left shoulder blade. It was identical to the one she had seen thousands of times on the same spot on her father's back. *Surely*, she thought, *these marks are the cursed stains of Satan*. Elise now knew, for certain, that Mace Madison was her little brother, as well as her son. She screamed wildly, "How am I going to cope with this?" She took Mace from the washbasin and dropped him naked into his crib. Then she ran from the room like a crazy person. Mace was abandoned again. He was all alone and crying for anyone to pick him up and care for his needs. He was left unbathed, unfed, and unloved until he left the world for his dreams.

# CHAPTER 12

Five and a half months later, Willie Stutzman sold his farm and almost everything on it before the winter's first snow. He did it to help prevent Elise from having another fall on ice. He did it to help prevent himself from having to go through life without the woman he loved. Elise's dreams had frightened him. They were so real and vivid when she had expressed them. He placed credence on them. Many characters in the Bible had dreams that came true. Willie believed that God sent people dreams to help save themselves or to help them do wonderful feats. Why should Elise be any different on both counts?

For everything that Willie sold, his final take was $437,253.85. That meant that the sum of Willie's assets as he and Elise left for Florida was $1,325,550. This included $110,000 in bonds, mostly given to him by his father, and the interest he received on his savings in Toluca Bank. He was pleased that at 5 percent interest per year, for the prior year, he had earned $36,600. Willie had no financial fears about moving to Florida. He had no fears about getting a carpentry job either. He knew he was good. He knew he would be needed wherever he landed. He was humble about his wealth, not a hoarder. He knew that most of it had come to him due to the early deaths of his grandparents and parents. He felt sorry for the impoverished and every Christmas drove to Peoria and gave generously to homeless people who were not begging. He loved them.

Willie loved Elise too, and he gave generously to her. Elise had no idea of how much money Willie earned from the farm or carpentry. She had no idea of his net worth. It was all merely manna from heaven, and it never stopped falling.

Michael Stutzman, Willie's father, had always told his son that if all else failed, he would still have his coin collection. The collection was filled with gold and silver coins and bars that had been collected all the way back to Willie's great-grandfathers. Michael spent hours with Willie teaching him about coins. He told Willie stories about Jewish people during the Holocaust who bought their ways out of the gas chambers by bribing guards and other officials with gold. Willie could not wait to teach Mace Madison about the history, value, and beauty of these precious commodities. Nearly seventeen months into their marriage, Elise had no idea that Willie had a coin collection worth about $10,000. The coin collection would go to Florida with Willie, as would the gun collection. The collection was marvelous, and Willie began to teach Mace about guns when Mace was only four. At the tender age of twenty-seven, Willie made a will, leaving the coin and gun collection to Mace.

Before leaving Toluca, Willie and Elise decided to buy an eighteen-foot motor home. Willie convinced Elise it would be a good investment. They would save so much money on hotel rooms. It would be fun. Willie had not yet learned that Elise had only two ideas of what fun was. She was happy when things went her way and when she was having sex with Willie. A 1966 Clark Cortez was what he purchased. He drove all the way to Chicago to buy it. For its day, the Clark Cortez was expensive, at $25,000. Willie had no problem shelling out that kind of money. He was wealthy.

Willie had also told Elise that it would be fun to see all the beautiful sights along the way from the windows of a motor home. She was wildly excited to see as much as she could. The little sheriff had never taken her or her mother anywhere. She was so curious about everything she saw.

There was only one problem with the Cortez when Willie bought it. There was a minute crack about halfway up the driver's side window. It measured about one-eighth of an inch, less than that in width. It appeared that it would take forever for that crack to pose any threat. Willie, a shrewd negotiator, was able to talk the salesman down $500.

With a large trailer behind them, filled with the gun cases, the coins, and a few other sentimental items and furniture behind them, the Stutzmans were ready to take off. It was the start of a long trip, the destination unknown to either mate. Willie teased Elise a little during their first mile.

"Well, Elise, we're off to who knows where. Maybe it will be Georgia."

Elise screamed. "No!" A serious pout overtook her face.

Willie chuckled. Elise did not.

Willie's prized Chevy truck remained in Toluca. He sold it to Mike Pescetelli, a friend since childhood. Willie loved the Chevy brand but figured he could buy a new truck when he landed.

As the trip south began, the adventure of the Stutzman's parenting continued. On the farm, when Mace cried to be changed and Elise was home alone, she was always slow to do so. Mace developed feelings of abandonment because of this. Every task related to Mace was difficult for Elise. She begrudged all she had to do for him. She had no love for her little boy. As the baby's infancy trudged by for her, Elise continued to think Mace was ugly.

When Willie was around and Mace cried, Willie was like a sprinter, getting to him. Changing diapers, bottle feedings, changing his bedding, making formula, it was all easy for Willie. He did it all with unbridled love in his heart for the little guy. By the time Mace was three months old, he felt infinitely closer to Willie than he did to Elise.

Willie was becoming more accustomed each passing day, to the fact that he was married to a quiet woman. Nothing made that fact more poignant than when they drove hundreds of miles in near silence. When Willie became bored, he would often whistle. Most of the time, the songs were from the big band era. They were songs he picked up from the records his parents and grandparents listened to on their Victrola. Sometimes he would break into a classical piece. These were also taught to him by his grandparents and parents. They enjoyed listening to a radio station that featured classical music. Elise never minded Willie's whistling. In fact, while driving through

Georgia one day, there was a long moment of silence in the car. Elise broke it.

"I like it when you whistle, Willie."

Willie was surprised. He was also deeply touched by her compliment.

The miles passed quickly. Five days after starting the trip, they reached Florida. For the next few days, they explored Jacksonville, St. Augustine, Ocala, and Orlando. Elise found several things to like about each city. Unfortunately, after a serious evaluation of each city, Elise would simply say, "I'm not feeling it for living here Willie. Can we drive further south?"

Elise asked, and Willie complied. He headed for Tampa. As the Clark Cortez racked up miles on its new odometer, Willie noticed that the crack in the window beside him was becoming larger each day.

Tampa was not far from Ocala. Elise hated it immediately.

"Too much concrete," she bellowed. "This certainly isn't paradise." She had found tremendous beauty on Bayshore Boulevard and in many of the old houses near there, but she hated the beach. It was simply too small. She asked to go to St. Petersburg. Willie pointed the Cortez that way. It started to rain. It started slowly, and within a single minute, it was pouring. Though the weather was annoying, it did not deter the couple from driving. Willie, behind the steering wheel, was totally focused on keeping the motor home and trailer safely on the road. He slowed to twenty-five miles per hour while passing over the Howard Frankland Bridge. He looked to his left as a foolish driver sped by. He noticed that the crack had grown substantially in the last few hours. It was now four and a half inches long and nearly three inches wide. Willie began to worry.

Suddenly, the rain came down so strongly it seemed as if it would slash through the roof of the Cortez. Willie could hardly see the road in front of him. He slowed the vehicle to ten miles per hour. A few minutes later, they were off the bridge, the rain still battering the motor home.

Willie's eyes could go nowhere but straight ahead. Suddenly, he heard a loud engine noise that belonged to another vehicle. It was upon him in a flash, a crazy truck driver and his huge cab and trailer. He must have been going sixty-five, passing Willie less than a foot away. As the truck passed Willie's Cortez so closely, it caused a suction force so strong that it pulled the cracked window out into the pouring rain. Willie saw it fly a few feet in the rearview mirror, bend at the crack, then shatter on the ground behind both trailers.

Even Willie Stutzman could get upset, and he thought the truck driver was a real jerk. The rain pouring into the Cortez forced him to forget about the truck driver and think about getting the window fixed. Elise was not at all happy. The semitrailer was long gone in moments, the driver oblivious to what he had done. In a minute, Willie was soaked. The gusting winds blew the rain all the way across the front seat and wet Elise as well. She was not soaked like Willie, but she was uncomfortable. Mace was asleep on the bed in the back of the motor home. The rain reached him too.

"We've got to get this fixed immediately," Willie said, intensely.

"Where?" Elise asked.

"At a glass repair place, I guess."

"But where?"

"I'll have to stop at a gas station and ask or find a phone book and look up the address of a glass repair place."

As they exited the highway, they made their way through the streets of St. Pete. Finally, a frenzied Willie found a gas station at Fourth Street and Fourth Avenue North. When he located a phone on the side of the station, he pulled his long vehicle and trailer onto the property, taking up most of it. He hopped out of the motor home and went directly to the phone. Beneath it was a phone book. As he thumbed through the pages, the rain slowed to a drizzle. A1 Glass Repair was located at First Avenue South and Twenty-First Street. He memorized the address and ran immediately into the gas station to ask for directions.

"You're lucky, buddy. A1 is only about two miles away," the friendly store clerk said.

Once he passed on the directions, Willie was off. Ten minutes later, he pulled up onto A1's property. He jumped out once again, this time heading straight to the office and the boss. At the same time, the baby started crying, and Elise reluctantly dealt with him. He was slightly wet from the rain, and his diaper needed changing. Willie found the boss quickly.

"Excuse me, sir, but I've got a motor home that needs a driver's side window."

"Well then, let's go have a look. I'm Frank, also known as A1 Frank, due to the commercials on TV." He gave Willie a great first impression.

"I'm Willie. Nice to meet you."

When they walked outside, the sun was shining, and the sky held only a few clouds. In a couple of minutes, it had turned into a completely a new day. Willie thought that remarkable.

"Does this happen often?" Willie asked.

"What's that?"

"Pouring rain, then it's sunny a couple of minutes later?"

"All the time around these parts," Frank answered, noticing the Illinois license plates.

"This is a beautiful motor home, Willie. Are you planning to move here?" he asked as he noticed the trailer behind the Cortez.

"I don't have any idea. Somewhere in Florida, I guess. It depends mostly on my wife. Wherever she is happy, I'll be happy."

"You couldn't do any better than St. Petersburg, son," Frank said affectionately. "In my opinion, it's the most beautiful small city in the United States. While I fix your window, you should rent a car and drive out to Pass-a-Grille. You will fall in love with it immediately."

"I'll do that. Remember, though, whatever Elise wants, goes."

Willie made the remark from the heart. He felt no malice toward Elise because he decided to allow her to have that choice. Anyway, he had fallen in love with Florida from the first day he spent on tiny Amelia Island. St. Augustine had made his soul soar. He knew Elise enough to trust that she would pick a place of such intrinsic loveliness that it would make them both happy.

Frank looked at the empty space in the motor home. He had seen this kind of thing thousands of times.

"About twenty-four hours, Willie. You can pick it up anytime between 11:00 a.m. and 5:00 p.m."

"Thanks," Willie said. "Now can you give me some advice on how to rent a car here?"

"Hertz is probably the best, but you have to be twenty-five to rent a car. Are you or your wife twenty-five, Willie?"

"Not yet, Frank," Willie said with concern.

"That could be a problem, but there's Rent a Wreck. They rent cars that have not-so-good bodies but great engines. I'm not sure what their rules are, but we can give them a call."

"Let's do it," Willie said, hopefully.

They made the call inside the office, but the clerk on the other end told Willie there was not a car on the lot. Willie was upset. He knew he was in a jam. Frank felt sorry for the kid.

"You look like a pretty responsible person, Willie, are you?"

"Yes, sir, I am," he answered humbly.

"I've got an old car out back that I drove all the time for thirteen years until I bought a new Impala a couple of years ago. It's a 1950 Chrysler Imperial, a big straight-eight with fluid drive. The body is perfect, and I keep the engine in top shape. It runs like a charm even though it has a hundred thousand miles on it. I would be willing to loan it to you for the day. Do you know how to drive a stick on the column?"

"You're talking to a lifetime farm boy, Frank. I have been driving them since I was eleven. Fluid drive, I've never tried."

"It's really easy. Come out back, and I'll show you the car and how to drive it."

"Okay, Frank, but let me tell my wife where I'm going."

Willie went to the empty space where the window used to be and called out to Elise. She was still in the back of the Cortez, sitting with the baby.

"Elise, I've got something important to do for about the next twelve or thirteen minutes, then I'll be back with a surprise for you."

"Okay, Willie," she said sweetly. Underneath, she was seething at having to stay with the baby so long. She was perspiring and antsy but a surprise.

When Willie entered the backyard of A1, he saw the big black beauty immediately. It was the most prominent of the seven cars parked there. As he approached the car, he noticed the lovely long lines that adorned the front of the car. There was more room on the inside of a vehicle than he had ever seen. The trunk was enormous. The gray cloth upholstery looked brand new. He saw no scratches or dents. The car shined. This vehicle had been loved, and now he loved it too. He looked at Frank. He was smiling.

"Hop in, Willie. You're driving."

Willie was excited. He scooted into the car and placed his hands on the steering wheel. He felt like a king.

"Pretty nice, huh, Willie?"

"My gosh, it's beautiful, Frank."

"I couldn't agree more," Frank concurred. "Now let's learn to drive her."

Frank taught Willie the subtleties of shifting and putting his foot on the gas pedal gingerly if he decided to use that instead of the stick. It was cool. Not only was Willie enjoying his drive around the neighborhood near A1, but he also enjoyed Frank. Frank was kind, and it reminded him of his own father, whom he had lost at such a young age. By the time he had driven two or three miles in the Imperial, he was proficient at working the clutch and the pedal. Once back at the shop, there were about three minutes of paperwork about the Cortez, then Frank told Willie how much it would cost.

"Am I good to go, Frank?"

"You are, Willie, after you catch these." Frank tossed Willie the keys to the Imperial. Willie caught them and thanked his new friend. They shook hands. "See you tomorrow, Willie."

Elise was more than ready to travel by the time Willie returned to the motor home. She had packed enough food and clothes to last a day outside the motor home. She was remarkably efficient when she wanted to be.

"So where is the surprise?" Elise asked her husband rather impatiently. "Come outside, and I'll show you." Willie was excited.

"Do we have a rental car?"

"Sort of."

"I'll carry the supplies if you carry the baby," Elise said spritely.

"Okay," Willie said.

He stepped out of the Cortez first with Elise right behind. He headed straight for his surprise.

"Voilà!" Willie said, gesturing with his free hand toward his loaner car.

"Oh my god, it's atrocious." Elise could not help herself.

"It's not," Willie snapped uncharacteristically. "This is a wonderful car, and the owner was generous enough to loan it to me for nothing."

"It looks like some kind of Nazi officer's car."

"It does not, Elise. This car is 100 percent all American. I'll tell you about some of its special features later."

"I don't know if I want to hear them."

"Elise, can we change the subject or not talk at all for a while?" Willie scolded in a never-before-heard tone of voice. "You should be thankful, and you're not. It's shameful."

Elise knew she had said the wrong things. She felt childish and embarrassed in front of Willie. They were feelings she did not like.

"You sit in the back seat with Mace, okay, Elise?" Willie said, softening.

"Okay, Willie," Elise answered, an apology in the tone of her voice.

Ironically, upon entering the back seat, she thought to herself, *This is the most spacious and comfortable back seat I've ever seen.*

Willie pulled out his map of Florida, found St. Petersburg, and looked for Pass-a-Grille, as Frank had suggested. Getting there would be easy. As they drove, Elise complained about the lack of air-conditioning. She shifted her position while holding Mace, placing her back against the door behind Willie. Then she put her legs up on the seat. It was like a bed. To save the like new upholstery, she left her feet dangling off the seat.

"Comfortable now?" Willie asked as he saw Elise shift her position.

"I am," she said pleasantly. Elise was not always a bitch, especially with Willie. The problem with her was that whenever she was, she never believed she was being one.

As they drove to St. Pete Beach, suddenly the restaurants that dotted Gulf Boulevard stopped. They passed a small motel on the left and several small houses on the beach to the right. Then bam! A mammoth structure appeared before them. It rose several stories above the water, which began about 250 feet behind the giant building. Nothing else that they had seen in the area could compete in size with this structure. And it was colored pink.

"Elise, are you seeing this?" Willie asked, excitedly.

"Holy shit, yes." Elise was enthralled. Ahead, an enormous building arose like a giant birthday cake but made of brick, stone, and mortar, and it was pink. They were going too fast to see that they were passing the Don CeSar, a once-magnificent hotel built in 1928. It was being used now, by the Veteran's Administration.

"We'll have to come back here and see the place from a better angle. Would you like that, Elise?"

"I would, Willie. I surely would." At that moment, she felt like an excited little girl. "I think that's the most beautiful building I've ever seen."

"Maybe someday we can explore inside."

"I'd like that," Elise replied.

The road narrowed after the Don CeSar, with mostly quaint old houses and a few new ones along the roadside. There was a first impression allure about the place. It felt special, with a rich history. Willie noticed the numbers of the avenues going down, Twenty-Ninth, Twenty-Eighth, Twenty-Seventh. At Twenty-Sixth, he could not help but notice an old house, painted green and white, with the writing Hurley Realty on it. Also written on it was the phrase "Since 1926." Interesting. The street numbers continued counting down. At Twelfth Avenue, the road turned slightly to the right, revealing an intercoastal waterway spread out over a mile to the east, leading to land and lush green mangroves that extended to the south before they abruptly ended. The waterway extended to the south for over a mile before it merged with an enormous amount of bay water.

"Look at this behind you, Elise. It's gorgeous."

Elise was facing the opposite way, seeing only tiny cottages. She moved her feet and turned her head and saw what Willie was talking about.

"Holy shit!" she said again enthusiastically. "First, we see the giant birthday cake, and now we see this. What a place! I'm sitting back upright again. I don't want to miss a thing."

They kept driving. Willie enjoyed every beautiful sight he was seeing, as well as driving the old but smooth Chrysler Imperial. At Seventh and Pass-a-Grille way, Willie saw a small tree to his right. The branches were filled with over a hundred parrots, all singing what seemed to be joyous tunes. Whatever they were singing about, it sure made Elise and Willie laugh. Neither one of them had ever seen anything like that before. They wished they had a camera.

The blocks became shorter as the avenue numbers continued to drop. At land's end, Willie could only turn right. The road was only one block long before there was another right turn. Before he turned, both he and Elise saw the beach and water before them. Both he and Elise realized that after the Don CeSar, they had been traveling on a peninsula only one block wide. Willie made the right turn, driving only five miles an hour to be able to take in all the sights. From the road to the water's edge was about 175 feet of pristine sand. Elise's heart leaped when she saw it. Elise's heart never did much of that. At the far south end of the beach was a small concrete pier, about 125 feet long. Iron bars had been built into the last fifty feet so that visitors and fishermen could have something to hold onto. The wind was blowing strongly after the morning's fierce rain and large sprays of salt water came up over the pier's end. It looked like the front of a ship was being battered.

"Can we park the car right here, right now, Willie?" Elise shouted like a small wild child. There was a wonderful tone in her voice that Willie had never heard. Her request was undeniable.

Willie pulled the car to the curb wordlessly as he felt a new type of joy spring up inside him. After the car stopped, Elise, with baby in her arms, made a beeline for the water. As Willie watched how gracefully she glided across the sand, Elise stopped and made a quarter turn to the right, the north. Something had caught her attention from her peripheral vision. It was the Don CeSar, the enormous pink birthday cake. She saw it from a completely different angle than she had a few minutes earlier, and this was a much more beautiful view. Her current view showed much more detail. She saw the exact height, the building's marvelous angles, how many windows there were, and the little houses that surrounded it. The wonderful building that she was seeing, made her think that the Don CeSar was a jewel of the sea. It was breathtaking. In a moment, Willie caught up with her, and by that time, Elise thought this place was the garden of Eden.

"Willie, can you take the baby for a minute? I want to try the water."

Elise placed big Mace into Willie's arms before he could utter a word. Elise always acted quickly when she wanted something. She slipped off her thongs and entered the water. It was warm. Even though it was late October, the summer warmth lingered in the water. As she went deeper into the water, her lovely summer dress with the tiny roses pattern began to get wet. Suddenly, she took a deep breath and dived. She inadvertently began swimming to the northwest. It was a lucky decision too. Had she swum to the southwest, she would have swum into the powerful pushing, swirling current that always existed near the pier. Even powerful and experienced swimmers were grossly challenged by those currents.

Willie sat down on the soft sand after he saw Elise dive. Mace Madison had awakened and was cooing in his father's arms. Since he did not have a bottle with him, Willie decided to kiss his son all over his face, blow fart sounds on his neck, and tickle his tummy.

"I love you, little boy. I will always love you, Mace. I'll always be there for you."

Over and over, he repeated those things and variations of them. He laughed and giggled, and the seven-and-a-half-month-old Mace did the same. A bond was being created between father and son. Each glance from Willie was a piece of heartfelt yarn being woven into an emotional sweater of love that Mace would wear forever. It would be the only love that Mace the baby, the young boy, and the man would receive from any human being for a long time. Willie thanked God for these wonderful times with Mace. Outside sex with Elise, these sharings with Mace were his favorite activities.

Willie and Mace were both startled when Elise came running out of the water, yelling, "I love this place, Willie. I absolutely love this place." She had said the word *love* twice. It was a rare word for Elise. Willie suddenly had a pang of sadness. Elise had never said "I love you" to Willie. She had not told Willie that she loved Mace. He had never heard her say "I love you" in any fashion directly to Mace. In fact, he had never seen Elise show Mace any affection. He also wondered why Elise never reached out to hold his hand. She never pulled away when he took hers. In fact, when he did that, she seemed to hold on for dear life. She simply never initiated hand-holding.

"I'm glad you like this place, Elise. I'm beginning to fall for it too."

"Like? Like is too little. You have to love this place the way I do."

"Give me some time, Elise. Can we explore and see if it's as beautiful all the way up the street as it is here?"

"Let's do it." She was talking like an excited small child again. "Let's go after my dress dries a little, okay?"

Elise walked north, away from Willie. She did not offer to share baby holding time with him, but Willie did not mind. Elise was in her own reverie. Overwhelmed with the water, the coastline, the warm sun, the magical Don CeSar, she scanned her inviting surroundings joyfully. A gentle wind blew steadily from the west. It would take no time at all for her sheer garment to dry, especially since she was walking and skipping and not sitting down. Though she never had a chance, she could have been a good, maybe even great, athlete in high school. She fantasied now, about running the beach beyond the Don CeSar, thousands of times over the next thirty years or so. She was not thinking about her crossed eye or her crooked nose. There were no mirrors here to reflect her shame about these things. There was only beauty to gaze upon. It made Elise feel that the second dream of hers had come true.

About a thousand feet up the coast, Elise turned back toward Willie. She skipped all the way back to him. She could not wait for the next part of their adventure. The entire time she played, she had not thought of Mace. She only took him into her arms when Willie placed him there when it was time to drive. At that moment, Elise felt resentful. Mace Madison had infringed on her joyous sense of freedom. She would nurture those resentments deep within her. She would then sew them into the fabric of her son's, her little brother's, fragile psyche.

Fate, serendipity, and synchronicity are of like mind and enjoy surprising you when you least expect it. But when all three act together, it is like being hit by spiritual lightning. Willie pulled away from the curb. He felt the pull of first gear and, at twenty miles an hour, raised his right foot slightly and felt the smooth transition into second. Willie was in his own reverie with the car he wanted to call Princess when Elise started shouting, "Willie, stop. Pull over!" She almost stood straight up inside the car. She accidentally banged Mace's head against the glove compartment. Shocked and in pain, he began to wail. Elise kept yelling. "Park this black tank right now." Her loudness made Willie think the end of the world would occur if he did not comply immediately. Elise did not care if she had hurt Mace. It was an accident. He would get over it. Willie wondered what was happening with Elise. Was she having a heart attack, a nervous breakdown? She could hardly breathe, but she forced her words out through her anxiousness while frantically pointing with her right hand to something that was close.

Willie was anxious too. The dissonance between Elise's frenzied yelling and Mace's crying was annoying. Willie wanted one of the sounds to stop. He pulled the black beauty to the curb and turned off the engine. He looked at Elise like, "What now?" Elise tossed the baby on the seat and took off from the Imperial.

"Come on, Willie. Come on." What was she running toward like an attacking soldier? Mace was still crying as Willie reached over and pulled him into his arms. Mace opened his eyes and met Willie's, who smiled. Mace smiled too and stopped crying.

"Come on, Willie. Hurry up."

"I'm taking care of Mace. I'll be right there." Willie kissed Mace on his bruised forehead, then his eyes, then cheeks, then flush on his pretty little lips.

"There now, big boy. Now let's go join Mommy." Mace frowned. "Hurry up, honey. Come look at this."

A split second later, Willie saw where all of Elise's excitement was coming from. A few yards ahead of him was a for sale sign, and the realty was Hurley, one and the same as the company he had seen on Twenty-Sixth Avenue. Elise had seen that For Sale sign, and it had driven her into a different dimension. Now she was looking through the front picture window of a one-story house. Willie's interest was piqued. He did a cursory look at the house as he approached his wife.

Concrete block, strong, grayish blue with white trim. Everything looked new at first glance. He joined Elise at the window. She grabbed Willie's arm tightly, almost causing him to drop Mace. Elise began telling Willie what to look at, like a realtor trying to sell him this house.

"Look at that living room. It's huge. And look at those pretty tiles on the floor."

They were beautiful, each one looking like the sand of the same color had been pressed together to make them. At the same time, Willie was thinking that the living room was perfect for entertaining a large group of people. Plus, he would be able to see the water from his easy chair.

"Look at that kitchen counter, how far it extends from the appliances. I could make meals and glance at the water from time to time." Elise was beaming.

Willie, who didn't drink much, saw a big cabinet and thought he could fill it with alcohol to serve his friends. He could not wait to fulfill his dream of being a gracious host. Unfortunately, Elise could care less if anybody ever came over. She was an introvert most of the time. Willie was a friendly extrovert.

"Let's go look through some more windows, Willie," Elise said, pulling away from Willie and Mace."

She hurried to the next window to the north. It was partially blocked by a handsome bush that rose to a height of eleven feet. She had no idea what it was. She reflected for a moment on how back home, she knew almost every bush, tree, and plant. Here, she only recognized palm trees, and there were many varieties of them. She certainly did not know those names. She knew she had a great deal to learn. Paradise had much to teach her. She brushed the bush back, and she and Willie peered inside. Again, a closed white curtain made it slightly difficult to look inside. They were looking into a back bedroom. Nothing special, small, square, same tile on the floor. It was acceptable. Next, they scurried to the back of the house. Another bedroom. It was 25 percent larger than the first bedroom. Very good. Willie thought the room would be perfect for Mace. Elise's excitement was now embedded into Willie.

They peeked through the next window to the kitchen, a room of maximum importance to Elise. First, she saw the silver-covered oven built into the north wall. The refrigerator was silver, and so was the stovetop. These were all suited to her taste. The counter was her favorite. She would use that item the most in her growing fantasy. She imagined herself cooking ten thousand meals for Willie over the years, growing old there.

Next was a small utility room off the east wall, opposite the kitchen. Together, they saw a second door in the utility room. It was opened, allowing them their first look into the huge master bedroom. The room looked perfect, with voluminous closet space. A person could peek out of the bedroom to the south and west and see the water. Even from outside the house, looking through those windows, the views were breathtaking.

Elise asked herself, "What more could I want? It's the perfect home at the end of the garden of Eden."

"It's wonderful, Willie. You and I could be so happy here."

"And Mace, too!" he blurted.

Elise's face showed her true feelings about Mace by staring blankly.

"I like this house too, Elise, but how 'bout we take a ride up the street and see if there's a house we like more?" Willie said, logically.

But Elise's mind was made up.

"We'll never find another house like this, Willie. There are only a couple of houses between here and the tip of the peninsula. The farther up the street we go, the more houses and people there are. I need space."

Willie was sympathetic, but they took the ride up the street anyway. They were not disappointed. From Third Avenue and Pass-a-Grille Way to Twenty-Sixth Avenue, there was nothing but beauty. Cozy little cottages that faced the beach, a couple of tiny hotels and restaurants, a few houses larger than the one Elise had fallen in love with, dotted the street all the way to Twenty-Sixth Avenue. Elise, though ecstatic with Pass-a-Grille Way, saw nothing that changed her mind. She wanted that house way down the street near the tip of the peninsula.

Willie kept his promise and parked on the street outside Hurley Realty. Inside the business a minute later, they met the boss, Mr. Hurley. He was the only person in the house. When Willie and Elise walked in, Hurley rose from his chair at his desk and greeted the young couple. It did not take the kids long to see that Mr. Hurley was all business. They told him why they were there, and he was surprised because they were so young.

"That's a lovely house. Would you like to see it?"

Willie and Elise said yes at the same instant. Hurley wondered if he might be wasting his time. When Hurley locked the office and walked outside, he noticed the old Chrysler.

"I've seen that old Imperial around here for many years. Did you buy it?" Hurley was curious.

"We're borrowing it, but I'd like to buy it," Willie answered.

Elise cringed, thinking that all little boys needed their toys.

"Let's use my car."

Everyone got into Hurley's car, a 1965 Cadillac that still had the new car smell.

Inside the house, Elise fell in love with it even more. Unaccustomed to talking with Willie about business, especially in front of a stranger, Elise could not contain herself.

"Can we afford this, Willie?"

"Of course, we can, Elise," Willie said confidently. "Mr. Hurley, what's your asking price?"

*Here comes the deal breaker*, Hurley thought. "Twenty-nine thousand dollars."

Willie stuck his hand out unexpectedly.

"Deal!" He shook Hurley's hand hard and firm, to Hurley's complete surprise. There was no negotiating, no hesitation, no hint of doubt in Willie's eyes. In thirty years as a realtor, Hurley had never made a quicker deal. Elise almost dropped the baby as she threw one arm around Willie and kissed him unabashedly, with tongue and passion, on his unsuspecting lips. Hurley, a bit miffed at such a public display of affection, was still skeptical of the young people's ability to pay that large sum of money.

"You realize that there will be quite a bit of paperwork and that closing will be in about a month if everything goes right?"

By 4:30 p.m., the paperwork was complete, and it was time to find a place to spend the night. Elise had her heart set on the Castle Hotel, a cute little place she had seen only a city block from her dream house. They said goodbye to Mr. Hurley and drove directly to the Castle Hotel. After walking into the building and ringing the bell for service at the check-in counter, they were met by a tall attractive lady in her early sixties. Her brown hair, lightly infused with gray, was pulled into a tight bun.

"Good afternoon and welcome. I'm Mrs. Gibson. What can I do for you?"

Willie answered her, as Elise expected, while she found a comfortable chair to sit in inside the comfortable waiting room. "We need a room for the night and quite possibly for a month or so. We just bought a house down the street from here, and we don't know when the closing will be."

"You mean the old Palmer house?" Mrs. Gibson asked.

"I'm not sure of their name, but it's on Third Avenue."

"That's the one. They were such nice people, married for over sixty years. They got sick about the same time and wound up in the same nursing home. They died six months apart. You will be buying it from their daughter, who's happy living on Cape Cod all year. Kids today might be your lucky day in more ways than one. I have an apartment right above us. It's a one-bedroom, faces the water with a huge picture window. I think you will love it. I can give it to you for $275 a month in advance and a hundred-dollar deposit in advance. Wanna see it?"

"Yes, ma'am," Willie answered. His handsome, trustworthy face and midwestern manners endeared Willie to Frances Gibson immediately.

"Let's go up now."

When Mrs. Gibson opened the door to the apartment, Willie's and Elise's jaws dropped. Everything was white. Everything! That included a couch and two matching love seats, three white chairs, and a white countertop. Even the floors were white slate. It was an amazing space. Nothing was the slightest bit off. Every item was the color of freshly fallen snow. Dishes, towels, forks, knives, spoons, stove, fridge, ashtrays were white. The coffee table was white. The end tables were white.

After being blown away by the living room and kitchen's wintry look, Mrs. Gibson said, "Follow me, guys." In a moment, when she opened the bedroom door, chins dropped again. The Stutzmans were about to enter "the black room." The young couple immediately saw the concentrated effort to coordinate everything impeccably.

"I feel honored to stay here, Mrs. Gibson. This apartment is pure art."

It was Willie who was doing the talking although Elise's thoughts were identical to Willie's.

"I wanted to make a statement," the lighthearted Mrs. Gibson said. "There is nothing in the world that is completely black and white, except for this apartment," she shared, tongue firmly in cheek.

Willy gave her a wry smile while Elise pondered exactly what she meant.

"Do I pay you here or downstairs?" Willie asked.

"Let's go downstairs. We can do the paperwork there."

It was the third time Willie had done paperwork, but his attitude was still super.

"Willie, do you have $400 cash on you? The rent is due in advance, along with the deposit."

Willie had taken $10,000 cash out of Toluca's bank. He still had seventy-four crisp $100 bills in his pockets. "I just happen to have that amount with me, Mrs. Gibson."

Mrs. Gibson was happy. When she finished the paperwork, Willie reached into his right pocket and felt for the exact amount. When he handed it to his new landlady, she gave him two keys to the apartment. As she walked out of the front door to help her new tenants carry things upstairs, she noticed the old Chrysler.

"I recognize that car," she said. "It's been coming to Pass-a-Grille for years."

"This is the same car, Mrs. Gibson. Al Frank loaned it to us while we have a window replaced at his business. He bought a new Impala a while back, and he uses that car now. I'm thinking of asking him if I can buy it."

Another jaw dropped. This time, it was Elise's. She almost hated the car, thinking it was an ugly beast. However, she knew it was not her place to tell Willie how to spend his money, especially after he had taken such good care of her these first few months of their marriage. She just thought the Imperial was ugly. She had no idea that Willie would soon lovingly buy her a car of her own.

It only took one trip to carry the things the couple would need to be comfortable in their new digs.

"Good luck, Stutzmans," Mrs. Gibson said before heading back to her own apartment, which was located downstairs in the hotel.

Though Elise did not have anything directly to do with Willie's money, she was already thinking of ways to ensure that Willie would get his deposit back. Elise had her problems, but she still thought of herself and Willie as a team.

That night, they went to dinner at small joint about three miles from the quaint Castle Hotel. They came straight home after dinner, put Mace to sleep in his bassinet, and were in bed themselves, by 9:30 p.m. They had not watched a moment of TV on the white television with the painted white rabbit ears.

*****

The next morning, Elise was up at 5:45 a.m. She changed Mace's diaper, fed him a bottle of milk, placed him back in the bassinet, and dressed herself. Then she walked out of the apartment. She went down the stairs and out of the hotel. She turned left on the sidewalk and sauntered to the house that Willie had just bought for her. It was dark, not a soul around. When she got to the house, she walked to the left of the living room picture window, spread her arms, and hugged the house. She nearly cried as a rush of emotions crashed upon her. It was the most grateful moment of her life. She was grateful to her hero, Willie, and to the Fates, for granting her true wishes of a lovely home in Paradise.

Willie and Mace slept in. When Elise had placed Mace back in the bassinet, he knew she would not return for a long time, so why cry? He was used to it. Elise disappeared to the beach for a walk all the way to the Don CeSar and back. When she returned to the hotel, she began to cook. Willie woke up to the smell of bacon, eggs, cheese, toast, and coffee. Among her positive character traits that this poor, flawed girl possessed was that she was a dutiful wife. The couple ate breakfast on the white barstools that were turned slightly so they could look at the water as the sun was beginning to enlighten it.

"This beats Illinois, don't you think, Elise?"

"By far. Here, we will never have the kind of winter we're used to."

Willie asked Elise to come with him to A1. She said yes reluctantly. She had wanted to spend her first day on the beach. When Willie met Frank at A1, it was Frank who began the pleasantries.

"Did you like the car?"

"I sure did, Frank. It runs like a charm."

Frank scanned the car and immediately realized there were no new scratches or dents on the car.

"How's the motor home?"

"The glass is in, and you're good to go."

"Frank, I want you to meet my wife. Frank, this is Elise."

"How do you do, Frank," Elise said on her best behavior. "We're staying at the Castle Hotel, and Mrs. Gibson told us she knows your car."

"That's true. I've done work for her over the years. Nice lady."

"I almost forgot," Willie continued. "This is my son, Mace Madison."

Frank reached over and took the tiny hand of little Mace and shook it. "How do you do, Mace Madison?" Mace could feel the affection, and he cooed. "Let's settle up inside where it's cool," Frank said.

Willie paid with another crisp hundred. When the bill was paid, Willie surprised both Frank and Elise.

"Say, Frank, might you consider selling the old Chrysler? If you are, I'm sure interested in buying her right now."

"I hadn't thought about it, but I'd consider it for a fella like you."

"What might you ask for it, Frank?"

"I hadn't thought about that either, but I guess she's worth about a thousand dollars."

Willie was ecstatic. That was the exact price he hoped Frank would say. Willie reached into his right pocket, pulled out one of his two wads, and started peeling off hundreds. Frank was as surprised as Elise was. He was pleased. Elise was not. Frank reached out his left hand to take Willie's money and his right hand to shake Willie's. It did not take long for Willie and Frank to complete their business with the motor home and the car. When they were finished, Willie immediately taught Elise how to drive his new baby. She was not happy about it, but she found the fluid drive concept fascinating. She learned to drive the beast as smoothly as the fluid drive functioned.

After their goodbyes to Frank, the rest of the day was filled with driving. First, there was a drive to the Department of Motor Vehicles, then to Allstate for insurance, and next to a storage unit to keep their things till they could move into their new home. Finally, they dropped off the trailer to U-Haul. By the time they finished their dinner at Mamma Lucia's, on St. Pete Beach, they were both revitalized after the day's exhaustion. Their dinner, full of carbs before anybody talked about carbs, was the reason. Back on Pass-a-Grille, they both took a swim with Mace.

After that night, the young couple slipped into the pleasant routine of beach people. Willie decided to spend the next month or so with his family. He could find work easily after they were comfortably moved into the house. It was a wonderful month. Marvelous memories were made, especially the times Willie and Elise made love in the water when no one was around. Closing for the house came quickly. The move in was easy, and the passage of days melded into a living painting of sky, ocean, sunshine, and relaxation. One day was different. Elise told Willie she was going shopping for a new bathing suit. She bought the suit but did not tell Willie she had an appointment with a doctor whose name she found in a phone book. Elise did not want another child. Mace was an intrusion in her life. He had spoiled the privacy and solitude she and Willie had before he arrived. She needed to talk to a doctor about it. The doctor explained the methods she could use to assure that. She decided on birth control pills. Elise achieved her goal. Not only did she not have another child, but she also never told Willie about the pills or the fact that Mace was not his blood heir.

*****

Elise could have gone stark raving mad with all the pressure she carried in her soul, but Willie and Pass-a-Grille saved her. One day, while taking a walk up the street, she heard a beautiful sound. Seven Australian pines lined the street near the Castle Hotel. Though it was afternoon's middle, the wind was blowing rather strongly. As it filtered through the pines, Elise heard a strange and pleasant sound, unlike any whisper of the wind that she had ever heard. She loved those dulcet sounds. They made her feel joy to the core of her soul. Not many things made Elise feel this way, but for the rest of the years she lived on Pass-a-Grille, she listened for those sounds every time she took a walk.

# CHAPTER 13

The next two years passed quickly and rather happily for the Stutzmans. Willie got a job with Miner's Construction Company Inc., and his skills and work ethic earned him a supervisor's position in his twentieth month with the company. Elise was still a bad mother, neglecting Mace as much as possible, until he absolutely had to have the attention she could provide. Instead of Mace behaving terribly while he was two, Elise was the one who behaved horribly toward Mace. Potty training for the little boy was pure hell when Willie was not around.

"Hurry up! Aren't you finished yet? Haven't you learned how to do this? Are you ever going to be a big boy?"

Elise could not help herself. She despised the creature who required so much of her time and energy. She dragged him everywhere with her. She loved to swim. She dragged Mace into the water, determined to make him a great swimmer. By two and a half, he was. A great teacher, she was not. She was always yelling at Mace, always impatient, incessantly critical. Despite the verbal and emotional storm Elise was imposing on the little fella, Mace still learned all the tasks that she demanded of him. By the time Mace was three, he was a terrific saltwater swimmer. Elise already had vision of him competing against other kids his age over the years and destroying them.

Because of Elise, Mace was growing up tough. At his first haircut, he wanted to cry but did not. Already, Mace was a feelings stuffer, taught to him well, by Elise. No, Elise was not a good teacher. She was a bad teacher because she wanted Mace to grow up to be tougher than any other boy. She told Mace that smiling and laughing and having fun was a waste of time and unmanly. At three, Mace did not understand what Elise was saying. At seven, he knew all too well. She was an effective spiteful mother. Each of her godforsaken loveless parables assured that Mace would never be a balanced human being.

Thank God, Willie was different from Elise. He was less powerful and influential, mostly because he spent so much less time with Mace. Willie spent quality time with Mace. He laughed with Mace and always wondered why Mace was so withholding of his laughter. At fairs and carnivals, Willie bought Mace ice cream and cotton candy, simple treats, certainly. Elise would never do that. He whistled around Mace often. Mace never whistled. Willie taught Mace the names of birds, the names of the songs that he was singing. He showed Mace his coins and his gun collection. He explained the history and value of things, one by one. Mace loved this part of his life, the flip side of his agonizing life with Elise. Mace was a smart little boy. He listened intently to everything that Willie said because Willie had a refreshing way of revealing the essence and beauty of things. Mace was mesmerized by Willie's style of sharing information. By the time he was five and a half, Mace knew more about gold and silver than most adults.

At seven, Mace knew the names of seventy-five big band era tunes. Willie had played them hundreds of times on old 33 1/3 records and his old Victrola that his paternal grandparents had given his parents. They, in turn, had left Willie the music machine and the records to him. After years of listening, Elise knew the music of Duke Ellington, Tommy Dorsey, Glen Miller, Guy Lombardo, and more. She grew fond of the music of the '30s and '40s. The music brought peace to her. It was all connected to the times Willie whistled the tunes when they first met.

On April 15, 1972, Elise's life changed forever. Walking the tightrope between portraying a normal life in front Willie and being a certifiable paranoid schizophrenic, Elise responded to a knock on the front door at 3:15 p.m. It was the mailman, Fred Winthrop.

"Good afternoon, Mrs. Stutzman."

"Same to you, Mr. Winthrop."

"I brought your mail to today, junk mail, mostly, but there's a certified letter for you and I need your signature."

"There is?"

"There sure is. Just sign right here."

"Who is it from?"

"I have no earthly idea, but you will certainly know in a moment."

Elise signed. Winthrop handed her the important letter and everything else and was off. Elise walked to the couch, sat down, and put every other piece of mail to the side. She was extremely nervous. Everything on the envelope was typed. The return address said "John Robert Watson, Esquire, P.O. Box 217, Toluca, Illinois."

"Who the hell is that?" She opened the envelope.

Dear Mrs. Stutzman,

My name is John Robert Watson, Esquire. I am the attorney for and the estate of your father, Mr. Herbert Short.

Before she could read another word, a wave of dread drenched her with no warning. She turned away from the letter and looked outside. She saw Mace Madison swimming alone, confidently and strongly. Suddenly, spiritually scorching tears began streaking down her cheeks. Her thoughts were assaulted by myriad negative memories of her father, the little sheriff. Because the name belonged to her father, she had begun to hate it long ago. She knew that Herbert raped her for years. Little Edna began to teach her this almost a decade ago when they were both young women. As the years passed, she had learned so much more about rape and childhood incest. Most of her information came from Father Velkos, her primary priest, and Father Confessor. Her anguish this moment was overwhelming. She wiped her cheeks and chin and returned to the letter.

I am writing to inform you that your father passed away on New Year's Day of 1972. Several months before his death, he began coming to me regarding his last will and testament. Together, we forged a plan first to give you what he had in his safe deposit box in Washburn State Bank. Since your father was not an investor, what he held in the box were his only assets beside the farm and his belongings therein. The contents of the safe deposit box include a significant amount of cash, gold and silver coins, old currency, your mother's and father's wedding rings, and a few other pieces of jewelry he bought for your mother. He asked me to apologize to you for being a hoarder of valuables and depriving you and your mother many things that you deserved, like clothes, birthday presents, and even food. He told me that he fell in love with gold and silver from reading his westerns. Whenever he made some extra money, he would buy a coin here and there and watch the amount grow in the safe deposit box. He did not care about how much money was there. He only cared about the volume. He never told you or your mother any of his secret. He also told me that he always planned to leave it all to you when he died.

My fees have been paid for from the sale of your father's farm, the house, the contents therein, and all the machinery, tools, etc. I assure you that the amount left to you is quite sizable. It was not difficult to track you down because friends of Willie Stutzman's were forthcoming when answering my detective's queries.

The tragic aspect of this communique is that your father took his own life. I had no idea that this would be his final course of action. During our time together, he told me that he had a debilitating illness that would take his life shortly. I had no idea that there was anything else going on with your father until I read his suicide note. I did not include the entire note here because I believed that some parts of it were inappropriate due to content. There were some tender words that I will share with you now.

My dear Elise,

I cannot bear to live without you any longer. You were always such a faithful and loving daughter. Not knowing where you were these many years has been a terrible cross to carry. I know it is my fault that you left and never contacted me. I am sorry for whatever I did to hurt you.

At that point, Mr. Herbert Short chose to express the things about Elise that he loved the most about his daughter, most graphically. She would never see those words, thankfully.

She would have collapsed. So far, this letter had hurt her more than anything had in the last seven years. She was shaking, but there was still more letter.

Elise, I am leaving you everything that I will have after the farm is sold. You always were and still are my beloved daughter.

Love,
Dad

"Love Dad? Was he crazy? He dared to use the word *love*. He never used the word when he was alive. Why was he using it now? And what in the hell was love anyhow? How dare he?"

I would like to conclude my letter to you at this time, Mrs. Stutzman. Please call me, and we will discuss all this further.

Until then, I remain sincerely yours, John Roberts Watson, Esquire.

Elise put the letter on her lap and looked outside again. Mace Madison was stretched out on an orange towel, soaking up the rays of the sun. Now the rage she had stuffed for so long began to pour forth. She had seen the name Herbert again, a sissy name she had never wanted to hear or say again. She hated it. There was the other name she hated too, Short. Her father was short in stature. She had remembered the many times her father told her how he was teased when he was a boy. "Here comes 'short, short!'" they would yell. When Elise got older, kids tried to hurt her by saying, "Here comes the tall short girl."

So many people trying to be cute were hurtful. The jokes, insults, and ridicules kept coming for years. After this letter, she relived all those torments over and over for the next several days. The dark secret compartment into which she had packed her past was now open as a monstrous Pandora's box. She wondered if her father had taken his life with the same weapon she contemplated using before she ran away with Willie. In about an hour, Willie would arrive home, and she had to tell him. Doing so was soon to send arrows from her psyche that pierced her heart unmercifully. She could not handle this business on her own. She needed Willie's help, desperately. Still, she could never tell Willie the whole truth about her father.

Willie did not disappoint her. He never found out the reason Elise always had a sadness in her eyes, but he was determined to fuck away her sorrows. He could not, but he never stopped trying. No matter the difficulties he had dealing with her, he was undaunted in his profound love for her.

Seven weeks later, the Stutzmans were back in Toluca to pick up a check from the little sheriff's attorney. There were also the items in the safe-deposit box, as well as the few remaining items Herbert bequeathed to his daughter. Elise and Willie were shocked at the amount of the check for the share of the Short farm, the machinery to run it, and the lion's share of Herbert's personal belongings. The check was for $217,435.86. Next was the safe-deposit box. It was the largest box the bank had to offer. There were ten ounces of American gold, $725 in 90 percent silver coinage, $315 in 40 percent silver coinage, and a stack of currency totaling $11,250. Altogether, this was a staggering amount of money for Elise, who knew little about managing money and nothing about Willie's finances.

"I don't know where to begin to deal with all this money," Elise said in Watson Esquire's office.

"I'll help you," Willie said sincerely, immediately soothing Elise's anxiety. When she realized that her father had left her nearly a quarter of a million dollars, she initially felt no joy. She saw the money as a burden.

Going back to St. Pete brought something akin to joy to Elise's heart. She was now a dutiful wife and reluctant mother. Sure, she now had money. But all she really wanted was to raise Mace as strong and tough as possible so she could get him out of the house as young as she could so that she could live at 315 Pass-a-Grille Way with Willie Stutzman and no kid. Though she did not want Mace around, she continued to raise him with continual rudeness and disrespect. Once, at a swim meet when Mace was eight, he was racing against five boys his same age at North Shore Pool. The place was packed with parents, coaches, and friends of swimmers of various ages.

Mace was deeply involved in a four-hundred-meter race, leading by a full body and a half. That was not good enough for Elise. On the second lap, Elise noticed a little boy inching up on Mace. Oblivious to the scores of people around her, she shouted, "Faster, you little son of a bitch, faster!" Much of the crowd heard her. They were shocked, as was Mace, who proceeded to push his body harder. A lady near Elise strode boldly toward her and came right into her personal space.

"Ma'am, I'm sorry to have to say this, but that kind of language is not appropriate for this venue."

Elise, a full five inches taller than her criticizer, flexed her taut mesomorph body and screamed, "That's my son, and I'll talk to him however I want! Now get the hell out of my face!"

The unknown lady returned to her seat, somewhat embarrassed, but certain that she had been in the right. Elise was a fearsome force, especially when she was angry. Also, Elise was not interested in making friends on any day or anywhere. This moment she was completely focused on Mace's swimming.

Mace won the race that day, as he did almost every time. When he won, his mother was never all hugs, smiles, kisses, and words of praise. What she did say were things like "Now that's how you're supposed to swim" or "See how much better you are than those other kids." Everything she ever said to him and the way she said it was designed to humiliate him and protect him from harm that any person could do to him. She incredulously wanted him also to feel superior to other boys and eventually men. Somehow, it worked. Combined with Willie's limited loving, Mace continued to grow. Mace did not like girls. He preferred the company of boys and men. He was not gay.

When Mace was nine, Elise enrolled him in karate classes. Again, she pushed him hard. There was no room in Elise's fractured mind for failure of any kind for Mace. Driving around with Mace in the beautiful yellow Dodge Charger she bought with some of her inheritance money, it seemed like they were together all the time. Since Elise did not know how to love, her relationship with Mace kept pushing him to a dark protective place within himself. He did what his mother told him to do, but he was never happy around her. She was mentally ill, the mother who did not believe in laughter or happiness for her beleaguered son.

On the other hand, Willie began teaching Mace about his gun collection. He taught him how to sail on a fourteen-foot catamaran. He taught Mace the names, appearances, and habitats of scores of birds. They continued to share their love of big bands. As times passed, Willie taught Mace the music of the 1950s to the 1970s. When Mace listened to music with Willie, he was relaxed.

There was no pressure to excel, to win at any cost. When Mace hung out with his dad, he felt real joy.

Elise admired how smoothly Willie contributed to Mace in ways that she never could. She was also happy when Willie and Mace were together because that meant Mace was out of her hair. When Willie and Mace left the house together and drove off in the old Chrysler that Willie had named Princess, Elise felt peace. It was the same type of peace she felt when she ran away from her father. Mace was gone. That was happiness for her.

When Mace was ten, Willie taught him how to kill. It was in a forest near Weeki Wachi, where the mermaids performed. Willie began teaching Mace about guns months before they drove to the forest. One by one, Mace learned about guns until he knew the names and actions of all of Willie's thirty-five firearms. The ones they picked for their adventures were two pristine old Winchesters that once belonged to Willie's paternal grandfather. They were going for wild boar.

It was a large animal for a first kill, but Willie had faith that Mace could handle the challenge. At ten, Mace was built more like a thirteen-year-old. He was five feet five and weighed a solid 135. The swimming he had done all his life had made his muscles long and sinewy. He had a six-pack already. Mace was a strong boy, and Willie knew he was ready and capable. They had shot hundreds of bullets from those Winchesters before they came to the forest. Practicing had been wonderful for them.

Mace had looked forward to this day. Even though he looked older, he was still just a little boy.

He was ten, and he knew this would be the most exciting adventure of his life. Finally, father and son were walking into the woods side by side to find a good waiting spot for the vicious animal they hoped to kill. Willie was more than a father to Mace. He was Mace's best friend. Willie was the only person on the face of the earth that Mace loved. Willie had saved Mace from complete internal devastation. Mace had learned about love despite Elise. For her, his feelings were a jumbled mess, impossible to sort out.

"We're here, son," Willie said after they had walked about a mile into the woods. "See the girth of this tree. It's perfect for me to hide behind, and you can hide behind me. Let's gather a good amount of brush and build a small wall on each side of the tree, slightly in front of it. This way, if we miss the boar and it charges us, this wall may make the boar change its path at the last minute and we might get a second chance at it. Remember, under no circumstance, fire a bullet toward the highway. If the boar runs past us, he wins. We let him live, all right?"

"Okay, Dad."

Fifteen minutes later, Willie and Mace had stacked enough fallen branches, pine cones, and brush to make a wild boar rethink his charge.

"Now we wait," Willie said. "Do you want to sit down?"

"Sure, Dad."

"Do you remember how we are dividing our shots?"

"I do, Dad. You get the first three shots. I get the next three, and we keep rotating like that."

"That's right, Mace. Till we bag one. You ready?"

"I'm more than ready, Dad."

"Okay, Mace, let's get started. The first part may be the most difficult. We have to be very quiet and very still. We keep our eyes peeled in about this general area."

Willie spread his arms to indicate their general area to fire into if they saw a boar.

They did not have long to wait. Eighteen minutes after they began to lay in wait, with only an occasional smile between father and son, Willie saw an ugly creature enter his line of sight. It was moving through the forest as if on an afternoon pleasure walk, without a care in the world. Willie soundlessly took aim and gently squeezed the trigger. The bullet sped through the open spaces between the myriad trees but missed its true mark, smashing into the boar's left hind quarters. The creature faltered but recovered quickly and began limp, running across Willie's and Mace's line of sight. Willie's second shot put a pock mark in a tree between himself and the boar. Mace stood up behind his father, excited beyond belief, to take his first shot in a couple of seconds. Willie's third shot missed everything, disappearing far into the woods.

Mace, who was standing almost straight up, took aim. The boar, unknown to the hunters, was heading for its home. Slowed by extreme pain, it began falling every few steps then righting itself and trying again, by the sheer power of its instinctive will. Mace observed the number of steps it took between falls. The next time it went down, Mace fired. His shot zipped through the air and slammed like a speeding train into the hog's brain. The bullet flipped that forest monster right on its back, its four frozen feet pointing plaintively toward the sky.

Willie exploded with happiness and pride for his son.

"You got him, Mace. One shot, and you brought that beast down. You are amazing." The praise felt wonderful.

"But you helped me too, Dad. You slowed him down for me."

"Yeah, but your first shot knocked him on his butt. I am so proud of you."

Willie moved to Mace and hugged him powerfully. It was the greatest moment of Mace's young life and one of the greatest for Willie.

"By gosh, my son is a marksman."

Together, they dragged that huge animal the near mile it was to Willie's truck. That was a challenge. Lifting the animal into the truck bed was impossible for them. Thankfully, a couple of other hunters came by and helped them complete that task. Once home, Willie ran to the back patio and grabbed a wheel barrel.

"Shit, Mace. I should have thought of this wheel barrel before we left. From now on, we take this with us every time we go hunting, okay?"

"Sounds like a plan to me, Dad. It's better than killing ourselves dragging those things."

Willie bounded into house with the same exuberance he had shown Mace a couple of hours earlier. He was proud of his son and wanted Elise to know it. Mace sprung into the house with the same bubbliness as his father. He felt tall and strong this warm, delightful evening. Willie found Elise in the kitchen cleaning the inside of the fridge. He bent down, lifted her to a standing position, and spun her around. He pulled her to his more muscular body than when she met him and kissed her long and hard.

"What's that for?" she asked, having thoroughly enjoyed the kiss.

"First, I love you. Second, you are beautiful. Third, I have great news. Your son killed a wild boar with his first shot today. Bam! One to the head and done."

Mace hoped, this one time, that his mother would show some happiness, maybe even affection for his accomplishment. She did not.

"It seems your father taught you well, Mace Madison. I would expect nothing less from you."

There was no love for the little boy, and his soon-to-be many achievements were unlikely to soften her heart.

"Now let's go outside and skin and cut up that thing as quickly as possible."

Three hours later, the family sat down to a marvelous dinner of wild boar chili, prepared by Willie and Elise. Again, what should have been a night of praise from both parents was only half that. During the meal, Willie complimented Mace at least thirty times. Elise merely nodded and purposely put an expression on her face that was more enigmatic than the Mona Lisa's. Willie wondered more this dinner than usual why Elise was not more affectionate with Mace tonight. But then again, she was not affectionate with Willie or any-one else for that matter. Willie put it off as shyness and quietness, which was the result of living with a cruel father. Willie would never know it was so much deeper than that. So many times, Elise wanted to tell Willie the truth, unload her enormous burden. As she grew older, she learned about counseling services that were available to her. TV taught her. So did newspapers. So did sermons at church and books she read. But she never did anything to help herself heal.

Elise's past was hers alone, and it would remain that way. She would never allow herself to be embarrassed by revealing the depth of her abuse or the complex feelings of love she thought she had for the little sheriff for so long. Mace did not have a past to be ashamed of. He just had a future. He was damaged since he was in the womb. That would never change. Millions of physiological interconnec-tions had been wounded by the closeness of the biology between real father and Elise. How much injury this caused to Mace's ability to form properly, to care about others, to be a balanced human being, to love, only a one true God could know for sure.

# CHAPTER 14

Willie Stutzman meandered through life a carefree soul. He was oblivious to the extent of damage Elise was doing to his son. Mace engineered his way through emotional life lopsided and awkward. Externally, he developed magnificently. His muscles were huge, due to swimming, karate, wrestling, and weightlifting. His high school wrestling record ended at 118–0, largely due to Elise's raging ragging on him at every match. She was a nonfiltered, wild woman, who was repeatedly warned by school officials to cut out the cuss words or she would be banned from the matches. On those occasions, she would flex her own large muscles and back down even men. She clenched her teeth, as if she would attack like a lioness. She never attacked, but she was never banned either.

Mace Madison Stutzman developed socially inadequate. He did not like girls, and he rarely made meaningful friendships with males, but Willie was always there for him. Together, they went on several father-son adventures. Willie was a great teacher. By the time Mace was eighteen, he knew the names of birds like most young men knew their favorite professional athletes. Mace loved Willie unabashedly. Even when Willie was silent, Mace could feel love flowing from his dad to him. On countless nights, the two of them would listen to old records or look at coins. Some nights, there were few words that passed between them. It did not matter. Willie was a legend to Mace, and Mace was a legend to Willie, who always believed his son was special.

Willie began teaching Mace about the family finances when Mace was only thirteen. Willie did not trust the stock market. He did not want to take the time to study it. Instead, he was content investing his money in a variety of CDs. Interest rates were high when Mace was young, and returns on investments were substantial. Willie taught Mace the Rule of 72, how long it would take for money to double. He taught him to read the paper every day and see what gold and silver prices were. The more Willie taught Mace, the more curious Mace became. It was easy to be that way. Willie always taught with joviality. He made everything interesting and exciting. No other teacher could compare.

Elise was the worst teacher. She went with Mace almost every-where when Willie was working. She was always scolding, pushing him to excel. He did. Of his many accomplishments, earning a black belt in karate at sixteen years and ten months was one. His wrestling earned him All-American honors. He was not a perfect swimmer, but he was All-State. Elise was relentless in her agitation of her son. When Willie was around, she was a completely different behavioral study. Her cruelty disappeared, but the best she could do was, "Come on, boy. Come on, Mace." Elise lifted weight with Mace five nights a week at a local gym. She forced the tired athlete to do this.

There she screamed and nagged also even though, at first, she knew nothing about lifting. She learned, and within a year, she was built like a competitive bodybuilder. Mace looked great too, but he did not compete, though he had become huge. By the end of his senior year, he was six feet five inches tall and weighed 285 pounds.

Lastly, she was vitally concerned with Mace's schoolwork. From first grade through senior year in high school, Elise made certain that Mace did his homework every night. He was a smart kid besides her nagging. He made the honor roll in high school six times. In his youth, everything Mace did had to be sanctioned by his mother. He played the sports she wanted. The hobbies he shared with Willie received her stamp of approval. Elise wanted Mace to have a sound mind in a sound body, but she had no idea how her influences splin-tered Mace's mind into countless emotional fractals. What she got from Mace was a brave heart, a massive body, with a wounded child-like emotional makeup. He was a well-mannered boy, trained mostly by Willie in that regard, but he would not take any crap from any-one. He had a short fuse when it came to perceived bullshit.

By the time Mace graduated from high school, he had worked his way into the top 10 percent of his class. He learned fast. His classmates viewed him as a shy but formidable presence. He was primed to go any direction he wanted to in life, but since early junior year, he had been talking with Willie about a career in the military.

"I love to shoot guns, Dad. I love hunting wild boar with you. I love this country, and I want to do something for it and make you and Mother proud of me. College seems too slow. I've been fighting all my life, one way or another. I think I would make a good soldier. That way, I can go to where some real action is. College would be too slow for me. I'd be stuck in one place. As a soldier, I could see the world."

When Mace started talking about the military, he was beginning to talk about his feelings. Neither parent had ever talked with Mace about his feelings. Elise did not care. Willie, though he loved his son dearly, was more of a father of action, of sharing adventures with Mace, not talking about feelings.

But Mace had them. Though rarely expressed, they were deeply felt. Mace had seen many mothers in his lifetime. He had seen them hug and kiss their children and encourage them without profanity and the anger his mother exhibited. Elise would not even touch Mace once he was old enough to care for himself. On the few occasions, he tried to kiss her on the cheek, she thrust her head and body away from him as if a lightning bolt had crackled between them. He was profoundly saddened by his mother's lack of affection. Yet he yearned for It. Despite the countless rejections, the unending scolding, the overt public put-downs, he pined for her affection. This abject lacking that he had felt all his life had disassembled his emotions as if they were a complex thousand-piece puzzle comprised of distorted images, almost unrecognizable.

*Thank God for my father*, he often thought. *He's a gem.* Mace Stutzman wanted to please Willie more than anything else he wanted to do in life. Willie was his best friend. On Mace's sixteenth birthday, Willie gave him the 1950 Chrysler, Princess.

"You have earned this, son," Willie told Mace. Then he hugged Mace with his own taut body, and Mace felt like a kid on Christmas morning.

"Thank you, Dad," Mace said jovially, then he tightly bear-hugged Willie, lifted him off the ground, and kissed him repeatedly on the top of his head. Willie began to laugh hysterically even though most of his face was pressed against his son's muscular chest. Mace was on top of the world, sharing one of the best possible moments a son could share with his father. How sincerely Mace wanted the approval of this little man who stood like a giant in his mind.

"Take care of her, Mace."

"I will, Dad."

"I'll help you, Mace. It will be fun. Maybe we can keep it running for a few more decades."

"I sure hope so, Dad."

Mace knew what love was, and he knew what love was not. But he could never reason the answer to the questions, Why would my mother spend so much time with me if she doesn't love me? Why would she always come to my events and push me to be the best? Why would she hover over me like a mother hen if she didn't love me? As corrupted as Mace's soul was, it was Elise who did not know how to love, for reasons Mace would never know.

To the immense heartache of Willie and the sublime delight of Elise, Mace enlisted in the United States Marine Corps on August 8, 1982. Willie shed tears. He hugged Mace as if for the last time. Elise's heart was absurdly empty as she reached out a tepid hand to grasp her son's.

"Take care of Princess for me while I'm gone, Dad."

"You bet I will, son."

"Thank you for all the wonderful memories, Dad, and all the amazing things you taught me."

"You're welcome, Mace. I hope those things will help you have a more enjoyable life."

"I'm sure they will, Dad."

"I love you, Mace."

"I love you too, Dad."

Then Mace Madison Stutzman kissed his dad on the cheek, then slid down a little and blew a fart sound on his neck—as Willie had done so often to him when he was little. They both had a good laugh during a sad day. When it was Elise's turn to say goodbye, all she did was grab Mace's hand, strongly pulled him toward her, and positioned her lips next to his right ear so only he could hear. She spoke tersely but with controlled softness.

"Make me proud, Mace Madison. Don't embarrass yourself or me."

His lips were so close to hers. He wanted to lean in and brush his across hers just once, in this intimate farewell. Could she grant him one moment of kindness before he left? She gave nothing, pulling away immediately after she spoke. His dream of a token of affection was dashed. She could have eased so much of his anxiety with a pinch of kindness. She was unwilling, and her insensitivity rendered Mace a more fractured spirit than he already was. Mace was off to his next adventure, with the last words of his parents resonating in his brain.

Though totally different, those words were enough to propel him to excel. At Parris Island, basic training was fun for Mace. In combat training with other soldiers, he was unbeatable. When drill instructors go up into Mace's face, trying to humiliate him, he simply looked right through their eyes to the backs of their skulls. He was unflappable. As difficult as it was to imagine, compared to Elise, they were amateurs. Mace was a silent soldier. In fact, his lack of language use was legendary with his fellow soldiers. Mace needed to be the best. There were enormously driving forces within him. The obstacles he faced were challenges he faced with aplomb. No task was too large that he did not shine while performing it. If cleaning a toilet, he would scrub so hard that he almost cracked the porcelain.

Mace used the activity to fill the myriad holes within himself. It was a futile pursuit because movement was temporary, porous, emotional concrete that dissipated as soon as it was poured. Only true peace could fill a single hole. Mace Madison had no peace.

Thirteen weeks can be a universe of time. Each day stretches agonizingly from a predawn wake up to falling into bed without being able to spend another ounce of sweat or blood. Time and tasks force every man to learn to share duties with barracks mates. Name recognition, acquaintances, enemies. Most guys deal with those things. Mace had no enemies. Not only was his size intimidating, but he was also a consummate gentleman with every young man in the barracks.

Even when he whipped them soundly, they did not despise him. They knew going in they would lose, so why hate a gentleman champion? Besides, they learned to be tougher because of him. That was a good thing. They knew that they were fighting the best, and there was honor in that. Their losses now may save their life later. Mace's parental voices drove him, for sure; but despite all the abuse that befell him, Mace was becoming his own strong driving voice.

Tyler Frailing was Mace's best friend. He was a farm boy from Quincy, Illinois, about 170 miles from Toluca. He was fresh out of high school, where he had played basketball and averaged 17.3, sixth best in his conference. He was an imposing young man in his own right at six feet three and 192 pounds. Although he was two inches shorter and 60 pounds lighter than Mace, they made a powerful impression when they stood side by side. Tyler's muscles were long and lean. He looked like a point guard, which he was. Mace's muscles were short, tight, and huge. Tyler had red hair. Mace's was blond. The biggest difference between them was that Tyler was always smiling and joking around, sort of like Willie. It was no wonder that Mace would like the kid. Mace's was wry and as rare as a Goudey Babe Ruth card in a high grade. Both boys were incredibly handsome, though Mace never thought he was because Elise had always told him he was ugly. Tyler knew he was a good-looking kid because his parents were well-balanced and told him so, often.

The new friends were also bunkmates—a phenomenon that has happened tens of thousands of times in the military. Words between them were few, but they bonded over numerous small things. One soldier would tell the other that their bedsheets were not tight enough, or they had an open button on a dress shirt. They did not talk about sports much. They talked about how to be good soldiers. They talked about and wondered where their first deployment would be.

They did not have to wait long to find out. Two weeks after basic training, followed by extended firearms training, both boys were deployed to Lebanon. It was part of a vaguely organized peace-keeping force designed to protect the integrity of the capitol building and grounds. The boys and their mates were told on the plane, that President Reagan believed that it was imperative that Israel withdraw from Beirut. Mace, Tyler, and each of their fellow soldiers had not even reached legal drinking age or voted yet, but fate had brought fifty of them here. Seven were from the same barracks as Mace and Tyler were in basic training. Here, in this frightening place, Marines had significant losses in recent battles. Their presence in the area was significantly reduced. However, a surprise was waiting for twenty-five of the fifty soldiers on the plane. US powers to be had decided to order them on a humanitarian mission while the remaining twenty-five were sent to various sites that had recently lost men and needed renewed strength. These locations included the perimeter of the capitol building and grounds and the Beirut Airport.

When the soldiers landed, they immediately saw many American Marines guarding both the outside and the inside of the terminal. None of the new arrivers knew where they were going until they were briefed at nine the next morning. Mace, Tyler, and twenty-three others were ordered to go into the mountains in helicopters to rescue hundreds of Lebanese civilians who were trapped in the snow. When that assignment was complete, they would resupply several isolated villages where the inhabitants were starving. They would begin tomorrow. One day of rest. Mace and Tyler would be accompanied by six of their basic training mates. Familiarity in these circumstances was a good thing. All the other soldiers were recent basic training grads. There was one experienced man among them. It was their leader, battle-hardened Second Lieutenant Riley Walker. He was quieter than Mace until he needed to speak. Then watch out.

The Upper Brass had, for once, come up with a good idea, sending the youngest soldiers on a humanitarian mission. This would be a relatively easy way to jump-start their careers. One bright colonel came up with the idea that this endeavor would create sympathy for the Lebanese people and make it easier to fight for them later. He was right.

Tyler and Mace had picked adjacent bunks the day before, in an uncomfortable barracks. After the meeting, Tyler was in a jovial mood. As they sat down on their bunks, Tyler said, "We made it, buddy. Tomorrow is the next step in our new lives."

"I wonder where that step will lead us," Mace answered softly.

"I hope we can take quite a few of those steps together, Mace."

"Me too, Tyler. Me too."

Mace thought of Tyler as the little brother he never had. For a moment, he wondered why his mother never had any more babies. Then he thought about how wonderful a dad Wille would have been to more children.

The day before they embarked on their first assignment, they spent their hours in a class led by Lieutenant Riley. He educated them on what to expect from the snow and the people they rescued. For the remainder of the day, they prepared the gear and weaponry they were to take. Then they rested.

Morning and adventure came quickly for the rescuers who slept lightly, at best. There were six Marines aboard two ACH 64s. The third carried seven, including Lieutenant Riley. The mission was dangerous, first because of steep precipices and angles between hateful-looking masses of mountains. There was also the concern for the few enemy forces that may be lurking, with the intent of doing harm to defenseless civilians. At the designated coordinates, Tyler and Mace were the third and fourth Marines to climb down the rope ladder to the frozen earth while the ACH 64 hovered above. At the first stop, there were only four people to be rescued. All four were over fifty, but capable of climbing the rope ladder to the helicopter, which was only about fifty feet from the ground. The whirring of the blades above the helicopter soothed Mace, as he watched the first four people enter the airship. By the end of the day, he had lost count of the people he had rescued.

Four days later, the warm fuzzies were still there, as the fading afternoon sun signaled the end of their brief but heartwarming mission.

"I wish I had $5 for every thank you I've received in English and Lebanese from the people I've plucked off that mountain the past four days," Tyler said.

"They're so appreciative," Mace responded. "I guess that's how good people respond when their lives are being saved."

"War is fun, isn't it, Mace!" Tyler said jokingly.

"So far it is, Tyler."

And Mace and a couple of their buddies, who had been listening, laughed nervously.

# CHAPTER 15

Six days after receiving their next orders, Mace learned what it was to receive enemy fire. While standing guard outside the capitol building, a single shot rang through the morning air and hit one of his basic training buddies in the neck. The young Marine fell, unaware that his life had been taken from him in an instant.

Mace and Tyler took greater cover, as did the rest of their friends, around the front perimeter of the capitol building. Each man's frightened eyes darted left to right, right to left, over and over to find the sniper. At first, no soldier saw any sign of a shooter in the buildings around the capitol. Mace, who long ago had learned to peer deep into the woods for wild boar and deer, spotted the assassin six blocks away, sitting comfortably on his buttocks. His feet propped were against the raised ledge of the building's roof. He was holding his weapon almost affectionately. Mace raised his weapon, as if he had done it dozens of times, aimed his M-14, set his eyes, and pulled the trigger. An instant later, the enemy's life fled from him, as the bullet hit him squarely in the heart. It raised his lifeless body half a foot before it slammed backward onto the hard roof.

"I got him!" Mace yelled, not to brag, but to give his buddies a moment of relief. "He won't be killing anyone else today or any other day."

"Nice shot," Tyler said.

"Thanks, Tyler," Mace said, his eyes still peering into the distance.

"Hold your positions, men. We have no idea what else might be out there." Lieutenant Riley Walker's voice boomed over the sudden silence that hung in the air above the young soldiers. Most of them had taken positions on the ground, not knowing what might happen next. A single bullet had stunned an entire squad of capitol protectors. The quiet seemed unbearable as the Americans watched the birds fly away from the area.

Ten minutes passed. Nothing but a group of jittery nerves. Two of the Marines had to urinate badly. Both hoped they would not have to engage in a firefight in that condition. Lieutenant Walker worried that he might be responsible for his downed Marine's death. He had all his men standing while on guard. He felt bad, whether responsible or not. He had seen many men die during his years as a Marine, but this was the first loss he experienced in Beirut. Walker was crusty on the surface but sensitive deep inside. The death of every soldier saddened him, and he did everything he could do to minimize the loss of life under his watch.

Only moments before Walker planned to order his men to change their positions and carry the dead soldier into the capitol building, all hell broke loose. Bullets began pinging off concrete all around the Marines, as thirty enemy soldiers began what appeared to be a suicide charge of the capitol grounds. It did not matter to Mace what enemy of the Lebanese government this was. They were shooting at him. He would kill as many as he could.

Mace was the boldest of the new soldiers, as well as the veterans, who were considerably more experienced in firefights. He was very smart to go along with his senses of daring and invulnerability. He began to strategize, quickly glancing to see who was fighting beside him.

Tyler Frailing, his handsome best friend, was still on his left. Mace was certain that Tyler could be trusted implicitly. To his right, was Darius Green, Mace's second best friend in basic training. He was black, five feet, ten inches tall, and another strong, silent type, which suited Mace perfectly. His mesomorph body was laden with magnificently sculptured God-given biceps, thighs, triceps, back muscles, and pecs. He could have competed in bodybuilding contests without ever lifting a weight. But like Tyler and Mace, he was a gym rat. Having been one added tremendously to his formidable appearance and fighting ability. Mace trusted Darius.

Mace, standing behind a concrete pillar, reached around it and fired his M-14 for the second time. It was a perfect headshot, straight through to the brain. He had killed again. A sense of exhilaration coursed through his mind as he pulled back again behind the ten-foot pillar, determining to conserve his bullets and make everyone count.

A split second later, as if scripted by God and furthering Mace Madison Stutzman's legacy, he noticed a single running enemy soldier, making his way around to the left side of the capitol complex. He could have wreaked havoc on the Americans, beginning with Tyler Frailing, who was unaware of him. Hiding behind trucks on a nearby street, the crafty enemy was hidden from view from Mace and his buddies for several seconds each time he hid behind a different vehicle. His buddies were completely blind to what the attacker was doing. Mace's eyes peeked through the black iron bars that were attached to the concrete pillars that were implanted in the earth every twelve feet. He had not taken a shot in over a minute, as Tyler and Darius fired unceasingly.

They wondered what was going on with Mace. Suddenly, he spotted the antagonist about thirty feet from where Mace had last seen him. The enemy soldier was now behind a 1979 Mercedes. He raised his weapon to the trunk and took aim directly at the torso of Tyler Frailing. Without hesitation, Mace ran three steps to his left, braving an almost complete lack of cover, and knocked Tyler to the hard earth. All the while, except for the push of Tyler, he kept his eyes on Tyler's would-be killer. While falling on top of his friend, Mace took a split-second aim and fired. The bullet, not his best shot, ricocheted off the trunk of the Mercedes eight inches in front of the insurgent and slammed into his breastbone, shattering it into twenty pieces.

Three shots, one a near miracle, three kills. When Darius saw Mace move so dramatically, out of the corner of his eye, he turned his head and witnessed Mace's amazing shot, as he was falling onto Tyler. He saw the bullet bounce off the trunk and fracture the enemy's torso. He allowed himself to be in awe for a split second as his eyes darted right to left, left to right, hunting for any more combatants in the kill zone. He saw nothing, no movement of man, beast or vehicle, but he did see Mace practically lift Tyler off the ground back to his feet.

"I felt a bullet fly by from that direction, Mace."

"So did I, Tyler."

"You're bleeding, Mace."

"It's nothing."

It was not much. It was still significant. The bullet had skimmed across the top of Mace's left shoulder and back, drawing blood. A couple of inches to the right, and it would have been a headshot. The injury did not frighten or stop Mace. After propping Tyler up behind the relative safety of a pillar, he dropped to the ground and began taking one measured shot at a time. *Pop, pop, pop*, three more down.

*Goddamn, this is fun*, Mace thought. *It's a lot more interesting than target practice or shooting defenseless dear or even charging wild boar. These sons of bitches are maniacs.*

While hundreds of bullets were whizzing around him, Mace was measuring each shot amid the rage. He was ice amid the rage. He was unflappable.

Three minutes of warfare later, the din abated, and a tenuous silence hung in the air above the Americans. It was another time of waiting.

Nothing. Then more nothing. Moments, then minutes passed before a single crow flew overhead and landed on a powerline a hundred feet away. It was then that Lieutenant Riley yelled for some of his men to get the wounded into the capitol building. It took two men each to carry the five men who had been shot, into the building, leaving ten men to guard the perimeter.

"Get back out here as fast as you can after you drop the boys at the trauma center."

Mace did not go into the building.

"Thank you for what you did for me, Mace," Tyler said. "I figured it out a moment after it happened."

"You would have done the same for me, right?" Mace said.

"You're goddamned right about that, brother."

Tyler was not kidding. Four times in the next seven and a half years, Tyler would lay himself out for Mace Madison Stutzman.

Darius had grabbed the legs of a fellow soldier, who was bleeding badly. He could not cease talking about what he had seen between Mace, Tyler, and the deceased enemy soldier. First, he told it to his carrying buddy, Johnny Paige, who claimed to be a distant cousin of the great pitcher, Satchel Paige. He was wiry, like Satchel, a couple of inches shorter, at about six feet, but darned if he did not look a lot like ole Satch. Plus, he had been a good pitcher in his own right. In high school, he was 25–10 overall and 13–3 as a varsity pitcher his junior and senior year. No college offered him a scholarship, so he joined the Marines and dreamed of someday playing baseball for the Marine team. Johnny, listening intently, was fascinated by what Darius was saying.

"I saw Mace leap on top of Tyler and fire his weapon as he was falling. He kills the attacker. His bullet ricocheted off the trunk and tore that guy up. No doubt, he saved Tyler's life."

Johnny was convinced of Mace's heroics. He thought about it all day as if he had seen a good movie. The wounded soldier and his carriers made it into the mini hospital in less than a minute. Darius kept talking. He told the doctors who received the wounded soldier. He told a nurse on his way out of the building. Somehow, his story made its way all the way to the upper echelon of the Lebanese government.

Lieutenant Riley heard the story by the end of the shift, but it was hours before he could talk with Mace. When it came time to change the guard, Tyler noticed blood was still oozing from Mace's shoulder.

"I insist that you go inside the capitol building and at least be seen by a medic," Tyler said strongly to Mace.

"You can't insist," Mace said jokingly, like he was speaking to a little brother.

"Oh yes, I can," Tyler barked and grabbed Mace by the uninjured shoulder and pulled him toward the mini hospital.

Mace felt strange. No one had ever grabbed him that way. He felt Tyler's power, and he felt his affection. He had never felt that from a friend before. For one brief moment, he basked in the uniqueness of the feeling. Immediately, he considered that the affection from Tyler was almost as joyful as annihilating nine enemy soldiers today. He knew that Willie would be proud of him and that even Elise would be proud.

Mace's comrades also noticed how many men he killed. Only thirty men attacked the capitol, and Mace killed 30 percent of those. These Marines knew who owned the kills. None of them was brave enough to shoot as rarely as Mace and with such accuracy.

Before bedtime, Lieutenant Riley sent a soldier to get Mace.

"What happened out there today, Mace?"

"Nothing much, sir."

"That's not what I heard, Mace. I was told by several men that you saved Tyler Frailing's life."

"I don't know about that, sir. I do know that Tyler was in the direct line of fire from an enemy combatant I spotted slipping around the left side of our perimeter. Things unfolded quickly, and I did what I had to do."

"Did you fire a shot while you were falling?"

"I did."

"That's pretty cool, Soldier. I've seen and heard of many marvelous heroic deeds in my time, but I've never heard of the kind of shot you took today."

"Thank you, sir."

"I also heard you only took a limited number of shots. Where did you learn that?"

"Nowhere, sir. I just felt today like it was the right thing to do. I didn't want to shoot haphazardly. I worried that everyone else would run out of bullets, and I wanted to have a bunch left, if that happened."

"It was also a consensus that you killed quite a few of the enemy. Is that true?"

"I took nine shots, Lieutenant, and knocked nine guys off their feet. I never saw any of them get back up again."

"You did some good work out there, Soldier. I'd like to shake your hand."

Lieutenant Riley stood up and walked all the way around his desk to meet Mace rising from his chair. Riley extended his hand to Mace, who reached out his own.

As the two men's hands connected, the veteran spoke to the humbled rookie.

"I'm proud of you, Mace. If you continue to do in the future, what you did out there today, only God knows what you will achieve as a Marine."

"Thank you, sir."

"How is that bullet wound, Mace?"

"It's okay, sir."

"Your doctor told me that the bullet splintered a piece of your collarbone. Are you sure you will be ready to take your post tomorrow?"

"Yes, sir." Mace was purposely minimizing his words.

"Most men would have to spend several days recovering in the infirmary with your type of injury. If you choose to do so, it wouldn't detract one iota from what you accomplished today."

"I'll be ready to go tomorrow, sir."

"Only if you say so, Mace. I want you to know that we've got some leeway here if you need it."

"Thank you, sir. I really appreciate you saying that."

"Not more than I appreciate you, Soldier."

Both men stood and saluted each other.

On the way back to his barracks, Mace thought about how proud his father would be of his actions today. He thought that Elise would be proud of him too, no matter how much of a bitch she was.

*She could never do what I did today*, he thought. *All she is, is a bag of hot cruel words.*

Elise was more than that. Unfortunately, Mace would never know even the depth of her or the why.

A few minutes later, he crawled into bed, feeling more pain in his back and collarbone as his breathing slowed. In a darkened room of relative silence, Mace heard two soldiers weeping, obviously distraught at having killed for the first time. Mace pondered how different their feelings were from his. He was happy, and if he did weep, he would cry tears of joy. He did not have anything to be sad about. He had helped to defeat an enemy in a bloody battle. He saved the life of his best friend and possibly the lives of several more of his lesser friends and acquaintances. He had been a true hero. While two of his barracks mates were expressing their pain, he was looking forward to his next shots. He would not shed a tear for the bastards he had annihilated. Some, in this darkened room, mourned their actions of the day. Mace was convinced that he had catapulted to the level of a stone-cold, remorseless serial killer.

# CHAPTER 16

Mace's stay in Beirut lasted five weeks. Back home, President Reagan had promised the American people to bring the troops back home soon. By March of 1984, he had kept his promise. Mace did not experience another firefight. He left the war-torn city with nine kills. He would not be immediately deployed. He would be going home; his heroic deeds having preceded him.

Willie met him at Tampa Airport with a bear hug that lifted him off the ground. Once again, Mace thought about how this was what real affection looked like. They walked together, proud father and son, from baggage claim to the elevator, then up to the open-air level nine of the parking garage. It was eighty-two degrees, bright sun, soft wind of early evening, and Princess, his beloved 1950 Chrysler, waiting for him to drive her home. Wille had made her look pretty, by slapping a $2,000 black paint job on her. Though Mace was carrying a heavy duffel bag over his left shoulder, he was able to catch the car keys when Willie tossed them.

"Take her home, Soldier."

"I will, Dad."

He walked to the back lock, opened it, and tossed his duffel bag into the enormous trunk. It looked clean inside. A moment later, he walked to the driver's side door, unlocked it, and hopped in. Right away, he noticed that everything inside Princess was immaculate. Not a grain of sand disgraced the interior. Willie had also shined all the surfaces, so they gleamed as brightly as the paint job.

"The car looks great, Dad."

"Thanks, Mace."

"No, thank you, Dad. You did all the work."

"Don't get what I did with the car, mixed up with work, Mace. That's fun stuff."

"Is spending a small fortune on me, fun, Dad?"

"I have a large fortune, Mace. So why can't I spend a small fortune on my son?" Willie was not kidding about his finances.

They both chuckled.

"You're my hero, Mace?"

"Come on, Dad," Mace responded, feeling deep tenderness toward his father.

"I'm serious, Marine. You deserve my complete admiration."

"Thank you, Dad. That's the most wonderful thing anyone has ever said to me."

They drove over the Howard Franklin Bridge in silence. Willie rested his left hand on Mace's right shoulder.

When Mace saw the Don CeSar, his heart soared. He was only a moment from his beloved and missed Pass-a-Grille. A couple of minutes later, Mace observed that Willie had put a fresh coat of paint on the house too. It was a great welcome home so far. But something dreadful waited for him only a few feet away.

*Behind four walls is where she belongs*, Mace thought. How odd it was that he had more fear approaching his own house than he had while in the middle of a gunfight. Life is strange. Even a young warrior like Mace Madison Stutzman can feel odd anguish.

When the door opened and Elise got a good look at her son waiting to come into the house, she was stunned. With his face perfectly framed by his hat and the collar of his dress uniform, Elise saw, for the first time, how ruggedly handsome her son really was. She looked closely at his frontal features. Certainly, they were not the curmudgeon face of her father looking back at her. It was her own beauty that she saw staring into her eyes. She was immediately and unabashedly attracted to him. In a moment of swift firsts, she took him by both shoulders, pulled his upper body down, and kissed him on the right cheek.

Mace's knees buckled. An uncomfortable here-to-for emotion coursed through his body like lye. It caused his stomach to become upset and the tips of his fingers tingled. His face flushed.

What should have been a moment of joy, was, instead, filled with confusion. Within a maddening two seconds, Mace decided to gently take his mother's shoulders, pull her toward him, and kiss her on her cheek. Elise flinched and backed away. Now he was more confused. One moment, Elise seemed to share genuine affection; two seconds later, she was back to being an unaffectionate ice goddess.

Elise was confused too. She knew she had given Mace a mixed message, but she could simply not resist kissing her own beautiful reflection. Her self-control was so tightly wrapped that she would never commit the same error twice. She did not realize she kissed her own reflection. She explained to herself that she had kissed Mace because he looked so handsome, and he acted so admirably in combat. She did not suffer from her mistake.

Mace suffered. Then he thought, *Thank God for Dad*. Willie validated Mace constantly. Mace had been a respectful and lovable little boy. It was easy to validate a boy like that. The happier Mace was, the happier Willie was. Willie loved Mace as he had been loved by his father and grandfather. He realized that Mace was grown now and that time they spent together would become shorter. He was determined to make the next twenty-eight days the most memorable he had ever shared with his son.

# CHAPTER 17

Twenty-eight days passed far too quickly for Willie, who was able to achieve his dream of sharing his most adventurous chunk of time with Mace. Together, the father and son, good friends, went wild boar hunting and bagged one on each of two hunting days. They bird-watched, peacefully at Weedon Island. Several evenings, while listening to big bands and classical music on the old Victrola, they would open the gun cabinet and spend an entire evening researching one gun or rifle. Willie had a magnificent *Encyclopedia* of firearms, and the father and son would revel in the history of each gun's usage, advantages, and disadvantages. They often took a gun completely apart until all the guts were spread on the living room coffee table. There would be more conversation about where it was manufactured, what metal was used, and what it was worth. Then they would reassemble the gun and go to bed.

Through this bonding of father and son, Elise stayed embedded in the distant background, cooking, cleaning, and trying to make sense of her not-so-holy Bible. Willie thought little of her behavior. Elise had been reading the Bible since he met her. Also, he had long ago concluded that Elise was a girly girl, preoccupied with her beautiful face, her muscles, her toes and fingernails, and her thick and luxurious long hair. These facts did not bother Willie. Her beauty made her more desirable. Sex was still exciting and creative for them. If Elise's preoccupations made her happy, then so be it. Willie had no idea Elise still had doubts about her beauty because of her unnoticeable crossed eye and indistinguishable crooked nose.

Mace was used to his mother's distance. Since he had enlisted in the service, he questioned it more. What bug was so far up her ass that she had such disdain for him? What had he ever done to her, except to be born? For all the effort he had given on her demand, shouldn't she love him and be able to show it? What the hell was wrong with her?

Mace's life at home continued as he had become used to it. The twenty-eight days had passed too quickly for him also. His goodbye from Willie was a hug-filled love fest between a father and son who genuinely loved one another.

"I love you, Dad, more than anyone in the world."

It was the greatest expression of emotion for a person that Mace had ever asserted.

"I love you too, Mace. Thank you for being my amazing warrior and my best friend."

After grabbing his duffel bag and before entering the terminal, Mace ran his fingers tenderly across the full length of his beloved 1950 Chrysler Imperial.

"We'll both be here waiting for you, Mace," Willie said.

"Thanks, Dad."

Then they headed for check-in.

Forty minutes earlier, Mace's goodbye from Elise was quite different. Standing next to each other in the Pass-a-Grille house, Mace had made no effort to touch or speak to his mother. Instead, Elise made an unusual move. She took Mace's shoulders, stood on her toes, and lightly touched her left cheek to his.

"You made me proud, Mace. Keep it up."

In what was again an awkward moment, Mace wanted to get away from her. He sidestepped her, not wanting to waste a single touch on her.

A few days later, he was on his way to his next deployment. How excited he was to add to his one day of bravery and incredible shooting ability. More medals would be nice. He knew how proud Willie would be and how he would admire those medals. Ironically, five of Mace's basic training buddies followed him to his next assignment: Tyler Frailing, Darius Green, Johnny Paige, Marcus Smith, and Robert Anthony. Marcus Smith—a tall, lean, fighting machine—was from the South Shore district of Chicago. He was a handsome black man, who could have been a model. What made him special to his friends was that he was a magnificent storyteller. When Marcus told a story, everyone in earshot would listen. He talked of the gangs he was in and the gangs they encountered while growing up in a tough neighborhood. His tall mother, a waitress, taught him the art of sharing tales. She came home from work each day and told Marcus about all the interesting characters she waited on each day.

Robert Anthony was another six-footer, daring, almost reckless, the antithesis of the calculating measured Mace. His bravery was unquestioned. Robert was not a conversation initiator, but he could more than hold his own, once engaged. He was a farm boy from Tennessee. The land he grew up on was a wonderful place for a boy to grow up. The creek was his favorite place, filled with fish just waiting to be caught by him. There were forests beyond the main farm. They were great places to make forts and play cowboys and Indians with friends.

From that point forward, the months flew by for Mace. He and his friends faced one war after another. Those wars *were always* fun for Mace. He was a driven man. It started with striving never to lose, instilled in him by Elise. Currently, it was his commanding officers who were always demanding the best of all the Marines in his unit. Performing superbly for his officers was as important to him as being a superb son for Willie. It was not only externals that drove Mace Madison Stutzman. Much of his drive came from deep within, where his love of country lived. When he was a little boy, he watched TV with his father. One of his favorite times was when he watched Audie Murphy's cowboy movies. The first time they watched one, Willie told him that Murphy was the most decorated soldier in World War II. His dad told Mace that the war hero was only five feet seven. When he was older, Mace thought, *If that guy could do what he did at five seven, I wonder what I can achieve at six five.*

As Mace experienced other nations, he was disappointed at how little they had, compared to his beloved United States. He felt protective of his fellow Marines. His deep concern for them was something he thought about often. He could thank Willie for those feelings. Willie had been a nurturer. As big and screwed up as half of Mace was because of Elise, the other half of him was a true big brother type. When his friends had troubles, it seemed like Mace was always there to listen. Despite his beliefs, that he was a serial killer, he considered himself a good person. Like the old cowboy movies and shows that he loved, the guys he killed wore black, and he wore white. And he had no regrets. Mace Madison was absolutely enamored with thoughts of saving the lives of his comrades as often as battle dictated.

*****

Seven months after leaving Pass-a-Grille, Mace received a letter that struck him to his core. It plummeted him into severe gut-wrenching depression. It was from Elise.

Dear Mace,

It is with grave sadness that I must tell you of your father's passing.

He had a short bout with a fast-moving type of leukemia that took his life.

Your father was kind enough to share with me the terms of his will before he wrote it down and gave it to our attorney. He left half of everything to you, Mace. He wants you to have his gun collection and half of what he has in the Safe deposit box. He also left you many lesser things, which I will wait to show you when you come home on leave. Willie left the house to me, for the duration of my lifetime.

I am terribly sorry for our mutual loss.

Sincerely,
Your mother

Tears began cascading down his rugged face.

"How could this be?"

Willie was only in his forties. What the hell kind of leukemia could take down his strong father? In the quiet of his barracks, Mace began to sob. The tears and the sobbing were new and horribly uncomfortable for Mace. Pressure built slowly inside him, till suddenly, an almost primal scream emerged from his soul.

The boom of it rocked the room. The seven men who were present were caught off guard, scaring the shit out of them. Tyler Frailing got to Mace in a micromoment while Mace's head was still facing the heavens.

"What's wrong, Mace?" Tyler said with grave concern.

The other soldiers in the room joined Tyler, asking similar questions.

"My father died, and my mother didn't even tell me he was sick."

He was speaking uncharacteristically loudly, acute anger driving his decibel level.

"I could have gone home and spent time with him before he died. My mother is the most selfish person I have ever known. She wanted to have him all to herself, even when he was declining. I hate her." He raised his decibel level again. "I hate her."

The room shook again, as Mace revealed to his friends his true vulnerability. During his horrendous pain, Mace experienced something new. Several hands were rubbing his back and shoulders. They were the hands of friends who cared about him. He heard the muffled whispers of their encouragements. His upper body fell to the mattress. He was exhausted. He curled into a fetal position as his friends sat all around him like guardian angels.

Mace's body was reeling from his outburst. Sleep came to him like a bullet from an enemy rifle. It snatched his wakefulness as an unplanned form of instant death, sparring him from any further conscious grief. He plunged into a deep place of subconscious darkness. He dreamed he was twelve years old, hunting wild boar with Willie. The two of them were waiting peacefully, but expectantly, in an idyllic piece of verdant forest. A boar appeared, snorting insouciantly along. It was Mace's turn to shoot, but a split second before he fired, an enormous crow landed on a branch near the boar. It let out a loud caw that caused the boar to stare in the direction of the startling sound. The fired shot slid under the boar's chin and disappeared into the woods. Willie saw the boar rear angrily and charge in the direction of the gunshot. He quickly aimed and moved to stabilize his right foot for the shot. His foot slipped on a tiny branch, and his shot flew one inch over the beast's brain. Mace began in dream slow motion to protect his father from the charging creature. He was pitifully slow and helpless to defend Willie. The incensed boar barreled into Willie, pushing him through the forest air for thirty feet before slamming him into a tall evergreen. Then the boar raised on hind legs like a stallion, let out a giant snort, and sped off into the woods triumphantly.

Mace raced to his father and gathered his limp body into his arms. He fell to his knees, and once again, he screamed his pain so loudly that his barracks mates were exaggeratedly startled. The primal yell was followed by uncontrollable sobbing and an avalanche of tears. He was awaked by the commotion he created, as his friends came for a second time to assist him, like angels. Shock, horror, burning, as if being shot with a shotgun at close range, raged through his body.

Completely understood by his buddies, they placed healing hands upon him, trying to ease his pain. Mace's body was shredded. In another moment, he had fallen asleep again. This time he slept through the night. When he woke the next morning, there was a pain in his gut that would not abate for many months.

His friends thought nothing less of him for his outpouring of feelings. Ironically, they thought more of him. He was just like them. He was emotional and vulnerable. He could fracture. He was a human being.

# CHAPTER 18

Mace did not fly home for his father's wake and funeral. He was, instead, the embodiment of pure, stuffed rage toward his mother. Simultaneously, he was filled with the pain of losing his father. He became a quieter man, as he pushed those feelings into dark, murky emotional substrata. After his emotional outbreaks in the barracks, he never had another one. Embarrassment put a stranglehold on any expression of what was going on inside his head or heart.

There were other ways to release those gut wrenchers. Oh, how badly he wanted to kill somebody, not just anybody but a piece of shit who deserved it. That would make him feel better. So Mace simply stayed deployed—the Persian Gulf, Panama, Bolivia, the Philippines, Saudi Arabia, excelling everywhere. His six best friends followed him. When it came to war and deployment, the seven friends petitioned to go everywhere together. Their responses from commanding officers were always positive because the boys were ideal soldiers, and they earned the right to fight together. In battle, they played a game of sorts, a round-robin of saving each other's lives, as well as the lives of countless other Marines. Winning medals became commonplace for them.

Mace was the heralded kingpin among them. Not one of his cronies volunteered for more dangerous missions than he did. His success rate in achieving mission goals and coming back alive cemented his role as an alpha dog within his elite group. Reputation came immediately for Mace, despite his outbursts over his father's death. Those moments were easily forgiven and forgotten. Notoriety came swiftly for Mace's friends as well. They came to be known as the Super Seven.

As his reputation was being embellished by feats of incredulous strength and courage, so was Mace's number of kills. Nine became ten and ten became thirteen. He was acutely sensitive to every prick he killed, no matter how intense the fighting. Each kill was exemplified by a heightened sense of awareness. Killing was still fun. What if he got hit with a bullet anyway? That would be merely physical pain. It was so much easier to deal with that than the emotional pain that had ravaged him since his days with Elise.

Now there was fresh pain since Willie had died.

As the years passed, Mace reenlisted, never returning home. He preferred to spend his leaves on one of the Hawaiian Islands, lying on a beach, sipping a beer, and swimming in luxurious warm water. Over time, he investigated Kuai, Maui, Hawaii, Molokai, and Oahu. He loved the friendliness and kindness of the indigenous people. He was never alone. Unbeknownst to Mace, all six other members of the Super Seven had entered a pact to protect Mace emotionally. They agreed to always have at least one member of their group accompany him on every leave.

Each member of his close-knit group knew that something gloomy was the base, the core, of Mace's being. No normal person could be so quiet, laugh as little or crack smile so seldomly. Protecting him from himself was the least they could do after the countless times he saved them from a multitude of enemies.

As his number of kills rose, Mace wondered how many other soldiers loved killing as much as he did. How many serial killers were there just like him, who kept the measurement of their deeds eternally hidden? There was no shame in numbers fourteen, fifteen, and sixteen. To the contrary, there was pride, glory, and honor.

\*\*\*\*\*

Years passed, and still, Mace did not return to St. Petersburg. Awards piled up for him. So did promotions. He even incurred two more bullet wounds: one to his left thigh, and one to his right bicep. Both bullets hit flesh and did not shatter bone. The injuries occurred while he was pulling a wounded warrior to safety, under heavy enemy fire.

The first wound happened in the Persian Gulf on a 107-degree afternoon during a routine patrol. The Super Seven and twenty other Marines were attacked by a feisty enemy that felt secure in the higher ground than the Americans. Amid the melee, a small rocket hit the right front tire of a jeep three vehicles in front of Mace. The impact lifted the vehicle off the ground, flipped it over, and propelled it thirty feet from the road. When it finally tumbled to a stop, it was a crumpled shell with three dead marines inside.

Mace was acutely aware that Darius Green was driving the jeep, but initially, it was impossible to tell if anyone was alive in the wreck. Slowly, the sand settled around it, and Darius Green emerged beneath a rain of bullets. He was bleeding from his forehead and face and was terrified by his precarious position. Suddenly, Mace saw a bullet hit Darius in the collarbone, drastically accelerating his emergence from the vehicle and slamming him violently to the unrelenting earth.

"Get to that jeep!" Mace screamed at his driver.

Complying with the intense command, the driver could only come to within seventy feet of Darius because of the rough terrain. Mace was determined to save his friend, but he would have to run through a torrent of bullets to be able to do it. Mace leaped from his vehicle and began what looked to his buddies to be a death run. Mace made it to Darius in four seconds. He jumped onto his six-pack stomach and put his right arm over his quivering friend.

"Is anybody alive in there, Darius?"

"I don't know, Mace."

Mace thought about how beautiful the red blood was against his friend's black skin. He would not let this man die. He peered into the wreckage. He had seen so much death before, and that was all that was left inside that jeep.

Suddenly, Darius said, "Jesus Christ, thank you, man."

Mace saw the first trickle of tears come, as Darius spoke, "Jesus Christ, thank you man," again.

"It's okay, Darius. You're my friend," he said with utter tenderness.

Darius could not stop thanking Mace for something Mace had not even done yet, save his life.

"Jesus Christ, thank you, man." The number of times he said that kept adding up—five, ten, fifteen, twenty. Darius was hoping that Mace was invincible. He wanted to live, but he also knew that Mace's chances of making it back to the rest of the unit were slim. Was that what was prompting the outpouring of thank-you from his nerve-racked lips? Was Darius hoping that Jesus loved Mace more than the average soldier and had bestowed special powers upon him?

"Jesus Christ, thank you, man," the repetitive sentence kept coming, as Mace picked up Darius over his right shoulder, the farthest from the flying bullets, and began sprinting back toward his men. In the same instant, two tank commanders had taken the fight to the enemy. Their barrage caused the number of bullets coming from the hills to become a drizzle rather than a torrent. Still, the danger of being shot was extremely high, but Mace's friends were doing everything they could to help Mace and Darius survive.

Darius was heavy, and Mace, though unafraid, labored to get any traction on the rough, uneven terrain. When he did, Darius could not stop saying, "Jesus Christ, thank you, man." Faster and faster, he spoke the words, until there was not a heartbeat between sentences. Eighteen feet from his jeep, an enemy bullet tore through the fleshy part of Mace's left thigh. Immediately to the ground went Mace and Darius. Mace's knees hit first and hard, breaking his fall. Darius's face planted into the earth, breaking his nose, ripping skin from numerous places on his face, and snapping his neck so violently, it almost broke. Mace did not have time to assess his friend's or his own new injuries. He had a goal to achieve, and time was of the essence, no matter how excruciating the pain he felt.

"Push the pain away!" he screamed internally as Darius lay unconscious and silent. "Push the pain away, Mace Madison Stutzman. You have a duty to perform. You must save the life of your friend."

Blood and pain were not enough to stop Mace. He righted himself and barreled the final feet like a fullback, with Darius on his shoulders. When he reached the back of the jeep, he set his friend on the ground with the tenderness of a big brother. Then he hit the ground and passed out. The last thing he heard was "Jesus Christ, thank you, man."

For this act of bravery, Mace won the Navy Cross. Both men fully recovered, Mace in five weeks, Darius in twelve. Fourteen weeks after their injuries, they were deployed together again. Then it was business and friendship as usual.

Mace received his arm wound rescuing three pinned down soldiers in another of countless firefights within which he found himself. On that day, Mace was himself fifty yards from his wounded comrades, close enough to see their slow, painful movements and nothing from several downed marines near them. An altogether too familiar feeling befell Mace. It was severe emotional suffering for whatever pain his fellow warriors were enduring at the moment. Mace Stutzman was a quiet, calculating man but also an impulsive one, an unusual blend of characteristics where your life might be on the line. In combat, Mace not only wanted to kill but to save. Rescuing fellow warriors was absolute truth and an implicit mission for him. Rescuing them meant almost sure death for him, but he did not fear it. He loved it when the power of life and death was in his hands. On this day, his joy was his own heartache for the three sons of bitches, bleeding and afraid that their lives may ebb away in the next few minutes.

Without more than his initial analysis of the situation, Mace raced from his position in an S pattern to the soldier nearest to him. As the bullets streaked past him, he bent down like a gray ghost and picked up the wounded soldier. He did not look to see where the man's wound was. Too many bullets, too much risk. He grabbed up the soldier, slung him over his right shoulder, and began running back toward the safety of his men and equipment. This time, there was no "Jesus Christ, thank you, man." There was only the soft moaning of a man in dire distress. Mace was alone, in no man's land, but he talked out loud to himself.

"Come on, Mace, you can do this. You'll be okay. Nothing has ever stopped you before."

His father's voice was in his ear. "Come on, Mace, my strong, beautiful son." His mother was there too. "Don't you let me down, boy. Once you take on a challenge, you must succeed. Do you hear me, kid?"

He heard her all right, and he argued with her, though she was not there.

"Don't call me boy, you bitch. You could never do anything like this, you loudmouthed coward.

His inner dialogue stopped only after he ran through his troops to the rear of them, where a hospital had been set up under a huge tent. Inside, he quickly identified the operating area and placed his rescued body on a surgery table, as gently as he could. There were all kinds of voices around him, outpouring all manner of shit to him. He distinguished none of it. He distinguished no faces either. He was only focused on objects, rocks on the ground, soldiers' bodies and vehicles in his way, the hospital tent, and the operating table. In his current state, he was unreachable to other human beings. He was in rescue mode, an intuitive, instinctive, unrelenting mode, to which only true heroes can relate.

After depositing his delivery to the operating table, Mace turned for the exit and began sprinting again, the length of a football field, from the hospital tent to the next wounded soldier. Mace picked him up and sprinted back toward his men. Thirty yards later, Mace was nearly knocked off his feet when an enemy bullet tore through the entire width of the injured man's back. The bullet skimmed the nape of Mace's neck as it exited the injured man's body. A solitary second later, another bullet ripped through Mace's right bicep. The pain was excruciating, but his pace was delayed only a microsecond as the rude metal's impact moved his body several inches to the left. Mace did not know that he would place a dead man on the second operating table. The bullet that had ripped through his body had crashed through several vital organs, and he was bleeding out on Mace's shoulder, the last ninety yards to the hospital.

The second body on the table, Mace lit out for number three. Again, he could hear the voluminous outpouring of emotion around him. Again, he distinguished no words. This time, his lifesaving mode was enhanced by the pain in his bleeding arm. Not hearing words was easier this trip, as the pain seemed to silence everything but his resolve.

Mace was enjoying the experience. He lived for these types of moments, enjoying saving lives as much as taking them. His body count for kills was twenty-five. He had thirty-seven saves. He had long ago created a secret game. He called it "My Favorite Numbers." It was the number of people he killed, plus the number he saved.

Right now, that number was sixty-two. In a moment, it would be sixty-three. He was proud of himself and his secret number. Then he put his head down, not wanting to take a bullet to the face, and continued running toward victim number three.

The pain in his right bicep felt as if someone had sawed through it with a butter knife. Distracting as it was, Mace pushed through it. Reaching the next wounded soldier was his focus. Approaching the body, while bullets sped past him at incredible speeds, he noticed it was twisted into a tight, protective fetal position. Its left shoulder was three inches above the small rocks that shielded the rest of its anatomy. An instant later, he reached the body. He turned it over enough to see the face and better position the body to sling it over his shoulder.

"Oh my god, oh my god, oh my god!" Mace cried out in agony. "Oh my god, oh my god, oh my god!" He screamed the words this time. The soldier he was rescuing was his best friend, Tyler Frailing. A man of few prayers, Mace begged the God of the universe to save the life of his friend. He could not cease saying the words "Oh my god." He remembered the words Darius Green had yelled a year and a fraction before when he was rescued by Mace. "Jesus Christ, thank you, man." Not thinking of his own serious bleeding, Mace only pitied the profuse bleeding of his cherished friend. Mace's fatigue shirt was saturated. He had been showered in blood. When he reached his men, they all stepped aside and saluted, in awe and respect for his accomplishments. Then Mace reached the hospital, tenderly placed his friend on an operating table, and collapsed onto the hard, cold earth.

For this tremendous act of bravery and loving, Mace received the Bronze Star.

# CHAPTER 19

In St. Petersburg, Elise had successfully moved on with her life without Willie and Mace. Money was never an issue for her. Willie had not only left his assets to his wife and son, but he had also left a substantial life insurance policy for them to share. Therefore, Elise was able to live a life of relative luxury. She rarely cooked, enjoying instead dining almost nightly at one of the scores of restaurants that dotted Gulf Boulevard between Pass-a-Grille and Clearwater. Sometimes, she would go inland to discover a new restaurant or return to a favorite. Occasionally, she would take the drive over the bridge to Tampa and explore the eateries in Ybor City. Her favorite restaurant in Tampa was Bern's Steakhouse. Willie had taken her there for some special events. They had even taken Mace with them a couple of times.

Finally, once in a very great while, Elise would drive south to Bradenton and St. Armand's Circle in Sarasota. Her favorite restaurant south of St. Pete was Sizzler's. She could get a tasty steak there and loved the single rose on each table. Always alone, she was forever the cross-eyed, crooked-nosed queen who acted as if she was better than everyone else. The reality was that Elise was dominated by an inferiority complex. As the years passed, she remained stunning, a true beauty, her facial flaws seen only by her.

Restaurants were not all that Elsie was about. She had taken scores of art classes throughout the bay area. She became quite the painter of local water scenes. She became equally skilled in the use of acrylics as well as oils. She loved colors and often used unusual ones where you would not expect to see them. She became like a small child when she painted, splashing color onto the canvas, always the consummate experimenter. She loved the gulf and the bay and inlets and bird islands and restaurants on the water. She became a prolific artist and sold hundreds of works at art shows, fairs, and galleries.

Men found her alluring and were drawn to her. She was not interested.

Instead of ceasing her relationship with the Bible and church because they were not making her happy, she delved deeper into both. At St. Jude's Cathedral, on Fifth Avenue and Fifty-Eighth Street North, Elise had two priests to choose to listen to each Sunday, for over a decade. One was Father Berigan, twenty-nine, handsome, on his second assignment. He was happy-go-lucky, progressive, always encouraging his flock to be happy, to love one another, to forgive transgressors. He was an eternal optimist, who believed that Jesus was the kindest, toughest man who ever walked the earth. He often told his audiences, "Jesus Christ was the greatest hero the world has ever known. This gentle warrior is risen and is alive, still saving souls each moment of every day."

Elise did not care for Father Berigan. She was, however, quite fond of her second choice at the church. His name was Monsignor Christian Velkos. When Velkos was a young priest, he deeply cared for a beautiful young woman his own age, whom he knew since the second grade. As a teenager, they dated for a couple of years, but the calling to the priesthood outweighed his romantic interest in the girl. They remained only good friends after that, absolutely nothing more. Her name was Evangeline.

Unfortunately, many of the townsmen pursued Evangeline with no luck at all. She rejected her suitors and for good reason. They were uncouth, unsavory characters, for whom she had no attraction. Instead of accepting their rejections and going about the business of their lives, a group of five men plotted revenge against her. Three of them attended the church of Father Velkos. One night, when Evangeline was returning home from a visit with Father Velkos, the five men attacked her as she opened her front door. The first injury was a blow to the head. This was followed by a powerful shove, which forced her into the living room. There they beat and raped her. The abuse continued for several hours, leaving the tiny woman barely alive. When Evangeline did not show up to her teaching job, coworkers found her and got her medical attention that saved her life.

When Father Velkos heard about the attack, he was livid. From the day he found out about Evangeline's brutal rape, he vowed, from the pulpit, to find the perpetrators and bring them to justice. Each day, he ranted the same words. If he had to find the men himself, he would, and his justice would be powerful and swift. He was outnumbered. The three men who attended his church grew tired of his threats. Together with the other two thugs, they planned their own comeuppance against him. On a cold winter night of his twenty-ninth year of life, Father Velkos was attacked outside the rectory by Evangeline's rapists. He fought with tremendous fury but was ultimately beaten into unconsciousness. There, on the frozen earth of church property, the rapists cut out half of the priest's tongue.

After recovering, Father Velkos went after his assailants. He had seen all five men, and it was just a matter of time before they were rounded up and prosecuted. They should have killed him. Three months later, Evangeline died of pneumonia. Her tiny body never regained the strength it had before her rape. The surviving priest was left with a raging bitterness toward all sin. He brought it with him from the old country to the new. He was a sad, unhappy man, the perfect person to become Elise's Father Confessor.

# Chapter 20

The years passed by quickly for Mace Madison Stutzman. He was a superb soldier, who had a marvelous circle of six true friends. He was a quiet and happy man. He loved killing bad guys, and now he had a secret, favorite number of seventy-two. The number represented twenty-seven kills and forty-five extremely fortunate human beings saved. He was proud of himself. He was proud of his ribbons, medals, and most of all, he was deeply satisfied with his saves. Killing was where he built his badass reputation. Whenever there was a dangerous mission or a job for one man, Mace Madison would volunteer for it. Unlike many Marines, he would always come back. Everyone he fought with had come to believe he was bulletproof, at least to the extent that they could hit him but could not kill him. He recovered quickly from physical wounds and had no new emotional scars. He only felt badly when he reflected on Willie and Elise. He longed for Willie. He despised Elise.

Almost a decade in the Marines and Mace had only been home once. He had no idea how rich he was. He did not care. Oddly, he only hoped that when he got home someday, his mother had not sold his beloved car. The 1980s slipped into the mist of time, and the 1990s held promises of new adventures and growth for the Super Seven. Having been promoted several times, each and decorated frequently, they displayed a formidable presence when together, whether in battle or in dress uniforms. They were a controlled wild bunch, brave, and powerful gentlemen.

On December 20, 1992, the Super Seven were deployed in dangerous Mogadishu. The day's schedule called for a routine after-dark patrol consisting of all of Mace's special buddies, plus a few acquaintances. About ten clicks from headquarters, enemy gunfire commenced from the patrol's right flank. Five seconds later, an IED exploded beneath the lead Humvee, sending it soaring into the air above the road. When it came down again, there was little left of it or the men inside. The explosive was enormous, and Mace saw it all. Once again, his lips formed, and spoke the words, "Oh my god, oh my god," over and over. Five of the Super Seven were in that vehicle. They had all been killed right in front of his eyes. "Oh my god," these spoken words proved that Mace believed in God. This was his way of expressing how angry he was with a divine being who could allow this kind of tragedy. In an instant, Mace had lost most of his friends. Now there was only one left. It was his dear black friend, Johnny Paige, and he was sitting right beside him.

"Did you see that?" Johnny hollered.

"I did," Mace said, "and it's killing me."

"Me too," Johnny said as tears welled up in his eyes.

There was no way Mace, Johnny, and the living marines could retrieve the remains of their friends. The sniper fire was too intense. The recovery mission would have to come another day when the sky was silent and safe. The pain of losing five friends in a microsecond was happening this minute. Johnny and Mace were devastated. Each man felt as if large sections of their own flesh had been torn from them, never to be replaced. Mace felt the loss worse because these men were the closest he had to a family. Johnny had a big family back home. He had plenty of shoulders to lean on. Mace had none, except Johnny, and he did not like to talk about his deep feelings anyway. He began to sink, down to a dark, hellish place within himself.

"Why was I always so quiet around them? Why didn't I laugh more with them? Why didn't I share more with them? Because my mother told me that laughing was a waste of time. Whose business is it anyway? It's my life, not hers. How can I go on without those guys?" And snap, he was gone. Mace Madison Stutzman was no longer in touch with himself. He had lost control. Catatonia swept over him like an unrelenting tsunami. Though his physical eyes could no longer see reality, his inner eyes kept seeing his friends destroyed in a blaze of fury. There was nothing left of them but unfulfilling memories. He saw himself always holding back from his friends, always striving for some unattainable standard of excellence and superiority his mother had programmed him to achieve. This is what he saw on an endless loop in the new darkness within which he lived.

# CHAPTER 21

Mace was on a pitiful psychic vacation from life for five months. His first psychiatrist got nowhere with him. Thirteen visits, and the shrink had not elicited an audible response from him. Mace was all the way inside himself now, and hospital staff all around him began to think he would never come back out. It did not help when the first psychiatrist let out his frustrations in front of a group of health care professionals.

"I've tried thirteen times to help Mr. Stutzman, but it doesn't seem like he wants to come out and play. I have tried every technique I ever learned in school and in all my years of practicing. Nothing works. Stutzman has an incredibly strong will. No one is ever going to break through his shell and get in there. It looks like Mace Madison Stutzman has simply had a little too much war. It's going to take a miracle to bring this guy back. And I don't even believe in God."

How insensitive. Then he quit the case. His name is not noteworthy.

His second psychiatrist, also, did not have a stitch of success at first. Colonel Ruppert Rafferty, a rare black Marine psychiatrist, had seen Mace four times with no alteration of the patient's facade. When the doctor began writing notes after seeing Mace, he was filled with doubt that he could help him. He did not enjoy writing that Mace was continuing to drop weight. Mace was now a physically different man. The forty-three pounds and multiple inches he lost rendered him an average-looking big man.

Bored with his work, Dr. Rafferty began whistling a part of Gershwin's "Rhapsody in Blue." The pitiful Mace still sat in his interview chair, his mouth slightly open, certainly not the look of a normal decorated war hero. Only occasionally did the doctor glance at his patient. He whistled and wrote. Though his physical body was not moving, Mace's brain was processing the environment with unusual rapidity. It was making millions of connections, sensing something different, searching for reality for the first time in many weeks. His eyes could still not see, but his mouth moved without his consciousness knowing it.

"Dad?"

Rafferty, not expecting any sound from across the room, much less this plaintiff utterance, turned.

"What's that, Mace?"

The worn-down soldier raised his head and scanned the room with his well-rested eyes.

"Where's my dad?"

As Mace squinted a look around the room, Dr. Rafferty turned toward him in slow motion.

"I'm afraid he's not here right now, Mace," he said with the tenderness of a father speaking softly to a child at bedtime.

"But I heard him whistling one of his favorite songs."

"That was me, Mace."

Mace looked at the gentleman with whom he was communicating. He did not know who he was, but he noticed the color of his skin.

"Do you know where Johnny Paige is?" he asked in a childlike tenor.

"I don't know, Mace?" the doctor said, making sure he said Mace's name each sentence so that the patient might grasp onto it and stay connected to reality. "Who is Johnny?"

"He's my best friend. Do you know when my dad will be back?"

"I don' think he will be back, Mace."

That was not the answer poor Mace's fractured brain wanted to hear. A billion more connections and Mace began to feel the pain of Willie's death. He felt the onrushing unfairness of his mother's disdain for him. He agonized over the dreadful loss of the Super Five and the thought that he might never see Johnny again. It was too much for his splintered mind to handle. Mace slipped away again.

No number of words from Dr. Rafferty would bring Mace back again on this day.

*****

Dr. Rafferty had something to work with now. Over the next few hours, he took copious notes about what he had experienced with Mace. It was not a miracle that brought Mace back. It was simply whistling. He wondered if it could work again. He had also learned that deep within Mace was a little boy who missed his dad. He wrote that Mace's best friend was Johnny Paige. He was already sure that in the future, he would use these bits of information to help his patient emerge from his cocoon.

Two days later, Dr. Rafferty met with Mace again. He saw Mace in the patient's private room. Mace had that room because top brass wanted him isolated, as a reward for his former gallantry. They did not want him interacting with a bunch of crazies while he, hopefully, recovered. What they hoped for was a brilliant psychiatrist to bring him all the way back so he could fight again. Mace Madison Stutzman was an incredible asset, and the Marines needed him healthy.

Dr. Rafferty sat in a nicely cushioned armchair near Mace's bed. He crossed his right leg over his left and rested his hefty pile of notes on his lap. He looked at Mace for several moments. He wondered how deeply Mace was incased in his psychological cocoon. He began with soft words.

"Hello, Mace. I am Dr. Rafferty. I talked with you a couple of days ago. Do you remember me?"

There was no light in Mace's vapid eyes. Then there were more soft words, all of which amounted to a variety of hellos. Nothing worked, as he anticipated. He decided to try whistling. Certainly, it was nothing he had ever read in his textbooks, but if it worked, wasn't that what good psychiatry was about? He sat back in his chair and began whistling "Rhapsody in Blue" from the beginning, every note he could remember. With eyes closed, he thought Gershwin must have been a kind man. No composer could be cruel and create such lovely music.

"Dad?"

*Could this really be happening?* Dr. Rafferty thought.

"Hello, Mace," he said, tenderly.

"Is my dad here?"

"He isn't, Mace, but we can talk about him as much as you would like."

"But I heard him whistling."

"That was me, Mace. I like Gershwin."

"My dad likes Gershwin too. Concerto in F was his favorite. He also liked big band music." Mace was engaging. Dr. Rafferty stayed on topic.

"Do you like the same music as your father, Mace?"

"Very much. We listen to music on our old Victrola."

"Did you learn a lot of songs that way?"

Millions of connections were occurring inside Mace's brain. He still did not remember his father's death.

"I have scores of titles in my brain. Sir, I realize that we're having a nice little conversation here, but who are you, and why are we in a hospital room?"

"Mace, I'm Dr. Rafferty." He did not tell Mace he was a psychiatrist. "It seems you have had a few issues as a result of a firefight you were involved in a while back."

"Was I wounded?"

"Yes, Mace." Dr. Rafferty was not lying. He wanted to tap dance around complexities that might drive Mace back into the cocoon. He continued with his gentle voice. Mace was so fragile, so breakable. Dr. Rafferty wanted to jump-start Mace. Even a loud sound might cause this prized patient to slip away. It was time for his next calculated statement.

"I've got good news for you, Mace."

"You do?"

"I have located your *friend* Johnny Paige, and I'm going to bring him here for a visit."

"You are?" Mace's brain was reconnecting once again, racing to make sense of the last minute of his life, though he felt a subtle joy.

"When?"

"As soon as I can, Soldier."

Dr. Rafferty smiled as he relayed this news to his patient. Mace did not think about his five dead friends. Instead, his emotional brain latched onto the sheer elation it would be to see his friend. The previous three minutes had taken a toll on Mace.

"Dr. Rafferty, it's a pleasure to meet you and all, but I'm feeling really tired. I want to take a long nap now. And thank you for telling me about Johnny Paige. I can't wait to see him."

The man was inching back. Then he fell asleep. Dr. Rafferty was relatively sure that Mace's anticipation of seeing Johnny Paige would keep him from slipping into his darkness once again.

Dr. Rafferty saw Mace two days later and two days after that and repeatedly, in the same pattern, for the next three months. Each session proved more productive than the last. As time and talking moved forward, Mace became more forthcoming with information about himself. Gradually, Dr. Rafferty became aware of the key details of Mace's life. He learned about his love of birds, guns, old cars, music, and how Elise treated him. Dr. Rafferty took the tack of being extremely gentle with the big soldier, always encouraging him. He realized that Mace was fragile, tentative, at best, about everything else in life other than warring.

The good doctor knew that he could not fix everything that was wrong with Mace, but he was determined to patch Mace's heartaches one small piece at a time. In their sixth meeting, Mace was lucid enough to understand when Dr. Rafferty explained what had happened to him. Nobody likes to hear that they were catatonic. Mace was mortified when he learned that he was so uncontrollably human.

As damaged as he was, Mace still had pride, and he was about to stun Dr. Rafferty.

"Doctor, is there a gym in this place?"

"A gym?"

"Yeah, look at me. I've withered away to nothing."

"There's not a gym, per se, but there is a nice rehab center on the first floor. They have weights, pullies, exercycles, treadmills, mats, and all kinds of equipment to help you get back into shape."

"Thank you, Doctor."

"Would you like to walk down there with me?"

"Sure."

Mace scooted his legs to the edge of the bed. When his feet hit the floor with about 235 pounds above them, his knees buckled, and his body collapsed. He was quick enough to grab the guardrails and pull himself up partway to the bed. Dr. Rafferty, tall at six feet two and strong at 210 pounds, jumped from his chair and, in one swift move, helped Mace into the bed. The soldier was out of breath.

"It looks like you are going to need some therapy to help you stand and walk again, Sergeant. You've been in that bed for weeks."

"I guess you're right, Doc."

Mace got that therapy to stand and walk. A few days later, the physical therapy department staff put together a plan to help him recover his strength. Mace did not stick to the plan. He exceeded it.

Dr. Rafferty learned a great deal about Mace by watching him exercise. He learned of his compulsive spirit to excel. He came to know how his mother pushed him relentlessly and ragged on him incessantly. He studied how his father motivated him with love and praise. He learned that Willie had died young and that Mace had not been home in almost a decade.

He discovered that Mace enjoyed talking the most when he was exercising. When Dr. Rafferty moved his sessions from Mace's hospital room to his office, Mace began to shut down. The room was too sterile, too small. He did not like being shrunk in there. He felt mentally ill in there. Though Mace was still a quiet man, he felt more prone to talking while working out. Exercise was his element, and whoever he spoke with while doing that was an equal, no matter who it was.

The most important aspect of Mace's life that Dr. Rafferty came to understand about Mace, was his deep love for the Super Six. They were Mace's surrogate family. When five of them first died, Mace felt the loss of their corporal bodies. An instant later, he felt overwhelming remorse for not knowing each of them better and for not sharing more of himself. Without warning, that is what broke him.

"What do you want now, Mace?"

"I don't want to kill anymore, Doctor."

"I certainly understand, Mace," Dr. Rafferty said softly. "I think you lost your stomach for it when you saw your friends die."

"I think I lost my soul too."

"Maybe not. Would you like to stay active in the Marines, maybe learn a new trade?"

"I want to go home, Doctor. It's not because I want to see my mother. It's because I'm tired of war, of seeing men die, of killing them, I miss St. Petersburg. I especially miss Pass-a-Grille."

"Where is that, Mace?"

"It's a tiny peninsula only one block wide and two miles long, adjacent to St. Petersburg. My family owns a cozy home there on Third Avenue, only a couple of hundred feet from the land's end. It's beautiful, a great place for a kid to grow up."

"I want a discharge, Dr. Rafferty, but not a crazy person's discharge."

"Mace, your service record before your hospitalization is impeccable. You are a genuine American hero." Dr. Rafferty's eyes were twinkling. He was sincerely honored to be seeing this veteran. "I am certain that we will be able to give you a regular discharge, and by the time we do, you will have a clean bill of health. I promise."

Dr. Rafferty's confidence put the troubled Mace at ease.

*****

Seven weeks into their conversations, Dr. Rafferty provided Mace Stutzman with the best surprise Mace ever had, in his nearly ten years as a Marine. It happened on an innocuous, overcast Tuesday afternoon. At about 3:30 p.m., while Mace was doing curls with twenty-pound weights and talking with Dr. Rafferty about birds, Johnny Paige sauntered into the rehab room. He headed directly toward the nearest treadmill. Mace did not notice Johnny at first. A moment later, when he looked up to see who he was sharing the room with, he noticed Johnny. He nearly dropped his weights to the carpeted floor. He set them down, jumped up, and raced to Johnny. His hug of his friend nearly took Johnny's breath away. Dr. Rafferty, a sensitive man, as well as a skilled psychiatrist, felt incredible joy when he witnessed a white and a black man share such fondness for one another.

"Easy, big boy, you're crushing me," Johnny said, 25 percent jokingly, 75 percent seriously.

Mace released his grip, stepped off the treadmill, and faced Johnny eye to eye. Johnny had already seen that Mace had lost several inches from his once-massive frame.

"How did you find me?" Mace asked dumbfoundedly.

"Dr. Rafferty found me, told me you were in the hospital, and asked me if I could come to see you. I couldn't get leave till now, so here I am."

Mace's heart burst with love for Dr. Rafferty. Nobody had ever done anything like this for him.

"How long can you stay?"

"For a week, then I'm flying back home to stay with my family for a while."

The child in Mace sprang out from deep within.

"Maybe we can go to dinner a couple of times, see a movie or two, do whatever the fuck you want to do."

"Sounds good to me, Mace. But whatever we do, it'll be better if we spend some quality time just talking."

"I can promise that," Mace replied. He turned to Dr. Rafferty and almost pleadingly asked, "Dr. Raffferty, will it be okay if we do those things?"

"Mace, you cannot only do them, but I also highly recommend you do everything you can with your friend."

Mace, having no behavioral filter, came across the room, lifted Dr. Rafferty from his chair, and gave him a gentle bear hug. "Doctor, you have no idea how much this means to me."

"I might just a little bit, don't you think?"

"You got that right, Doctor."

That was the happiest moment that Mace had experienced in years and the most emotionally healthy he had been in months. To Dr. Rafferty, he almost looked like a normal guy.

\*\*\*\*\*

The seven days that Mace spent with Johnny were glorious and healing. Though they had spent two thirty-day leaves together in Hawaii, Mace grew to love and admire Johnny Paige more deeply than in the prior thousands of days they had spent close to one another. The reason, they talked deeply and honestly to each other. They also listened intently. It started at dinner that first night.

"How are you now, Mace?"

"I'm definitely better than when I blanked out with you a few months ago, but I still miss the guys terribly. I have lost my love for killing, Johnny. Can you believe that? I don't even want to continue my career in the service. I want to go home, though I dread seeing my mother. She's a cruel woman, a true heartbreaker. I want to go home, grab my old stuff, then start a new life. I am afraid of doing that alone."

"It's good to want to start over again, Mace. When our friends were killed and you wigged out, I had to start all over without any of you. You can do it too."

"I'm not so sure, Johnny."

"Have you considered finding a nice girl and settling down? You are a great-looking guy. You should be able to find a gorgeous female."

"Thanks for the compliment, but when it comes to women, I don't know where to begin to deal with them."

"No one really does, Mace. It's all trial and error."

They both chuckled, though Mace immediately thought of his mother and all the times he had tried to please her. He never did. Elise, who long ago told him that laughing was a waste of time, never laughed with Mace. She rarely smiled. When she did, it was more of a smirk. Johnny took him away from those thoughts.

"How are you handling the loss of our friends now, Mace?"

Mace's eyes filled with water.

"Not well, Johnny. Without you, I would not have anybody. Those men were my family. You are my family."

Something rare happened when Mace spoke his next words. A single tear fell from his left eye and rolled slowly down his cheek.

"Promise me, we will be best friends for life." Johnny reached his hands across the table. "Give me your hands, Mace."

Mace willingly obeyed. Johnny took both of Mace's hands into his and covered them.

"I swear on these heroes' hands that we are best friends for life."

The two friends stared into each other's eyes. The stare was another way to cement their commitment to each other. Neither man could know how this bond would play out over the years, but they sensed that good things would come from it. They were both right.

# CHAPTER 22

Time rocketed by the next six days, but it was more than enough time to bring the soldiers closer together than they had ever been. This week span included two sessions with Dr. Rafferty. Mace preferred to call them visits because he did not consider himself crazy, and he did not even remember being wigged out for a while.

"How did it go with Johnny last night?" Dr. Rafferty asked with his usual concern.

"It was great, Doctor, a night filled with eating and good conversation. I must have packed in 3,500 calories."

"What was the most important thought or feeling you came away from last night, Mace?"

Mace squinched his face uncharacteristically, as he thought about his answer. It came to him a moment later.

"Sir, Johnny, is my lifeline to almost my whole military career, and he will be my lifeline to the future, as well."

"Why do you say that, Mace?"

"Doctor, Johnny and I have saved each other's life on the battlefield. He's my link to the Super Five that died, and he's my friend for life. Of that, I am sure."

"That is a good takeaway, Mace. From what I have learned about Johnny, so far, I think it's a good bet that you will be lifetime friends, and I think it will be good for both of you."

"Thanks, Dr. Rafferty. Do you mind if I ask you a question now?"

"Not at all, Mace. Fire away."

"What do you take away from our visits, Doctor? Am I like all the rest of your head cases, or am I different?"

Dr. Rafferty chuckled softly at Mace's choice of words, then so did Mace.

"Please do not disrespect yourself by saying you are a head case. You are not. You are a good person, Mace. You were traumatized by the deaths of your military family in a flash. I believe you blanked out because your mind could not take that loss, combined with the knowledge that the only family you had at home was a loveless mother. You are completely unique, Mace. There is no other man like you. I am asking you to believe that every human being has the right to break apart when faced with a high degree of trauma. People are a little like Humpty-Dumpty. They fall off a wall and break apart. A rare person can be put back together again. I have concluded that you will be one of those rare people. You possess a rare brand of willpower and determination. I am betting that you are coming back stronger than ever. I am convinced that your mind needed to hit the reset button and that while you were away, your subconscious contemplated where to take you in the future. The trauma you endured and your escape from it signaled the end of your military career and much of your emotional life up to that point. So far, Mace, that is what I take away from our visits."

Mace did not reveal to Dr. Rafferty this visit or any other visit that he considered himself a serial killer. He did not reveal to him that there was more to Mace Madison than he would ever know. In fact, he would never tell anyone of his secret instinct for and delight taken in ending the life of his and his country's enemies. Mace's likewise would never know, nor would Dr. Rafferty, that Elise held a secret she would never reveal, that Mace was a product of incest. Mace appreciated Dr. Rafferty's assessment of him, but before he thanked him, he relished, for a long moment, joyful thoughts of his twenty-seven kills.

*****

Shrinking someone back to health is a daunting challenge, to be sure; but in this case, had it not been for the whistling of a rhapsody, Mace Stutzman might have never come back from within himself.

Psychiatry, with endless pursuit of truth, was at its best with Dr. Rafferty. Each visit, he would try to bring Mace out a little bit farther from his secret world, into which he would not allow anyone to enter for several weeks. He knew he would never know all there was to Mace. He knew that about all his patients, but he especially knew that about the super quiet ones. He had contemplated the phrase, "still waters run deep" thousands of times, hundreds of times regarding Mace. All he wanted for the soft-spoken soldier was for him to be able to cope with the rest of his life with limited support systems.

When Dr. Rafferty found out how much Mace loved his father, he decided to take a fatherly approach in their interactions. It worked. Mace grew to feel a real connection with this good doctor and developed a wish to have him in his life forever. How he would achieve that, he did not know, but he would try.

*****

Sixteen weeks later, Mace was ready to go home. By the time Dr. Rafferty declared him certifiably normal, Mace had been in the hospital three quarters of a year. Looking fit, Mace had gained back twenty of the forty-three pounds he had lost. He was also able to add a couple of inches of muscle everywhere on his body. He liked the way he looked, but he knew he could do better. He planned to join a gym as soon as he returned to St. Pete.

Dr. Rafferty was all smiles during their final session.

"Are you excited about heading home tomorrow?" he asked.

"As excited as I can be when I have to consider what I have to deal with when I get to my house. When I think about my new life and career, I truly am excited."

"Are you still sure you want to be a police officer?"

They had talked about this transition many times.

"I have always been a police officer, Doctor. For almost ten years as a Marine, I was policing the world. Policing St. Petersburg should be much easier."

"Do you still have an aversion to killing?"

"I do, now. But if I absolutely had to do it, in the line of duty, I could. You may know, already, that I'm a pretty good shot. I could do quite a bit of damage to someone without killing them."

It was different for Mace to listen to himself speak. He was a different man than he was only a year ago. Since seeing his friends die so horribly, rivers of PTSD had cut pathways through numerous chambers of his brain, nervous system, and emotions. He still had nightmares about it, but after months of therapy, he could cope with them better. He simply no longer had the stomach for killing.

"Who are you now, Mace?"

"I'm a different man, that's for sure. I find myself looking forward to many unknown things. I want to make new friends and try other hobbies."

"I am happy to hear those statements, Mace. Please remember that you have every right to chase all your dreams, the way you choose. Never let one person's negativity slow you down. In the future, it is full steam ahead, but pursue what you love."

Mace listened intently to every word, as he always did. At the same time, he would think his own accompanying thoughts. He knew, after all the talking with the good doctor, that he had more tools with which he would step into his future. He had begun to buy into the doctor's positivity. He believed, now, that he had the intrinsic right to be happy, no matter how much a parent might have hurt him as a child. He was ready for his new beginning, which he would begin tomorrow. He felt ashamed to be in the hospital. He was ashamed that he had been a big, strong, Marine who had allowed his wounded mind to fracture into some dark nether world for, God knows how long.

"How are you feeling right now, Mace?" Dr. Rafferty asked, seeing Mace drift into his own dimension of reflection.

"I'm okay. I was just thinking about how ashamed I am that I lost my mind and got stuck in here for so long."

Dr. Rafferty became visibly upset, a rarity.

"Mace, I've told you this before, and I'll repeat it. It is vital that you comprehend this concept and take it with you wherever you go. There is no shame in what happened to you or any human being whose mind undergoes severe trauma. There are a complex series of unknown mental and physical equations that precede a breakdown. If anyone knew those equations, they would try to divert the breakdown. But nobody knows those equations, and far too often, a person is already broken down before anyone can even try to save them. There is no shame because a person is experiencing something out of their control. You came back a stronger and better man. Count your blessings. Do not waste life's precious moments beating up on yourself. You woke up from a horrible nightmare. You have awakened, however, and reconstructed your mindset to be able to handle future challenges and disappointments. Facing your future will not be easy, Mace. There is no panacea for successfully facing it. You know how or when your PTSD will manifest itself, cause you pain, and affect your behavior. You must face every day with courage and even pride in yourself, no shame. You are a true American hero, Mace. You performed many honorable feats for your country, yourself, your brother Marines, and for humanity. When you embark on the next segment of your life, you will do a great deal more for yourself, your city, and humanity. Of that, I am certain. The main thing you must do first, Mace, is to eradicate shame from your personal equations."

Mace noticed Dr. Rafferty's face. It was the perfect blend of a determined psychiatrist with the twinkling eyes of Santa Claus. This man cared about Mace more than most people ever had.

Mace needed time to digest Dr. Rafferty's comments. It only took a few seconds to wonder whether these words from the graying doctor would be enough to erase the shame he still felt.

"Thank you, Doctor. I promise to try to eradicate that shame, but it's still gnawing at me."

"That is all I can ask, Soldier," Dr. Rafferty responded. Dr. Rafferty's face remolded itself into a more concerned facade. "We have talked at length about your mother, Mace. I would like to share some parting thoughts with you about her. Is that okay with you?"

"Go ahead," Mace said, his eyes dropping to the floor.

"I know that your mother hurt you terribly, as a child and young man, Mace. After thinking about your case for many weeks, I have done something I enjoy doing, and that is to create a backstory for her life before you were born. It was not you, as a baby and little boy, that deserved her poor treatment.

"Something was off-center with her. We know that she was just a simple farm girl, only child, tons of chores, no siblings younger or older to share with. She simply had no experience with babies or children. Plus, she was so young. Those things in themselves do not usually make for a bad mother. I suspect something hurt her very deeply in her own youth that restricted her ability to love you. I have no idea what that might have been, but it was something painful. Life presents a myriad of trials that can ravage your youth. I believe that you were both damaged. That backstory might be reason enough to give her another chance when you get home."

"I can certainly give her that chance, Doctor, because that is one thing I know how to do very well. I have already given her a million chances. I think can give her a couple of more. I don't think she has changed. You don't know her like I do."

"If that is true, Mace, then you probably need to show her that you have changed. You are stronger now. If you have it in you, perhaps you should confront her. If she still is the same cruel woman, you might become a catalyst for her growth."

"I've never seen myself in that role, but I'll give it a try if that's what you want me to do."

"I do, Mace, but what I want most from you is not to allow your mother to hurt you anymore. You have paid more due in life than most men ever do. You have had an exemplary military career. You have every right to live a free and happy life. Try different approaches with her. If one does not work, try something else."

"I'm not sure I can behave that way, Doctor. Elise is a frightening woman."

"Approach your future like you did war and your wrestling career. You were fearless. You were unbeatable. You were heroic."

"That might all be true, Dr. Rafferty, but would you believe that through all my life, I have had my mother in my ear? For wrestling, it was literally. For war, it was figuratively, but she was always there."

"Is she still there now, Mace?"

"Yes, sir, she is."

"She may always be there, Mace. That is a fact of your life. There is a way to combat it."

"What is that?" Mace asked quickly.

"Your inner voice must become stronger than hers." Dr. Rafferty looked older than his forty-five years. His hair was already gray, his face, a furrowed map of a million concerned thoughts for his patients. He was a dashing black man, and Mace admired him. He wondered what courage the man might have on a battlefield.

"That would be a trick."

"But it is one you can perform, Mace. Add your father's voice to your inner voice. It is probably there already, but maybe you can turn up the volume. Add my voice. Add the voices of all your Marine friends, dead or alive. Add the voices of anyone else who ever cared about or appreciated you."

"Who might that be, Doctor?"

"How about all those people you saved all over the world?"

"That's fair enough, Doctor, but when it comes to friends, there are not too many around. I scare most people away with my quietness. People mistake it for sullenness or meanness. I was never mean, Doctor. I was only painfully shy. The result is still the same. I am alone. You are right. My father's voice is in my ear, but it's a whisper. Mother's is a scream. I don't know how loud your voice will be till I've been away from you awhile."

"I hope my voice is loud enough to be heard sometimes, Mace. If that much occurs, then we will have achieved something remarkable here."

"I know that we have, Doctor."

"Try to remember that the love and encouragement you receive from people who care about you should carry far more weight than the discouragement you receive from people close to you."

"That is a pretty cool equation, Doctor, but I'm not sure that it's absolute truth in the real world."

"Someday, somewhere, when you least expect it, someone will enter your life, and through love and logic, quiet your mother's voice to a minuscule peep in your ear."

"That's a lot to expect from one person. And I'm not much of a ladies' man. I don't ever see that happening, but who knows, you may be right. I'm curious to see what unfolds, myself."

"None of us can see the future, Mace. One thing is certain. We will all die. Many of us will suffer greatly before that eventuality. Because of that, we should try to develop some compassion for each human being, despite their faults. When you do that, it should help to reduce the pain you may have felt from someone who has wronged you. Forgiveness for someone who has hurt you can also strengthen you."

"How, Dr. Rafferty? How can forgiveness strengthen me if I forgive my mother?"

"You ask a good question, Mace. Answering it is as almost difficult as it is to achieve forgiveness. Harboring a grudge against or having hatred for someone is like wearing a horse collar. Everywhere you go, everything you do, its overwhelming weight drags you down. Somehow, you must come to understand the humanity of your abuser. There is no doubt that your mother began her life as a sweet little girl, but somewhere along the path of her early years, someone abused her enough that it changed her adult behavior from normal to unloving and cruel. It is my firm opinion, Mace, that your mother was broken before you were born. As a result, she took her pain out on you. Had she been able to forgive her abuser, she might have been a nurturing mother. She also, probably, never had anyone to talk with about her damaging experiences."

Mace listened intently, his head resting in his hands, his elbows on his knees. He looked like a curious lad.

"Does that make sense so far?" Dr. Rafferty asked, furrowing his brow, hoping he was reaching Mace.

Mace nodded.

"Before I continue, I want to digress a moment to tell you that forgiveness is not one of my greatest attributes. Being a black man in America, I have encountered a broad variety of abusers in my path through life. People especially tried to abuse me as a child and a teenager, simply because I was black. I am still trying to forgive some people from my past who treated me poorly.

"Mace, in order to forgive, we must disconnect from our abuser's grievances against us. If we can do that, we can remove that horse collar from our neck."

The pensive patient thought for a moment, sat upright in his chair, and said, "I don't think I can do it."

"Can you try?"

"I can think about it."

They talked well over the allotted time of one hour for a visit. Philosophical concepts, principles, and emotional equations flowed back and forth freely between Dr. Rafferty and his respected client. Mace listened carefully, internalizing everything. He ate up Dr. Rafferty's words as if they were manna from heaven, necessary to sustain him for a long time.

When Dr. Rafferty said, "I think it's time to say goodbye," Mace looked like a little lost boy.

He stood up almost simultaneously with Dr. Rafferty as he reached out his hand to shake his client's. A nonfiltered feeling of sadness leaped from Mace's stomach and spread out through his upper body.

Instantaneously, he bypassed the outstretched hand and with each of his own reaching hands, placed them on the doctor's back, and pulled him into a tight embrace. Dr. Rafferty, not at all surprised at Mace's response, merely relaxed his muscles and allowed Mace his almost son-like display of affection. Toward the end of the tender moment, Mace slowly lowered his face into the crook of Dr. Rafferty's neck between his chin and shoulder. He smelled the pleasantness of the doctor's cologne. It was soothing and refreshing, reminding him of something from long ago. It was a musky smell.

After a moment, Mace felt two taps on his right shoulder. He knew they meant it was time to release his grip. He gave himself a mere three more seconds to feel the goodness flowing into him and the appreciation he wanted to convey. Then he simply relaxed his arms and backed away. He straightened and stiffened his body and strongly raised his hand to the position of salute. Dr. Rafferty followed suit, straightening and stiffening and returning salute with extreme dignity. Mace dropped his hand and arm a split second after

Dr. Rafferty dropped his. Mace turned on a toe and walked out of the room without looking backward. The moment left the two men with completely different thoughts. The kindhearted Dr. Rafferty believed that it was over between them, that he would never hear from Mace again. Mace Madison Stutzman left knowing that he would do whatever it would take so that the two of them would be friends for the rest of their lives.

# CHAPTER 23

The next day, Mace left the hospital, wearing his dress blues. He was not going to be discharged for several weeks from now. He looked amazing. Pinned onto the left side of his dress jacket, were the reflections of his incredible military career. Displayed were numerous ribbons, two Purple Hearts, a Navy Cross, a Silver Star, and a Bronze Star. He carried a duffel bag filled with only eighty-two pounds of stuff he had accumulated during his long tenure in the United States Marines. It was extraordinarily little stuff, really, because he collected nothing excepted his ribbons and medals, of which he was extremely proud. When he thought of them and the moments he had earned them. There was no shame. In fact, his pride in his achievements was so deep that he knew it would help to sustain him through difficult times in the future. He also had four Hawaiian shirts he had bought on leaves in Hawaii that would serve him perfectly in St. Petersburg.

An hour and a half later, that duffel bag was safely tucked away in cargo, and he was sitting on the plane flying to Tampa. He was not a reader at this time in his life, so he merely sat bookless, looking out the window, thinking about home. What a strange word *home* was to Mace. Instead of a word filled with air and buoyancy, it was laden with fear and discomfort. It was an uninviting word, filled mostly with pain. With his father long dead, home was just a place where his belongings were stored. A cruel woman stalked the rooms of that house and whatever home it should have been, she had destroyed it. These were the thoughts that drew him into sleep that flight. He was awaked by the bumping of the wheels upon the tarmac upon landing.

After picking up his duffel bag at baggage claim, he stepped into a Tampa Yellow Cab and headed for his tiny corner of the world.

"Third Avenue and Pass-a-Grille Way, please."

"Sure, thing, Soldier," the middle-aged driver responded. He turned on the meter.

"It's been a long time since I've seen that many medals on somebody's chest, if ever, Soldier."

Mace enjoyed being called soldier even though he realized that his time for being one was coming to an end. His only response was "Thank you, sir. I worked hard for them."

"I can only imagine what you had to do to earn those. I feel honored to say thank you for all that you did for your country. And welcome home."

"Thank you again, sir."

"I just met you, soldier, but I can honestly say that I'm proud of you, and it's an honor to be driving you home."

"Thank you, sir." Mace was not always the consummate gentleman. His calm demeanor belied the fierce behavior that earned him those medals.

They were coming to the Howard Franklin Bridge. How beautiful the calm bay was in the early evening sunlight. Mace took his hat off, stared at the water a moment, then closed his eyes. He did not want to hear any more compliments. He certainly did not want to start thinking about his battlefield achievements or losses.

The cabdriver was silent as Mace slipped into a light slumber. Though the driver was not speaking, he stared repeatedly into his rearview mirror at the wondrous chest of medals and ribbons, the likes of which he would never see again. A couple of loud horn beeps from an impatient driver woke Mace in time for him to see the Don CeSar looming ahead. The enormous pink edifice had not changed overtly since he had last seen it. He thought he would have dinner there in the next day or two.

"Have a nice sleep, Soldier?"

"I did. Almost home."

"I'll bet your wife will be happy to see you."

"I'm not married," Mace said, not taking offense to the cabdriver's statement. "But my mother will be there."

"That will be nice. I bet she's mighty proud of you."

Mace did not respond. Instead, he began to feel butterflies in his stomach. They passed by the Laundromat and the pizza place at Twentieth and Pass-a-Grille Way. Nothing had changed. It felt homey and inviting. Mace had eaten there many times and remembered exactly how delicious the pizza tasted. The butterflies turned into a churn. He was more upset than when he went into battle. He had written his mother a letter, informing her when he would arrive home. She responded with a single sentence, "I'll be waiting for you." Mace agonized over that sentence. How was he supposed to interpret it? Was it an implied threat? *Is she so angry that she would try to hurt me?* Fear still dominated his thoughts of her. *Why should I be worried about her? I am a highly decorated soldier, and she is just a crabby old lady who has no composure or class. I will show her what composure and class is the moment I see her.*

Mace paid the cabdriver, got his change, then slapped a $10 bill into the guy's hand.

"Thank you, Soldier. I greatly appreciate that. You made my day in more ways than one."

He was not kidding. He had been working since 7:00 a.m., and this was his most profitable ride so far.

"Would you like me to carry that duffel bag for you?"

"No thank you, sir. I can handle it."

The friendly driver hopped out of the cab and quickly opened the back door for Mace. Mace grabbed his duffel bag and left the cab.

"Good luck to you, Soldier."

"Same to you, sir."

The cab pulled away as Mace walked to the front door, noting a fresh light-blue coat of paint on the house. He leaned his bag on the wall to the left of the front door. His key, long ago lost, forced him to have to let Elise show him indoors. Then he thought that even if he did have a key, he would knock first and wait for Elise so he would not frighten or offend her by entering unannounced.

The moment Elise opened the door, Mace picked her up and kissed her three times on the neck, like Willie did to him, except he did not blow fart sounds. Elise stiffened like a two-by-four, but instead of putting her right down, Mace spun her around for a circle and a half. While spinning in the air in Mace's strong arms, she remembered how Willie used to do the same thing with her in the privacy of their bedroom and how much fun it was. But this was her son. This was not right. Or was it? She was not sure.

It was the boldest gesture Mace had ever made toward his mother. Dr. Rafferty's voice was in his ear. "Try a different approach." He certainly was. There was nothing sexual to Mace's behavior. He was merely expressing that he loved this woman somehow, for whatever good she had done for him, and that he wanted to try to live in his future with her without angst.

"What in God's name are you doing, Mace Madison Stutzman?" she asked. She was not angry.

"I'm showing you genuine affection, something we should have shown toward each other a long time ago."

It was quiet for a moment.

"Did that feel good, Mother?"

"I'm not sure how to answer that, Mace. No other person has done that to me since your father, and that was a long time ago. It felt good when he did it, and I felt that sense of memory when you did it. But it doesn't seem right between a mother and a son."

"It is right, Mother. Genuine affection is always right between people who care about each other. I have seen it all over the world. What is not right is when people stuff their good feelings for each other, for whatever reasons."

Elise was miffed. She did not know what to say. She had not expected to encounter such a depth of logic, intelligence, and expression from her son.

"There is no reason to yell and scream at me to excel anymore because I've been doing that for many years on my own. You and I are entering a new phase in our lives. I would like to live it with kindness and civility."

Elise was speechless, finding the truth in what her son was saying. She also could not take her eyes from him. He was ruggedly handsome, her features dominating his face. His chest was a rainbow of ribbons and medals, very impressive, indeed. She wanted to take him everywhere with her, dressed as he was. Certainly, he was his own man, brave and honorable. Though pondering what he had said to her, she was also giving herself credit for how she raised him. Look at what he had become. She could take him places, and his awards and bearing would reflect on her and her parenting skills. She had not failed. She had succeeded marvelously. She remained silent.

While no one was talking, Mace had the opportunity to look at Elise. She wore a red-and-yellow bikini, not an ounce of fat on her. She had probably come in from a swim minutes before he arrived. Her long blond hair cascaded down her back to the tailbone. With her deep tan, she looked like a wild brown mustang with a yellow mane. Her muscles were tight and cut splendidly, reflecting a woman dedicated to serious weightlifting. She was gorgeous. She might be crabby, but she was not old. She presented as a person of great discipline. Mace wondered why this goddess had not been snatched up by some local bachelor, divorced man, or widower. In all his travels around the world, Mace had never seen a woman more beautiful than Elise.

"Would you like me to make you some dinner?"

She was diverting, not wanting to talk seriously anymore.

Mace answered, "Yes, ma'am. I'd love that." He dropped the conversation, sensing he had made a little headway with his mother.

"Is Princess still here?" he asked hopefully.

"It's in the backyard," the crabby goddess answered, still not wanting to use the car's nickname. "You can't miss it. It's under the blue tarp."

Mace chuckled. She was the same stubborn woman, still unfriendly toward an old car.

Mace forgot about his duffel bag, tossed his hat on the couch, and headed out the back door. One quick look to the left, and there was the blue tarp. Under it was Princess, the big old plump 1950 straight-eight, his most prized possession. He had shared Princess with his father. They had worked on her engine together. That is how Mace learned the basics of automotive mechanics. They had loved her together. Her paint job was only slightly faded and kept hidden under tightly cinched ropes. When he opened the hood, he was stunned. Willie must have worked scores of hours working on the engine to surprise Mace when he returned home. The engine was pristine, reflecting the diligence and patience of his dad. He slammed the hood down, walked to the driver's side door, and sat on the still new looking upholstery. Willie had left the keys in the ignition, believing that Mace would be home soon. Willie never saw Mace again. He hurt terribly when Mace did not come to visit him when the leukemia was killing him. Elise had lied and told Willie that Mace was on a special mission and could not get leave. Of course, Willie had no reason to doubt his Bible-reading darling.

Mace began to smell a faint whiff of a pleasant scent. He began to think of Dr. Rafferty, more of Willie and even Elise. Why was he thinking this way? What was that smell of long and not so long ago? In a couple of minutes, he figured it out. It was the smell of musk, the cologne of choice for his parents and his psychiatrist. It was not odd that Elise used a man's scent. Willie wore musk, and Elise loved the way it smelled on him. When she tried it, many years ago, she loved the bouquet, and it made her feel closer to Willie when he was not around. Mace grabbed the steering wheel, dropped his head upon it, and sobbed tearlessly, for several moments. A short time later, he raised his head, opened his eyes, and looked at the gas gauge. He started the car. It sounded smooth. The tank was full. Willie and Mace had filled it about nine years earlier. They had just finished working on the engine the day before Mace returned to regular duty, after his first and only leave. Mace wondered if the gas was still good.

Mace felt no shame for his outpouring of emotion. Instead, he felt rare joy. He was surrounded by the warmth of his father's adoration in a sacred place, that was akin to a love shrine.

"You wait a little while longer, girl. I'll take you for that great spin that we've been waiting for a long time after dinner."

He talked to the mass of metal as if it was a real person. Real or not, it was a true friend. Elise could have gotten rid of Princess, but she did not. For that, Mace appreciated her. To her credit, Elise had made up her mind not to sell the car, long before she ever saw that Willie had willed it to Mace. Besides, she knew how beloved that car was to Mace, and she felt Willie's presence all over it.

*****

The first dinner Mace and Elise ate together was pleasant. Elise made fillet mignon, mashed potatoes, and macaroni and cheese. Mother knew they were her son's favorites. Elise never scrimped on food. She may not have felt love for her son, but she did not want to starve him to death either. Elise told Mace she was proud of him for what he had accomplished. Interesting first night home. First dinner together, first compliment. *Are things looking up?* Mace wondered.

*****

Three days later, Elise took Mace with her to the eleven o'clock mass at St. Jude's Cathedral. He decided to wear his dress uniform since he had not yet been officially discharged. Elise was extremely proud to be with her soldier. Always a woman to stand and walk erect, this late sunny morning her shoulders were farther back, and with her highest heels on, she stood almost as tall as Mace. She chose to wear a blue-and-white dress, cut one inch above the knee, which also showed the perfect amount of her ample cleavage. With their beautiful colors and height, they were an amazing and formidable tandem. They both felt as good as they looked. Before they left the house, Mace told Elise, "Mother, you look spectacular."

"So do you, Mace Madison."

It was Mace's first ever compliment of that nature from Elise.

Then came the homily of Monsignor Velkos. There was not a compliment to be found in his Sunday sermon. There was only ranting in his rambling sermon. He ragged on sinners of all kinds. It was difficult for Mace to listen to this miserable priest. He was trying to turn his life around, try new approaches, and his mother takes him to listen to this guy. What a bummer.

"Brethren, sin is darkness all around us. If the devil were an artist, he would paint one black canvas after another. His soul is a black hole devoid of light. Sin is everywhere. It is the devil's full-time job to suck you into this vacuum of pain. Once you get sucked into it, it is unlikely that you will ever get out. If you spend too much time there in life, you will surely wind up there in death. Do not count on God helping you either. He is too busy with his compulsive creating of new worlds. He is an artist too. Every time he starts a canvas, he paints a new world. He wants the inhabitants of these new worlds to seek out the inhabitants of the previous worlds he has created. Why should he pay attention to sinners who sin all the time then try to back into heaven at the last minute? Maybe Jesus will listen to you a little if you want to toss a prayer his way. But he is busy too. What you should realize is that Jesus does not have to answer your prayers. The prayer itself should be enough for you, no matter what the outcome.

"Sin, pray, sin, pray, over and over, day in, day out. It's exhausting watching everyone go through these motions. We all go through the same motions in different ways. The worst of us repeat the sin without the pray. We are all sinners, you and I. There are no exceptions. We must leave this church today and strive for even the slightest degree of purity of thought and action."

This was only a small piece of the sermon, but it made sense to Mace. He knew he was a sinner, and a killer, as well. Even though he considered himself a serial killer, he hoped God forgave him. He would do it all again if he had to in order to protect his beloved America. Mace's mind began to wander. His mother could never imagine how dangerous or courageous he really was. If she did, she would never rag on him again. He could snap her neck like a toothpick, no matter how tall and strong she was. What kind of man would he be if he killed his mother? He would be guilty of matricide, a word, and concept he despised. He never really wanted to kill her, though many times he wished she were dead. He did not wish to be a black hole soul. Neither did he think he could be a pure soul that could help humanity the way the deities wanted from him. He did think that perhaps he could live life about three quarters to the good side, and that would give him a better chance of getting through the pearly gates.

At this point in Mace Madison's life, he wanted to be a good person. He wanted to serve his beloved city of St. Petersburg. He wanted to add to his favorite number, which now stood at seventy-two, but he wanted those new numbers to be lives saved. Killing people was easy. Rescuing a life was much more challenging.

Taking a bullet while saving someone's life was much more joyful than putting a bullet into someone and snatching their life away in a microsecond. He fantasized about his future life as a cop. He wanted to be remembered as the brave cop who saved countless lives and never killed anyone. Mace shut off the rest of the Velkos sermon and got caught up, thinking about Dr. Rafferty, wondering how he would stay in touch with him. He dreamed about the good times he would share with Johnny Paige. He even confidently wondered if he could repair the profoundly damaged relationship with his mother.

In his own odd way, Mace was happy. He was living a new life. He did not want to think about sin, heartache, and eternity. He wanted to live in the moment, try to love his mother, and help her to love him. He truly felt like a better man than the one whose mind ruptured about a year earlier. When mass was over, Elise asked Mace, "Son, would you like to go to brunch at a nearby Denny's or Bob Evans, my treat?"

"I sure would," he said, thinking that she was being sweet to him.

He did not realize she wanted to show him off. Fifteen minutes later, they sat down in the last booth in a crowded Denny's. While they waited for their ice water with lemon, Mace broke the ten minutes of silence that had passed between them.

"Does Monsignor Velkos usually give sermons like that?"

"Pretty much," Elise answered matter-of-factly.

"That kind of sermon could certainly keep the parishioners depressed."

"I listen to him every Sunday. He doesn't depress me. He fortifies me in what I believe now and about life in general. Monsignor Velkos had considerable pain in his early life. It reminds me of my early life. I feel terribly like him, and because of that, I feel close to him."

"I don't understand how anybody could feel close to a man like that. I tuned out after a couple of paragraphs. I certainly won't be going to eleven o'clock mass anytime soon."

Elise felt an unusual sense of disappointment, a moment after she realized that this was the beginning of the most interesting conversation she had engaged in for many months.

"That's your right, Mace, but I will miss your company."

Her statement had slipped out. That was not the way she talked. What was she thinking? She never needed or wanted anyone's company except Willie's, and her daddy's, when she was a foolish, needy child.

Elise's statement had touched Mace in an incredible way. Had his cruel mother remarked that she would miss his company at church? Where was she coming from? Had she changed so much over the last several years?

The truth at this moment was that she was curious about this new man with all the stripes, sitting across her. She wanted to know how he became decorated this way. She was willing to go against her defensive nature and become action-oriented. She wanted to ask him outright and stimulate conversation. She could not believe her own behavior. She kept noticing how handsome he was, movie star looks, no doubt. He was not the ugly creature she had thought he was when he was a little boy. In fact, his facial features were almost identical to hers. She stared at his face to see if his nose and eye were flawed, as she believed hers to be. They were not. He was perfect, as she once was. He was prettier and stronger than she was. He was straight-faced. He rarely laughed or even smiled. He was everything she had spent all those screaming hours molding.

She did not think it during the years she was a demeaning mother monster. Now she thought that she raised a consummate man. She believed nothing could hurt her son. He was invincible, like she was. She did not know how badly Mace had fractured when overwhelming grief infiltrated his supposed unconquerable spirit. He kept that fact from her, as she had kept her father's sins secret. He was a perfect clone. He was taller, stronger, and braver than almost any man alive. What she knew of him, now, was exciting. Mace had succeeded in making her proud, something she thought he could never do. Her curiosity was soaring. She wanted to know everything about him. For the first time ever, Elise wanted to talk deeply and humanly with Mace. Elise's eyes sparkled as she spoke next.

"I must admit, you look mighty handsome in that uniform, Mace. You must have gone through hell to get it decorated that way."

She had never engaged him this way. He liked it.

"I did." He paused. "But it was all worth it."

She did not respond. He saw her staring at his ribbons, not his eyes.

"I won't be wearing this uniform much longer, Mother. I'm getting discharged soon."

"Why?" She was startled. She was enjoying being with her son while he was dressed this way.

"Too many bullets and too much shrapnel have taken their toll," he lied.

"I'm sorry, Mace." First apology.

"Ten years is long enough, Mother. I want to be here now, in St. Pete, and become a police officer."

"I would have never expected that in a million years."

"None of us has a million years, Mother. I have almost been around the world already. I just want to live out my life here where I love it and be of service to this community."

"I'm sure you will be a great cop. I'll bet that someday your police uniform will be as decorated as this one."

"I hope so," he said this with utter humility.

"Mace, will you tell me exactly how you earned those decorations if it doesn't hurt too much?"

He wanted to tell her every bloody detail. He yearned to tell somebody besides Dr. Rafferty. Now his heretofore emotionally aloof mother was asking. He would be overjoyed to share, but he would keep that joy hidden from her.

He began to tell her in his best storytelling voice, which he had never used before. His details were impeccable and thrilling. Though

Mace was somewhat monotonic, Elise saw the wonder of his experiences in his eyes. Elise was spellbound. She felt as if she was in a movie theater, watching an Academy Award-winning war movie with the Academy Award-winning star narrating the story right in front of her. And he was handsome to look at, with such a soothing voice, to share such horror.

As she listened, her feelings for him began to change. It became clear that she could never bully him again. He was not only a physical giant compared to her. He had paid so many honorable dues. He was a true American hero and a good person. It was far from love she was feeling for him at this moment, but she decided that in the future, she could at least be civil with him. He deserved that.

When he finished, having not been interrupted by his mother, Elise could not speak. She was overwhelmed by his story and conflicting feelings of a keen sense of pride for him and what she always thought of him as an unlovable mongrel. Her thoughts darted to Willie and whether she ever loved him, then to if she even knew what love was. She knew what civility was, though she rarely employed it. She was almost always angry, short with nearly everyone.

Time was passing, and no one was speaking. They each took about four forkfuls of sausages, waffles, and eggs. This gave Mace Madison time to contemplate, telling her the unthinkable. He decided that he had the courage to tell her part of the happening but keep the outcome to himself.

"Mother, something happened at the end of my duties that completely changed me. I enjoyed killing those twenty-seven enemy combatants. Then one day, on a routine patrol, the vehicle ahead of mine rolled over an IED and blew up. Five of my true friends, including my best friend, were killed. Nothing in my life impacted me the way that did. After that, I lost my desire to kill. I was damaged to the core of my being. My heart was broken. I asked the brass if I could get an early out. They said that, after all that I had endured physically and mentally and what I had done for my country, there would be no problem. What they told me made me feel a bit better when I was feeling the worst I'd ever felt in my lifetime."

Compassion arose from the darkness within Elise. When Willie died, she was heartbroken. She had one friend to help her. It was Monsignor Velkos. She remembered asking him a question.

"Can a person have a broken heart if they are not even certain that they loved someone who died?"

"Yes, my dear one. The human heart has complexities that stretch out to infinity. It can love without being aware that it is doing so."

At the time, she thought his answer was poppycock. Right now, she was remembering the depth of pain she felt when Willie died. It was the worst pain she ever felt. She could relate to Mace. She understood how he loved his friends. But even as she thought of the mere mention of the word *love*, she wondered whether real loving would detract from the invincible Amazon concept she had of herself.

"I'm sorry that happened to you, Mace. To lose one person that you love can be devastating, but to lose five at once is impossible to describe."

Although half of Elise was doling out what little compassion she had, the other half was angry that God had ever allowed that damned broken heart. All it did was spoil the image she was trying to create for herself, that she was invincible. Now she had learned that her son was human and vulnerable, despite his medals. He could suffer heartache like anyone else. She could not control it. Mace dropped a notch in her mind. After building his image so strongly with the bulk of his story, the last small part damaged it. He was human. It would be much more difficult living near a human man than an illusion.

*****

Three days later, Elise drove Mace in her perfectly restored 1974 Dodge Charger to her lawyer's office in downtown St Petersburg. His name was Michael Fitzpatrick. He was not only her lawyer. He was her financial adviser. Fitzpatrick had practiced law in St. Pete, his entire forty-eight-year career. He was seventy-three now and was in superb condition. He was still running marathons, and four times a week, he still ran ten miles a day to stay in top running form. His great benefit to Elise was to make tremendous money on her substantial investments. She may have been a farm girl, but Elise was a fast learner. Willie was her first financial adviser. Fate was her second when Willie died. Fitzpatrick was her third. He was good, really good. He also represented scores of Major League Baseball players, who came to St. Pete every spring. He had the knack for making money, and the word got around.

Elise had used Fitzpatrick for seven years. She was always professional with him. She addressed him as Mr. Fitzpatrick, never once as Michael. That is how Elise rolled, vigilantly tightly wrapped. Fitzpatrick long admired Elise's acquired acuity with high finances. Since Willie died, Elise spent most of her time painting, reading the Bible, working out, and protecting and growing her money. Since childhood, she determined not to let anybody take anything of value away from her. She was not going to allow that to happen with her money.

For some reason, unknown to Elise, she would not tolerate anyone taking anything away from Mace, either. She rationalized that if someone stole from Mace, they would be stealing from Willie, and that would be unconscionable.

Mace immediately noticed the difference between his and Fitzpatrick's body types when they met. The finance man was only five feet ten and lean, maybe 4 percent body fat. His grip was just the right tightness to make Mace feel he could trust him. A moment after that first handshake, Mace began to peer around the room at the twenty-five, or so, pictures Fitzpatrick featured on his desk and shelves. They depicted a happy family. The financial guru's wife was gorgeous, about twenty-five years his junior. Mace thought she was not as beautiful as his mother but a trophy wife, for sure. The couple had four beautiful children, all at various stages of life. There were wedding pictures, camping shots, views of Disneyland, and grade school and high school pictures. There were also pictures of the kids' sporting events and Fitzpatrick's runs. There were a few photos of his professional events, where his wife was stunning in various gowns and jewelry.

"Beautiful pictures, are they not, Mr. Stutzman?"

"That they are, sir. Please, call me Mace."

He was unaware of the formality between his mother and his new lawyer. Elise was not pleased with Mace's relaxing her unspoken protocol. While she seethed for a moment, Mace wondered how it could be possible for a man to have so much love in his life.

"Mace, we're here today to discuss the conditions of your finances, according to your father's will and the diligent efforts of your mother all these years, to help your money grow."

Elise smiled demurely. Compliments were always appreciated, especially this one.

"Thanks to our joint efforts during these almost ten years you were away, the original amount your father left you has more than doubled. Your father divided all his cash assets equally between you and your mother. The gun collection and his gold and silver are entirely yours. The coins, bars, and ingots are housed in a huge safe in your home and in three safe-deposit boxes at the Barnett Bank in St. Pete Beach. In his will, he left instructions that I do not give the combination or the safe-deposit keys to anyone but you unless you met your demise in the service."

He opened a brown folder, looked through a few pages, and found what he wanted.

"I'm going to write down the combination of the safe now. I advise you to memorize this sequence as quickly as possible, then fix the number in a safe place, in case you forget it."

He gave Mace the address of the Barnet Bank and gave him the safe-deposit box keys.

"Your mother graciously paid the fees for these boxes all these years."

"I'll pay you back, Mother."

"That's absolutely not necessary, Mace."

"Thank you, Mother."

Fitzpatrick was fascinated by the degree of formality between Elise and Mace.

"I almost forgot, Mace. The Victrola and old records are yours. The house Willie left to you and Elise until she dies, then it's yours."

Elise thought for a moment of all the contented hours she spent listening to those records while Mace was chasing the world's bad guys. The closest Elise ever came to pure joy was when she was painting and listening to those records at the same time. She wondered if she should tell Mace about those activities. A moment later, she decided to do so. She thought that it would be appropriate, from now on, to ask whether he minded her playing the records.

"I have the entire will here, Mace. I would like to give it to you to read at your leisure. It is very personal. You may feel some strong emotions when you read it. I think you might want to experience those feelings in private."

"Thank you for considering my feelings, sir."

Elise reflected that Mace had feelings. She had never considered them before.

"You're welcome, Mace. Now I would like to share the bottom line of why we are meeting today. After all your investments are tabulated, you have cash assets that total slightly south of $4 million."

Mace was speechless. His insides were bubbling. He was thinking about Willie—from farmer to carpenter to millionaire. Then he thought about himself—from the son of a carpenter to soldier to a multimillionaire. The silence in the room was palpable. Elise was thinking too. She wondered how the young man would spend his newfound wealth. There was not a droplet of jealously in her heart toward her son. Strangely, there was a happiness that she nursed for Mace. He was, after all, an extension of herself. Who could hurt him now with all this additional power?

"So, Mace, do you have any comment?" Fitzpatrick asked curiously.

"Thank you, sir. I'll call you when I need some money." That was all he said. He rose to shake Fitzpatrick's hand.

"Anytime, Mace, anytime."

Their meeting ended with a few well wishes and pleasantries.

"He's an awfully nice fellow, isn't he?" Mace said as he and Elise walked to the elevator.

"He certainly is," Elise answered sincerely.

"Mother, what do you say we go out for lunch to celebrate my good news. How about the Don CeSar? My treat."

"That sounds great."

At lunch, Mace revealed that he was always conservative with his money. He had saved several thousand dollars, but it was spread out only between his checking account, his regular savings, and two CDs.

"I don't know anything about money management, Mother. Do you think you could teach me some of what you know?"

The question fell easily on Elise.

"There is a great deal to learn, Mace. Some of it is complicated, but you'll be better for it the more you learn."

Then Elise reflected that this was Willie's money, another reality that kept him alive. While Mace was away and she was responsible for the money, she made up her mind that nobody would ever steal a penny from her or her husband. No one stole any money. If they would have, Elise would not have been above murdering them for their crime.

Lunch passed smoothly, with civility flowing freely between mother and son. Civility transitioned to an odd companionship but one they did not have in the past. Both souls, though damaged severely, felt instant merit to it.

Three hours after the unusual pair arrived home from lunch, Elise told Mace she was going grocery shopping.

"I'm going to Publix. I'll be back in an hour."

The ice was breaking between them, but the waters they tread still seemed cold and dangerous.

A few minutes after Elise left the house, Mace became curious about the gold and silver safe that Fitzpatrick mentioned. Mace put down a nine-year-old *Sports Illustrated* and headed for Elise's bedroom. He figured the safe would be in there because Willie would have wanted to look at his treasures whenever he wanted. The memories of trying to go into that room, however, were excruciating. Once, as a little boy, he walked into that room accidentally. Elise reacted like an angry wild animal.

"Get out of here! And don't you ever come back into this room."

Mace was stunned. Willie was shocked and frightened.

"Honey." He paused a moment. That was enough time for Elise to cut him off and continue her screaming.

"Do you hear me, little Stutzman boy? From now on, when you see that door closed, you knock first, then you stand there and wait. After someone answers, then you can open the door, but you cannot come into this bedroom again, ever. This room belongs to your father and me. It is not a room for a little boy to be walking into. Are we clear, Mace Madison?"

For reasons known only to her, the bedroom suddenly became sacred. Little Mace stood in that doorway, shivering, forgetting why he had come to the bedroom in the first place. Mace felt that long ago shiver, but this was 1992, and he was no longer a frightened tyke. Grown Mace turned the knob and walked into his mother's bedroom. To his surprise, the room was spotless. There was not a grain of sand on the floor. Odd, since this was a beach house and Elise spent most of her time on the beach. The bed was tightly made. The sheets were white, with a dainty pink rose pattern. The bed was brown, new, with a beautifully carved horse on the thick headboard. An antique vanity sat on the floor to the left of the king-size bed as he faced it. To the right was a gorgeous antique chest of drawers.

It was what Mace saw on top of the vanity that made his eyes well with tears. Four framed pictures of Willie and Elise rested there. The most prominent was of Willie and Elise standing at the altar during their wedding at St. Anne's Church in Toluca. Another picture was of the pair vacationing at Starve Rock in Illinois. One was of the honeymooners laughing on Navy Pier in Chicago. The last one showed them standing in front of Buckingham Fountain. A magnificent spray of pink water lit up the night sky behind them. It was the tiny votive candles in front of the pictures that almost made Mace weep. The vanity was not only a place to do her face and hair; it was Elise's shrine to Willie. This was such a tender gesture for a woman not known to them.

There was no safe in the bedroom or closet. Slowly, the smell of his mother's and Willie's cologne wafted into his nostrils. The tears remained in their place. Mace stared at the pictures for a few more seconds. There were no other pictures of Willie in the house. It was nice to see his dad again. Mace wondered if Elise had any more pictures of Willie somewhere. She did, boxes of them in her closet. What he saw was bewildering and satisfying. There was more to his mother than he knew. Why she did not share her sensitive side with him during his childhood, he could not figure.

The only other room the safe could be in was the guest bedroom. That was another room he had not been in for years. His senses sprung to life when they were bombarded with the myriad sights and smells of an artist's workshop. Everywhere his eyes fell were paintings of landscapes, sunsets, people, and buildings. There were four easels in the small room. Each of them held an unfinished picture on their ledge. The pictures were painted with vibrant hues. Every space of wall, from floor to ceiling, had a picture of some kind, hanging upon it. The floors were littered with paintings. They were stacked four or five deep all around the room. More paintings leaned against the two tables that held paints. The studio was all about painting, except for the northeast corner.

The safe was a monster. It is a sure bet that the people who created it, never imagined it to be standing in a corner of a beach house in Pass-a-Grille, Florida, in 1992.

The safe was a Halls, produced by the Halls Safe and Lock Company in 1876, the same year as Custer's last stand. It had two thick doors that made it look daunting to break into, which is exactly what Halls wanted. Mace could hardly wait to try the combination, but before he began, he was compelled to leaf through some of the paintings that surrounded him. Thumbing through the paintings was like peeking at different parts of his mother's mind. Almost everything she could have cast her eye upon through the years was represented. Elise was not afraid to tackle anything. She even painted about twenty pictures of Willie, in various activities. In each painting, he exhibited an angelic demeanor. He was happy in each picture. Each picture was imbued with the love Elise felt for Willie. Mace's heart ached for his father.

There was not a single painting of Mace Madison. Elise's son finally moved toward the safe. He was thinking that maybe someday he might have three or four of his mother's paintings hanging on his own walls.

Mace pulled the combination from his pocket and slowly and excitedly opened the safe for the first time. Again, he was surprised. The enormous space inside was filled with gold and silver coins and bars that represented three generations of collecting. There were several more guns inside that could not fit into the gun cabinet. The colors were different, but it looked like Christmas in there or a candy store, and Mace was the kid. He felt no stress, no PTSD, no anxiety about his future. Mace felt like he was among friends. He did not care that they were amorphic. They were good company, no matter what they were.

Suddenly, he heard the unmistakable sound of his mother's muscle car pulling up to the front of the house. He stopped what he was doing, closed the powerful safe doors, and quickly walked outside to help Elise carry the groceries. He could not wait to talk with her.

"Thank you for coming to help me, Mace Madison."

"It's no trouble, at all, Mother, but there's something wonderful I want to share with you."

"What's that?" she asked while filling her hands with grocery bags.

"I found the safe in the bedroom."

She cut him off.

"You didn't go into my bedroom?" she asked curtly. The muscles all over her body tensed.

"Of course, I did not, Mother. You should know me better than that," he lied without a hint of it.

Elise became calm again.

"Anyway, when I walked into that room, I was overwhelmed with your paintings. They are gorgeous. So many different settings. So many different birds, skies, sun colors, oceans in different moods. Your night scenes and clouds are hauntingly lovely. I am utterly impressed with your talent and prolific production."

Elise took the compliment into a sacred place with whatever soul she had left. For a moment, she did not know what to say, but her next words flowed quickly and humbly.

"Thank you for your kind words, Mace. You've only seen a fraction of my work. I've sold hundreds of paintings over the years, all shapes and sizes, some on pieces of driftwood, palm fronds, bricks, and even a couple on walls here and in Bradenton."

"I cannot contain my pride for you, Mother. You are utterly amazing."

"Let's not talk about that now. Help me put the groceries away, and you'll see what favorites of yours that I bought. Then I'll tell you what we're having for dinner."

"Okay, Mother."

Elise, still beaming over the compliments, showed Mace at least a dozen of his favorite foods, including steaks, cream of wheat, Quaker Oats, mozzarella cheese, Tootsie Rolls, and much more. It was like a foody Christmas for Mace. He felt comfortable. What a remarkably different feeling it was for him. It almost felt as if he was hanging out with a pleasant female friend. Was Elise being nice, or was she merely not being cruel?

A minute before the last of the groceries was put away, Elise spoke again.

"I've been noticing you're wearing your bathing suit. What do you say we take a short run and a swim before I cook those fillet mignons?"

"Okay," he said unhesitatingly.

He had run with his mother hundreds of times before, but this was the first time in ten years. In the past, she would always nag him to run faster. She would yell at him and criticize his inability to keep up with a girl.

Then she would increase her speed, so she stayed a couple of strides ahead of him. He never beat her. Never. He wondered how she would run now.

*Hell,* he thought. *She's in her late forties. There is no way she can beat me now. I am still a Marine and in my late twenties.*

A couple of minutes later, Elise emerged from her bedroom, wearing a red bikini and carrying her red tennis shoes, red socks, a cream-colored top, and skimpy shorts that matched the top. Elise, the strong mesomorph, wanted Mace to see her body, every inch of it, except for what was covered. She wanted him to marvel at the size and cut of her muscles, from head to toe, especially the six-pack that still adorned her stomach.

Mace watched her finish dressing as if she was the lead actress in a movie, preparing for a running scene. Elise did not speak, and her quiet intensity matched an actress contemplating a scene. She was beautiful. No other woman he had ever looked at could compare with his mother.

"Let's go to the Don CeSar and back," Elise said as she finished tying her second shoelace.

"Okay," Mace said, though he thought four miles was a bit much for a guy who had only run about twenty miles in the last three months.

After their towels were on the sand and they stretched for a few minutes, the two runners headed for the Don CeSar. Mace was appreciative that his mother jogged at a slow pace all the way to where they turned around about the midpoint of the Don. Along the way to the Don, many onlookers wondered what the handsome couple was to each other. Some thought they were boyfriend and girlfriend. Some thought they were husband and wife. No one saw them as a mother and son who had been at extreme odds with one another all their lives until the last few days.

About Twentieth Avenue and Pass-a-Grille Way, Mace noticed something subtle and unnerving. Elise was picking up speed. It was not much, just enough to put her a single step ahead of him. At first, he allowed it, as they approached Nineteenth Avenue. By Eighteenth Avenue, he could not take it anymore. The single step that she was ahead of him felt like a mile. She did not look back at him and yell, like she did years ago. She simply ran ahead of him with a shit-eating grin on her face.

*Bitch*, he thought. *Ten years have gone by and she's still pulling the same crap.*

By Fifteenth Avenue, they were running side by side. Mace felt a sense of satisfaction. Only twelve blocks to go. Suddenly, Elise was a step ahead, again. Her legs were stretching out now, from a jogging pace to a run. At Twelfth Avenue, he caught her again, but he was breathless. By the snack shack, Elise was two strides ahead. In past years, they had stopped their run where they had placed their towels or beach chairs on the sand. The couple lengthened their strides. Onlookers marveled at their gracefulness. With less than two blocks to go, Elise turned on the afterburners. She was giving every ounce of her energy and spirit to the sprint of her lifetime. She raced past their towels and turned to see her son a full seven strides behind. He was running at his full speed. He was noticeably upset. She beat him again, and at her age.

"That was a really good run, son."

Son?

"Thank you, Mother."

"I can see that you haven't been running much lately. Is that true?"

"Yes, Mother."

"Well, since you're home now, you'll get back into top running condition, right?"

"Right."

*She was not really insulting,* he thought, *or was she?*

*There was a compliment thrown in there at the beginning of what she said. She never complimented me after a run until now. I can't figure out this woman.*

Dinner was served an hour later. It was fillet mignon, as promised. There was a different touch on the table this warm, muggy evening. Elise had placed and lit two tall white candles and turned down the dining room light to nearly nothing. The mood was lovely, almost romantic. Strangely, their dinner conversation went beyond civil. It was cordial.

# CHAPTER 24

The next several weeks were a whirlwind of getting things done, for Mace. He joined a gym, began lifting weights in earnest, and stepped up his running and swimming. He applied to, and was accepted, by the St. Petersburg Police Academy. He called Johnny Paige and wrote a warm thank-you note to Dr. Rafferty on a large Hallmark card. Mace's favorite activity, after his run with Elise, was visiting the three safe-deposit boxes that Willie had left for him. After going through a few minutes of introductions and paperwork, Mace, with help from two other staff members, took the large metal boxes to the viewing room. Surprises galore awaited him. The first two boxes were filled with more gold and silver coins and rolls of Indian Head pennies, wheat pennies, and 1943 steel pennies. There were scores of gold and silver coins from all over the world. There were hundreds of coins with white stickers on them that Willie had bought at various auctions. Mace did not know what the white stickers meant, but he would soon learn. Willie had picked up the auction hobby after Mace left for the service. He had become lonely without Mace. He also became bored, as Elise began to paint more. Mace was serene as he looked at the coins. He felt he was sitting with hundreds of speechless friends, who told curious stories just by their appearances. There was no trace of the serial killer he once believed himself to be. There was no mother hatred. He also felt Willie's presence, as he sat quietly and alone in the viewing room.

The last box was filled with totally unexpected treasures. It was American currency, in multiple stacks, from bottom to top. Before he perused the money, he could not help but notice a large square white envelope resting atop a few stacks, with his name written on it. He took the envelope into his hands and opened it. It was not licked shut. He pulled out a letter, which was written on lined paper. It read:

Dear Mace Madison,

You will always be my beautiful, strong, intelligent, and brave son. I am so proud of what you have achieved in sports and in the service of our great country. I wish I could have seen more of your athletic events. I also wish I could have been with you to see and help you with your military experiences instead of merely imagining how marvelous they were. I want you to know that I was always with you in spirit and am with you now, as you face your life without my physical presence. As you know, I have been fighting a fast-moving and virulent form of leukemia. I have given beating it my best shot, but if you are reading this without me, I have probably lost to the illness. That means these coins and currencies are now yours. I encourage you to study the history of these items. When you pass, you can leave whatever you have then, to your son(s) and daughter(s). Please also consider using some of these items to do acts of kindness for your fellow man. Please remember that you are blessed with this enormous volume of treasures. Most people are not.

I also hope that you will continue to listen to our old records and that you will keep the Victrola in tip-top shape so you can pass that on too. Keep watching the birds. They can be very amusing. Keep hunting. And will you think of me when you bag those big boars?

Finally, always try your best to love your mother. She was awfully hard on you while you were growing up, but she always had your best interests at heart. I think something was always bothering your mother, but she was extremely private and never shared much of her deeper self with me. The outcome of her rough approach to you was that you become the best at everything you ever did. You were the top dog wherever you went, and everybody knew it. You went into the service and did not miss a beat. Your heroic scenarios were beyond brave. And I am far beyond proud to be your father.

Again, please try to love Elise. No one needs more love than she does. She is not an easy woman to care for. She is an incredibly quiet woman until she gets riled up. Then she becomes a tiger. She is complex and unrevealing. Do not ever expect a straight answer from her. You will not get it. She will, instead, give you an ironic response that will baffle and bewilder you. Still, try to love her. If you can learn to love your mother, it will undoubtedly help you to love the woman of your dreams, should you be lucky enough to find her. By the time you return home, both you and your mother may have grown enough that loving each other will become easier for both of you. Who knows, you may become good for one another.

Once more, please remember, Mace, that I will always love you, my once beautiful boy and now my brave and decorated American hero.

Love,
Dad

The words of his father were almost too much for Mace to digest. In the silence of the stark little room, he bowed his head, rested it upon the closed third box, and wept for several minutes.

# CHAPTER 25

A few days later, after swimming and running with Elise, Mace was relaxing in the living room, reading a *Sports Illustrated*. Elise was preparing a protein snack for herself, consisting of turkey and mozzarella cheese roll-ups. Mace liked them too but not right now. Elise poured herself a glass of water, tossed some ice cubes into it, and walked into the living room. She picked up a recent issue of *Vogue* magazine and began to turn pages. Mace was itching to tell her something important.

"Mother, may I interrupt you for a moment?"

"Certainly, Mace. What is it?"

He could tell that she was in one of her friendly moods.

"I deeply appreciate all the nice things you've given me since I've been back home." He felt he needed to be somewhat formal with her, as he had always been until recently. "Your shopping, cooking, cleaning, working out with me, and your companionship has been greatly appreciated. Despite all that, I feel it's time for me to start looking to buy a house."

Elise dropped her eyebrows. Her beautiful face could not conceal the shock and disappointment that had beset her. She did not speak.

"I'm going to walk to Hurley Realty tomorrow and start the process of finding a house on Pass-a-Grille. You know how much I love it here."

Elise's gorgeous tanned face with the two flaws that nobody but her saw softened. Mace had never seen her look this way before. Her effect was tender, sweet, and loving. When she spoke, her vocal tone was the most dulcet Mace had ever heard emanate from her lips, which suddenly became sensual and alluring.

"Mace, there is absolutely no reason to look for your own house. All your things are here where you're comfortable. And I have grown accustomed to your company. I like being around you. You are my best friend now, even better than Monsignor Velkos. You can stay here with me as long as you like."

*What was she saying? Best friend? Accustomed to my company? I can stay with her indefinitely.* Suddenly he smelled the sexy scent of her musk perfume, which he had grown to love long ago, despite her meanness. It was wafting across the few feet between them in tantalizing, seductive waves.

Everything was coming together within and outside of Elise to make her sexually desirable to him for the first time. He fantasized about being with her in hers and Willie's bedroom, which had been sacred to her for many years. He fantasized about being the first man to be with her since his father died. He saw her in his imagination, coming to him wildly, raw passion exuding for him from every pore in her body. If she did not allow him to enter her bedroom, then his would be fine. He saw himself carrying her over the threshold of his bedroom, tossing her onto his king-size bed, and thrusting his virginity inside her—his friend and equal, finally.

Across the room, Elise was thinking similar thoughts, deciding she would keep her room sacred and devouring Mace in his room. She wondered if it would be his virginity he would be propelling inside her. She wondered how it would feel being with such a big man. Mace was six feet five. Willie was five feet seven.

As soon as these thoughts flashed through them, they both tried frantically to dismiss them. Each felt shame and acute disdain for allowing such forbidden ideations. However, neither Mace nor Elise could eradicate the fantasies. Once thought, the secret dreams were savory and not to be discarded. These imaginings would haunt them from this day forward. To act upon them or not to act upon them—those were the questions.

\*\*\*\*\*\*

Elise was still a self-centered bitch with almost everyone else but Mace and her favorite priest. Everywhere the mother and brother-son went, Mace witnessed her nasty behavior. She was the worst with waiters and waitresses, condescending toward them as if she were a queen and they were peons. Please and thank-you were rarely uttered by her. She was also horribly argumentative with her almost girlfriends at church. For her, there were too many rules and regulations in the Catholic Church and not enough love there or in the Bible. She hated the idea of confession. Why should anyone keep the Lord's Day any holier than the rest of the days of the week? Eternal hell? What was that all about? Love? In the privacy of her sacred bedroom at night, Elise wondered whether what she felt for Willie was love or dependency or great sexual attraction and gratification. She wondered why she was faithful to him. She wondered how she could have ever fallen in love with her father when she was a teenager. She remembered the joy that she felt with her father and Willie before and during sex. Was that love? Was receiving what she knew was Willie's love for her love? She had no idea what love was. Or friendship either. All these questions bugged the hell out of Elise. Now she had to wrestle with the razor-sharp sexual inclination she was having toward Mace.

Elise was a totally bewildered human being when it came to genuine feelings for anyone. Maybe that was the reason she could not help being a bitch most of the time. Seeing her sell paintings was a different story entirely. She was smart enough to change her affect from grumpy to cheery and schmooze potential and previous buyers. She was excellent at acting and selling. With her real physical beauty, fake charm, and marvelous art working in unison, Elise was able to sell tens of thousands of dollars of her craft. When an art show ended, Elise would merely flip a switch and return to the person she really was.

Mace witnessed all of it, accompanying her to art fairs on Corey Avenue, in Gulfport, downtown St. Pete.

He especially observed how she worked the men. She gave herself over completely to their flattery. So many men wanted to be with her, that they bought her paintings to impress her with their money and personalities. Doing this made them feel they had the inside track to her bed. Little did they know that there were no tracks that led to Elise. She would give men her business card early in their acquaintance, getting their hopes up. Then she would ruefully lure them into a sale with her irresistible luminescence. Occasionally, Mace would make a sale. Ironically, his rugged handsomeness worked wonders on the women. He did not have to change his affect one bit. His gentle manner and calm, sensual vocals were a turn on too, though he never knew it. In the deepest part of himself, he still thought of himself as ugly. Problem was, when he looked into the mirror, he saw a handsome face. He could not reconcile what he felt with what he saw. Elise's continual cruelty when he was a little boy had damaged him that much.

He was not interested in women. Nearly thirty, after a decade in the Marines, the only woman's approval he sought belonged to Elise. That was despite the weird behavior he observed from her from day to day.

For the next several months, Elise and Mace lived in a semicongeniality between them, fused with Elise's lack of feelings for others, and a seething, mounting, nerve-grating sexual tension. Thankfully, for each of them, Mace was away from their odd little household most of the time while training to become a St. Petersburg police officer. By the time he completed his training, Mace had established the same reputation he held as a Marine. It was that of a soft-spoken man of few words, a superb shot with either a pistol or rifle, and a man of incredible physical strength.

When Mace finished his training, Elise came to his graduation. She wore a sleeveless, fire engine red dress, matching shoes, and a stunning red garnet necklace that plunged perfectly to the middle of her breasts, which were firmer and lovelier than when she was seventeen.

When Mace saw her, he thought, *Wow!* Then he looked around at all the other women present at the ceremony. There were scores of girlfriends, along with plenty of sisters, wives, and mothers. He thought, and rightly so, that there was not another woman there who could begin to compare with Elise's beauty. He was suddenly attracted to her fire engine red lipstick, wondering what it would be like to kiss this beautiful woman flush on her full sweet-colored lips. She was not his mother now, in his current reverie.

She was simply the most beautiful woman in a crowd of people, the one that any man would be attracted to, and many of the men at the ceremony were. It was so much easier to be attracted to this woman, who was not picking on him anymore, though she was a bitch to most other people most of the time. He did not kiss her on the lips this brilliant afternoon. He only dreamed about it.

Two weeks later, Mace had a couple of days off in a row. He told Elise, who had been painting prolifically since Mace had entered the Police Academy. They agreed to spend his first day together on the beach in front of their house, at the end of Pass-s-Grille. They began their day on the beach under a sunny sky at about 1:00 p.m. They started a fun swim together. It began at Third Avenue and lasted all the way to Twenty-Sixth, where Hurley Realty was. When they saw the small gray sailboat that never moved, embedded in the sand, they turned back around toward Third Avenue. Mace could not help but notice that Elise was not competing with him. They were having a relaxing swim, the kind you share with a friend.

They swam past Third Avenue, and the strong current around the pier began pulling them swiftly toward the concrete. As they had a thousand times, they stroked powerfully out of the dangerous water flow. They both hit the beach running and plopped tiredly onto their multicolored towels. Mace dropped to his stomach, and Elise reclined on her back. Mace almost fell asleep while Elise kept her eyes opened and stared into the calm blue yonder. When she dropped her eyes from the sky, she noticed how pale Mace's skin was. She thought it might be a kind gesture to rub some suntan lotion on his back. She grabbed the lotion, raised up, and impulsively straddled her son. Mace shuddered when he felt his mother on top of him. A moment later, he felt her hips undulating back and forth on his buttocks. At the same time, she firmly pressed the number 70 sunscreen into his back and arms. He had never been this close to a woman. Her movements were thrusting his manhood hard against the resistant sand. It took less than thirty seconds for the blast of orgasm to spasm every muscle of his body with heretofore unrecognizable joy.

If Elise had wondered before this moment, whether Mace had ever been with a woman, she knew now that he had not. He had just got his rocks off like a twelve-year-old boy. Elise was feeling nothing like a young girl. She was feeling womanly, with an inherent right to have her own turn at some explosive sexual fireworks. She knew her body. It would not take long. She closed her eyes and slathered an abundant amount of lotion over the massive muscles of the man beneath her. Her mind wandered to thoughts of Willie and how beautiful his body was. Then she made the subtlest tilt of her pelvis until her powerful private parts made just enough contact with Mace's tailbone. Time stood still, as her intense concentration and swift, fluid movements, transported her to other worlds completely undiscovered. Then she also exploded, not once but several times before she allowed her torso to fall onto her son's back. She slid her hands down Mace's triceps and arms all the way to his fingertips.

There, she rested her hands and plummeted into a sublime hour-long sleep. Mace did not move, except to breathe. He did not feel bad, a little odd. He thought that this was not an entirely unpleasant way for his mother to apologize for her abject cruelty to him for over half of his lifetime. Then he fell deeply into sleep. He was unaware when his sister rolled off him onto her own towel.

The next time they saw each other, Elise was dressed in a pure white pant suit, cooking dinner. Neither of them said a word about their self-directed interlude. Both were shy because of their peculiar life experiences. Neither person could think of the first word to begin a dialogue about it. Underneath the quiet was a raging river of wonder, confusion, joy, doubt, and guilt. Deep inside, mother and son was incessant thought revolving around their incestuous moments. It was as if a twenty-piece orchestra was playing powerfully inside each of them, chests heaving and falling, cheeks puffing out and collapsing, fingers flying wildly over keyboard and buttons. The players stood up when featured and dropped to their chairs when their special moment was over. All that frenetic activity within their minds and souls and not a single sound was being emitted.

# CHAPTER 26

Though behavior grew cordial between this odd couple, the Stutzmans did not become loquacious people. They were both shy and almost introverted souls. Beneath their relative shyness was the relentless noise of the sexual tension between them. The gnawing irritation was an itch that neither of them was daring enough to scratch again. Whatever was happening between them now was far better than how they related years ago. Days passed, taking on a sameness. Mace went to work five or more days a week, made new acquaintances, and assumed more responsibilities. Elise continued painting, but her colors became more vivid, brighter. Amid her generally soft and muted hues, there appeared the greenest greens across sunset skies. Cherry-colored suns graced canvasses, which before would be beautiful, but now were tickled with happiness, fun. Bold colors invaded her paintings. There were bright yellow sailboats and deep blue fishing piers. Even her strokes were friskier and more playful.

Each canvas seemed more unique than the one before. Elise did not even realize what had happened to her. She did not realize she had playful qualities. As weeks passed, colors continued to pour from soul to brush to canvas. All this was triggered by her special moments with Mace.

Around the usually quiet house, save for the big band music they both enjoyed, different nuances emerged. Mace especially enjoyed it when Elise would wink at him, smile like the Mona Lisa, then walk away. Elise enjoyed the rare smile that Mace would give her from deep within his heart. Though never discussed, the seething sexuality that filled the house with electricity was providing them with a strange and oddly satisfying reason to live. Mace, who allowed himself no social life whatsoever, thought of his mother every day like a boyfriend thinks of his sweetheart. Mace would never make a move on Elise for fear of embarrassment if she rejected him. Conversely, he did not think he could handle the overwhelming guilt and shame he would feel if she accepted him.

Elise thought of her father, the little sheriff, and the damage he did to her. As much as she hated Mace when he was younger, she did not want to scar him as she had been scarred. Intercourse would do that. As the months passed, there developed a comfort within the discomfort that passed between mother and son. That feeling can be likened to a person who was thankful that they had a regular irregular heartbeat.

Soon, 1992 turned to 1993. Almost as quickly as the last few months of 1992 passed, 1993 disappeared into 1994. The Stutzman household remained the same. Valentine's Day had just passed, with Mace having looked through the greeting cards for a romantic one for Elise. He did not find one. He knew he was kidding himself before he started looking, but he also thought there was no harm in trying. The card hunting helped to keep his fantasies of his mother alive.

On February 18, after a quiet shift, Mace was relaxing at home, eating a couple of hamburger patties, no bun, with a side of micro-waveable broccoli and cheese. Mace was enjoying the lengthening of the days and the fact that he could swim under the last rays of the sun even though the water was cold. He was planning to turn on the television in a couple of minutes, maybe watch a cop show. At 8:17 p.m., there was a rare knock on the front door. Mace answered it. His boss, Commander Johnathon Braxton, stood outside.

"Hello, Commander. To what do I owe the pleasure of your company? Would you like something to drink?"

"No thank you, Mace. Do you mind if we sit down for a minute?"

"Not at all. Have a seat on the couch."

Mace directed the commander with a wave of his arm. Mace sat on a chair near Braxton. He wondered if he was going to receive a commendation for one or more of his many excellent pieces of police work during the last several weeks.

"I'm afraid I have some disheartening news for you, Officer."

Mace's inner thoughts changed from positive to concerned. He stayed silent. Braxton did not speak for a moment while seeing Mace's affect change.

"There's been an automobile accident, Mace."

Big, strong Commander Braxton was as gentle as a small child. Mace could not swallow.

"Your mother was driving on First Avenue North at Forty-Second Street. Unbeknownst to her, a police chase of a very drunk driver was taking place nearby. The drunk driver had already hit two cars in traffic, so the chase was intense. Suddenly, the drunk turned off Central onto Forty-Third Street and made a split-second decision to turn right and go against traffic. The problem was that your mother was driving in the left lane. Less than two seconds after the guy turned onto First Avenue North, your mother saw him and swerved sharply to the right to avoid him. When he turned abruptly onto first, his momentum took him halfway into the center lane. Your mother's swerve was not enough. She was T-boned on the driver's side door. The impact disabled both vehicles, and your mother was seriously injured."

"Is she ok?" Mace asked with little breath behind his words.

"I'm afraid not, Mace. She survived till she made it to the hospital, but she succumbed about an hour into surgery."

Braxton chose his words carefully, trying to soften the harsh finality of death. Mace was overcome with grief. He did not cry. He did not move externally. Internally, Mace instantly began the life-altering process of stuffing his feelings relating to his mother's demise.

*Don't cry*, he thought. *Don't show the commander any weakness.*

Meanwhile, Braxton was staring at a man in shock, whose face was drained of blood. Braxton felt that Mace's spirit had left his body.

"Are you okay, Mace?"

"Yes, sir."

Braxton knew Mace slightly from work. He knew of his reputation for toughness, from numerous coworkers. He thought Mace was being very brave right now. He did not see that inside. Mace was a catastrophe.

"Thank you, Commander, for telling me what happened to my mother."

"There is something else, Mace. Your mother is at Bayfront. The staff agreed to keep her until you get there."

"Thank you again, sir. Is there anything else?"

"We are here for you, Mace. I am here for you. The department has psychologists to help you through this. All you have to do is ask."

"Thank you again, sir." That was all he could say, short sentences that took little effort. The catastrophe within was nearly paralyzing his vocal cords. He wished to God the commander would leave quickly.

"If there's nothing else, I can do for you, Mace, I think I should go."

"I'll be fine, Commander. Thank you." He wanted to scream.

Braxton stood up and extended his hand. Mace extended his.

"You're a good officer, Mace. Why don't you take a couple of paid weeks off while you take care of things? The first week, you will be terribly busy. In the second week, you can rest and get your head straight. Does that work for you, Mace?"

"Yes, sir, it does. Thank you again, sir."

They shook hands again, and the compassionate commander left. Mace watched him drive away, then he walked into his bedroom, fell onto the bed, and brought his legs to his chest. When he felt safe in a totally unusual fetal position, he let out the most horrific primal scream ever projected on Pass-a-Grille. Tears began to cascade from his eyes, though he made no sound other than his primal outburst. The multitude of tears he shed in the next fifteen minutes was the last he ever shed over the passing of his mother.

# CHAPTER 27

The next week was a blur for Officer Stutzman, beginning with his trip to Bayfront Hospital, twenty-five minutes after Commander Braxton left 325 Pass-a-Grille Way. Staff at Bayfront cautioned Mace not to look at his mother because her face was severely cut. Each of them wanted to use the phrase "beyond recognition," but no one did. No one wanted to hurt the quiet policeman more than they already saw he was. Mace thought about looking at his mother one final time. He almost did. Then he thought he might stare into the face of a female Dorian Grey, a hideous creature, that reflected the evil she had inflicted upon him when he was young.

He decided not to look at her. He wanted to remember her as the most beautiful woman he had ever seen. He wanted to recall only the last several months when she was the quiet, sexy, flirtatious siren. That is the way he wished to remember her. Unfortunately, he could not dismiss his memories of his eighteen years of abuse. He could not forget the cold letter she sent him after Willie died. Mace sat in a waiting room, unable to reconcile the good and bad qualities of his mother. No matter what he thought about her, it was painful. He suffered silently and muddled through the next several days.

When it was all over and Elise was in the ground, loneliness and exhaustion consumed him. On his drive home from the cemetery, Mace began talking to his beloved 1950 Chrysler Imperial.

"It's just you and me now, Princess. Everybody is gone. But don't worry. I won't die. It's you and me forever."

He arrived at 325 Pass-a-Grille Way, walked inside, went to his bedroom, and plopped onto the bed. He fell asleep until the first rays of morning sunshine hit his eyelids. As soon as he woke, he called

Johnny Paige in Louisiana. Johnny was not at home, probably working, so Mace left a message on his answering machine.

"Hey, Johnny, it's Mace. Sorry, I haven't called you in the last few months, but I have a couple of important things I want to talk with you about. Call me tonight, about nine o'clock. I'll be home."

Precisely at nine, Mace's phone rang.

"Hey, Mace, you ole Devil Dog, it's Johnny."

"Thanks for calling me back so promptly."

"Your wish was my command, sir. What do you want to tell me?"

"My mother died about a week ago, and I'm feeling kind of blue. I sure could use some company. Do you think you could come down here and spend a few days with me at the beach? I'll pay for everything to get you here and keep you entertained while you're here. I'll even treat you to Bern's Steakhouse if you want."

"I'm sorry to hear about your mother, Mace. How did she die?"

"It was a car accident, Johnny. A wrong-way driver T-boned her." Mace wanted to change the subject immediately. "What about my offer?"

"Nobody ever made an offer like that to me before. I'd kind of be a fool not to take it."

Conservative Mace was more than happy to spend some of his fortunes on his friend.

"You can stay with me for as long as you want to, Johnny. When I go back to work, you'll have the beach, the girls, the restaurants. You name it. I'll even rent a car for you."

Johnny knew that Mace was loaded, but he never figured on being the recipient of such benevolence.

"Let me see if I can get some time off from the grocery store. I'll call you back during my lunch hour tomorrow, between noon and one o'clock. Does that work for you?"

"It works for me, Johnny. I'll be waiting for your call."

The phone rang the next day at 12:37 p.m. Mace answered. He was worried that Johnny would not be able to get time off.

"Hello."

"Mace, I've got great news! My boss is giving me a week off. If I leave here Friday night, I can spend about nine days. Then I'll leave on the second Sunday night. How does that sound?"

They worked out the details over the next few minutes. During the three days Mace had to wait for Friday, he wrote a lengthy letter to Dr. Rafferty. He debated whether to pour his heart out or to speak about his mother and his life conservatively. He settled on the latter. He could not tell the doctor about his sexual experience with Elise on the beach. That was the highlight of the last year and a half. No matter what path of correspondence he chose, it would help to unburden his aching heart. Besides the unburdening, he wanted to convince Dr. Rafferty that he was not crazy anymore. He wanted to tell the doctor that he was a successful policeman, and he was not in the frame of mind to kill bad guys merely because they deserved it. Mace went so far as to remind the doctor that he was a superb shootist and that he had already disabled two men with excellent shots when he could have killed them. Most of all, Mace wanted his letter to convey a friendly tone. He hoped that he would be remembered and that Dr. Rafferty would respond to him in a like manner.

When Mace picked up Johnny at TIA Friday night, Johnny saw Mace first. He jogged to Mace and hugged him. Mace's body stiffened for a second before he realized it was one of his best friends ever that was hugging him. Mace returned a modest, guarded hug.

"Let's head for home, Johnny. Let's go get as shit-faced as we want to in my living room."

"Sounds good to me, my friend."

Once together, it seemed to both men that no time at all had passed since their meeting in the hospital.

"What kind of beer do you have?" Johnny asked.

"Do you think that I could ever forget?"

"Sam Adams Boston Lager!" Johnny said, like a happy twenty-one-year-old.

"Of course. Do you remember the hundreds of times you ordered that beer in front of me?"

"I do, thank you."

Mace delivered the Sam Adams, and the two men began to talk deeply, the way friends often do.

"You look great, Mace. How do you feel?"

"Physically, I feel great. Six feet five, 280 pounds, all muscle, six-pack still. You'll see that tomorrow when we swim. Mentally, I'm a wreck. My mother's passing has left me torn into a thousand pieces." Mace wanted to tell Johnny most of the truth but not all of it.

Johnny was confused.

"All those years we were overseas, you told me your mother was rotten to the core."

"I despised her. How could I love a monster? But after I got home, she changed, little by little. She revealed different sides of herself. I found out she was an accomplished artist, who sold hundreds of her paintings. Sometimes, she had five paintings going at the same time. Her paintings were beautiful, dainty, serene, powerful, dynamic, and majestic. I'll show you what's left of them tomorrow when you're rested. They reveal an aspect of her that I could not have imagined existed. They show all the moods of the ocean, sky, clouds, and people on the beach. I wonder where she acquired all that sensitivity. I never saw any of it growing up. I saw the exact opposite of the wonder she exhibited in her art. I saw only coldness and cruelty and lack of praise."

"Did you two finally become friends?"

"I don't think so, Johnny. We didn't talk much. I guess we became compatible within the silences that existed between us."

"Did you grow to like her?"

"I did. She was physically stunning. She had a six-pack at forty-nine. It was impossible to look at her and not like what I saw, especially because she wasn't ranting and raving at me anymore. It was a beauty I never saw when I was a little boy or a teenager. I'm going to miss her."

"Do you have a girlfriend?"

"No, no girlfriend." There was a lengthy pause in the talking until Mace resumed. "What about you? Any prospects?"

"There's a lot of pretty girls going through that store, even for a small town. I've gone out with some fine ladies, but no one special yet."

"You'll find somebody wonderful, I'm sure."

Another pause. They both sipped their beer.

"Do you ever miss being on active-duty, Johnny?"

"Not really, Mace. I went around the block with them three times. That is enough. What I miss are all the friends I made there. How about you?"

"I miss the guys the most. The service, not so much. I have changed, Johnny. I am not into killing bad guys like before. Since our friends died, my heart is not in it anymore. I am a wounder now, not a killer. I give bad guys a chance now. That was not the old me. Don't get me wrong. If I had to terminate someone, I could do it."

"You sure were good at killing, Mace. You were the best and the bravest I ever saw. I would not be here if you had not saved my life a couple of times. Maybe someday, you'll find an excuse to eradicate some of those bastards from your beautiful city."

"You never know, Johnny. Life is funny that way."

"You have my blessing if you ever cross that line again, Mace."

When the beer became too much and the conversation slowed to a crawl, Mace noticed Johnny's head fall to his chest while holding his beer bottle. Mace walked to his dear friend and nudged him tenderly.

"Time for bed, Soldier."

Mace walked Johnny to his sleep site. It was Mace's old bedroom. The room was white-glove spotless. Johnny crawled under the brand-new sheets, which were pulled back at a perfect forty-five-degree angle.

Johnny fell quickly asleep.

Then came the hard part. Mace had not been in his mother's bedroom since long before she died. Now he would sleep in her bed. As he approached it, his eyes scanned the wedding and honeymoon pictures on the dresser and the candles that were almost brand new. A book of matches rested near one of the candles. Mace decided to light them. Then walked to the windows and closed the slats for the first time since Elise died. Once under the sheets and comfortable, Mace enjoyed the flickering yellow glow around him. His nerves were unsettled, however, because he was worried that Elise would scold him at any moment, for being in her bedroom. Though it was unusual for him to do so, Mace curled into a fetal position. As his head nestled into the pillow, the pleasant aroma of Elise's musk perfume infiltrated his nostrils. He felt close to her before sleep overtook him. She was the only woman he ever loved and hated. Now he was sleeping in her bed for the first of many hundreds of nights, completely unaware that he had lost not only his mother but his sister.

*****

Mace kept his promise to entertain Johnny. They swam together, ran, and ate at all the finest restaurants, including Bern's Steakhouse in Tampa. They nearly wept in the Holocaust Museum and enjoyed the Museum of Fine Arts and the Dali exhibits. They worked out at Mace's gym. There was also the Wagon Wheel Flea Market, where Johnny found a few nice 1950s baseball cards to add to his collection. Their friendship, which had blossomed years ago, ascended to a higher level spiritually. Their long deep conversations, aided by the relaxing qualities of a few beers, helped to heal sorrows embedded in each of them.

Mace had one problem with Johnny, and he told him so with acute sternness. They were sitting together one night on the outside patio at the Don CeSar. They were having a late lunch when Mace made his feelings known.

"Johnny, you know I love you, man, don't you?"

"Of course, I do, Mace. You know I love you too, man, right?"

"Absolutely. Our feelings for each other are why I'm bringing this up. It's not going to be easy to talk about this, Johnny."

Johnny Paige focused all his attention on his friend. He thought Mace was going to reveal some dark secret.

"Johnny, I'm worried about your smoking."

"Oh shit."

"There's no shit about it, Johnny. I'm genuinely worried about you."

"You have enough to worry about in your own life. Don't brood about me. It's a waste of energy."

"It is not, Johnny. I've seen you light up one after another. That's chain-smoking."

"It sounds like you're scolding me, Mace."

"That's the one thing I don't want to sound like, Johnny. I want to sound like I'm trying to save your life. It's almost a new century. Everybody knows now that smoking can kill you. Did you ever see those commercials with Yul Brynner that were released after he died?"

"I have. It's sad."

"That's what I'm saying."

"I feel great!"

"Maybe you do, but I hear you coughing and hacking up phlegm first thing every morning."

There was a moment of silence. Each man felt poorly about what had just transpired. The shy Mace, emboldened by his concern for his friend, tried to sum things up, finish the conversation, and move on.

"The bottom lines are these, Johnny. You are my best friend. I would be lost without you. I don't want to lose you."

"Can't you make new best friends at the police station?"

"Johnny, there will never be anyone else I will meet who will share as much as you and I have. Do you realize how many wars we fought together? How many times we had each other's back? There will never reappear in my lifetime a group of men as marvelous as the Super Six. You and I are the only two left to represent. Can you understand that I don't want to be the last man standing?"

Johnny took a puff of his cigarette with a smirk on his face. Mace smirked back.

"I know what you're saying, Mace, and I genuinely appreciate your concern. I have to tell you though, when you're not around, cigarettes are my best friends."

"Okay, Johnny, I get it. But I had to put it out there. Would you promise me one thing?"

"What's that?"

"That you'll try to give it up little by little?"

"I can't promise that I will succeed, but I will try. I can promise that I will not smoke anymore around you. Will that help?"

"I appreciate your offer, Johnny, but I am afraid that won't be enough to save your life."

"Are we good for now, Mace?"

"We are always good, Johnny. What would you like for dessert?"

That is how it ended, the first of many conversations about smoking over the next thirteen years. The ensuing dialogues about smoking were always brief but poignant. Mace always ended the conversation, telling Johnny he did not want to lose him.

Two years after that discussion at the Don, Johnny married a beautiful nonsmoking white woman, Cindy. A year after that, a handsome boy appeared, Henry. Two years later, a knockout of a baby girl arrived, Lila. As she grew, her head became enshrouded with the loveliest curly auburn hair on the planet. Johnny and Cindy decided they would never cut that hair. By the time she was three, she was a bold, loquacious charmer. By the time he was five, her brother Henry was a brave protector of his little sister. He was already good at sports, especially baseball. After all, his father had been a rather good high school pitcher. Besides, there was a family name to uphold. Johnny never smoked in his house or around the children or Cindy. He loved them too much to expose them to those nasty carcinogens.

However, he could not stop smoking no matter how hard he tried.

After Johnny and Cindy had Henry, Mace started taking vacations with the Paige family. This was convenient for Johnny because he did not have to pack up his family and deal with the commotion of a baby and a toddler. In 2001, Johnny asked Mace for a loan of $10,000 to add to his already saved $15,000 for a much-needed larger house. He told Mace he wanted four bedrooms. There would be the master bedroom for himself and Cindy. Each child would have a separate bedroom. Johnny told Mace that the last bedroom would be used, primarily for him, when he came there for his two or three-week vacations. Mace said yes to Johnny immediately. They kept things simple. Johnny would send Mace $1,050 every December 31 for ten years. Mace gave Johnny his loan in cash three days before his vacation that summer ended. The day he left, Mace said goodbye to sweet Cindy, little Lila, and Henry.

The final goodbye for the war buddies was private. They shared a light hug, with a few pats on each other's back. They expressed a deep desire to be able to spend more time together. Each man felt real sadness deep in the gut. Goodbyes were always this way. The feeling of genuine affection between the Marines was palpable.

Mace slid into his Cadillac Escalade, turned the engine on, put the vehicle into drive, and opened the window. For a reason known only to him, Mace kept both hands on the steering wheel. Johnny, expecting the usual final handshake, merely patted Mace on his massive left bicep and said, "Take good care of yourself, my brother. And thank you for the loan. It means the world to me."

Mace, with an unreadable look on his face, turned his head and looked directly into Johnny's eyes. "About that loan, Johnny, I'm not happy with our loan arrangement."

"What, why?"

"After recalculating all the figures, my math shows that you have a zero balance. You don't owe me anything. We're even, okay?"

A fraction of a second later, with the hint of a smile on his face, Mace lifted his foot off the brake and drove quickly away.

*****

Eight years later, Johnny Paige died of lung cancer. Mace took an emergency leave to be with Johnny as he passed. Cindy had called Mace to tell him that Johnny was close to dying. Unfortunately, she waited a little too long and Johnny was comatose when Mace arrived at the hospital. At the moment of Johnny's last breath, petite Cindy sat in a chair on one side of her husband's electric bed. She held his right hand between both of hers. Mace sat in the chair on the other side of the bed, holding Johnny's left hand in the same manner. After Johnny's death, Cindy stood up and wrapped her arms around her husband's strong upper body. She pressed her head against his chest and allowed her tears to fall profusely. She made no sound. Mace looked at his friends for a moment and dropped his head. He felt as if a major portion of his own spirit had just left him, at the same time Johnny's soul was departing for who knows where. He sat there, tearless, feeling an ethereal presence ooze ever so slowly from him. He knew that the disappearing essence would never return, that this new hole in his being would remain forever.

Mace spent his next two vacations with Cindy and the kids. They were not the same after Johnny was gone, but there was still lots of love and fun to be shared. Mace smiled and laughed almost all the time he spent with Lila and Henry. He did not think, in those moments, that laughter and frolicking were useless exercises, as his mother preached when he was young.

In 2012, Mace did not spend his vacation with the Paige family. A couple of months before his vacation, Cindy called him and told him that she was marrying a man she had met almost a year earlier.

"He's a great guy, Mace, a carpenter, just like your father. You will really like him. You can come down your regular vacation weeks because that's when we set the wedding date, just so you can be here."

Mace was not shocked by Cindy's announcement. She was a doll. He knew she would marry again. In fact, he hoped she would find a great guy and be happy. He certainly did not want the children he loved to be fatherless. What he did not expect was the crash of emotions that bombarded him after Cindy's announcement. Immediately, he did not want to attend the wedding. He no longer wanted to spend his vacations in the same house with a man who was not Johnny. He wanted to remember the Paige family as it was, with Johnny as the head. He suddenly felt joyful and saddened. These emotions flooded him in the single second before he responded.

"Congratulations, Cindy. I am so happy for you. He must be a great guy because you are a spectacular woman. How do the kids feel about him?"

Joy and sadness struck him like a lightning bolt with two personalities. He thought of his genuine love for Johnny's children, the first kids he had ever spent time with. They taught him the wonders of giving love to and receiving love from little people.

"That's great, Cindy. The kids deserve a good father, especially now through their teenage and young adult years."

"Thank you, Mace. Your approval means a lot to me."

"I more than approve, Cindy. You deserve a fabulous life. If you believe he is the right man for you, I'm all for it."

"Thank you, Mace."

"I would like to talk longer, Cindy, but I have some paperwork that needs my attention. I'll call you soon, okay?"

"Okay, Mace, I'll look forward to it."

"Bye, Cindy."

Mace did not call Cindy soon. Instead, two weeks later, he wrote her a letter. It was the deepest, longest, and most sincere letter he ever wrote to anyone except his father.

> Dear Cindy,
>
> My heart aches as I write to you. I regret that I will not be able to attend your wedding. It is because I am weak, and my heart aches when I think of your family with any other head of household than Johnny. I want to remember the wonderful times had by the five of us, then the fun times the four of us had after Johnny died. I am afraid that my presence might rain on the parade of your new lives together. I am afraid that my being there might alter the precious balance a family needs to be happy. I hope you are not upset with the reality of my feelings. Please remember that I have always admired and respected you. My feelings for your children have been the most sublime I have ever felt for two youngsters.
>
> Please accept my gift as a token of my thankfulness for the good times we had together. Use some of it for your honeymoon, and please put some of it away for Lila and Henry's college funds.
>
> Remember me fondly.
>
> Love,
> Mace

Inside the envelope was a check for $25,000. As soon as he signed the check, a memory entered his mind and would not vacate for several days. It was the recollection of the countless times he read bedtime stories to the Paige children when they were young. It was an activity they yearned for every night that Mace spent with them while he was on vacation. It was a real treat for them. When Mace finished his outpouring to Cindy, he was overcome with loneliness. His missing of the Super Six was embedded in this loneliness.

When Cindy finished reading the letter, a cluster of thoughts began to swirl in her mind and did not vacate for several days. She wondered why Mace had never expressed an interest in being with her as her mate. He had always been so kind to her, so polite. Beyond that, Mace impressed her with his kindness to Lila and Henry. He would have made an excellent father. He was so good with the kids. He was handsome, muscular, not loud, or vexatious. She wondered why he muffled his laughs, why he only smiled like the Mona Lisa. She wondered what dark experiences in his distant past had contributed to his reserved nature. She pondered the pain in Mace's soul. She correctly surmised that she would never see him again. Because of that, she felt as if a piece of her heart broke off into a lifeless abyss, from which it would not return. She knew she had to keep that fragment tucked away in a place where no one could ever find it.

*****

Life changed forever for Mace Madison Stutzman. He became a quieter man. For a time, his feelings of caring for others disappeared. He was not sullen, just wordless, unless circumstances dictated that he spoke. Days took on a relative sameness. First and foremost, there was work. Mace took pride in his profession. He made a few friends too, despite his guarded heart. He thought often about his favorite number, which had not changed in quite a while. One part of it, the saving life component, had blossomed to seventy-three. The killing score had remained constant, at twenty-seven. His favorite number rested at one hundred. He began looking forward to his next save. He no longer cared about killing, He increased his workouts. He became a revered presence at the gym. Walking in wearing his cut-off T-shirts in all kinds of weather drew silent oohs and wows from the women as well as the men. He was so buff he appeared to be a champion competitive bodybuilder.

When he was not lifting weights, running, or swimming, there were still plenty of hours to enjoy his other favorite hobbies. He had spent many days teaching the Paige children his beloved interests. Antique guns, bird watching, big band music and coin collecting, were his constant companions in time wasting. One of his special spots in town was David Reynolds Coins and Jewelry. A cozy little shop, it was filled with gold, silver and other coins that dated as far back as ancient Greece and Rome. He liked every staff person there. Each of them was always friendly and knowledgeable about coins and currency. It seemed that every time he went there, he learned some tidbit about old money. The jewelry part of the store brimmed with handsome and beautiful watches, bracelets, rings, pendants, necklaces, earrings, and more. Sometimes he wished he could buy a piece of jewelry for someone he cared for. He would dismiss that moment of angst by buying a St. Gaudens or a Krugerand. Over the years, he bought himself a Seiko and a Rolex that he wore with pride.

As time passed, the awards for Mace mounted. Situation after situation, no matter how dangerous, he faced them with extreme courage. At each annual policeman's banquet, his name was brought up for meritorious service. Three times he was voted St. Petersburg Police Officer of the Year. If not for foolish politics, he would have won the award ten times. He deserved it. He was the best cop St. Petersburg ever had.

Despite his decade long inability to give much of himself to anyone, Mace developed three significant friendships within the department. One was Bobby Banner, a St. Pete native, who attended St. Pete High, where he starred in baseball and basketball. He was six feet three and 220 pounds. He loved to gamble at the dog track when he was away from work. He was bright and intuitive in perilous conditions. He had a seven-year hitch in the Marines where he earned a Purple Heart. He respected Mace's pensive demeanor. He admired Mace so much that he would lay down his life for him if the situation required it. Mace would reciprocate in a heartbeat. Bobby was a loquacious soul, who tempered himself to be more compatible with Mace's reticence when they were together. He figured he would allow Mace to continue thinking about whatever was on his mind at any moment. He did not realize that most of the time that Mace was not talking, he was listening to a tune of some kind in his head. It was the way Mace relaxed and rejuvenated between calls. Small talk was too much like laughter—a waste of time. Even soundless music soothed the chaos of the day. As partners, Mace and Bobby were a fierce, well trained duo whenever they encountered the trash of their beautiful city by the bay.

What a character Pete Laughlin was. At five feet nine and 185 pounds, he was a gym rat mighty mite. He was an alcohol drinking, doughnut-eating jokester, who was Mace's partner for three years. They were opposites and mates who observed them wondered how the Giant and the Dwarf, as they were affectionately called, could ever work together. In the three years they worked together, they were cited for bravery four times. This included the infamous Charles Landry shoot-out at Twenty-First Avenue and Thirty-Second Street South. Landry was a well-known thug, who, on this day, felt full of himself enough to rob the Sun Trust bank on Central and Sixty-Third Street. He shot a security guard, took a black, tall plastic garbage bag a third full of money, and fled. He aimed his souped-up Cadillac toward the Sunshine Skyway, hoping to make his way toward Miami, where he planned to burn the Caddy and buy a new one with his loot.

When the Giant and the Dwarf got the call, they were only six blocks from Central and Sixty-Third Street. As usual, Mace was driving. He knew how to handle the squad car well and he was not afraid of speed. Mace punched the gas pedal to the floor. The police car lurched forward like a tiger springing toward prey. With siren blasting and warning lights flashing, they made a wild turn, through unyielding traffic, onto Fifty-Eighth Street, then an immediate left onto First Avenue South, clipping the rear bumper of a new silver BMW that was running a red light. It took a miracle of speed, daring and luck to catch up to within sixty yards of Landry at Forty-

Ninth Street. Mace gained no ground on Landry as the robber passed Thirty-Fourth Street.

Pete Laughlin took out his beautiful .38 Colt, given to him by Mace. He scanned the area for pedestrians. When he saw none, he began taking extremely measured shots at Landry's rear tires. Suddenly, the die pack in the flimsy money bag exploded, covering Landry with red splat. Instinctively, he thudded his foot on the brake, slapping at his face as if he were being attacked by a swarm of bees. At the same instant, a raging piece of metal from Pete's .38 shattered the right rear tire of the Cadillac. There was no controlling Landry's vehicle. It careened spasmodically into the concrete light pole on the southwest corner of Thirty-Second Street. Still battling bees, Landry pulled out his own .38 from his right sweatpants pocket. Having heard a siren and seen only one cop car chasing him, he figured he stood a good chance of winning a gun battle between himself and one or two cops. He crouched behind the open car door.

When he won the gunfight, the still confident Landry planned to grab the damaged money bag, which still had lots of loose and rolled coin in it. He would run east. That would get him into the neighborhood he knew well. He would take refuge in the house of one of his multitude of friends who lived there or, in the worst case, an open garage.

Landry began firing toward the police car. Still partially blinded, he saw shadowy figures, which were not good targets. Fear began mixing with Landry's adrenaline as he realized he was in a terrible spot. Several yards away, Pete ran out of bullets and reloaded his weapon. Meanwhile, Mace was planning to risk his life in a maneuver he had practiced many times. He stepped out of the cruiser. With his head above the door, he took dead aim. One shot, that is all it took. Mace's zooming lead struck Landry squarely in the right shoulder. The strike of lead through bone and muscle lifted Landry through the air to the concrete. Anger coursed through his being. He lifted himself and fired two shots at Mace's blurry figure. Mace, not wanting to kill, put a shot into Landry's left shoulder. Again, Landry came up off his feet, but the angle of the strike caused his body to swivel and smack the concrete with a crushing upper body and face plant. Bleeding profusely from his hands, forehead, and shoulders, he worried that the cops would come up on him and shoot him in the back. He sprang up from the street, an adrenaline-fueled wounded jack-in-the-box. He painfully resumed his position behind the car door and raised his weapon.

Pete Laughlin was waiting for him. He had moved to the front bumper of the police Crown Vic after Landry was hit the second time. When Landry's head came up over the door's window ledge, Pete fired once, with as much precision as Mace, and hit the stupid criminal right between the eyes, taking his life.

When Mace got home that night, he wrote Dr. Rafferty for the thirty-first time. He shared how proud of himself he was that he did not kill a deserving bastard when he had the chance. He told his ex-psychiatrist of his two perfectly placed shots that were intended only to wound.

"I almost had him completely disabled," he wrote, "but my partner, Pete Laughlin, lined him up and took him down forever, with a single shot to the cranium." What Mace enjoyed telling Dr. Rafferty the most was "After all these years of not taking anyone out who really deserved it, I no longer consider myself a serial killer. I was once, but I'm not anymore."

Dr. Rafferty, who was now in his late sixties, always answered Mace's letters. His endings were the same: "I'm proud of you, Mace." How deeply Mace came to rely on the emotional support of the kind psychiatrist.

The last of Mace's nearest friends was Ellis Wong, who came from interesting stock. His father was a small-in-height powerhouse who idolized Charles Atlas and his bodybuilding tenets. His mother was Scotch Irish, taller than Elise had been at six feet one. She was a stocky mesomorph, chiseled like a block of ice carved into a statuesque beauty by Rodin. She taught Ellis love for humanity, especially the oppressed. His father taught him physical strength and to protect his mother and sisters. Ellis Wong was well-constructed, physically. He stood six feet three, and his muscles were cut sharply from hours of work in the gym. With his father as his mentor and workout partner, he achieved competitive bodybuilding stature. He won several awards for his age category, in almost thirty amateur competitions. He was a gentle giant, much like Mace, but two inches shorter and fifty pounds lighter. Though they were never partners, Mace liked Ellis and felt as if they had been. Time after time, Mace watched Ellis handle tough situations on the streets with cool levelheadedness and bravery. Off duty, they often shared conversations about work and life at a Starbucks or Dunkin' Donuts. They were strong mellow friends.

All three of Mace's friends looked up to him. They had good reason. Mace was the top cop in the department. He was the "giant," the bravest, the most selfless, what every other cop in St. Petersburg, strove to attain.

# Chapter 28

In May 2013, during Mace's nineteenth year of police work, Dr. Rafferty died. Mrs. Rafferty, while going through her husband's desk drawers, found a stack of thirty-seven letters from Mace that were bound together by an enormous rubber band. Every return address was the same. She noticed how many different return address labels there were. For a moment, she wondered if Mace contributed to the charities that sent the label or if he just kept them when they came in the mail. She would never know the answer.

Mace gave generously to a variety of charities and causes. He felt sorry for everyone who was oppressed or physically suffering from an illness. He felt compassion for anyone who was controlled or manipulated.

Ironically, Mrs. Rafferty had also seen a partially written note to Mace on her husband's desk. It was dated the same day he died. The letter was the last piece of personal business he was attending to before he had a heart attack later in the day. At first, she had no idea who Mace was. When she found the letter stack, she quickly saw that the person her husband was writing to was Mace Stutzman. Her curiosity led her to read her husband's incomplete penning.

Dear Mace,

Thank you for your letter. It is always a pleasure to hear from you. It warms my heart to read the stories of you and your three policemen friends. You have bonded with them over so many life-or-death situations. Certainly, your life is infinitely more exciting than mine.

I also appreciate hearing that your favorite number has increased to 107, without having to kill anyone. You are a good person, Mace. You have incredible discipline.

You have saved many more lives than you have taken. I believe you have been too hard on yourself, Mace. You are not a serial killer. They usually pick on innocents to abuse. You have never taken that path. As a soldier, you were fighting for your own survival, as well as performing your sworn duty. I encourage you to stop suffering because of your negative self-judgment.

Over the years, I have grown to look forward to your letters, Mace. I deeply appreciate you always being so honest with me about your feelings and experiences.

I no longer consider you merely an ex-client. You are my friend. You have brought to my life table the gourmet meal of a complex and sensitive man. You have served me with stories only a few men can tell. Your heroic deeds are legend. I am trying to say that it has been an honor to know you. Since I am now retired and we have communicated so deeply, I feel it is safe to say that you are the most interesting—

That is where the letter ended. Dr. Rafferty had felt a sudden stomachache and went upstairs to take a nap. He died in his sleep. Mrs. Rafferty felt compassion and fondness for Mace after reading her husband's partial letter. She immediately felt the need to send the latter to Mace, along with the stack that her husband had kept. Surely, these mementos would provide Mace with some solace for the rest of his life. How honored Mace would feel to know that the unfinished letter was Dr. Rafferty's final piece of personal correspondence.

When Mace received a touching letter from Mrs. Rafferty, along with the stack of his old letters, he fell from his precarious emotional precipice into a deep depression. He did not draw comfort and solace from Dr. Rafferty's letter and the stack. Instead, he felt overwhelming sadness over losing the man who had given him the second most moral support of his lifetime. Willie had been his biggest supporter for a long time. Now they were both gone. Dr. Rafferty's death was a complete disconnect from the heart that held his sanity in check.

With the hole in his soul deeper than it had been in several years, Mace began to look for an outlet to express his pain. He had lost six of the Super Seven, Willie, Elise, his cherished relationship with the Paige family, and now Dr. Rafferty. His stomach and chest began to hurt. If by some godforsaken quirk of fate he was to lose any of his three police buddies, there would be little to nothing left of him. No longer was working on Princess to keep her running and beautiful, as satisfying as it used to be. Bird-watching became boring. He had seen all his guns and coins hundreds of times. He even stopped listening to his favorite music. When he was quiet, he did not hear it in his head. That head was bristling with negative thoughts.

One day, when the boredom became unbearable, a thought flitted into Mace's head. *I wonder if there might be anything in my mother's art room that might interest me?*

Until that thought, Mace had not entered the room. He considered it somewhat of a shrine to her memory. Later that night, after dinner at home and a refreshing shower, he stepped lightly into Elise's art studio. He found it remarkably bright even though the slats were closed. It had been more than four years since he crossed the threshold of this sanctuary. It seemed that the paintings themselves were lighting the room. Mace opened the slats and turned on the lights. Before him was a carnival of colors. Mace sat on the floor and rested his back against the only open spot between the stacked paintings. He gazed at the amazement before him. Every painting reflected some special aspect of his mother.

"These are all beautiful. Therefore, Elise must have been beautiful. But why did she not show me any of this beauty while I was small? What did I ever do to deserve her abuse?"

He would never know his mother's secret. *Thank God, I had a few good months of flirting with her before she died,* he thought. *At least that bit of weird behavior was better than anything she shared with me when I was young. Might I be able to express something meaningful through art, the way my mother did? Is there anything inside me other than the pain of loss? What about my good memories? I have plenty of them, the Super Six, Dr. Rafferty, my dad, Johnny Paige's family. I even had some good ones with Elise. Why do I always think negatively, except when I'm trying to save a life? I could try to paint. See what happens.*

In the ensuing months, while a drug war raged around him at work, Mace spent his nonworkout hours trying to become an artist. He first bought new paints, every single color that his mother had in her arsenal. He cleaned her brushes so he could reuse them. He bought several canvasses, all shapes and sizes, and settled into Elise's old art room one hot afternoon, to paint. Mace had developed a strategy. He would take Elise's paintings that he deemed unfinished and, by his additions, complete them. A sun here, a wave there, some sand, a rotting fence, a lightning bolt; things like that would do the trick.

Before his first stroke, he remembered an assignment he had in the seventh grade, to paint a tree. He enjoyed that challenge. Each time he thought he was finished and turned the work in to his teacher, the teacher handed it back to him with a suggestion on how to improve it. This happened four times. The last time he turned in that tree, he was proud of his painting. He received a B minus. He was disappointed, but he learned something important about layering and shading that he never forgot. Now he would be the teacher. He would review each painting four times after the first time he thought it complete. Each time, he would add something of substance until, after the fourth redo, he would let it go. He was done with that canvas.

At first, Mace was sloppy. Too much paint went onto canvas; and how could he have known that there were a million ways to paint a wave or color the sun to tint the sky or design a beach? In the beginning, Mace's additions were more like subtractions from works of art that had previously been beautiful. He learned that he could paint over his mistakes and try again. The first piece of art he shared with Elise, he redid eighteen times before he considered the piece completed. All he had done to the canvas was to make the sky look more ominous. When he was satisfied that the menacing seascape was finally completed, a casual observer would not be able to tell where Elise's work ended and Mace's work began.

About a year into his artistic endeavors, Mace took twelve of Elise's completed works and eighteen of their shared works to Gulfport's Tuesday bazaar to sell them. He rented a three-side canvas kiosk and faced the open side to the sidewalk. He hung the paintings on the canvas, organized his money, then sat on a comfortable dining room chair he brought from home. When he used all the canvas space to hang paintings, he still had ten remaining. Now he waited behind a long picnic table to see if anyone would buy a piece of art. What a surprise awaited him.

Generally, a man of few words, Mace found himself in a situation where he would have to interact with a variety of people from all walks of life. His first surprise was that he found he was enjoying what he was doing before anyone at all appeared before him. When a parade of people began passing his stand, he felt good about the eclectic scene before him. He hardly laughed, but he was smiling a great deal. He slid into a better mood than he had been in many months. He was also surprised at how many people knew him and treated him kindly.

"Hey, Mom, there's the cop and his old car right behind him," one little boy of about ten said as he passed Mace's kiosk.

The day's greatest surprise was the amount of interest there was in the paintings behind him. Time after time, passersby remarked on the beauty of Elise's individual works as well as Elise's and Mace's joint ventures. The best part of the greatest surprise was that six of the paintings sold, for a total of $725.

Mace could not believe his good fortune. Though he absolutely did not need the money, he still realized that $725 was a great deal of cash. It could go a long way to helping some individuals or charity around town that really needed it. As he packed the remaining twenty-four paintings into the back seat and trunk of his beloved Princess, he fantasized how he would give away the $725.

# CHAPTER 29

Alonzo Johnson was a black behemoth. It took him eighteen years to grow to six feet eight inches tall and 260 pounds. It took him thirty-one more years to grow from a lowly bicycle-riding scout to the kingpin of St. Petersburg's lucrative drug industry. A complex warrior with few friends, Johnson was also a dedicated gym rat and ballroom dancer. Leaning toward paranoia, he had become, as he called it, a watcher long ago. He studied people with alluring eyes that complimented a keen analytical mind. At forty-nine, he was acutely aware of the crimes he had committed to achieve his current status. He knew, instinctively, that there were men and boys, both within and beyond his organization, who would love to end his life and take his place. Feeling somewhat invincible, he did not usually travel with bodyguards but went nowhere without his trusted .38 special tucked inside his brown leather shoulder holster.

Johnson had gone to the same high school as Mace, Gibbs, where he excelled as a wrestler. Where Mace had a 118–0 record, Johnson came close, with a record of 106–6. His record was marred by one boy, six-foot-ten, 320-pound Marty Phelps. They wrestled each other twelve times over a three-year period, breaking even. Johnson feared no man one-on-one in his current life. However, nearly thirty years after their final match, won by Phelps, Johnson wondered if Phelps might seek him out and try to destroy him. Johnson had no way of knowing that Phelps died of heart failure in Kansas City at age twenty-three while working on a construction site. His ticker simply could not handle his 393 pounds.

There was one more activity that occupied the rest of the free time that Johnson could get for himself, women. With his money, his smoothness, his dancing ability, and his rugged good looks, women gravitated to him. There was never a shortage of girls and women, of all ages, who were available to him. His favorite venue to meet them was the Blue Parrot. Each Monday night, he delighted in listening to the Tomcats Jazz Orchestra, an eighteen-member group, eclectic in their musical offerings, but favoring the big band era. Johnson loved jazz his whole life. His mother was a beautiful tall sultry singer, who had made quite a name for herself in St. Pete's and Florida's jazz communities. She was a well-educated, erudite sophisticate, who taught her son continually on the beauties and subtleties of her favorite genre.

Beatrice Johnson was a loving and lovable woman. Her kindness served to enhance her son's love of women, but he grew up picky. A woman had to be kind, or he had no fondness for her. Though he was never close to a woman for more than a few months, he was rarely unkind to his girlfriends. He was never abusive, but he did use them for their beauty, their bodies, and that necessary kindness. These were qualities he needed to be happy. They were not qualities he found on the streets in his drug endeavors.

Fate struck lovely Beatrice at the tender age of forty-three, with unpleasantness that would change the life of hers and her son, Alonzo, forever. The sultry singer was beset by a series of significant strokes, which left her partially paralyzed on her dominant right side. The strokes caused profound damage to her ability to speak and sing. Unruly fate also twisted the right side of her mouth into a perpetual frown. Seeing his mother stricken and suffering, first in the hospital, then at home, had an immediate and profound impact on the impressionable Alonzo. He suddenly felt the need to take care of her physically and provide for her financially. Though only twelve, at the time of his mother's first stroke, he felt responsible for her care.

In a single day, Alonzo Johnson would go from a good boy to a criminal, as street crime beckoned him as the only way to make the money, he needed to help make a life for his mother. At night, he would ride his bike through different dark seedy neighborhoods of south St. Pete. Drug buyers would approach him and ask if he could procure their drug of choice. Most of the customers requested crack cocaine. Alonzo took their order and money, told them to drive around for about seven or eight minutes, then meet him right there. Then Alonzo would sprint out of sight and take a quick, circuitous route to the drug house of the day. There, he took out the buyer's drug cash, which ranged from $20 to hundreds. He gave it to a trusted drug soldier, usually a young guy of eighteen to twenty-five. That guy would count the money in front of a third young stud. One of the two guys in the drug house would then get however many crack rocks the customers had paid for. If the customer asked for something else, he would grab that. Alonzo was handed the drugs, then he sprinted back to hand them to the buyers. Every minute, Alonzo was looking out for cops. Getting caught, especially by cops in unmarked cars, could be costly. Over the years, hundreds of scouts had been arrested and court-appointed to Operation PAR, St. Pete's drug treatment program for young people.

Alonzo excelled as a scout. He was likable, uncommonly articulate for a young black boy, trustworthy, and most important, he did not get caught. No doubt that luck played a big part in his six-year success on the bike. Along his life path, he met Lamar Singletary, the kingpin of St. Pete's drug trade in the '80s, '90s, and 2000s. Singletary took an immediate liking to the boy who everyone knew was working to help his mother. Singletary took the young boy under his wing and became his mentor in the business of distributing drugs. He did not teach Alonzo quickly, merely occasionally.

Meanwhile, Beatrice Johnson's health improved. She explained to Alonzo her personal insurances, her checking and savings accounts, her IRAs, and how her disability payments worked. Alonzo was learning personal finances from his astute mother, who wanted to make certain that her house was always in order. That included Alonzo finishing high school. There were many courses that gave him major problems. That included second-year Spanish, geometry, and calculus. He stuck with every course and made it through all of them even though there was a spattering of Ds on his report card. He told Lamar Singletary three times that he was thinking about dropping out of school. Each time, Singletary, a murdering psychopathic egomaniac, sternly demanded that Alonzo finish high school.

"This organization needs intelligent young men. Unfortunately, most of the guys that work for me are stupid losers, but you're not."

Singletary's words always motivated Alonzo for a few months, then he would grow discouraged again and head back to his drug king mentor.

"Stay in school, Alonzo. Graduating will give you options. You might even be able to go to college."

"My grades are not that good."

"I'm sure if you graduate, St. Pete JC will accept you. You will make me incredibly happy if you earn your diploma and decide to work for my army. I will make sure you climb through the ranks fast."

That was a good incentive for a seventeen-year-old boy with no dad in the picture. Singletary was not only Alonzo's mentor, but he was also his father figure. Alonzo did not realize it at the time, but that is what was happening in a deep part of his psyche.

What Alonzo never understood was that Singletary was as damaged as a man there could be. He had a mother once, whom he loved dearly. She died of lung cancer in 2007. Singletary paid copious amounts of money to make sure she was well cared for. He had that in common with Alonzo. His relationship with his mother was extremely personal for him. When she died, Singletary's psychopathology worsened, as he felt lost without her. He did not speak about her with anyone after she passed. The other secret Singletary religiously kept from Alonzo was that he had seen Beatrice Johnson sing at numerous venues. He had an unspoken soft crush for her for nearly two decades.

*****

The drug war that raged in St. Petersburg during Alonzo Johnson's reign was not between rival gangs vying for territory or from factions trying to overthrow Alonzo. It was between the St. Petersburg Police Department and Alonzo's well-developed criminal enterprise. On June 3, 2014, during Mace's twentieth year on the police force, one of Alonzo's soldiers made a terrible mistake. His name was Darrell Nichols. He was a career criminal, covering the entire ten years between his tenth birthday and the present. He was first arrested for arson on his tenth birthday. He told the police that he was angry because he did not have a birthday party, and he needed to see some action. He burned down an empty garage on the same block where he lived. In the ensuing decade, he was arrested eighteen times, for petty theft, breaking and entering, and assault with the intention of doing bodily harm.

On his mistake night, Darrell Nichols was standing on one of the most notorious drug corners in St. Pete. His location was Fairfax and Twenty-Eighth Street South. He was standing on the south side of Fairfax and Twenty-Eighth Street with two other thug buddies, facing north in front of Leon's bar. The three drug soldiers did not notice a squad car driving behind them to the south and approaching. The cops in the car were looking to break up whatever group was hanging around that infamous corner. When the cop car turned the corner, the driver immediately recognized Nichols, as the three men scattered in different directions.

The driver yelled to his partner as he pointed, "That's Darrell Nichols. He's got a warrant!"

His younger faster partner shouted, "I got him!" He jumped out of the car and began pursuit.

Nichols, younger and swifter than both officers, and not carrying equipment, quickly gained ground on his pursuer and, in a moment, was a hundred feet ahead of him. Into greater darkness, the young criminal ran. Suddenly, he darted to his left into the front yard, paused to open a rusty gate, then sprinted into a black abyss of a backyard. He took three more strides and tripped over an unseen foot-tall garden gnome, twisted his right angle, painfully, and fell to the ground. While writhing there in pain, he reached into his pocket and pulled out his gun. As he twisted awkwardly onto his back and looked up, he saw his pursuer above him reaching for his own gun. Nichols fired at the instant the cop was pointing his gun at him. His bullet found a true mark, slicing through the officer's neck and into and beyond his brain stem, to some uncharted space beneath the stars. The cop was dead in a split second, but his body quivered and quaked, his trigger finger twitched and fired a round. That tiny chunk of metal found Nichol's right inner thigh near the femoral artery. It was the same leg as the sprained ankle. He had been rendered immobile, but still, though writhing in agony, he aimed his weapon at the gate. Seven seconds later, the driver cop appeared, his gun unholstered and ready to fire. He had heard the gunshots, and his adrenaline was surging immeasurably. He had just sprinted a hundred yards, and his worry for his partner had skyrocketed.

As soon as Nichols saw the cop, he opened fire. The cop did not hesitate. Though Nichols was a dark black man wearing black clothing in a black hole of a backyard, his shooting gave him away. With each shot, a piece of the yard lit up like a firefly on steroids. Each man's bullets found the other, ripping through flesh, unwanted aliens, intent on destruction.

Two minutes after the shooting stopped and the gun smoke had wafted into oblivion, the backyard returned to pregun battle blackness. There was an eerie silence, as the three participants lay on the cool earth. The darkness was broken when lights went on in the two nearest houses. Both homeowners had already called the police but were afraid to turn on lights while the shooting raged. Within twelve minutes, there were three ambulances, two firetrucks, five police cars, and news trucks from Bay News 9 and Channel 10 around the house where three men lost their lives on an inglorious early morning.

The mistakes by Darrell Nichols were first beating his girlfriend so badly that he had a warrant issued for his arrest. This was followed by his killing of two police officers. What those mistakes caused was the exposing of the St. Petersburg Police Department's poor handling of the drug trafficking in their city. Beginning the next night, both Channel 10 and the *Tampa Bay Times* sent unmarked cars into the southside to see for themselves the depth of depravity the drug trade revealed on the city's streets. Unaware of each other's presence, they both came to the same conclusion. The streets of south St. Pete were an absolute mess. Driving down one street after another, they found over two dozen locations where two or three undesirables standing or a scout riding his bicycle waiting for some action. The newspeople were shocked to see three young men standing outside Leon's Bar the night after the murders in the black backyard. A multitude of cars, cabs, and trucks came into the quiet dark neighborhoods from all over the city, looking to get well, for a short time. Conversely, there was only a small spattering of police cars that patrolled those rough streets.

The media coverage of the cop murders revealed the lack of a skillful antidrug plan by the St. Pete Police Department. It created a lit firecracker of emotion within the ranks of the officers and Alonzo's army that threatened to explode at any moment. The police needed to crack down, and the drug pushers were dead set on keeping their operation running smoothly and their territory for themselves. The area that Alonzo wanted to control was all south St. Pete from First Avenue South to the Sunshine Skyway. It was a rather small area to be king of, but it was enough to make him millions of dollars a year. Beware any interloper into that realm. If it took murder to keep the police from their incursion into his kingdom, Alonzo was ready to commit it.

Mace hated to hear about the killing of the two police officers. His three best friends felt the same. The current police chief was livid when he heard of the deaths of his comrades. He became angrier when he read about the inefficiencies of his department day after day. When he went home at night, there were more discouraging words on television. His name was Robert Garrett. He wrote his true feelings into his speech at the officers' funeral.

"I'm putting the entire drug community of St. Pete on notice. From top to bottom, every boss, every soldier, we are coming for you, and I am personally coming for you. I promise that I will occupy a squad car myself and search this city's streets for anything untoward. When I find it, I will deal with it with the coldness I have in my heart for every one of you. To you, those police officers meant nothing. But I assure you that these were fine and loving men. Every day of their lives, they woke with thoughts of what good things they could do for their family and their communities. Unknown and unlike any of you, they had names they carried with pride. The officers whose lives you took from them were Kevin Corey and Mike Magneson. Let their names be seared into your brains because from this moment into the foreseeable future, their names will be mine and the police department's battle cry. Kevin Corey and Mike Magneson. These courageous men have not succumbed in vain. Many of you will suffer, I assure you. You have become the nameless soldiers for whom this department no longer will have any regard. Kevin Corey and Mike Magneson are who this day is about. I swear on my oath that if we find you breaking the law, you will suffer, one way or another. You will soon learn what zero tolerance means."

Garrett was pissed. Alonzo Johnson immediately put a hit out on him. Garrett doubled his security for himself and his family. The war was on. The newspaper and the TV stations wondered if Chief Garrett would keep his word. Garrett was serious. He made sweeping changes in department policies toward drug dealers. He promised to target every rung of Alonzo's army, from the scouts to him. He pressed investigators to dig deeper and faster for facts that would lead their busts to convictions. This would put scores of drug dealers behind bars and keep them off the streets of his beloved city. That would also assuage the guilt he felt for being somewhat lax on drugs prior to the deaths of Corey and Magneson.

Mace and his three friends looked forward to Garrett's war on drugs. Real action against the bustling drug industry for the first time in years. Mace remembered that the last time he fired his weapon was nearly five years ago, about two years after the Charles Landry shoot-out. A frightened fifteen-year-old black drug scout panicked one night when he thought he was being stalked by a slow-moving cop car a hundred feet behind him. He started peddling like a madman while the cop car sped up and quickly closed the gap between it and the kid. The young thug turned a corner, darted into an alley, jumped off his bike, and waited for the cop car behind a large round black garbage can. With gun drawn and scared to death, he started firing when the cop car was eighty feet away. Bobby Banner opened his window and began expelling bullets toward the shooter. Mace stopped the car and immediately opened his door.

Bobby Banner did the same thing on his side of the car. While slowly emptying his load, the right side of the kid's body stuck out ever so slightly from behind the trash bin. It only took one of Mace's slugs to shatter the punk's knee into uncountable fragments. He was arrested a moment later, cowering on the ground, crying like a baby.

"I wonder how far Garrett will go with these new policies?" Bobby Banner asked in the squad car one night.

"I hope he takes it to the max," Mace answered. "I'm sick and tired of the passive approach we've had out here for years. It's no pleasure being a cop when you're doing nothing to improve your city." He paused. Several seconds later, he spoke more sternly, "I'll tell you one thing, Bobby. I'm all in for as long as this purge lasts. How about you?"

"Me too, Mace. I got your back, buddy. Now let's set some arrest records."

Because Mace and Bobby were such decorated officers, they requested and received patrol assignments in the most heavily drug trafficked sections of St. Petersburg. After having extensive conversations with Pete Laughlin and Ellis Wong, Mace convinced both to take similarly dangerous assignments. Since Laughlin and Wong were also highly decorated policemen, they, also, were granted their requests. They had become partners seven months before the killing of Officers Magneson and Corey. All four of the officers knew the slain officers. The living quartet took the dead duo's deaths especially personally. Any payback they could give Alonzo Johnson and his army would be joyful, no matter how difficult it might be.

# CHAPTER 30

There were many excellent policemen who took Chief Garrett's new policies to heart. There were none finer in the performance of their increased duties than Mace Stutzman, Bobby Banner, Pete Laughlin, Ellis Wong, and Chief Garrett. When they trolled the streets of their fair city for bad guys, they found them in droves. Scouts on bikes, drug sellers standing on various corners and parts of blocks, throughout a multitude of neighborhoods, littered the streets of south St. Pete. There were so many drug thugs in south St. Pete that decent people were afraid to take a walk on theirs or adjacent blocks for fear of being harassed by the criminal element. Good cops began to scour the south side. It became them versus Alonzo's soldiers' sense of entitlement to the city's streets.

The crackdown grew intense. More and more scouts and lower-level soldiers began disappearing from the streets. When Alonzo added new scouts and soldiers, they were arrested too. Cops used any excuse to bust them. They also followed cars that came into the hood from Largo, Kenneth City, Woodlawn, Snell Island, and other communities north of Central. Soldiers would peek out of windows night after night and see the same faces hunting for them. The thugs got tired of it. There had to be a way to counter the cops and stop their own diminishing numbers.

Eight weeks after the purge began, Alonzo came up with an idea he shared with his subordinate.

"How 'bout an old-fashioned ambush, just like the 1950s westerns?" he told his second-in-command, DeMarkus James, his first cousin on his mother's side.

"We can do it at my favorite location, Fairfax and Twenty-Eighth Street. Instead of mountains, there are a couple of tall trees where we can hide guys up high with automatic weapons. We will get some big trucks to block the squad car from behind and in front when they come by one night on one of those goddamned slow cruises. These cops could never guess we would hit them that way. If it turns out to be Garrett's car, that would be the best. Chief Garrett had been driving the streets every night, accompanied by a squad car with two heavily armed officers in it."

"We'll have the men in the trucks armed with automatic weapons. Each guy in the trees will have a walkie-talkie, along with their weapon. So will the passenger in each of the trucks. The tree climbers will arrive on the scene first, about two fifteen a.m. They will take a cab to Leon's bar. There they will make a pit stop. A few minutes later, they climb the trees. When the trucks are in position to block the street, the tree guys will call them on their walkie-talkies. The start of the waiting time for a cop car to come by will be two thirty. Whatever squad car that comes down the block after that is the target. Everybody on the block should be asleep in their beds, so there should not be any casualties. We only want the cops. May they both be white. This all should be fun for the ambushers, don't you think, DeMarkus?"

"I do, Alonzo."

Alonzo was no longer the loving, innocent boy who became a scout to help his sick mother. He was a coldblooded killer several times over, though he was no longer pulling the trigger.

"Do you understand everything I've told you, D?"

"I do, Alonzo. It's an easily workable plan. Great idea, man."

"It may have come from my brain, but it's your plan to implement. I'll give you eight weeks to deliver. I'll give you a budget of $50,000. That includes paying the shooters, buying the walkie-talkies, any weapons the shooters don't have, and whatever other expense you might incur. If you run into trouble, come and talk to me. If you pull this off, there's a $5,000 bonus for you."

"Thank you, Alonzo," Demarkus said appreciatively.

"We'll call it 'Operation Crossfire,'" Alonzo said, feeling like a four-star general. "If you have any other difficulties working this thing out, you know you can always talk to me. Now I'm heading to the Blue Parrot."

It was a Monday night and the Tomkats were playing. Alonzo did not like it when he missed a performance.

*****

It took Demarkus the full eight nerve-racking weeks to implement every aspect of his cousin's plan. It took him six and a half weeks to find the participants for the policemen killings. Demarkus wanted to please Alonzo, so he worked hard on his project. There was a strong bond of trust between Alonzo and his little five-foot-eight-inch cousin. D, as he was affectionately called by Alonzo, was two years younger. Alonzo knew D since D was a baby. When Beatrice Johnson had her stroke, D was ten.

Instead of shying away from her, D would visit her often. Sometimes, he went grocery shopping for the Johnsons. Many times, he sat with Beatrice and shared small talk with her. He did odd jobs for her around the house when Alonzo was away. The two good little boys bonded deeply over the care of Alonzo's mother. That love and care continued long after the boys developed into hardened criminals.

*****

Mace and his friends were racking up arrests in numbers the St. Pete Police Department had never seen. Each of the four men was proud of the work he was doing. Chief Garrett appreciated them immensely. Finally, after years of being ruled by criminal kids and dangerous young men, the streets of south St. Pete were being cleaned.

Mace felt he was experiencing the zenith of his career. This was after tiptoeing through those rugged south of Central streets for years. He was happy, with a feeling of true purpose. He had friends he worked with, ate with, and sometimes even worked out with.

That was more than enough to satisfy him socially. No longer did he consider himself a killer. He considered himself a relatively well-adjusted middle-aged man.

*****

The early morning of Alonzo's planned massacre of two human beings arrived with no fanfare. Fairfax was quiet, as it usually was. Not too far away from Leon's Bar, ten men, in the soundless darkness of the night, were dutifully scurrying to implement DeMarkus's plan to take the lives of two policemen.

Curiously, moves were being made by the gangsters with extreme precision. Performing with no dress rehearsal, whatever tasks they did in the next several minutes had to be executed perfectly.

The tree climbers, names not necessary, arrived at Leon's Bar at 1:43 a.m., just enough time to have a drink. What could it hurt? Their automatic weapons and walkie-talkies were tucked into a large black athletic bag that each of them carried. The young black faces were well-known to Leon, the owner and sometimes bartender, so he had no worries about being robbed.

The trucks did not move into position in the alley north of Fairfax until 2:27 a.m. They did not want to be there long enough to draw attention from passing police cars. Two of the trucks were parked on the west side of the alley facing west. These would be the trucks to block the exit from Twenty-Ninth Street. The other trucks faced east and were parked on the alley's east side. They would block any escape attempts to Twenty-Eighth Street. All four trucks had their motors running, lights off, feet on the floor, not brake. Each vehicle would be able to drive into the blocking position in a few seconds. By the time the trucks were in their waiting positions, the tree climbers were in their trees with their weapons and radios strapped over their shoulders. Their athletic bags were hung on nearby branches.

At 2:30 a.m., the official waiting time began. The young men in the trees were thinking, *First cop car gets it.* At 2:34 a.m., a 1985 Cadillac turned onto Fairfax off Twenty-Eighth Street. The occupants, probably looking for drugs, would not find any on this street this unholy night. As the minutes ticked by slowly, nerves began to become frayed, and fear crept into the hearts of the ten killers. As 2:40 a.m. passed, there was nothing but poisonous, agitated butterflies fluttering in ten anxious bellies.

At 2:47 a.m., a lone police car coming from the south on Twenty-Eighth Street turned right onto notorious Fairfax and parked on the wrong side of the street in front of Leon's Bar. As the driver, jokester, Pete Laughlin, got out of the car, the tree-sitters wondered what was going on. All Pete did was to check Leon's front door to see if it was locked. He had figured that if there were people drinking in there after hours or engaging in some other nefarious activity, he would bust them. But the door was locked. Immediately, when the tree-sitters saw Laughlin turn around to face the squad car, they nodded to each other, pressed a button, and said, "Okay." As Laughlin drove away slowly, looking for any movement in the shadows of the yards that dotted the streets, the blocking trucks were rolling. By the time the cop car got to the midpoint of the street, both Laughlin and Wong saw a 1967 brown GMC step van and an old Tastee Cake truck park oddly at the end of the street. After a second of processing, Wong said, "What the—" Before he said another word, the shower began. It was not a cool refreshing rain but a torrent of bullets that seemed to be coming from God's heaven.

The thunderous storm was more violent than either officer had experienced or could have ever imagined. Instincts took over as the officers began to drown. "Mayday! Mayday! Car 213, Fairfax and Twenty-Eighth Street. Massacre." Breaths became difficult to take, as lead droppings from the sky began to shatter the windows and roof and hit against the officers' vests and body parts. The embattled officers could only cower to the floor, heads down, hands over them in a pitiable fetal position.

The two men in each truck got out and began firing at the helpless officers, whose heartbeats slowed.

Mace and Bobby Banner were cruising west on Fourth Avenue and Thirty-Sixth Street, a mile from the ambush.

"Oh my god, that's Ellis and Pete's car!" Bobby yelled.

"Let's roll," Mace answered.

He punched the accelerator, turned left on Thirty-Seventh Street North, laid rubber, turned left on Fifth Avenue, laid rubber again, and sped perilously toward Twenty-Eighth Street. Bobby pulled out his sidearm and started shaking.

"Massacre! What does that mean?"

"It means to be ready for a war zone."

Mace felt like a young soldier again, adrenaline coursing through his veins, unafraid, looking forward to saving his buddies and adding to his favorite number. It took the Mercury forty-seven seconds to reach the hell pit. Since the trucks were blocking Fairfax, Mace parked the squad car adjacent to the first truck he came upon. Sounds of copious amounts of bullets fired, overwhelmed each man's ears, as well as Bobby Banner's psyche. Mace motioned Bobby to go the farther truck. Mace jumped from the squad car and hid behind the rear of the truck, trying to surveil the battlefield while bullets whistled past his face and body. The block was a nightmarish movie scene, and he was the actor who had been hired to save the day despite all odds. He looked down the street into the trees to what seemed like the sparking of a hundred huge angry fireflies.

The shooting continued. It was a minute fifty seconds into it, but it was almost the agreed-upon time to stop shooting when Mace took aim at the punk in the north tree. He took his first shot as the kid looked at his watch to see there were three seconds left before the gang would cease firing. His watch was the last thing he ever saw. Mace's bullet tore through his heart. One down, nine to go. Mace did not like having to aim to kill, but after a quick sizing up of the situation, he felt as if he had no choice. The other nine shooters turned their attention to Mace after his shot. Mace jumped to the ground behind a large rear truck tire. Bullets flew into Mace's area like an apocalyptic hoard of killer hornets.

As the bullets continued, Bobby Banner took quick aim at the nearest young killer. His shot flew all the way through the killer's neck, nearly severing his head. Two shots by cops, two thugs down. For the first time, the killers feared for their lives. They began shooting desperately at the two police officers that come to the rescue. Mace's old instincts came raging back to him. He knew the situation was nearly impossible. His next two shots took out two more punks. Now there was a glimmer of hope.

The amateur assault team was sloppy when they began shooting in two directions into fire that was being returned. During the transition, one of Alonzo's henchmen was shot in the spine by one of his own fellows. The spine split like a cracked walnut. Four shots by the cops, five crooks down. Mace spotted two heads peek from their hiding places behind trees. One was the remaining tree-climber, one was some other punk twenty-three feet closer to the barrel of his gun.

The men in the squad car on Fairfax could no longer breathe. They had drowned in gunfire, their weakened hearts ticking for the last time, only seconds from one another.

Though under warlike fire, Mace contemplated his next shots for fifteen seconds. He would take out the closest ambusher first, the second tree climber next. The shots would have to be *boom, boom,* no time in between. He knew he had it in him to make two perfect shots in a row. Three or more would be impractical, foolish.

"Come on, punks, show me a little more skull," Mace muttered softly.

A second later, an enemy head emerged. Mace blew every bit of face into a nearby yard. His second shot cemented the fact that his second target would never climb another tree. After Mace took these shots, he scooted from under the truck and hid behind the left front tire and the engine compartment. Both Bobby and Mace were doing the same thing now. They figured that the bad guys would not shoot out their own engines. The officers caught sight of each other. Bobby shrugged his shoulders. His face showed extreme concern. Mace shrugged his shoulders too, but his face was angry and undaunted. Both men peeked around an engine to see five men still in the field of play, like a ghetto video game. No one had made a move yet to escape to a truck. If they did, the cops would suddenly gain an advantage.

A second later, Mace and Bobby looked at each other. Mace directed his partner to move to the other side of the truck. Then he pointed to himself and indicated that he would run the other way. Then he squatted a bit and put his hand on his head to indicate "Find cover as quickly as possible." Bobby got the idea. There were several cars parked on Fairfax Street. Each cop figured that he would run to the rear of the nearest car, crouch, and take cover. Both felt they could outrun bullets for a couple of seconds. They both also knew that this was a life-threatening risk, one they knew they had to take. In the distance, sirens could be heard. Help was near, but in massacre time, near was an eternity.

Figuring they could split the fire, on Mace's thumbs-up, they both darted for the nearest parked car. They both made it with their lives, but one bullet found Bobby's leg, an inch above the knee. "Fuck!" he yelled, loud enough for everyone on the street to hear. The injury hurt so badly that it prevented him from squatting. He fell to both knees and took a moment to catch his breath. He instructed his brain to cope with the pain and not allow him to stop attacking the gunmen.

On the other side of the street, about ten feet closer to Alonzo's thugs, Mace felt a moment of disadvantage. Exposing himself while taking his next shots would be a life-threatening risk, and that is what he thought he had to do. He now had to fire from behind the car, probably while leaning on top of the trunk. Still, that would leave too much body exposed. He replaced his used cartridges, took a deep breath, and prepared for the greatest fight of his midlife. Before he sprung into firing position, he noticed how many lights were being turned on in the houses that dotted this tiny piece of Fairfax. It was now five creeps versus the two top cops in the city of St. Petersburg. It was simply dumb misfortune that three automatic weapons were trained on Bobby Banner, and that only two were pointing in Mace's direction. Mace knew that he had to come away from the car and get an immediate beat on the killers. If he could, for only two or three seconds, without getting shot, maybe he could fire two perfect see and shoot shots and eradicate two more murderers.

When Mace took his peek, Bobby Banner simultaneously leaned around the right rear bumper and began firing before the angry black dudes could fire back. Since Bobby's firing occurred before Mace shot, all five gangsters turned their weapons toward Bobby. All this was happening at immeasurably fast speeds. Bobby was able to get one good shot off. He hit the youngest kid in the killer crew on the left side of his upper torso, missing all vital organs but rendering him writhing in blood on the street. A split second later, it was Bobby's turn to experience a thunderstorm of lead. It only took four seconds for two sizzling hot bullets to find him. They hit him a microsecond apart. The first got him in the middle of his right thigh, narrowly missing the auxiliary artery. The second, blasted through his protective vest and his armpit, slicing the brachial artery.

"Fuck!" he said loudly, as his body twisted to the right and faceplanted into the concrete. He was dying, fast.

Mace did not know this. At almost the same instant as Bobby was being shot, Mace rose from his crouch, leaned on the trunk of the car, and fired two shots. "Time's up, fuckheads," Mace said as he took his shots. They were perfect skull shots, destroying copious amounts of bone and brain matter, an instant before two more evil men left their souls in the darkness of Fairfax Street.

Instantly, after firing, Mace ducked down behind the car that was giving him protection against the last two gunmen who were still standing. The sirens were almost on top of them. It was then that Mace saw his dear friend on the ground in a blood pool. His emotions plummeted. As his heart broke, his anger soared. He knew that if there was any chance to save his friend, he would have to eliminate the two shooters immediately. Every big hand clock tick was crucial even though considerably more help was only eight seconds away. Mace leaped to his feet, leaned his entire upper body against the trunk, and began firing. The attackers returned fire with the last bullets of their reload. Mace hit them both. One bullet was a left shoulder hit. The other smacked a right forearm. After being wounded, each man instinctively turned and ran for Twenty-Ninth Street and the two parked trucks. Each had an ignition key for all four trucks. By now, the killers felt they were outnumbered. Mace shot one of the men as he ran. His bullet found the middle of the man with the shoulder wound's back. It struck his spine at T5, and he went down like a sack of concrete. His knees hit first before his face smashed onto the cold road. He was dead before he realized he broke his nose and several small bones on his face when he impacted the street.

When the young man with the right forearm wound began racing for the southernmost truck, Mace came out from behind the car. He sprinted toward the runner, shooting while running. The young black killer, fighting for his own survival now, felt something warm and moist on the upper right side of his back, before it began to sting and burn. Only three strides from the truck, he wheeled and fired his last spate of bullets in Mace's direction. Another of Mace's bullets struck the frenzied youth, this time in the fleshy part of his torso's lower left side. It was painful but not lethal. He turned and made it to the truck, thanking God for allowing him to still be alive. All his friends were dead or dying on the street or in the grass. He thought how he would speed the truck to Bayfront ER and get treated. He did not care if the police caught him in the hospital. He wanted to live.

By the time he threw his weapon on the seat, found the right key, and started the engine, a St. Pete police cruiser roared into the scene. The two cops inside wondered what the hell was happening. They were bright men and seeing two large trucks blocking Fairfax made them immediately think ambush. The driver of the police car parked sideways in front of the truck, seemingly blocking an exit attempt. When the truck driver saw what the police car did, he screamed, "Shiiit!" holding on to the cussword a long time in complete panic. Both police officers got out of their car as the killer kid turned his wheel and barreled into the right quarter panel of the squad car. He successfully moved the vehicle enough that escape seemed possible. During the three seconds it took the fleeing driver to move the squad car, the two cops were able to take perfect aim at him. The thug kid was out of bullets and out of time. He pushed his foot on the gas pedal as the cops placed a few bullets into the escapee's upper torso. His life was ended, but his foot spasmed on the gas pedal and the box truck lurched forward another hundred feet before smashing into a light pole at the edge of the alley.

Absolute silence returned to the street. As the scene revealed itself, the four officers entering it began to feel and express their horror to each other about what they were observing. The entire block was littered with bodies. They could smell blood. One officer discovered Bobby Banner's lifeless body. He teared up as he felt for a pulse on the wrist and neck of the fallen officer. Ambulances were called.

Eventually, all four of the officers who arrived on the scene immediately after Mace and Bobby saw the two bodies in the ambushed vehicle. They were, at first, unrecognizable. The pitiful corpses were still on the floor in fetal positions, their hands covering their head. That position did not save them. Some of each man's fingers had been completely shot off. They looked like little boys playing a game of hide-and-seek on Halloween, dressed as horrifying policemen.

One officer found a killer still alive. When found, the black kid begged the white officer not to kill him.

"Please don't hurt me anymore," he pleaded, Bobby Banner's bullet burning inside him.

"I wouldn't waste a bullet on you, you piece of trash. I want to see you rot in jail for the rest of your days until they execute your ass."

Finally, the cops found the biggest body of them all, unconscious upon the uncaring street. It looked like an injured manatee and its life force was quickly departing.

# CHAPTER 31

The hospital room was cold and devoid of any other person when Mace awoke three days later. His body ached all over. He saw an IV flowing into each arm. He knew something terrible had happened to him, but his memory was foggy, and he could not recall what it was. He had no clue how long his trip lasted into the netherworld. There had been no bright white light, not a dream, nothing but darkness.

He looked for the call button because his mouth was parched, and it was difficult to swallow. He found it, pressed it, and a minute later, a pretty, little natural redhead of about thirty entered the room. Her charm and bubbliness were the opposite of what Mace was feeling, but from the moment she started, Mace liked her.

"Hi, sleepyhead. You are finally awake. Good."

"Good morning to you too."

"It's nice to see those beautiful eyes open. You had us all worried for a couple of days." Bubbly was nice. So was a compliment.

"My mouth is dry. Would you please get me a glass of water and some ice cream, maybe two cups of ice cream? I'm a big man."

"I'll get those for you in a flash, Officer Stutzman."

"Oh my gosh, Nurse, please call me Mace."

"Yes, sir, Mace."

She left the room. She had called him Officer Stutzman. Certainly, his being in this uncomfortable icebox had something to do with that fact. Three minutes later, Nurse Peppy returned with a large Styrofoam glass of ice water and a plastic pitcher of the same. Mace wondered where the ice cream was, but a second after putting the pitcher down, the nurse pulled out three cups of ice cream from her pockets. Three ice creams further endeared his new acquaintance to Mace.

"Thank you very much, Nurse," he said before sucking up half his glass of water through a paper straw.

"You're welcome, Mace."

"What's your name, Nurse?" he asked through eyes that were not yet focusing properly.

"It's Riley, Mace. Riley Taylor. You can call me Riley."

"Okay, Riley. Can you tell me where I am?"

"You're in the intensive care unit at Bayfront."

"How did I get here?"

"I can tell you that you were shot three times."

"How?"

"All I'm allowed to tell you is that you were shot during a shoot-out on Fairfax."

All Mace could visualize was Fairfax at night, the way it usually was, dark and foreboding. He saw two or three drug thugs hanging out in the empty lot adjacent to Leon's bar.

"How are you feeling, Mace?" Riley asked, tenderly.

"I'm sore all over, even my head, and I can't remember the shoot-out. Why?"

"It has to do with your injuries, Mace."

"How? Where was I shot?"

"Your doctor asked me to tell you that he wanted to talk with you personally about your injuries."

"Are they that bad?"

"Nothing you can't handle, Mace."

Riley hovered over Mace for the next few minutes, checking his IVs, and taking his blood pressure, pulse, and respiration. She flitted around him like a confident, carefree butterfly. Her movements were smooth and lovely, as if choreographed. Her perfume was jasmine, and it lingered on both sides of the bed long after she left the room.

*****

He should have asked the nurse for a blanket because it was the feeling of cold that woke him again a few minutes before 7:00 a.m. He remembered a dream. Bobby Banner was on third base, and Mace was batting. Their team was losing 6–5 with two outs in the bottom of the seventh. The pitcher let go of the ball with the highest, most majestic arch a pitch had ever traveled. In slower than slow dream motion, the ball began to decline from its apex. As it did, Mace saw the blue sky, decorated with a pale-blue full moon behind it. Mace felt as if there was an eternity for him to flex his muscles and find the perfect instant to swing his mighty club. When bat met ball, a thunderous crack was heard in every nook and cranny of the stadium. The twelve-inch sphere exploded into the atmosphere, its trajectory loftier than any of the thousands of observers had ever witnessed. It sailed a hundred fifty feet beyond the left-center field fence before it felt the grass again. It rolled another fifty feet before it ended its once-in-a-lifetime journey by falling into a lime green creek with a soft kerplunk.

Mace had won the game with a towering home run. Starting his proud trot around the bases only after watching the entire flight and roll of the baseball, Mace noticed Bobby Banner waiting for him behind home plate. Mace jumped emphatically on the dish, stepped a foot beyond it, and was greeted with the powerful hugging arms of his best friend, Bobby Banner. A micromoment later, he felt his massive torso being hugged by two more extremely strong men. It was Pete Laughlin and Ellis Wong. Enormous smiles adorned their faces, as they heaped a mountain of praises upon Mace for his game-winning, myth, and legend-creating home run. But Mace deflected.

"It's all you, guys," he said to his three dearest pals. "None of this would have ever happened if you hadn't taught a muscle-bound cop in his forties how to play baseball. Thank you all so much."

The scene then faded into merely the memory of it. Mace pondered what he had dreamed. He realized it was one of those rare dreams that matched real-life frame by frame. What he experienced during REM sleep had happened to him three summers ago. He wondered when any or all three of his friends would come to visit.

After a few moments of reveling in his joyful, real-life memory, Mace's breakfast arrived. This was another joyful moment because the injured officer was famished.

The joy turned to disdain when he took the lid from his plate and discovered that everything was pureed. He found and pressed the call button angrily. A minute later, a big, busty nurse entered the room. Before she spoke a word, Mace lit into her.

"I know we haven't met yet, Nurse, but can you please tell me what the hell this shit is?" He pointed to his tray.

"Good morning, Officer Stutzman. Glad to see you are feeling so feisty."

"Come on, cut the crap, Nurse. Can't we get some real food up here?"

"Your chart says you're to stay on this special food until the dietician approves your ability to swallow."

"Well, I'm telling you right now that I can swallow fine. Here, watch me." He grabbed the ice water pitcher, poured a full Styrofoam glass of water, and gulped it down in a few seconds. He then opened his mouth and stuck his tongue out like a small child to prove he had swallowed every drop.

"That is very good, Officer, but I'm not qualified to approve you. Besides, that's just water, not solid food. There is a big difference, you know."

"I know, I know, but I'm not eating that slop. Can a good cop get about three cups of ice cream around here? I'm a big guy, you know."

"The rule is two in the ICU."

The yet-to-be-properly met nurse left the room. She could not wait to leave. It took fifteen minutes to compose herself and return to the ugly antiseptic room with the angry officer in it.

"Thank you," Mace said as he dug into a chocolate ice cream cup.

"You're welcome," the big girl said cheerfully.

"I'm sorry I was so rude before. That is the kind of behavior my mother always exhibited, and I am certainly not her. I'm frustrated, that's all. I don't know what my injuries are, and I don't remember how I got here. By the way, what's your name?"

"I'm Nurse Sandy Robertson. You can call me Sandy."

"Please, call me Mace. I'm not always such a grump."

"Okay, Mace. It is a pleasure to meet you. I have been instructed to tell you two things. The first is that you were in a shoot-out against a large gang on Fairfax Avenue South. That's how you incurred your injuries. Your doctor and surgeon, Dr. Franklin, has put in your chart that he wants to discuss your injuries with you before anybody else does."

"How long will that be?"

"Not long at all, Mace. He is making rounds now. I imagine ninety minutes, at the outset."

Nurse Robertson began hovering around Mace, checking his IVs, the machine he was hooked up to, and if all his wounds were clean and bandaged correctly. Before he fell asleep, Mace caught a whiff of Nurse Sandy's perfume. It was not his mother's musk or Nurse Riley's jasmine, but whatever it was, the faint hint of it was comforting, helping sleep to come easily.

Ninety-seven minutes later, Dr. Franklin woke Mace with extreme tenderness. Accompanying the short doctor were three other doctors, two men, and one woman. All were carrying clipboards. As Mace woke, he noticed that Dr. Franklin's were the daintiest hands he had ever seen on a man. The doctor's face was smooth and closely shaven, and his deep blue eyes exuded kindness and brilliance. He was wearing English Leather and his breath, minty fresh. Mace also noticed that the doctor's fingernails were groomed perfectly and covered with a clear polish. His voice was dulcet and a tick above soft. As Dr. Franklin began to speak, Mace became mesmerized by his captivating mannerisms.

"Hello, Mace. I'm Dr. Franklin. I'd like to explain your injuries if you are feeling up to it." He extended his beautiful hand, which Mace took and shook with care. Dr. Franklin's grip was surprisingly firm.

"I hurt like hell from my head to my toes, but I'm ready to hear everything you have to tell me."

"That is very good, Mace. You seem very alert and able to communicate well."

"Thank you, Doctor."

"Mace, when you came into the ER, you were in bad shape. I was called and performed three surgeries on you. The least troublesome was a bullet wound to your midright thigh. For the average person, it might have a through and through shot, but this bullet lodged itself in the thickest thigh muscle I've ever seen. I was able to extract it but with a relatively high degree of difficulty. The bullet caused considerable damage, but I quickly put things back the way they should be. With some therapy and your workouts, you should be walking without a limp in a few weeks."

"That's good news!" Mace said as all the doctors smiled.

"It certainly is, Mace," Dr. Franklin continued. "Your second injury is more complex. One bullet found its way around your protective vest and into the dense muscle of the left side of your chest. Thankfully, your muscle slowed the bullet considerably, but it still traveled enough to puncture and deflate your left lung. I repaired that problem. However, I had to put you on a ventilator because that problem, combined with your final wound, made breathing on your own an impossibility."

"What was my final wound, Doctor?"

"Here is where complete wonder enters the picture, Mace. A bullet nicked your brain. It did not stop in the brain. If it had, we would not be having this conversation. It simply made a fleeting visit. In the wake of its brief passage, it left some interesting damage. In my assessment, the bullet hit the back of your head when you were falling forward from your other wounds. It clipped off the back of your skull and skimmed over your thymus and hypothalamus. It took with it a significant amount of brain matter. You may know that these two areas of the brain are largely responsible for the emotions we feel as human beings. This includes how we react to stress and stressors, fear, anger, sex drive, even hunger. It is a wonder that you woke this morning talking with Riley. It's all in your chart, Mace. You have remarkable healing powers."

"Thank you, Doctor. Is that all there is?"

"Not quite, Mace, but I'd like Dr. Roland to explain this next part to you."

The lady doctor stepped forward. She was pretty, about the same height as Dr. Franklin, about five feet six. Her skin was no sunshine pale, also like Dr. Franklin's. Her lipstick was the faintest hint of pink, upon two extremely thin lips.

"The type of injury that your brain sustained, Mace, may cause temporary or even permanent loss to some areas of your past or future." She was all business in her delivery of confounding news.

"When Dr. Franklin performed emergency on you, removing damaged tissue was like picking away gossamer with a tweezer. We were extremely judicious in our movements, but we have no idea how many memories were stored in the damaged tissue or how much of it may be needed to store future memories. Consequently, you may experience a roller-coaster ride with all your memories. You may remember some, forget others, never knowing when one or the other will occur. When these memory lapses occur, they may become stressors to your emotional well-being. Since your thalamus and hypothalamus have been damaged, these stressors may cause depression, anger, or even rage. You may experience behaviors that are not your norm."

She stepped back to her original standing place and spoke one word to Dr. Franklin. "Doctor." The gentle little man stepped forward and began speaking again.

"None of us can say exactly how badly these injuries will affect you, Mace. We know that troublesome behavior will not occur all the time, but we know that problematic behavior will arise some of the time. How you control yourself during these episodes of memory loss, complex stimuli, and stressors is anybody's guess. In the final analysis, it will be up to you, but it will not be easy. You will be at a definite disadvantage, like a pitcher who is pitching with a fractured arm. How these things collectively will affect your social life and your career are also concerns. We do not want to say that you are permanently disabled, but getting back to being the magnificent police officer you have always been will be a considerable challenge. What I am saying, Mace, is that so far you have overcome some serious injuries, but the overall degree to which you overcome these will be a lifelong challenge for you."

"Do you know how I got here?"

"We do, Mace, but do you have any idea?"

"I don't," Mace replied humbly.

"That is not uncommon with your injuries, Mace. At the same time, it is not possible for us to know whether this memory lapse was caused by lost brain cells or because your mind is blocking a traumatic event. We also cannot say whether this forgetting is temporary. You may never recall this incident."

"Will someone please tell me what happened to put me here!"

Dr. Franklin spoke again, "Mace, when you first came into the ER, Police Chief Garrett was near you in the waiting room the whole time. When we finished your surgeries, I and my team discussed your possible memory problems, especially what went down on Fairfax. The chief asked us for the right to explain the situation to you, personally, and we agreed. He'll be here at 11:00 a.m."

"Thank you, Doctor."

"Do you have any more questions for us at this time, Mace?"

"No, sir. I'll take some time now to process what you've told me."

The four doctors checked Mace's IVs and wounds and once again concluded and told Mace that he had extraordinary healing powers. They left the room with a series of friendly goodbyes and "we'll see you again."

When the doctors were gone, Mace's emotions sagged. He remembered how he cracked up years ago when his five friends were killed in combat. He was not catatonic now, but was his memory loss a different form of insanity? Was whatever it was that brought him here so bad that he was subconsciously blocking it?

Sleep overtook Mace five minutes after the doctors were gone. A gentle nudge of five fingertips on his right shoulder woke him. His eyes opened to see a gaunt Chief Garrett, whose life had been pure hell since the massacre.

"How are you, Mace?" he asked while extending his right hand. He was surprised how strong Mace's grip was, as he answered, "I hurt like hell all over."

"The doctors told me that you don't remember how you got here. Is that true, Mace?"

"Yes, sir, it's true."

"That is why I'm here, Mace. I felt it was my responsibility to tell you those details. Do you mind if I pull up a chair?"

"No, sir."

Chief Garrett walked to the other side of the bed and scooted a wooden chair, with thick blue padding, right next to Mace. His eyes were bloodshot and sad.

"According to our investigation and our hypothesis, we have concluded that Alonzo Johnson and his cousin came up with a plan to ambush one of our police cars. It was retaliation for our stepped-up presence and arrests on the south side. We feel that was Alonzo because no one else has the power to organize a stunt like that. When we questioned him and his cousin, they told us they were in St. Augustine on vacation with two respectable women from St. Pete. We questioned the women too. Everyone told the same story. All, but one of the attackers, are dead. That survivor is not talking."

"What happened, Chief?"

"The ambushers had two guys climb a tree, one on each side of the street. Both had an automatic weapon and a walkie-talkie. At nearly the exact time, they planned for one of our cars to come onto Fairfax. The shooters knew our car would be going slowly. The tree men called a signal on their walkie-talkies, and in a few seconds, four large box trucks emerged from hiding and blocked any possible exit to Twenty-Eighth or Twenty-Ninth Street. Two armed men got out of each truck. They joined the tree men in shooting into the blocked police car. A torrent of bullets hit that police car, Mace. The officers inside had no chance of survival."

"Who were the officers, Chief?"

"It pains me to tell you this, Mace, but it was Pete Laughlin and Ellis Wong."

"Are they okay?"

"Neither one of them even got a shot off. Their weapons were still holstered. They were able to get a Mayday call out, and a nearby police car raced to the scene. It arrived in two minutes, the officers inside it, there to save the lives of their friends. That car was yours, Mace. Do you remember now?"

"No, sir. Who was my partner?"

"Bobby Banner. You were outnumbered, ten to two, but you and Bobby tried to take out the entire gang, one by one. At one point, you had both been wounded but kept fighting. According to ballistics, Bobby killed one ambusher, and you killed seven."

"How's Bobby?"

"He didn't make it, Mace. I am so sorry. I know he was your best friend."

"Bobby's gone, sir, and Patrick and Ellis?"

"Yes, Mace. Of the first four officers on the scene, only you survived."

"They were my three best friends, Chief."

"I know, Mace. We are here for you, each and every one of us. Everything the St. Pete Police Department has to offer is available to you. You are a hero, Mace. You nearly took down that entire hoard by yourself. All of St. Petersburg and the country want to see you. They want to see what makes you tick, where that bravery comes from. The *Today Show* called us, said they wanted to interview you as soon as you are up to it. My office has been flooded with calls from local and national broadcasting stations. Millions of people want to see me pin the medals you've earned on your chest."

"I don't want any publicity, Chief. I especially do not want people to see my face. If they did, I would soon become a target for all the crazies and wackos, including Alonzo. I'll take the medals. I can add them to my collection and stick them in a drawer and never look at them. You can hand them to me in a broom closet, for all I care, Chief. They are just little trophies. They can't talk. They're just metal reminders of the people I fought, to earn them. What I really want, Chief, is what I can never have. I want my warrior friends back."

Mace would not allow himself to cry although he wanted to do so. Instead, he closed his eyes and stopped talking.

"Are you tired, Mace?"

"No, sir. I'm empty."

"I think I understand, Mace." The chief was almost whispering. "I heard every word you said, and my heart aches for you. I promise that I will do everything in my power to keep the media at bay. I apologize in advance for anyone who slips through the cracks."

"Thank you, sir. Now I have to get my heart and head straight and figure out my next move."

"I haven't given you a direct order for a long time, Mace, but I want to give you one now. I order you to get well, Officer Stutzman. Do whatever it takes to regain your strength, emotionally and physically, and get yourself out of here and back home. Clear your head of the pain that you feel for your lost brothers as quickly as possible. Replace that pain with the knowledge that you saved countless lives by taking out those murderous thugs. They would have killed over and over, but your bravery circumvented it. That is something you can carry in your heart for the rest of your life. You are larger than life, Mace. You are a true hero."

"Thank you for the compliments, Chief, but I'm just a man, and a rather simple one at that. Believe me, I will follow your orders and get well. I have a lot of life to live, and I do not want to waste it at Bayfront Hospital."

"I believe in you, Mace. Whatever you decide to do after you heal, I will understand, and I will back you 100 percent. I hope you return and work with me. There is no better officer on this police force, Mace. I need you."

He reached his right hand out, and he and Mace shook with two of the firmest grips in the history of mankind.

"Thank you, Chief Garrett. Your encouragement and support mean more to me than I could ever express."

"I'll stop by every three or four days to see how you're doing. Is that okay with you, Mace?"

"That would be great, sir."

"I'll see you soon, Officer Stutzman."

*****

Mace still could not remember the massacre on Fairfax, but as he sadly pondered the loss of his three friends, he thought of his recent baseball dream. Amid great tragedy, his mind shifted to his subconscious fantasies. They depicted true friendship between the four friends. They offered him thoughts of joy and levity. Thinking of this dream was the exact sublime soothing that Mace needed to fall comfortably asleep. It was when he awoke that he would begin to experience the myriad difficulties that would intrude on the next chapter of his life.

# CHAPTER 32

It took Mace forty-two days to leave Bayfront. Looking back on the prior weeks, he realized that they were filled with constant reflection of what happened the night of the massacre. Not only was he agonizing over the deaths of his friends, but he was also incapable of replacing a memory where it should have been. He thought, too, about Riley, the pretty night nurse. He became well-acquainted with her during the six weeks he was stuck in the hospital. He developed a genuine fondness for her, and, to his surprise, a strong sexual attraction. This was only a second for him. The only other woman he felt that kind of tension with was Elise. As with his mother, he did not follow through with his desire. In fact, he fell slightly short of asking Riley on a date, for fear of rejection. Funny thing was, for several days after Mace was released, petite, redhead Riley missed him. She wondered why he had not asked her for a date. She had heard so many stories of his bravery, going all the way back to his service career. She would have enjoyed going out with him, if only he would have asked.

Mace was stuck in his head that was filled with hurt. The thoughts that went through him became more damaging for him the more he considered them. He reflected on his three friends and the ways they lost their lives. Those thoughts lead him to recalling five Marine friends who were killed by an IED. That totaled eight of his dearest comrades. They were not ordinary men, either. They were the finest of the fine, the bravest of the brave. Then he thought about Johnny Paige and his death from cigarettes. That made the ominous number nine. Mace could not measure the sense of forlornness that beset him.

When he could not remember the faces of Johnny's wife and children, he wondered if life was worth living with his various peculiar brain abnormalities.

Still, he trudged on, doing the things that made him Mace Stutzman, a solitary man. The doctors at the hospital put him back together well enough, physically, and their therapy took him to a better level. However, Mace knew that there were many more levels that he would have to pass through to become the physical specimen he once was. Though he had turned fifty in the hospital, Mace was determined to achieve lofty physical goals. Once Mace made up his mind to do something, no exterior or interior force could stop him. His depression, strong enough to paralyze an average man, he carried like Atlas with the world on his shoulders. It was mighty heavy, but he had carried extreme pain his whole life. He, long ago, learned to manage that weight and not let it stop him from doing the things he loved.

When Mace left Bayfront, he longed to take a ride in Princess to Weedon Island to see what birds were in town this year. He could not wait to crank up his old Victrola and listen to Count Basie and Glen Miller while he lifted weights on the patio. He wanted to look at his guns and coins. Like his records, they were amorphic friends. He looked forward to going to David Reynolds, to see what was new on the tiny electric shelves, and in the gold and silver case. He looked forward to seeing the staff. Always professional, helpful, and delightfully gregarious, they were the closest people in the city to his friends even though they did not share social activities. There was only one person he considered a friend these days. That was Chief Garrett. The chief had kept his promise to see him every few days. He was always encouraging, supportive. Their conversations were as deep as Mace would allow. They were more sensitive, significant, and sincere than Mace had ever shared with anyone. The chief also kept his promise to keep the press away. Mace believed the chief would do anything for him. There was no one else in his life that Mace believed in as much as Chief Garrett.

One day, about a week after he left the hospital, his favorite number popped into his head. Though Mace had no recollection of the massacre, he remembered the chief told him he killed seven men. He wished he could remember so he could derive some pleasure from it. Maybe the pleasure would help to assuage some of his pain. Over twenty years had passed before the massacre since he had killed. He wondered if he enjoyed doing his job that night the way he used to during the war. Though he did not feel any satisfaction from that heroics, he still had to add the seven to his former total of twenty-seven kills. That made a new total of thirty-four. Though his memory could not partake in his figuring of this number, his mind gave him extreme joy, reflecting on the amount of evil he had eradicated from his city. Unfortunately, when he recalled the lifesaving part of his favorite number, he realized that he had not saved anyone on the massacre night. He had failed to save his friends. That fact devastated him. His new favorite number of 137 meant little to him now.

Mace retreated farther into his world of unspoken grief, as the weeks passed, and he brought himself nearly back to his old physical self. During the time of body strengthening, he questioned his true manhood thousands of times. He had done horrible things twice, and knowing it was torturing him. First, he had not given enough of himself to his friends, nor had he extracted enough of their true personalities from them. How often had he escaped from sharing from them and listening to music in his head? He had not laughed enough with any of them, clinging to that bullshit his mother forced upon him. Second, when his five friends were killed, he cracked up, went insane, and became catatonic. Then when his three friends were killed, he could not remember anything about that. It could not be the loss of a few brain cells that caused his forgetfulness. It was because he was not man enough to accept and deal with tragedy, like a real hero. He did not consider himself a coward. He merely considered himself weak-minded when it came to handling tragedy. He certainly did not want anyone to fuss over him.

Ultimately, he grew to believe he was not someone worth knowing. He became more silent than ever, determined to speak only when necessary.

*****

Mace returned to active duty as a St. Petersburg police officer five months and one week after being shot three times in the Fairfax massacre. Still, he remembered nothing about it. He came back on August 19, 2015, a fifty-and-a-half-year-old stud unsure of whether he ever wanted to pull the trigger of a gun again. He came back having received three medals for extreme bravery. Chief Garrett delivered the trinkets to Mace in Garrett's office, exactly a week before. He was given a new partner and was asked to ride shotgun for a month so he could get used to the routine again. He was miffed for a moment about that, but he quickly realized it was not a punishment but a show of care on Chief Garrett's part.

*****

While Mace was healing from his bullet wounds, Alonzo was gloating over his success with the infamous Fairfax massacre. He had achieved more than he hoped for. Three of the four top arresting officers in St. Pete had been killed. The top cop was put out of commission, almost out of his misery. How could that cop, no matter how good he was, come back to his job whole again? Alonzo was so happy about his success that he took the hit off Chief Garrett. His assault struck an enormous amount of fear into the hearts of all the St. Petersburg policemen. They each came to believe that Alonzo would stop at nothing, to reclaim the streets of south St. Pete. Each officer thought horrifying thoughts about how or when he or she could be assassinated. They were vitally concerned for their safety. Chief Garrett gave a force-wide order to drastically cut back on minor drug busts. Even the mayor put pressure on Garrett to give that order. He did not want his beautiful city by the bay to become nationally known for cop killings.

Alonzo was interviewed by detectives thirty-two times about his involvement with Fairfax. He revealed nothing. He behaved as a consummate gentleman, always. He was Pierce Brosnan, Sean Connery, and Clark Gable in their finest performances, rolled into one man. He was as slippery as hot butter, and he taught and demanded his cousin DeMarkus conduct himself the same. DeMarkus was not an exact replicant of Alonzo, but he had learned well. He loved being second-in-command of Alonzo's army. He loved the power and the money and the women, who were available to him everywhere. He would never say anything to damage his beloved lifestyle.

Though each cousin was a cold killer, both men learned to compartmentalize the traits required to successfully run their drug enterprise. Detectives looked deeply into Alonzo's and DeMarkus's backgrounds. They found that years before Alonzo had purchased the extraordinary successful restaurant, Eldo's, on Eighteenth Avenue South. Deborah and Ethel were longtime friends of Alonzo's beautiful singer-mother. Alonzo loved them both, like close aunts. He went to that place his whole life to hang out and eat. El and Do, the aunt's nicknames, began teaching him to cook when he was ten. He loved cooking his whole life and even joined the head chef for a turn in the kitchen in the present time. He spent three hours a day there, on average, and his loyal employees loved and respected him.

No one knew that he spent most of his time in the office doing gangster business. Only but two black construction workers knew there was a carefully crafted hiding space behind the main wall. Finally, absolutely no one but Alonzo knew there was a four-foot-tall safe in that hiding space. That safe not only held a variety of his gangster papers; it held more currency than an average guy might handle in a lifetime.

DeMarkus owned the thriving little grocery store on First Avenue South and Twenty-Second Street. He, also, had a little safe in his office, the loyalty of his employees, and spent about three hours a day there. Vacations were the exceptions to that rule. Years ago, when DeMarkus bought his little gold mine, Alonzo told him to always be kind to his employees. He told him to never lose his temper, even if he had to fire someone, who might have been caught stealing from him. Even if a customer was caught stealing, the staff was taught not to call the police but to try to be sensitive to the real needs of the person stealing. Food was one thing. Beer was another.

"We want those guys who hang outside the store and who frequent the place to be our friends. Give away a little free food and some soda pop. We can afford it. Someday, trust me, these people will be our alibies."

Alonzo was not wrong. Never did his theory come more to fruition than after the Fairfax massacre. Everyone the detectives talked with about the two businessmen liked them. It was impossible to collect evidence against the two murderers when the people they knew spoke so highly of them. Alonzo also instructed DeMarkus to be kind to all his women.

"If you don't like a woman, don't get mad at her. Just get another one. Happy ex-girlfriends whom you're still cordial with make great alibies."

Alonzo was right about that too. Every ex-girlfriend and especially their current girlfriends said that Alonzo and Demarkus were great guys.

"This is the way we're going to roll. Can you handle that?"

After Demarkus said yes to Alonzo, they both lived by Alonzo's austere rules. They were in so much control of their behavior that at the end of each interrogation, the detectives felt a genuine fondness for them.

# CHAPTER 33

"I can't take it anymore, Chief," Mace said in the early part of their conversation. "I've tried to endure my anxiety and function successfully in my job, but I don't want to try anymore."

"Mace, if you think seeing a psychiatrist or psychologist might help—"

"Seeing those guys won't help, sir. They can't talk me back into something I simply do not want anymore."

"Are you sure, Mace? You know I can give you all the help in the world if you need it."

"Need is a funny word, Chief. It kind of goes along with that word *want*, and I don't want to be a police officer any longer. I don't even want to pull my weapon out of its holster ever again, less shoot it to kill someone."

"Are you serious, Mace?"

"As I have ever been in my entire life, sir. And the funny thing is, that I don't have a clue why I feel this way. That fact scares me because I have grown to hate something that I loved for an awfully long time. Emmerson talks about self-reliance. How can I feel self-reliant if I'm reluctant to defend myself if the situation demands it?"

It had been six months since Mace returned to active duty. They had been six agonizing months. The more he became used to the daily routine, the more he realized he hated every aspect of it. Twenty-one years as a cop and ten in the marines was enough.

"I'm twenty-one years in, Chief. I know it's time to take the uniform off and pack it away. I feel like I have fulfilled my duty to humanity. I feel empty, Chief. There's nothing left in my tank."

"Do you want to give a two-week notice, or do you want to leave right away?"

"If it doesn't hurt my official record, I'd like to stay on a few more days, give you a chance to fit someone else into my schedule."

Garrett thought for a moment, sadly.

"Can you give me five more workdays, Mace?"

"Yes, sir," Mace said with an emotionless face.

"If you had to draw your weapon and use it in the next few days, can you?"

"Quickly and efficiently, sir, just reluctantly."

"I am sorry to see you leave, Mace. I feel as though my right arm is being amputated."

"I assure you, it's still there, sir."

"You may be a quiet man, Mace, but you are a true American hero. This department takes a deep hit losing you."

"Thank you, Chief. May I be dismissed now?"

"You may, Sergeant."

Mace did not care that he had achieved the rank of sergeant in the department long ago. He wanted everyone to call him Mace. Then he saluted the chief as a sign of deep respect. Then the chief returned the salute with an even greater admiration for the man standing before him. Garrett knew that in his own personal career, he had not achieved nearly what Mace had in his. In his deepest, never spoken soul, the chief considered Mace a better man.

*****

It was late February 2016. Mace worked five more uneventful shifts. He asked Chief Garrett to keep his departure as quiet as possible. He wanted his ending to be seamless and wordless, no goodbyes. When he left headquarters across Ferg's Bar after his final day, he was done.

# CHAPTER 34

Mace Stutzman loved St. Petersburg, everything that is except for most of the south side. While policing the parts that he adored, he continually saw the criminal aspects of them. There were drugs, which led to murders, breaking and enterings, car thefts, purse snatchings convenience store holdups, etc. There were many different et ceteras, the kinds that made a police officer's life interesting. They were not much different from other cities, he mused. There were few criminals who were smart enough to come up with crimes that differed from the norm. Mace always found it interesting how criminals would leave similar breadcrumbs that would make it easy for them to be caught.

When he used to finish his shifts at work, Mace would usually head quickly back to his beloved Pass-a-Grille. He loved the tiny peninsula almost as much as he loved life itself. He swam in its pristine water, listened to guitar players and ate hamburgers at the snack shack, put down tasty grouper sandwiches at the Hurricane Restaurant. Now he wanted a great deal of that to change. He had become fixated with the tiny piece of land. Now he wanted to explore St. Pete as a carefree, curious retiree. He wanted to relax on the veranda at the Vinoy, to have dinner at 400 Beach. He wanted to go to the Cobb Theatre, order dinner in the lobby, then eat it at his seat while watching a movie. He had not been to a movie since he was on R&R in Hawaii when he was in the service. That must have been twenty-three, twenty-four years ago. It was not people that he was seeking out. It was the exploration of his city.

Three months into his retirement, while having dinner at Guy Harvey's restaurant on St. Pete Beach, he overheard a conversation that would change his life.

"I've never seen anything like it my whole life," a pretty old lady of about seventy-five said to her three tablemates. "All those musicians together in a tiny place playing their hearts out. There was not a cover charge, but if you reserved a table, your bill had to average $12 a person. That is how they paid the band members, and only $20 each, can you believe that?"

Her girlfriend, who had gone with her to listen to the music, jumped in.

"Those fellas were amazing. There were eighteen of them. They had trumpets, trombones, saxophones, a keyboard, drummer, guitarist. The middle saxophone player played the clarinet sometimes, and his solos on both instruments were terrific. I think he was my favorite of the bunch."

The first lady did not give her friend a chance to catch her breath.

"They're called the Tomkats, and my favorite was the trumpet player, second from the right, top row. Goodness, they were terrific."

The other lady chimed in again.

"They played Cole Porter, Count Basie, Gershwin. Sergio Mendez. Smokey Robinson, Benny Goodman. They were all over the place with music that spanned multiple eras. The dance floor was not designed to be one, but the dancers made do, and the floor was packed for almost every song. Betty and I danced almost every dance."

Betty spoke up again like an excited thirteen-year-old girl.

"Even though Tildy and I went alone, there were plenty of men there who asked us to dance. Pretty nice guys, mostly, a couple of odd ones, but we had a great time. The only time we weren't dancing was when we were eating. I'll tell you, we really had some great exercise that night."

Betty and Tildy were talking about one of Mace's favorite languages, music. It was not just any music. It was the music he had grown up with and always loved. When the pretty old ladies said the names of some of the creators of the music, Mace realized that he had records by those artists. He kept his ear to the conversation as he enjoyed his medium-rare fillet mignon. One of the ladies accompanying Betty and Tildy spoke.

"What did you say the name of the place is?"

"It's called The Blue Parrott."

Her girlfriend spoke next, "Where is it located?"

"Eighty-Five Corey Circle," Betty said, "almost right under the Corey Causeway Bridge. It's only a few feet from the water. I saw a big saxophone-player warming up under the bridge. It was cool."

Mace thought that the ladies seemed younger and more beautiful as they talked about this wonderful spot. He had never been to the Blue Parrott, but he remembered that before it was the Blue Parrott, it was a girlie joint whose name he could not remember.

"Don't forget, Patricia and Mary Ann, they play every Monday night from seven till nine thirty." It was Tildy's dulcet voice. "I think it would be best to make a reservation. The place was packed."

Mace had all the information he needed. Next Monday night at six, he would have dinner at the Blue Parrot, then stay to enjoy the music.

*****

The next few days passed quickly for Mace because there were a plethora of things to do in retirement. This week, he chose to concentrate on painting. He painted from his memory, his imagination, and his heart. What transferred from brush to canvas on a given day was anybody's guess. He had moved far beyond his mother's obsession with seascapes. At this point in life, he was wildly eclectic in style and content. Mace thought of painting as his silent music. The brush was his instrument. Each dollop, dab, swirl, line was his sixteenth or eighth, quarter or whole notes. Connecting lines were slurs, each one moving the piece through itself to the finale. Once completed and seen its entirety, he could almost hear real notes that leaped from the canvas.

*****

Monday night, Mace dressed informally in basic Florida style. He wore a bright yellow Hawaiian shirt, featuring stunning blue parrots. His black shorts were a perfect complement to his shirt. He looked like a blond Tom Selleck without the mustache, but his exposed body parts reminded onlookers of Arnold Schwarzenegger. No one in St. Pete looked better in a short-sleeve Hawaiian shirt and shorts than Mace Stutzman. He was not trying to attract attention. He simply wore what he loved: birds, color, flowers. At the Blue Parrott, he wanted anonymity and to relax.

Once the music began, Mace sat quietly, speaking only to his middle-aged waitress, Patty. When he had to use the restroom at about 7:30 p.m., he enjoyed a moment of rare humor. He noticed the ladies from a few days ago from Guy Harvey's. They were eating dinner.

"Hello, Betty, Tildy, Mary Ann, Patricia." He nodded to each lady as he spoke her name. He stayed long enough to see the look of shock on their faces, then ducked away to the bathroom.

"Who the heck is that?" Tildy said.

"I don't know," Betty answered, "but he seems vaguely familiar."

"I don't either," Mary Ann said. "I sure would like to know who he is. He's one handsome fella, don't you agree?"

Her three friends concurred, all smiling. Meanwhile, Mace had a wry smile on his face. *No memory problems here*, he thought. He was amused with himself. Oddly, his moment of humor moved him into a rare happy space for a couple of minutes. Add that to the feeling he had that the orchestra was over the top in their performances of the three songs he had heard, and Mace was suddenly in a pretty-good space. When he returned from the bathroom, the orchestra was playing "The Shadow of Your Smile" as a Bossa Nova. As he passed the table with the four ladies he had surprised earlier, Tildy spoke up.

"Excuse me, young man, but how do you know us?"

He was expecting that question from one of them. Before he answered, he could not help but notice how beautiful Tildy's gray-and-white hair was, cascading with a light curl, beyond the midpoint of her back.

*Seventy-five and still beautiful,* he mused.

"I sat next to you a few nights ago at Guy Harvey's. I overheard your conversation about this place, and I memorized your names in case I saw you again. You and Betty are the reasons I'm here."

"Young man, is it fair that I inquire as to your name?"

She was elegant.

"It's Mace, just Mace."

Betty chimed in quickly. "Do you dance, Mace?"

"I do not, Betty. That is one activity I have never participated in, and I probably never will."

"That is a shame," Tildy said sincerely.

For a moment Mace thought about how pleasant it might be to dance with Tildy. Though a quarter of a century older than he, Tildy was a stunningly beautiful woman. Then he flashed back to his own mother. Elise would have been about seventy. He wondered how beautiful she might look at this age. Betty broke his reverie.

"Between the four of us, I'm sure we could teach you to dance."

"Thank you, Betty, but I'm only here for the music. Have a great evening, ladies."

He was off to his table on the opposite end of the open-air room. On the way to his table, he thought that he could have said yes to being taught how to dance. It might have been fun, that elusive word he had dreamed about having, his whole life. "Night Train," by Jimmie Forrest, disrupted his thoughts. Over the next hour and a half, the music took him back over forty years, to the days when he and Willie listened to records on the old victrola.

At 8:30 p.m., Gershwin's Summertime was the featured song. Mace quietly mouthed every memorized word to himself. He closed his eyes for a moment and enjoyed the arrangement. When he opened his eyes again, he could not comprehend what he was seeing. Across him, about six feet from Tildy, stood an extremely tall black man, dressed completely in black except for a brown vest. Atop his head rested a cool-looking black felt hat. Mace's breathing became labored. His heartbeat increased substantially. Fight or flight activated inside him. In fact, it was far beyond the feeling of fight. It was kill. The sounds of the orchestra dissipated into a soundless dimension, as Mace tried to wipe the look of hate from his face and return to a more neutral persona.

Before him loomed Alonzo Johnson, dressed to wow! He looked dashing in his silence and demeanor. He looked like a movie star, towering over all the other men standing or dancing in the room. His beautiful eyes were scanning. For what, Mace was not sure. Was he looking for trouble? If so, why here? He certainly was not dressed for trouble. The son of a bitch was relaxing. The brutal murderer of his friends and countless other men was cooling it at the Blue Parrot.

Mace took a swig of his iced tea. His mouth had become a dessert. After the tea went down, Mace realized that Alonzo's presence there was something, about which he could do nothing. He decided to observe Alonzo, catalog his every move, thinking that maybe someday he could use those moves against him. Five minutes later, he almost snapped when he saw Alonzo escort his first partner to the dance floor. She was a gorgeous, tall brunet, forty-five, great figure, and no matter what her past might have been, she still looked wholesome. *What is she doing with Alonzo?* he thought.

He wanted to kill Alonzo right here, right now. He wondered if this was the kind of snap and rage Dr. Franklin explained to him at Bayfront. He knew he could take down Alonzo, no matter how tall and strong he was. His hands suddenly ached to strangle the big black stud. Mace watched the couple dance, They seemed affectionate with one another, maybe friends. "When I Fall in Love," the old Nat King Cole song, was playing. The woman wore a wide smile and looked utterly lovely, as Alonzo spun her. There their dancing was fluid and alluring, watching it made Mace nauseated. He did care that Alonzo was projecting a gentlemanly facade, punctuated with suaveness and savoir faire. Mace knew the depth of Alonzo's murderous tendencies.

For the rest of the evening, Alonzo chose a new partner for every dance. He even danced with Tildy, Betty, Mary Ann, and Patricia. When he danced with Tildy, the sickening feeling in Mace's stomach worsened. He felt unusually protective of Tildy, for reasons he could not identify.

"Slow it down, Mace. If Alonzo can be cool, you can too. Breathe, look away, focus on the orchestra, the musicians, how good they are."

The next time Mace looked around the room, he saw Alonzo dancing with a four-foot-ten-inch eighty-year-old woman that Mace thought was downright ugly.

*How nice of the son of a bitch to spread his dance choices to women of all shapes, heights ages, and looks,* he thought mockingly.

The last song "A Foggy Day" ended, and the room emptied quickly, as the musicians began to pack away their instruments and equipment. Mace watched Alonzo leave the building among a swift-moving group of music and dance lovers. Mace remained at his table for several minutes until his waitress brought the bill. After he paid up, Mace made a couple of decisions. He would not kill Alonzo at this amazing venue or anywhere near it. He would also keep coming to the Blue Parrot any damn Monday night he wanted, even if evil incarnate frequented the place disguised as a gentleman dancer.

# CHAPTER 35

When Mace arrived home that first night at the Blue Parrot, he painted his feelings into a new painting. He began it at 10:30 p.m. and completed it at ten minutes to 4:00 a.m. The theme did not matter to him. What did was that he expressed what he was feeling in the moment, completely. This had become his pattern in recent months. He did care what topic he painted; he was painting anything that came into his mind. He only wanted to pour his feelings into whatever picture appeared on the canvas. He had no one to pour out his feelings to, verbally. Painting was the next best thing.

Mace went to the Blue Parrot each Monday for the next several weeks. Each time he went, he saw Alonzo. One time, they met in the restroom. Alonzo was pleasant there too.

"How you doin', man?" Alonzo had asked.

Mace, not willing to reveal the tiniest bit of his disdain for Alonzo, simply replied, "Doin' fine, man. How are you?"

Mace learned to control his temper and focus on the music, the musicians, and all the interesting characters that frequented the venue. In the weeks he attended the Blue Parrot, Mace never saw Alonzo do anything untoward. In public, the former wrestler was a pleasant dance partner and customer. Mace learned why the rumors about Alonzo's smoothness were so prevalent among the detectives. Alonzo was the epitome of smooth.

Life had so much more to offer the ex-cop besides the Blue Parrot. He still was into his many hobbies: his running, swimming, workouts. Painting was where he spent most of his time. He developed a habit of watching Stephen Colbert's monologue, then beginning to paint at about midnight. The next four hours would pass peacefully, like the blink of an eye. At five minutes to four, the systematic Mace cleaned his brushes. At four, he hit the sack and slept soundly until 11:00 a.m. His alarm clock would go off to the music of 89.1 F.M. He would spring out of bed, shower, shave, make breakfast and eat, all while listening to and watching his, cannot miss, *The Price Is Right*. Though Mace did not engage people very often, he enjoyed observing humanity always. He did not feel isolated from people. He merely wanted to limit the number of interactions he had with them. Though Mace had experienced thousands of interactions with people in his two decades as a police officer, in his personal life, at age fifty-one, he was intrinsically and profoundly shy.

One of Mace's favorite things to do was to take himself out to dinner. He always treated his waiters and waitresses with respect. The nicer they were to him, the kinder and more generous he was with them. Mace had so much money in the bank and in solid investments, with nobody to leave it to, why not give a tiny chunk of it to good people who worked hard for their money? Besides, many of these people became his "almost friends," like the staff at David Reynolds.

On May 2, 2017, while walking through Tyrone Mall after buying a pair of tennis shoes, Mace decided to have an early dinner. Choosing Chinese food from among the ten or so choices of foods in the food court, he scanned the seating area for a quiet place to eat. The table he chose was farther away from any other where someone was sitting. It was the perfect spot for the quiet watcher.

A third of the way through his tasty chop suey, his peace was disturbed by two tall, thin young black men. It was the amount of their profanity and their decibel level that upset him. He almost picked up his tray and moved to the farthest part of the dining room. He decided to stay put, not wanting to create a scene. The moment became worse when the two foul-mouthed men decided to sit at the table nearest to him, not six feet away. He did not want to hear their conversation, but their loudness made that impossible.

"They're all white trash. I don't care what their jobs are. They're all white trash."

"The big shots act so cool in their big shot careers, but they come into our house and they're all greasy and sweaty and nervous. They're total wrecks."

The man who made the last statement was still dealing with a serious case of acne even though he must have been about twenty-three.

"White trash, dumbass honkies," the other guy, who sported orange hair and three gold teeth, added."

"They're all such easy pickin's."

"Like fucking ducks in a shooting gallery."

"I wouldn't spend the money I make, buying the shit we sell. That stuff will kill you."

"No, you spend it on gold teeth and orange hair."

"Shut the fuck up, Ronnie," orange hair said.

"Baboon butt hair," Ronnie fired back.

"That's funny, dumbass. You come up with the weirdest shit. You always make me laugh."

Mace saw that they were good friends when they laughed off the insults. Even Mace thought Ronnie's comments were funny.

"I'm serious about those druggies, man. When they first come to us, they are all handsome and pretty, nice bodies, but a few months later, they're all skinny, greasy ugly, pitiful nervous wrecks."

"And sometimes they die," Ronnie said.

"I like it when they do," orange hair, gold teeth spurted, hatefully.

"Why, it costs us money?"

"I don't care about that. Whitey just keeps comin' in waves. They never stop."

"Thank God, man. They hate us for everything else, but they come for crack and meth. They're willing to risk everything for that shit."

There was no trace of the humor Ronnie expressed a moment earlier. His true self was about to come out.

"I don't care if they die either. One by one or in clusters. It don't matter to me. They all need to die anyway." He paused for a second.

"Except for good-looking white chicks. I can always find something for them to do."

Mace's anger was heating up quickly. He had never used someone for sexual purposes, and he did not like Ronnie's implication. Both men were loud and vexatious. It seemed as if they wanted everyone within earshot to hear the venom they were spewing. Orange hair spoke again.

"They're all so stupid."

"Yeah, they are, Lavan. Beyond stupid. If they die, they bring it on themselves. No one forces anybody to come into our neighborhood."

Now Mace had two first names to memorize.

"You got that right, Ronnie. If they didn't come into the hood, we would be bankrupt. We'd have to rob stores and shit and shoot some people while we're doing that."

"We're lucky we have a great boss too. Look how he pulled off that ambush of the two white cops. That was brilliant, man. A couple of those a year and that'll really keep the cops off our backs."

Mace had heard something that ripped his guts apart. His heart broke when it was bombarded by thoughts of his dear friends: Pete, Ellis, and Bobby. Their lives were so carelessly disregarded by these thugs in front of him.

"I wish I could have been there," Ronnie continued. "Then you would have been dead."

"Maybe, maybe not," Ronnie said sarcastically.

"If it had not been for that one prick cop, all our guys would have made it out of there. It only takes one to spoil the fun for everyone else."

*Fun?* Mace thought, *If this guy has not killed already, he will certainly evolve to becoming a killer someday.*

"I'd like to find that tough cop myself and put one through his skull," Lavan said seriously. "I could make some big points with Alonzo. It would be in all the newspapers and on TV too."

"Good luck finding him, Lavan. And if you do, you' better remember, he's one bad motherfucker."

*I'm right here, dumbasses*, Mace thought. *Come and get me if you want.*

Mace was rightfully confident he could beat down the two men right now, but he would never reveal himself and precipitate a riotous scene. Now that he knew what was in these young men's hearts and minds, he realized they did not deserve to live. Whether it was brain chemistry, hatred, or the raw desire to make the planet a better place, Mace felt that it was now his responsibility to eradicate these two men from the planet. Considering what he had heard, Mace would not allow himself to be hunted. He was not a wild boar in the woods. He would be the hunter.

Mace listened to the two men for several more minutes. Their words were a continual litany of hatred for Whitey, their love of money, pursuit of white chicks, and their disgust for cops of all colors. Time and again, the same topics emerged, in an endless revolving loop. There was a little talk of the Tampa Bay Rays.

*So what if they're Rays fans. That is not a free pass to live*, Mace thought.

At the end of the thugs' meals, Mace heard Ronnie say, "Let's go talk to those white girls."

"I was thinking the same thing myself," Lavan said.

They pushed their chairs back, left their dirty trays, plates, and utensils on the table, and walked toward the girls. Mace raised his head and saw two adorable young girls sitting at a table about twenty feet from the guys. They wore pretty white sundresses with Florida designs, beach chairs, palm trees, pelicans, and flamingoes on them. They could not have been a day over sixteen, and both had blond hair that tumbled to their midback. They could have been sisters, fraternal twins even. They were beautiful and looked totally innocent and unequivocally wholesome.

When the young men approached the girls, they pulled out the two empty chairs and sat down, uninvited. To Mace's surprise, within a couple of minutes, the four young people were chatting up nicely. There was laughter at the table, and Mace could see the foursome pairing up. Their conversation lasted no more than ten minutes before the new acquaintances left the table for the heart of the mall. Mace noticed that the girls bussed their trash. Lavan said, loudly enough for the whole room to hear, "Leave that shit there, Karen." The petite debutante looked surprised for a second, maybe embarrassed, but she continued cleaning her portion of the table. Then she carried the slight mess to the wood-enclosed garbage can with the tray return on top.

Mace did the same cleaning as the young girls, then followed them into the mall, trying to be as stealth as possible. He wanted to follow the young men to their car so he could memorize their license plate numbers. The small group stepped into a couple of stores, but Mace was able to continue to follow them, by ducking into stores nearly directly across the youths. Finally, the odd-looking quartet, with both guys nearly a foot taller than each girl, exited the mall at Red Robbins.

Mace waited for them to get a small lead before going to the exit doors and watching them head for a specific vehicle. When Mace saw the young gangsters step into a brand-new black Cadillac Escalade, he went out the exit door. He walked quickly so he could read the plate before the impressive vehicle drove off. He made himself as inconspicuous as possible, and he read the plate in one long look. He was simultaneously making it look like he was looking for his own car.

Unfortunately, Mace saw something besides the license plate that made his stomach churn. It made him worry, more than he already was, about the girls' immediate and distant future. He worried about their parents' possible heartache. He worried about their fatherless children and how difficult it would be for biracial children to navigate through life. He pondered the pain the girls would endure if they did not continue their education.

Mace saw Lavan and Karen kissing. It was not a quick, little, shy peck on the lips. It was a long, no doubt, tongue-filled hold that lasted until the Escalade was out of sight. Mace's fatherly instincts were in full gear as he wished he could pull Lavan and Ronnie out of that black beauty and knock them out with one punch each.

"I hope you're happy right now, boys, because I'm not."

Mace did not have the opportunity to punch Lavan and Ronnie out this day, but he looked forward to the day he would be able to knock them out forever.

# CHAPTER 36

The next day, Mace took a ride in Princess to find out the registered owner of the Cadillac Escalade. At headquarters, he called upon an old friend for a favor. His buddy pointed to the equipment he needed. It was an easy task that Mace had performed scores of times. That friend and a few other cops and staff enjoyed seeing the shy, retired officer, if only for a moment.

The SUV was registered to Ronnie Spence, of 2915 Third Avenue South. That was the most important information Mace wanted. But as soon as he got that, he became interested in Spence's rap sheet. He was not surprised to see its length. Spence's life was littered with arrests, dating back to age thirteen. It started with three petty thefts, followed by grand theft auto, possession of and distributing drugs. Most recently were three assault charges. One was for pulling a tech wizard from his car and pummeling him during a drug deal. A second was for punching his girlfriend squarely in the face and knocking a tooth out. For the third assault, Spence had chosen to slug his landlord, who had come to collect the rent.

There was little doubt in Mace's mind that Spence had the money to pay the rent. He was just too lazy or annoyed when the landlord disturbed him. Mace hoped that he could eradicate Spence before he graduated to murder.

Since Mace had never killed a civilian, his next few weeks were a complex time of figuring out how to do it and not get caught. First, he bought an old black Toyota in Gulfport for $500. He did not expect the car to last a long time, just long enough for him to eradicate his targets, then work his way up to Demarkus and Alonzo. He wanted that car to be totally nondescript. He wanted it to be as much a ghost as possible. He wanted to drive through bad neighborhoods and rotten men and attract no attention. He wanted to park it and watch what the thugs were doing a block away.

Next, he had to figure out how to kill Ronnie Spence. Not wanting to shoot a gun again, he settled on garroting. It was quite by accident that he decided that. While jogging in the alley on Pass-a-Grille one afternoon, he spotted a piece of wire next to a garbage can. It was not anything special, simply perfect for the purpose of taking out Spence. He picked it up, put it in his pocket, and brought it home.

The most difficult part of Mace's self-imposed task was the actual stalking of his prey. For parts of the next twenty-seven days, Mace kept track of Spence's comings and goings. After he felt he had tracked enough, Mace was convinced that he knew enough about Spence's nightly patterns, that he had figured out how and when he wound end him. Ronnie Spence had chosen to sell drugs on a street corner only three blocks from where he lived. He worked that corner Tuesday through Saturday, like a real job, with real hours. It was in front of Leon's Bar. Yes, the street corner was still open for nefarious business. Watching Spence go there every night to sell drugs was heartbreaking and angering for the quiet retiree. Though he still did not remember the Fairfax massacre, he knew it had happened there, and he would never forget that he had been told that his three dearest friends had died there. When he pondered how two of those friends died in a downpour of bullets, he could not wrap his head around it. The mere concept of it was impossible to endure. What unfathomable evil preceded the formation of that murderous plot? Ultimately, the source of that evil would have to be annihilated; but for now, Alonzo Johnson would have to wait. It would have to be Ronnie Spence, an infected arm of the beast.

Ronnie Spence's night always ended about a half hour before the black sky began to turn into a dark blue. This way, he would always be home before sunrise. Where he would die was determined when Mace saw a magnificent live oak in the far southwest corner of the neighbor's house, directly to the east of Spence's house. The enormous trunk was more than large enough to hide behind without anyone from the street or sidewalk being able to see a body standing behind it. The only danger of being seen was if the owners of the husky live oak were aroused and, for some reason, walked into the living room, opened the blinds, and looked outside.

After weeks of observing and careful planning, the morning of the execution arrived. At the appropriate time, Mace parked his old black invisible Toyota one block from the hater's house. Dressed entirely in black, he left the car door unlocked and walked to the beautiful live oak. He was not nervous. He was excited. Eradication of this nature was a joyful process. He had killed so many bad guys before. Why should this one be any different? As he pressed himself against the tree, he felt her energy and vitality soaring within her, from her deeply embedded roots to the base of her bough and upward beyond his body.

*What a quiet, noble life she has had growing and giving her oxygen to everyone around her*, Mace thought. "Too bad Ronnie didn't expand like the live oak. He would not be in the position he is in now. The world needs this tree much more than they need that dirtbag."

Mace peeked out from behind the tree. He had darkened his face with black shoe polish. With the black knit cap he was wearing, he nearly blended in with the tree and became invisible. He peeked from behind the oak. As expected, Spence was sauntering across Twenty-Ninth Street. Mace quickly memorized Spence's pace so he could time his attack. Mace listened through the hush of the night only for Spence's footsteps. It was only a moment later that Mace heard Spence's footsteps growing closer.

Spence's body completely passed the live oak, heading west. Without hesitation, Mace sprung forward like a jaguar with hands. In a swift, fluid movement, he raised the killing wire over Spence's head and crushed it into Spence's throat. The force he used pulling the wire while yanking it backward at the same time was the most force he had exerted for a single action in his lifetime. Instinctively, Mace raised his knee and placed it where Spence's sacrum met his coccyx. This gave Mace better leverage, and it would make death come quicker. After all, Mace did not want to hurt Spence. He wanted to kill him. The tall prey struggled only a little. The blitz attack, where metal met flesh, was so brutal that Spence's life ended almost immediately. He did not suffer. His life left him there on the sidewalk, with a piece of garbage wire around his neck and Mace's knee in his back.

When Mace was certain that Spence was out forever, he rifled his black-gloved hands through Spence's gray sweat-pants pocket. In the left pocket, he found a wad of currency. He snatched it out and put it into his right pocket. He removed the wire from Spence's neck and began walking toward the car, as if he were taking a carefree pre-dawn stroll. On the way home, he turned right on Forty-Third Street off First Avenue. A moment later, he turned left into the alley at Third Avenue South. He turned off his headlights while making sure that all the nearby houses were dark and looked for a random garbage can suitable for his purposes. When he found one, he stopped the inconspicuous Toyota beside it. He exited the car and took the killing wire out of his money-laden pocket. With his still gloved hands, he opened the lid, then threw the wire into a mass of other garbage. Mace returned to the car and drove toward Pass-a-Grille.

Thirteen minutes later, he was home. He removed his clothes, pulled out the cash, and counted it. There was $670, mostly 10s and 20s. This made him happy. Finally, in death, Spence's money would contribute something wonderful to a segment of St. Pete's population that was in dire need. He tossed all his garments and his gloves into his outside garbage can and took an extralong shower. He turned off the alarm clock, and for one rare time, he did not care about watching *The Price Is Right*. He dried himself in the bathroom and hung up the wet towel. He walked into his bedroom, fell on top of the sheets, and for the next ten hours slept undisturbed, like a newborn baby.

# CHAPTER 37

For the next few days, Mace read the newspaper reports and watched Channel 10's coverage of Spence's murder as much as possible. Since Spence was a known gang member, the police jumped to the conclusion that the killing was gang and drug-related. They wondered why the killer used garroting. The only fact they had was they believed the killer to be strong and tall, for him to get the garrot over Spence's head and onto his neck. The killer had to be six feet two or taller. They also found a shoe print in the dirt, grass, and leaves near the live oak. The shoe size was 14, which helped the police to formulate the concept that the killer was six feet five, Mace's exact height.

Mace knew he made a big mistake leaving those shoeprints behind, but he did not care much. He guessed what the detectives would do with that information. They would go after all the known felons and gang members who fit that height estimate. Detectives would not compare a criminal's shoe print to Mace's. When Mace read in the paper that detectives had done exactly that, he took his boots and put them in a double Publix plastic bag and threw them into his garbage can on the patio.

*****

Exactly one week after killing Ronnie Spence, Mace took the $670 to the soup kitchen at Fourth Avenue North and Fourteenth Street. He asked for the manager by name, Bradley Walker, a selfless young man who poured his heart and soul into managing the soup kitchen and helping its clients. His master's degree in social work, master's in psychology, and five years of helping New York's indigent had landed him the St Pete job. He could not love the city of St. Pete or the clients he served, more. Walker, who preferred to be called Walk, had been on this job six years, and Mace had known him his entire tenure. This soup kitchen was Mace's favorite charity over the past ten years. Mace made a visit and donated a wad of money to Walk about once a month. The amounts of the donations ranged between five hundred and a thousand dollars.

Walk was not surprised to see Mace, but he was happy, as usual, to see him. The handsome brown-bearded manager would take Mace to his office, and the ex-cop would give him a wad of cash. Walk would count it, thank Mace, then put the money in a nearby safe. For the next five minutes, they shared the same conversation they always had. "How are you feeling?" "How's the soup kitchen doing?" "More money is needed to run the place." Talk about the local sports teams. "How is Princess running?" "She's great. She's right outside. Would you like to see her?" Sometimes Walk would go outside and gaze at the beautiful fully restored 1950 Chrysler Imperial. Whatever they talked about, it was small, routine, and swift.

Walk always ended their initial conversation with a variation of "Would you want to have some nice lunch or dinner?" depending on the time Mace had stopped by.

Mace enjoyed the dining part of his visits the most. He would sit at a table with a few homeless people who were already eating. He always sat quietly for a few moments, listening, observing. He would begin eating the sumptuous amount of food that was always served to him, and eventually, conversation would find him, and he would engage. Mace felt a kinship with people he met at the soup kitchen. He believed that most of the people in this room were here because they had been abused in childhood, by one or both parents or by somebody else. He could relate to a deep level of abuse. Elise had slit his little boy's heart apart with an endless array of insults, smacks, and spankings. If it had not been for Willie's love, he might have bled out emotionally and become a chronic depressive or worse. Though Mace was generally a man of few words, he saved most of them to share with the clients at the soup kitchen. He wanted to know everyone's story. What happened that broke them down piece by piece.

What was the final blow that severed them from living like a normal person in a house or apartment? He often asked them, "Where do you go from here?" He cataloged the hopelessness of their answers deep in his soul and genuinely felt their pain.

Mace felt comfortable here in this place of respite. Sometimes he would reach into his pocket and pull out three or four $50 bills and very carefully give them to people he thought it might help.

"Please do not tell anybody where you got this," he would always say. He figured that $200 or $300 would at least get someone or a couple at least two or three days at a decent hotel near downtown. There, they could relax, take a few long hot showers, watch some television, maybe even figure out a better path for their future. Mace even enjoyed talking with angry people, ones who seemed to like to start trouble. Almost anytime he talked with people who liked to bark at the moon, he quickly cut through their bullshit and got to the core of their emotional pain. He liked ugly faces. The worse it was, the more he sought it out and would sit at that table across it. The more lines, bruises, bumps, scars, sagging chins, and drooping cheeks, the better he liked it. Mace had the rare ability to see the depth of an ugly person's emotional pain from the instant he met them. He could immediately see how they had been shunned, excluded, teased, and ridiculed because their facial features were far beneath some acceptable societal norm. In the precious minutes he spent with them, he showed them his utmost courtesy and respect. In the hours he spent at the soup kitchen, Mace gave something deep, meaningful, and genteel to the clients he engaged. His gift was for their betterment.

This was the absolute contrast with the reactive, violent behavior he exhibited as a Marine, a cop, and in his current role as vigilante. His actions in these roles had caused the enemies he engaged their complete annihilation.

# CHAPTER 38

Tracking Lavan McCoy was almost the same as tracking Ronnie Spence. The Motley pair had been best friends. They hung out at the same restaurants, bars, and dance halls. They even asked Alonzo if they could have the same schedule and worksite. Alonzo granted both of their requests. Mace drove by the corner where both men stood most nights. Each time, he felt overwhelming anger and heartbreak. Now there was only one of the fated tandem standing on that corner next to Leon's bar. When the shy avenger saw him now, after pimple-faced Ronnie Spence was dead, orange hair Lavan was standing with a different buddy or two, waiting for druggies to drive into their hood to get high.

Lavan was no longer riding shotgun in his best friend's Escalade. He drove his own car, a partially restored 1961 Chevy Impala, the iconic white one with the red stripe.

*At least the two thugs had good taste in cars*, Mace thought. He wondered who would get their vehicles when they were dead.

Another thing that was different about tracking Lavan was where he hung his hoodie at night. Ironically, his house was only four blocks from Ronnie Spence's. He lived at 2604 Fourth Avenue South. It was a dark street. Lavan parked his Impala on Twenty-Sixth Street so he could keep his eye on it from his bedroom window. The '61 had a cool security system, with a state-of-the-art tracking device. Lavan loved the car and enjoyed looking at it several times a night.

Finally, tracking Lavan was different from Spence because Mace had seen him with a girlfriend three times. Each time, the girl was Karen, the beautiful little underage darling from Tyrone Mall. Each time Mace saw them together, it made him livid, especially when the couple spent hours together at Lavan's modest house.

*I wonder if her parents know what she's up to these days,* he wondered repeatedly. *Or if she even has parents? How could she make the choice to be with this guy and so quickly?* He wondered how much Karen would grieve Lavan's imminent murder. He was unequivocally convinced that she would be much better without him. One day while thinking about her, another thought came into his head that would not leave.

*I wonder if she is an abused child, and this is her way of acting out.* Whatever it was, Mace was going to end it.

\*\*\*\*\*

Figuring out the proper method of execution for Lavan was challenging for Mace. He debated whether to hurt Lavan severely before finishing him off or killing him quickly and efficiently. His heart yearned to hurt Lavan as much as he could. His logical mind told him not to give the kid any chance of hurting him while he was fighting for his life. Mace did not want Lavan to yell or scream after the initial assault. He finally decided that the execution had to be devastating and immediate.

The how came to him one evening while running on the sand on Pass-a-Grille. A family had left behind a metal spoon, half buried, among other unsightly amounts of their trash. Mace bent down, grabbed the spoon, and put it in his pocket. He picked up most of the other garbage and tossed it into a nearby trash can. He rinsed his hands in the showers south of the snack shack, then ran the last two blocks to his house at the end of the boardwalk.

When he went into the house, Mace immediately washed the spoon in antibacterial soap and hot water. How nicely the trough part of the spoon fit into his right hand. Some cutting and filing on the other end and the spoon would become the perfect weapon with the perfect piercing point.

In a couple of days, the spoon was ready, and so was Mace to use it. He killed Lavan at 5:43 a.m. on a nondescript Tuesday morning during a steady drizzle. He timed his walk down Fourth Avenue South till just before Lavan turned to open his front gate. Lavan felt a swiftly moving presence approaching from his right. Though he thought for a moment that he did not have any enemies, an oncoming fear made him turn and speak to the oncoming man.

"Yo, bro," he said meaningfully.

"Yo," Mace returned, his right hand holding the spoon in his pocket.

Lavan turned toward the gate's latch, his final thoughts whizzing through his mind.

"That motherfucker is large."

Fear welled up within Lavan as Mace pulled out the murder weapon and plunged it deep into the base of his target's neck. The spoon-dagger cracked through the skull, the brainstem and into the cerebellum, the body's balance, and fine motor control center. Lavan dropped near fatally, to the ground, with the killing tool stuck into his neck. His arms flailed, trying to pull the metal out, but they could not do it.

Mace did it for him. He forcefully flipped Lavan onto his back and embedded his weapon deep into Lavan's heart. Breathing ceased, and eyes froze open in a gaze of terror.

Mace rifled through Lavan's pockets and found a wad in the right pocket of his jeans. He put the money in the left pocket of his hoodie, pulled the spoon out, and put it in his right pocket. He quickly rose and headed back up the street to his scruffy Toyota. A few minutes later, he threw the bloody spoon deep in the same garbage can, in the same dark quiet alley as he had dropped the garroting wire.

Mace was excited that in a few days, he would be able to make another donation to the soup kitchen, this time on Lavan's unspoken behalf. Though happy about that, he felt himself withdrawing more and more, into a secret place. The world was a harsh place for him, and he had terrible work left to do. He wanted the killings to be over so he could live the rest of his life without the copious amount of vengeance he still held in his heart. Words to most people would be few. He made exceptions for his "almost friends" and the needy at the soup kitchen.

When he got home, Mace put every article of his clothing, including his relatively new boots, into a large Hefty trash bag. They were full of blood and bad memories. He put the Hefty bag into his patio garbage can the day before his little city's next pick up. He showered heartily, dried off, and walked nakedly into his small old bedroom, which was cluttered with paintings of his true feelings. He, once again, fell on top of the sheets, a whisper emanating from the fan above him. As his head hit the pillow, he longed for true companionship. He wondered what true love looked like, knowing intimately about hate. In the one dream he remembered the next afternoon, after ten hours of uninterrupted sleep, he was Michael the Archangel, and God was thanking him for his avenging.

# CHAPTER 39

The world was becoming a dark foreboding place for Mace as he retreated into himself while pondering how to eliminate Alonzo's cousin DeMarkus. The two young men, Lavan and Ronnie, had been easy kills. DeMarkus was a high-profile person, who sometimes traveled with a bodyguard or two, or a woman or two. After weeks of carefully stalking DeMarkus, an exhausted Mace decided that the best way to take him out was to catch him after a rendezvous when he was vulnerable and relaxed.

Mace developed tunnel vision during his quest to eliminate DeMarkus. His interest in his beloved hobbies, except staying strong and painting, disappeared. Painting, he needed desperately. He had no other way to express his deepest feelings. Art was no longer a hobby. During these bleak days, painting was an absolute necessity, an overwhelming urge. It was almost like breathing. Day after day, empty spaces in the house became filled with Mace art of all shapes, sizes, and themes.

The problem Mace was having was how to eradicate DeMarkus. *How could a man develop the construct to kill two innocent cops in a hail of bullets?* Mace pondered every day. Hate for DeMarkus burrowed further into the ethereal space inside his consciousness and grew like cancer cells. Before he ended the cop killer's life, Mace concluded that he had become nothing more than a killing machine. He despised the process that was happening to him as much as he despised the young men whose lives he had taken. The Mace he used to know and accept was disappearing. He wished he could become an invisible man, unseen by anyone, because shame and remorse for his murderous ways had moved into the same compacted compartment as his hatred. Mace Stutzman was a disturbed powder keg, ready to explode.

"I want to strangle him," Mace repeated in his thoughts. "I want to put my hands around his neck and squeeze the life out of him. I want to glare into his dying eyes and tell him that Pete Laughlin, Ellis Wong, and Bobby Banner were my friends."

Strangulation was the choice. It had the personal touch.

Mace was so tightly wrapped before taking DeMarkus to his final destiny, that he had to do something to relax the intense feeling of being a human pressure cooker. He decided to go to the Blue Parrot. He knew the music would relax him. He spent the evening with his lifelong unmet friends: Cole Porter, Duke Ellington, Woody Herman, Count Bassey, and Glen Miller. Alonzo did not show up this night of R&R for Mace. A bunch of smiling faces did, however. Because of this combination of lovely faces and uplifting music, a tiny boarded-up window in Mace's psyche burst open, and an abundance of emotional sunshine flooded in. The previously pitch-black control center of Mace's maudlin moods filled with joy for the next two and a half hours. The warm feeling lingered for an hour after the music stopped until the darkness of the night reminded him that it would have to be about this time, he would have to kill DeMarkus.

*****

On the twenty-first grueling day of stalking DeMarkus, Mace followed his prey's 2017 Mercedes to the Jungle Prada on Park Street. The JP, as it was called, was a popular local bar, restaurant, and hangout. The staff and the owner were exceptionally friendly, and long ago, Al Capone was known to relax there.

After DeMarkus entered the JP, Mace parked the old Toyota about three hundred feet from the building and waited patiently for DeMarkus to come back out. An hour later, when he emerged, he walked almost directly toward Mace. The pursuer's heartbeat quickened. He scooted down in his seat. He wondered if this was going to be the end of him. If DeMarkus had a gun, Mace might be a dead man. The rarely vulnerable ex-cop did not bring a gun. DeMarkus did not walk to the Toyota. He walked a hundred fifty feet down the street to a wooden plank pier about 250 feet long, built over Tampa Bay. Once on it, he continued walking its full length, passing a couple of benches that faced south and a couple that faced north. The end of the pier was built like the head of a hammerhead shark. At that part of the structure, there were five benches, three about three feet from the edge and two a few feet behind them, between the spaces of the forward benches. If the pier had really been a hammerhead, it would have been swimming toward St. Pete Beach.

Mace straightened up in the seat and watched DeMarkus sit on the right bench of the front row. There were people occupying the other front-row benches. Mace got out of his junker and watched DeMarkus sit quietly for twenty minutes, as all the other people on the pier gradually left.

*How convenient it would be for me to walk out there and strangle that son of a bitch right now,* he thought, "if so many people had not already seen me. What I wouldn't give to follow him out there one night when no one's around," he mumbled to himself.

When DeMarkus stood to leave, Mace quickly left the pier, got into his Toyota, and drove as quickly as he could toward Pass-a-Grille, without attracting attention. There was no way DeMarkus could have "made" Mace or his beater.

*****

The drudgery of tracking someone as intensely as Mace was tracking DeMarkus made days interminably long and physically debilitating. The time constraints Mace placed on himself caused his workout and painting hours to be seriously reduced. What made it worse for Mace were the thousands of times he thought about DeMarkus living the high life and his friends rotting in their graves six feet beneath the autumn grass.

On the twenty-eighth day of tracking, Mace's efforts finally began paying dividends. At 10:00 p.m., he followed DeMarkus from a drug house on Nineteenth Avenue and Fourteenth Street South to the Jungle Prada. It was a Wednesday night, the same night of the week he had gone there last week. Even though DeMarkus had come to the JP only two Wednesdays in a row, Mace wondered if that might be a pattern. He was correct. Each of the next two Wednesdays, DeMarkus showed up a little past 10:00 p.m. He stopped in the restaurant and took a walk on the pier to relax. Both weeks either a relaxing couple or a lone fisherman thwarted efforts to assassinate DeMarkus.

It was not until the following week, a worn-out Mace saw DeMarkus pull into the parking lot at 10:17 p.m. He walked right to the restaurant and bar and did not emerge until almost midnight. Again, he walked straight for the pier. This time, it was empty and utterly silent. Above them both, hauntingly beautiful clouds were doing their best to hide a bright half-moon. DeMarkus was stumbling. It was obvious to Mace that he had drunk too much. Mace knew he would have no fight in him. DeMarkus was almost asleep as Mace came up behind him, quietly. He offered no initial resistance as Mace slapped a devastating chokehold on him and began crushing. DeMarkus roused from his reverie in a desperate panic. He flailed his arms in an instinctive attempt to break the lock that had beset him.

"I'm killing you because you killed my friends on Fairfax. Do you remember that asshole!"

Of course, DeMarkus could not answer. It was Mace's long-awaited moment to terrorize the terrorist. Mace and DeMarkus could hear tiny bones breaking in the dying man's neck as Mace continued speaking.

"You never gave Ellis Wong and Pete Laughlin and Bobby Banner a chance." Mace had wanted to tell the executed man these things eye to eye, but his blitz attack from the rear robbed him of the pleasure seeing the horror on the gangster's face.

That was it for Mace's speech. He said what he wanted to say, and it was over. Mace concentrated on completing the business at hand as quickly and efficiently as possible. Mace denied DeMarkus his final breath. Once the executioner's enormous arms wrapped themselves around his victim's neck, not a molecule of oxygen would be able to get in or out. DeMarkus died without fanfare when his arms and legs stopped flailing and his body slumped. Mace knew there was nothing left of him but a corpse. He did not check for a pulse. The man before him was a broken shell. He lifted from his knee, removed the wallet from the pants pocket, and began walking toward his car. DeMarkus remained, appearing to be asleep. There was no one around, and the moon was still hidden behind the clouds. For a moment, everything seemed right. He got into his little nothing car, turned right onto Park Street, and headed for his beloved Pass-a-Grille. He drove slowly, feeling peaceful and satisfied. Justice had been dispensed.

# CHAPTER 40

After DeMarkus's body was found by a fisherman at 5:00 a.m., the local TV and radio stations were all over it. Since the corpse was found so late in the morning, the newspaper could only get a reporter to the scene but not get the story immediately into print. The broadcast media jumped on it with as much detail and depth as possible. Nobody in St. Pete, outside Alonzo's army, could prove that DeMarkus was second-in-command of the organization, but when Chief Garrett and the St. Pete police officers heard the news, they were almost celebratory.

Who killed DeMarkus James, was the question of the day around town. Was it someone from within Alonzo's army, or was it someone from the outside trying to make a move to the inside? Was it Alonzo? Nobody could get closer to DeMarkus than Alonzo. Had the cousins fallen out and had Alonzo taken care of business at the end of a quiet pier? Was it a random mugging? No wallet had been found. Was it a professional hit made to look like a mugging?

These questions and a multitude more filled the airwaves and minds of the greater St. Pete viewing and listening area. The good thing for Mace was that there were no immediate answers forthcoming to these questions. And there never would be.

\*\*\*\*\*

Unfortunately for him, Alonzo was the person about to suffer the most because of his cousin's murder. The police, knowing his daily routine well, arrested him at his restaurant in the early afternoon in his office. They arrested him for murder in the first degree.

They marched him through the kitchen and the dining room and out the front door in handcuffs, in front of his cherished staff and customers. Alonzo, who genuinely believed he was slick and a gentleman, was mortified and visibly shaken as he was pushed into the police car. He could never have imagined this happening. This was not part of his overall life plan. Someone had murdered DeMarkus. He wondered if he might be next. His bewilderment was the first seed of paranoia that took root in his soul and psyche. Within five minutes of the police bursting into his office, Alonzo's nerves and emotions were irreversibly damaged.

\*\*\*\*\*

Mace woke rested when his alarm clock went off at 10:55 a.m. He sprang from bed, made a beeline for the kitchen, poured himself a large glass of orange juice, and plopped down on the couch. He grabbed the remote, turned on *The Price Is Right*, and began thinking about how he would kill Alonzo. His first several ideations were pure fantasy, but about the time of the first spin-off, he had an idea that intrigued him.

"How about wrestling him for his life?"

Both men had been great wrestlers when they were young. Now Mace wondered if he could pin Alonzo now.

*I wonder if he's in good shape from all that dancing?* he thought with a laugh. *He's got a flat stomach under all those pretty shirts he wears. I wonder if he's got a six-pack like mine,* he thought with a sense of pride for his abdominals.

During the next commercial, Mace gathered every stitch of clothing from the night before, walked to the patio, and threw them away in the big black trash bin. Then he counted the money in DeMarkus's wallet. It was only $280. Within a week, he would take that money to the halfway house, augment it with a chunk of his own cash, and give it to people who were in dire need of it. Doing that made him feel like Robin Hood.

The fast-moving game show moved quickly to Mace's favorite part. It made him ecstatic to see a feisty seventy win a patio set, a trip to Lima Peru, and a brand-new car. All totaled she won $43,437 worth of cash and prizes. Mace thought it odd that he could feel such happiness for a stranger's success. As soon as he heard that total, he walked to the fridge and pulled out all kinds of fixings to make himself a big breakfast.

Three minutes later, Channel 10 news led with the discovery of DeMarkus's James corpse on the Jungle Prada pier. Mace walked back into the living room, grabbed the remote, and turned the TV off. He knew the story better than anybody. He did not have to hear what Channel 10 had to say about it. After breakfast, he spent most of the day painting, listening to music, and napping. At the end of the day, he lifted weights on the back patio for an hour, took a six-mile sunset run, and capped it off with a fillet mignon at Outback Steakhouse.

***** 

A few miles away, in downtown St. Pete, Alonzo was not having a relaxing day. He was stuck in a claustrophobia-inducing room with a chair on both ends of a metal table and two crusty veteran detectives. He had been interviewed many times, over the years, by James Glade and Robert Stone, the longest-tenured and partnered pair in the department. They were also the best detectives.

James Glade, fifty-six, was a native of St. Petersburg. He was six feet three and a solid 210 pounds. He had been married to the same pretty woman for thirty-five years and had three adult children. He had a master's degree in criminology from Florida State and joined the police force at the age of twenty-six. He was a handsome, well-mannered gentleman, who had an intellectual way of questioning his suspects. He was patient and logical. In the good cop / bad cop scenario that partners often utilize, Glade was always the good cop.

Stone was the bad cop in the interrogation room, but beneath that facade, he was a feisty and fun person.

His long partnership with Glade had lasted longer than his first two marriages and was on the verge of adding his third to that short list. Stone loved women, especially new ones with whom he had no commitments. He was six feet six, with Sean Connery's good looks, and his playful nature attracted women to him naturally. Eventually, his wives felt utterly neglected, due to his prolonged hours at work and his dalliances. In an interrogation room, he was at his intimidating best. Most of the time, he would play "antsy standing man" while Glade would calmly relax on his chair as "sitting man." He would walk around the room, an angry look on his face, walking uncomfortably close to a suspect. If he thought the person being questioned was being a smart-ass, he was not above smacking the guy on the back of his head. Occasionally, he would smack a suspect hard in the face to get to the truth. Three times in his career, he had punched a suspect in the gut, immediately before saying, "Have a seat." Those three times, he was almost certain the suspect had committed a serious crime.

On this day, they were being civil to the suspect. It was, after all, Alonzo, the larger-than-life criminal that had always treated them with respect, no matter why he was being questioned. Alonzo did not appear to be his normal cool self. He looked beaten and worn. Neither Glade nor Stone really believed that Alonzo had killed DeMarkus, but they had no choice but to question him. Perhaps they could catch their suspect in a flub up when they questioned him about his drug empire. Catch him now when he was down and out. After three hours of questioning, nothing of value to the detectives had emanated from his lips. He could have had a lawyer present, but he knew he had nothing to hide in relation to his cousin's murder. When asked about something other than the murder, his head dropped, and his eyes closed in unfeigned exhaustion. During these moments of personal examination, Alonzo began to see the seeds of paranoia growing into an ugly tree that was strangling his psyche. DeMarkus was so close to him, and he had just been murdered.

*Had he been stalked before someone crushed the bones in his neck?* Alonzo wondered during one of his quiet moments. *Am I being stalked? What about Lavan and Ronnie? Could their murders be connected? Was it multiple killers? Was it the same man? If it was, then what kind of monstrous thug must he be?*

Alonzo had a multitude of quiet moments during his interrogation by Glade and Stone on the day that DeMarkus died. There were times his voice was barely audible in the stark room. His mind, however, was a large manufacturing plant producing relentless questions about the three murders and his safety.

Eventually, Alonzo grew intolerant of the multitude of questions being put to him. At 7:10 p.m., he called for his lawyer to be present. When Herbert Wylie arrived, all five foot four and 133 pounds of him, he turned on his human dynamo powers and immediately commanded the respect that his personal strength and the law dictated.

"Unless you're going to charge my client, you have no legal grounds to keep him here!" he barked in a commanding voice that was larger than his size. "I wager you do not have a shred of evidence against Mr. Johnson. Therefore, it is quite an unfair leap to consider him a suspect merely because he is the victim's cousin." Wylie was chastising them.

"You're right, Wylie," Glade said softly. "Your client is free to leave." Then he more than doubled his decibel level and said, "Just make damn sure Mr. Johnson doesn't leave town for any reason, anytime soon." Glade felt better, having taken back some of the power of the law.

# CHAPTER 41

Ten days after killing DeMarkus, Mace returned to the Blue Parrot on a busy December Monday. He had not begun stalking Alonzo, but he figured that this was as good a venue as any, to begin. Mace arrived at the restaurant at 6:15 p.m. and was finished with a huge piece of meat loaf by the time the orchestra began the evening by playing Henry Mancini's Moon River. Alonzo arrived at his usual time, 8:00 p.m. He was dressed well and looked okay, but he was wearing sunglasses well after dark, and Mace wondered why.

*Did he have eye surgery? Does he have conjunctivitis? Could he still be grieving over his cousin's death? What else could it be? A new fashion statement?* Mace pondered these questions while Alonzo was suffering from a poor facial image. He had cried several times in the days following his cousin's murder.

Worse than that, he began to worry whether he was next in the sights of some grotesque killer. Finally, he became emotionally ravaged by the degree of critical comments the local news media was piling upon him. These painful stressors, plus having to plan for and burying DeMarkus yesterday, made their way into Alonzo's sleep patterns. A usual eight-hour sleeper, his normal time had been cut in half. While trying to sleep, his thoughts were filled with negativity. When he first heard that DeMarkus had been murdered, his stomach felt as though it had been struck by a thousand pellets from a shotgun blast. He felt palpable agony from that moment to this night at the Blue Parrot. When he awoke during the night, he attributed it to that torment. When he tried to return to sleep, his aching stomach made it almost impossible. His dreams were jostled like palm fronds in a hurricane. There was no place accessible to Alonzo to escape his unusual condition.

He did have one meaningful diversion. Her name was Kate Faraday. She was a fair-skinned white woman, intelligent, well-educated, and a banker by trade. In order to date Alonzo, a woman had to be beautiful by his standards. Kate exceeded those requirements.

She was beautiful by everyone's standards, model lovely. Her gait was lithesome and conveyed an innate sophistication. Most noticeable was her kindness, to everyone, without exception. Being near her was a joyful experience for Alonzo. They had met a couple of months earlier in Gulfport, at the Backfin Blue Café. Alonzo was there for the corn chowder. Kate was lunching on a rare weekday off. Kate spoke to Alonzo first.

"Sir, may I use your ketchup for my French fries?"

"You certainly may, ma'am, but I'm not sir. I'm Alonzo."

"Pleasure to meet you, Alonzo, and I'm not ma'am, I'm Kate."

He was so gentlemanly and articulate. She was beautiful to look at, and her long, thick, brushed curly red hair held his gaze. Her playfulness was charming. His strength and good looks were appealing. That is all it took. Introductions had been made, but more importantly, Fate bestowed its rare, elusive, and fickle spark into both people. That was the seal that brought them together, and each wondered how much fun it might be to pursue the attraction.

Much had happened to Alonzo since he met Kate. The worst was the loss of DeMarkus. That was followed by the consistent harassment by Detectives Glade and Stone. There was also the incessant deriding of him by the local media. These things combined to bring his emotions to the lowest ebb of his lifetime. His pride had been dashed. His swagger disappeared because before this shit befell him, he thought he was above it all. He considered himself invincible, as well as untouchable, a tall black superman. His recent suffering taught him that he was just as human and vulnerable as any other person, maybe more. He figured that the average schmuck did not know what it was like to be dragged through the mud by every broadcaster and newspaper columnist in the city. He knew that the average guy could find a place to get away from people and find refuge somewhere. He did not know where to go for solace, except to Kate. And he worried from moment to moment that he was being targeted to be murdered.

His thoughts became heavy and foreboding. His damaged ego and newly felt exhaustion caused his long upper body to bend forward. He began to look like a depressed man, carrying the weight of the world on his shoulders. He was alone tonight because Kate was out of town on one of her many business trips. He missed her, and the missing caused him more grief as he watched many in the crowd look away from him when he looked at them. When he spotted Mace, who was across the room at a back table, he made eye contact and touched his right index finger to the brim of his black felt cap. It was his way of saying, "Hi, buddy. Hi, Pal." He added a little smile to the gesture. Mace, in turn, gave a similar smile, raised his right index finger to his forehead, and brought it back down. It appeared to Alonzo that Mace was saying, "Hi, friend." These friendly sharing's occurred only after these two men had exchanged hellos in the Blue Parrot, one time. That was it, not counting the occasional eye contact they made at the restaurant.

Mace turned his head back toward the orchestra, which was playing a swing version of Duke Ellington's "I'm Beginning to See the Light" from 1944. He thought, *I wonder if wrestling Alonzo to the death would be a good idea? He is a big dude. He could tear me up.* Alonzo, the watcher, kept his eyes on Mace for several seconds. He could not help but wonder whether the quiet man who never danced was the stalker who would someday kill him. *He certainly has the size and strength to sneak up behind some unsuspecting soul and crush their neckbones to ash," he thought.* In that singular instant of conjecture, Alonzo came the closest that any human being ever would, to surmising that Mace could have killed DeMarkus. Then the thought was gone.

For the first time ever, among his Monday night visits to the Blue Parrot, Alonzo did not dance. Instead, he sat stooped forward on a backless barstool and waited for his better friends to give him condolences for his terrible loss. No one stopped by. As loud as the music was, Alonzo did not hear it. Instead, he listened to an unmelodious inner dirge that zapped the light from his eyes and warped his gregarious personality. By 9:00 p.m., he had experienced enough of the Blue Parrot and left. Mace let him go. He would start to stalk his already bruised and battered friend tomorrow.

# CHAPTER 42

Seven days after Mace began stalking in earnest, Alonzo's mother, Beatrice Johnson, had a serious stroke. Already living in the finest assisted living facility that drug money could buy, Beatrice was found on the living room floor of her apartment. When she did not show up for lunch one day, an orderly was dispatched to her quarters. Within minutes, she had been whisked from her rooms to an ambulance and was speeding toward Northside Hospital.

Mace was on his self-imposed stalking duty and was shocked to see Alonzo sprint from his house to his jeep on a Blue Parrot Monday afternoon. Mace was not the only one following Alonzo that day. There were two other vehicles that trailed Alonzo that day when he drove away in a frenzy. One was a Bay News 9 truck, and the other was a pretty woman in her new Lexis. Mace had no idea who she was, but she was a reporter for *The Times*. She was gathering info for a three-part story on Alonzo that she was planning to publish in three Sundays. Mace had no problem following the small convoy through light traffic, all the time wondering where they were going with such urgency.

When Mace and the others arrived at Northside, he was not surprised. He knew well about Beatrice Johnson, having read several articles about her and her relationship with Alonzo in *The Times*. He had also been briefed about her a few times, by the duty sergeant when he asked where Alonzo spent his free time. He was 100 percent convinced the convoy's brief excursion revolved around Beatrice when Alonzo ran as fast as he could from his parked jeep into the hospital.

A short time later, Alonzo was told by a doctor that his mother had suffered a severe stroke, but she was stable. Her outlook was grim due to her age and prior history of strokes. Alonzo felt like his physical heart was bleeding in his chest. This was in addition to his stomach pain, which was still dominating every aspect of his life. He called Kate for support, and thirty minutes later, she was at his side. Beatrice was Alonzo's number one girl. Of that, there was no doubt. But Kate was becoming securely entrenched in position number two.

Alonzo stayed with the mother he loved dearly, throughout the day and night. Kate stayed till 7:30 p.m., then apologized for having to go home, study some documents, and sleep well before another busy day. She was only forty-six but was at the apex of her career. Work had to come first, but she was also a one-man woman. Deeply personal behaviors had already occurred between them that convinced Kate that Alonzo was her man. Uncharacteristically, Alonzo wondered what it would be like to have Kate as his wife. He concluded it would be a joy to have her at his side. However, part of the pain in his stomach was caused by his worry about what Kate's cronies would think about her being with him. He also worried about what people in general would think if they saw him and Kate together, and they knew the nature of his business. Despite his worries, he fantasized about buying Kate a huge engagement ring and an even larger wedding ring at David Reynolds.

When Beatrice finally awoke at 10:14 p.m., Alonzo was slumbering in a chair on the right side of her bed. He was holding her tiny right hand between the bars of the hospital bed, with both of his huge hands. A guttural sound emerged from his mom as if she were trying to speak. It roused him, and he raised his head from his chest enough to make eye contact. Her face exuded a faint smile while her eyes expressed worry and fear. She shrugged her shoulders. Alonzo correctly interpreted her movement to mean, "What happened to me, and why am I here?"

"You had a stroke yesterday in your apartment, Mom, but no worry, the doctor told me you would recover real soon."

He softened the blow. He did not share with her the severity of the stroke, nor her vulnerability to more strokes in the future. He would not worry her more than she already was. He would speak no negativity to Beatrice. He would force himself to believe that his mom would recover and live for many years.

*****

The night before, Mace waited for Alonzo to emerge from the hospital till 10:18 p.m. When Alonzo did not appear, Mace drove to the nearest Taco Bell, ate some tasty food, and drove home. The next morning, Mace woke at 8:00 a.m. and stopped at the McDonald's near Northside. After he drove into the parking lot and saw Alonzo's jeep parked in the same spot, he ate breakfast. As soon as he realized Alonzo had spent the night, he felt sorry that Alonzo had to suffer through his mother's grave illness. He also felt compassion for Beatrice, that she was probably living through the aftermath of a fall, a heart attack, or a stroke. He knew Beatrice's story for many years, as well as that Alonzo doted on her.

*How can I have these feelings for someone I'm planning to kill?* Mace wondered.

Alonzo emerged from the front door of the hospital at 12:45 p.m. He was beat. He walked directly to the jeep and drove home with no side stops. The same small caravan as yesterday, followed him back to Snell Island. There, his followers waited while Alonzo showered, caught a few hours' sleep, and emerged, shaved, well-dressed, and looking refreshed at 6:30 p.m. He drove straight to the hospital, oblivious to the curious caravan that was stalking him. He certainly did not give a damn that they were dogging him. Comforting his mother was his only focus.

*All my other interests will have to take care of themselves till Mom gets better*, he thought, hopefully. Again, he spent the entire day and night in the hospital. Almost the entire time, he held his mother's right hand. Once he removed it to stand, greet her doctor, leave the room, and find out that Beatrice was doing remarkably better. His heart soared at the news. For a few minutes, he did not feel the painful pit in his stomach. He also released his mother's hand when Kate

325

arrived. He hugged Kate and, a few minutes later, accompanied her to the cafeteria.

"How is your mom, Alonzo?" Kate asked.

"The doctor says she is doing much better, thank God," Alonzo answered, honestly believing his spiritual reference.

"That's wonderful news, Alonzo. I'm so happy for you and your mom."

Kate thought about how strange it was to meet someone in Beatrice's condition. She also pondered the wonder of how love could grow quickly for a person who could not even speak but who was able to convey a heartfelt smile and warmth with her eyes. When they returned to the hospital room, Kate sat on the opposite side of the bed from Alonzo and held the left hand of Beatrice with her two dainty hands.

"We will give her as much energy this way as we possibly can, okay, Alonzo?"

Alonzo got it and softly said, "Okay, Kate." Holding his sleeping mother's hand, believing her condition was improving, and sitting near Kate's spiritual and physical beauty, vanquished the devastating pit in his stomach. For the next hour, he felt at peace. He did not worry about the press that was following him. He did not think about a stalker who wanted to kill him. For a rare time, he was mesmerized by the love that flowed from Kate to his mother, through her to him and back again, over and over.

When Beatrice awoke, her face reflected joy that her hands were being held.

"The doctor says you're getting better, Mom. Isn't that great news!"

Beatrice gave a wry smile and a soft head nod. For the next two hours, Kate and Alonzo said as many loving and encouraging things to Beatrice as they could create. Beatrice felt filled with more affection than ever before. Kate felt honored to be there. Watching Alonzo give so much love to his mother endeared him to her. She had no clue as to the depth of Alonzo's depravity. She also had no clue that these were the first times Alonzo had ever brought a woman to meet his mother. In her stroke-muddled mind, Beatrice hoped her

6 THE MAKING OF MACE STUTZMAN

son had finally found his eternal mate. When Alonzo watched Kate give his mother so much attention, she endeared herself to him to a degree he did not think possible.

Kate left the hospital about the same time as the night before. There were more documents to peruse and thinking and planning for the next day at work. Alonzo stood up and met Kate at the foot of the bed. There was no shyness as each of them walked into the other's arms. They hugged tenderly for an extended moment, wordlessly. Then they kissed with genuine affection as a tear formed in each of Beatrice's eyes.

"I'll call you before I go to bed," Kate whispered.

"I'd like that, Kate."

When Kate was gone, Alonzo returned to his chair and resumed his comforting hand-holding. Sometimes he spoke soothing phrases to his mother. Sometimes he snoozed when Beatrice snoozed. A few times during the night, Beatrice woke and tried her best to speak. Only unintelligible sounds emanated. Her face showed shame and sadness at her inability to verbalize. She shook her head a couple of times and closed her eyes, trying to hide from embarrassment.

"Don't worry, Mom. You'll be talking in a day or two. So what if you can't talk right now, Mom. You are still the prettiest lady I've ever seen."

Beatrice was pretty, except for that tiny droopy part of her mouth. She put way too much emphasis on that flaw, probably because she felt she could never sing in public with it again. She never sought the attention of a man, either. She could have, easily. In her forties, fifties, and sixties, she maintained a stunning figure— big breasts, a slim, perfect waist. In her seventies, she lost weight when she chose to eat only one light meal a day. Beatrice Johnson looked better at seventy than she did at fifty. Sometimes, she stood in front of a mirror, facing her good side, and sang, remembering her glory days. Those were both sublime and bittersweet moments for her, always in front of an appreciative audience, present for her impromptu performances. Beatrice always made certain there was no other flesh and blood person in the house with her when she per-

327

formed this way. These lovely a capella concerts were performed only for herself and her imaginary band and audiences.

*****

Mace waited patiently for Alonzo to come out of the hospital. He did not. In order to stave off boredom and partial insanity, Mace spent the day reading, his new practical hobby. At the Blue Parrot last week, he overheard a quartet of women talking about their book club and their current read, *One Hundred Years of Solitude* by Gabriel Marquez. He was enthralled with it, reading each paragraph with keen interest. As he read, his thoughts drifted. He had one more thoroughly rotten person he wanted to dispatch to his Creator, and he wanted to get the job over with as soon as possible. Reading about the Buendia family, especially Meme and the butterflies, was a much-appreciated diversion.

*****

Alonzo spent the entire night with his mom, holding her hand, except when necessity dictated otherwise. Each time his mother woke up with that frightened look in her pretty eyes, Alonzo roused from his light slumber and comforted her. Each time, she tried to speak. When she failed, she shook her head, closed her eyes, and went back to sleep because there was nothing to say. She did this seven times before sunrise and nine times before her liquid breakfast arrived. Before eating, she tried to speak again, but her utterances were garbled, unintelligible. It sounded worse than a small child's idioglossia. She shook her head, closed her eyes, and tried to retreat into sleep.

"Not this time, Mom." Alonzo was louder than normal. "You have got to get some food into you. It will help you get better." He had not meant to be rude to his mom with his loudness. He wanted to be sure he woke her. Beatrice could fall into a deep sleep in two seconds.

Beatrice drank one-third of the food that Alonzo presented to her through straws that stuck out of twelve-ounce cups. She drank all the coffee. To let Alonzo know she was finished, she pinched her lips shut and shook her head no ferociously. They were adamant gestures, which conveyed an unmistakable command, no more food.

Two seconds from these three gestures, Beatrice was in dreamland. She did not hear Alonzo say, "I'm proud of you, Mom, for eating so well." A moment later, he took his mother's right hand, and though knowing she was out, said, "I love you, Mom." He hoped that she could hear his feelings somewhere in a deep crevice of her subconscious. She did. She pondered them in that secret world where there are no audible words but where everything you have ever experienced is discussed and analyzed in proximity, silently.

# CHAPTER 43

As deeply as Beatrice slept, Alonzo fell into a similar one. Mace continued reading, in his own solitude, until he, too, succumbed to a dreamless sleep of a similar depth. For two hours, the oddly intertwined individuals escaped their personal sorrows. As Mace continued to sleep in his car, Beatrice awoke and broke the silence of her hospital room with a single word, "Alonzo." Alonzo was awakened and jettisoned into a state of unexpected bliss.

"Mom, did you just say my name?"

Beatrice swallowed hard, her Adam's apple taking forever to make its journey from down to up then down again. With a strained face, she forced his name out again, somewhat awkwardly. There was no doubt about it, the single word she said was *Alonzo*. The ecstatic son raised from his chair, reached over the bed, hugged his mother, and kissed her affectionately on her neck. Her eyes sparkled with tears of hopeful joy.

"Do you see what this means, Mom! You're getting better. You can talk now. You said my name. What an honor."

Beatrice tried to say something else, but it came out garbled.

"Don't struggle to say anything more, Mom. Let's just celebrate this momentary success, okay?"

She smiled warmly, and the droop was gone.

"How about I go get us some ice cream and we can have a little party?"

Her smile enlarged as Allonzo turned around like a frisky nine-year-old and fast-walked to the nurse's station. He got chocolate for himself and a strawberry, her favorite, for his mother. Alonzo fed Beatrice the whole cup, complimenting his mother's spoken word several times during the process. When they were finished, Beatrice was worn out, and Alonzo observed it.

"Why don't you get some rest now, Mom? The next time you wake up, I will probably be gone. I need to get a few hours of sleep in my own bed, get out of these clothes, and get cleaned up. I'll see you at about seven o'clock. Oh, and Kate will probably stop by after she finishes work. See you then, Mom."

Then he bent over the guardrail and kissed Beatrice on the right cheek. Her eyes were closed in sleep before the kiss ended.

*****

The same small train-like caravan, with Mace as the caboose, followed a happy Alonzo to Snell Island. Though his physical body was weary, a fantastic new energy coursed through his spirit. It was hope. His mother was getting better, and she had chosen to speak his name, twice. What an honor it was that she chose his name above all other words.

Once inside his luxurious home, Alonzo removed his clothes, showered, put on a pair of white boxer shorts, and plopped down on the couch. He grabbed his landline home phone and called Eldo's, asking the manager if everything was all right. Things were fine there. He told his friend at Eldo's that his mother was getting better. Next, he called the Corner Store, which he inherited when DeMarkus died. Everything was okay there too, according to the manager. Well, it should be. The manager there knew that if he fucked up too badly, he might not only be fired, but his boss might also have him killed. Alonzo did a little more phone work, more than he had done in several days. His operations were still running smoothly although his drug empire was showing signs of being in transition. Soldiers were already vying for the number two position now that DeMarkus was dead. Clearly, no matter how anyone looked at it, Alonzo was still the kingpin. He had the deep pockets and all the primary, secondary, and tertiary connections. After an hour of personal work and beginning to ponder who he would promote to the number two position, he fell dead asleep for the next four and a half hours. He slept in a fetal position, the only way he could fit on the couch.

When he awoke, he showered again and, after dressing sharply, drove back to Northside happily. He was planning to tease his mother a bit while complimenting her at the same time by greeting her by using her first name, Beatrice. He never did this. He fast-walked from the jeep to the hospital, smiled at the seventy-five-year-old receptionist at the front desk, and took the elevator to the ICU. His eyes brightened as he walked down the corridor and saw Kate sitting next to his mom's bed. As he got closer to the room, he noticed that Beatrice was not in her bed. His eyes darted across the empty bed to meet Kate's. He had not noticed a moment ago that Kate's eyes were worried.

"Where's Mom, Kate?"

"She's in the OR, Alonzo."

"What's wrong with her?"

"No one could tell me yet, Alonzo. It all took place a few minutes ago."

"What happened?"

"She was sleeping peacefully, and with no warning, all these bells and whistles started going off." Uncontrollable tears began streaming down her face.

"I guess there's nothing to do, but wait, right?"

"That's right, honey," Kate said soothingly. A moment later, she interjected, "We could pray."

Kate dropped her head and began praying immediately. Alonzo did not. He knew how evil he was at his core. He knew he had no credibility with any of the Holy Trinity. He simply moved his chair to Kate's side of the bed, held her hand, and hoped for the best for Beatrice. His eyes, too, filled with tears. Both were silent for the next thirty minutes.

A doctor that neither Kate nor Alonzo had ever seen before entered the room.

"I'm Dr. Morgan," he said softly. There was a modest amount of drying blood dotting his surgical scrubs. "I'm the chief of the team that just worked on your mother, Alonzo. At first, we all thought it was another stroke. To be sure, we continued our lifesaving efforts and discovered that Mrs. Johnson had experienced an aneurysm." He was choosing his words carefully because he did not want to hurt Kate and Alonzo more than they would be in a moment. He had wanted to use the phrase "massive aneurysm," but he refrained. "In all likelihood, this aneurysm is the reason your mother passed away at 7:23 p.m. I am terribly sorry to be the bearer of this news."

Alonzo felt the urge to go crazy, to rant, to rave, to scream, but somehow, he stuffed those feelings into a dark and dangerous place within his soul.

"Did she suffer much, Doctor?" he asked intently.

"I can assure you that she did not suffer at all."

Alonzo and Kate thanked the doctor at the same time. Dr. Morgan said nothing more, turned, and walked out of the room, leaving the two mourners to their own devices. Alonzo hoped that emotional strength would pass through Kate's hand all the way through to his shattered heart. Kate wished she could stand by her wounded man and support him from collapsing. It was her love that kept Alonzo from drowning in his sorrows.

*****

A bit later that night, Mace saw Kate and Alonzo leave the hospital arm in arm, as if they were holding each other up. Their eyes were bloodshot and tear-filled. Their heads and upper bodies were bent by the drag of sadness. From these easily discernable pieces of evidence, Mace concluded that Beatrice had passed. He decided to leave Alonzo to his grief and not follow the devastated killer to either his or Kate's home. He knew that he would not kill Alonzo anytime soon. One part of him felt sorry for Alonzo's pain. Another part of him wanted to see Alonzo suffer through every fraction of heartache that accompanies the death of a mother. He wanted him to feel the final closing of her casket. He wanted Alonzo to drop a rose on her casket and the dirt that splattered upon it. He wanted Alonzo to feel the finality of every action that was done to Beatrice's corpse. He wanted each of those actions to help to rip his heart into uncountable fragments.

*****

While Mace was in a state of homeostasis, waiting for the right time to stalk Alonzo again, the grieving killer was in a state of free fall. With a cracked and splintered psyche, he moved like a zombie, going through all the motions a responsible son must go through when his beloved mother passes. Every part of the after-death process was difficult, heart-searing. Kate made herself available to help as much as she could, and she was great. She was not enough to stop Alonzo's emotional plummeting.

Of the many bad moments he experienced, the wake was the worst. It started sweetly enough. Scores of Beatrice's fans, friends, and family, many of whom had attended the wake of DeMarkus, stopped by to pay their respects. Almost all those people got along with Alonzo, the public gentleman. Unfortunately, to his extreme dismay, Detectives Glade and Stone showed up. They respectfully approached the coffin, stopped, and made the sign of the cross while stopping a moment to view Beatrice. Then they walked to Alonzo, who was standing next to Kate, shook their hands, and offered their genuine condolences, and left. That was all good. Why they came at all was the question Alonzo had. Kate asked him who the men were, and Alonzo told her. When he finished, the subject was dropped, leaving Kate to wonder whether they were friend or foe.

The answer as to why Glade and Stone had been there developed fifteen minutes later. Two uniformed St. Pete's policemen walked into the funeral parlor, side by side, in complete silence. Their faces were beyond somber. Their effect was anger. They marched like automatons to the casket. There they stood, not making the sign of the cross or any other religious gesture, for about thirty seconds. Then they turned in unison and walked directly to and past Kate, made eye contact only with Alonzo, with that lingering stare, and left the building. It was obvious that they purposely avoided eye contact with

Kate. They continued their choreographed zombie march through the parking lot to their squad car and drove off without looking back.

"What the heck was that all about?" Kate asked with concern.

"I have no earthly idea," Alonzo answered, quietly.

Oh, but he had clues all right, lots of them, all bad, not one he would like to share with kindhearted Kate. In fact, Alonzo was so flooded with clues and questions he almost drowned in them while projecting a brave face to his girlfriend. Were these cops here to represent all the other St. Pete cops who hated Alonzo? Were they letting him know they were stalking him more closely now? Were they warning him without words that they were going to arrest him soon for his drug activities or for the Fairfax massacre or for the murder of DeMarkus? Whatever they were there for, it was rude and inconsiderate. They were not welcomed, and besides their somber faces, they were threatening something.

They were gone now. The show was over, but Alonzo's negative thoughts continued, beginning with a frightening conspiracy theory. Could they have all conspired to kill Beatrice? Any reasoning as to the why of their presence was as plausible as any other. Because of these newest unanswerable questions, Alonzo's spirit continued to plunge into cavernous inescapable darkness.

He was squeezing Kate's hand a little too tightly fourteen minutes later when the second pair of police officers entered the funeral parlor with the same gait and projecting the same intimidating effects. Their movements and timing were almost identical to the preceding officers. They did not look at Kate, and the dirty looks they gave Alonzo hurt and angered him. After their measured passage through the parlor, Kate's discomfort became palpable. She was not a stupid woman. She had recently heard rumors about her man. She did not think it was the right time to talk with Alonzo about whether they were true. Kate was ignorant when it came to the deeper truths about Alonzo. She was new to St. Pete and a workaholic. She did not buy newspapers or watch the news. She had two radio stations, and both were classical. Alonzo thought that Kate would be above all his transgressions against humanity. Little did he know that if Kate knew his true crimes, she would leave him in a flash. If she did, that would be like a third death to Alonzo, something he could not take.

Fifteen minutes later, another duo of police officers arrived at the funeral parlor. This time, it was a tall cop and a short police-woman. Same walk, same attitude. Same everything in a roomful of sorrowful souls. It was awful. Both Kate and Alonzo cringed as the officers passed by them. When Kate saw the female officer's ice-cold stare squarely into Alonzo's eyes, all she could think of was the phrase, "If looks could kill."

Fifteen minutes later, another solemn, angry tandem entered the scene and behaved the same choreographed spiteful way. This time, it was two strong six-foot women. That was all Kate could stand.

"I've got to go home, Alonzo," she said softly. There was no anger in her voice, just exhaustion, and disappointment. "These police officers are trying to tell us something, but I don't know what it is. I certainly don't like the way they are trying to tell us," Kate said.

"I'm trying to figure that too."

"Call me later, Alonzo. I'll wait up for it."

"Could you please stay, Kate?" he asked, like a nine-year-old boy who loved his babysitter and did not want her to leave.

"I really have to go, Alonzo. I'm truly not feeling well." She was not lying, but her ill feelings were coming from her emotions rather than the physical side of her nature. Kate knew herself well. It would only be a matter of time, if the police officers kept coming, that her feelings would cause her stomach to churn.

"Go ahead, Kate. I'll try to call you when this day is over."

He was being his gentleman self on the outside, though his chest and stomach were already on fire, and he needed an antacid fiercely.

Kate kissed him hurriedly on the cheek, reaching high to do so, and wasted no time exiting the funeral parlor.

When she was gone, Alonzo continued his decline into hell on earth. Paranoia continued its ugly maneuvering through the channels of his psyche. He began to think the worst thing possible.

"Could the police presence here be their way of telling me they killed my mother? They have the means to pull it off. A couple of payoffs here and there and the evil deed could be accomplished."

This was the nature of his thoughts for the rest of the day and beyond. Once this singular thought process overtook him, it never relinquished its grip. His personal paranoia, already heightened by the death of his two soldiers, his cousin, and now his mother held him crushed beneath a mountain of fear, distrust, and rage. To make things worse and to cement the possibility there was truth to his ruminations, two more police officers entered the parlor and behaved the same as those who had come before. There was no variation in attitude, time spent at the casket, or their method of departure. They were in complete control of their faculties and their wordless roles. There was no adlibbing, though some of the players wanted to, especially when standing face to face with Alonzo, the killer of their friends, Bobby Banner, Pete Laughlin, and Ellis Wong.

By visitation hours end, Alonzo's temperament was indelibly stamped with aggression toward the St. Petersburg Police Department. He wanted to kill again, more of these rotten cops. He now believed they killed his mother. By ten o'clock, he was stuck in the mire of hypothesizing that they probably killed DeMarkus. By 10:30 p.m., he was convinced that they killed Lavan and Ronnie and that he would be next.

Alonzo did not call Kate that night. He needed to feel love in his heart to be able to talk with her, and tonight, all he felt was murderous rage because the walls of death were closing in on him. He knew that if the cops had killed all these people in such a short time, his time on earth was limited, and he faced a horrible sneak attack death.

No one in the St. Petersburg Police Department had killed anyone close to Alonzo since the Fairfax massacre. Alonzo would never know that. The truth about the officers and their austere attitudes at the funeral parlor is that the whole thing was choreographed by Detectives Glade and Stone with the hearty approval of Chief Garrett. Their idea was to put pressure on Alonzo to make him think that they were close to arresting him for the murder of his cousin or the Fairfax debacle. They wanted him to think that maybe they had just enough evidence to arrest him for being St. Pete's drug kingpin. They certainly could not have imagined that Alonzo would make the leap from what they hoped to achieve, to believing that one or more officers or detectives were killing his soldiers and family.

Kate waited for Alonzo's call till nearly 2:00 a.m. Sleep overtook her as she was reading *Mistral's Daughter* by Judith Krantz. Worried and tired the next morning, she called Alonzo at 10:30 a.m. from her office.

"Hello," the tall killer answered simply.

"Hello, sweetie. I was so concerned when you didn't call last night. Are you feeling better today?"

"Not really, Kate, and I am sorry about not calling you last night. I was overwhelmed by what happened at the wake yesterday, plus having to bury my mother tomorrow. I didn't have the heart to call you even though you're the only person I need right now."

He was telling the truth in his gentlemanly manner. He was also completely withholding the depths of his fears, his rage, and his desire to kill the killer or the killers of his family and soldiers.

"I wish I could be with you right now," Kate said, her love passing through the phone straight into Alonzo's fractured heart. "But I made a deal with my boss to work all day today so I could be with you tomorrow."

"I understand, and I appreciate you making that deal with your boss. I really don't want to be alone tomorrow."

"Will you call me tonight, say between nine and nine thirty?"

"I promise I will call you, no matter what happens today." Alonzo was speaking to Kate from a spec of his fractured heart that could still feel love for someone.

"Thank you, Alonzo. I had better excuse myself and get back to work. I'll look forward to your call all day."

"I will look forward to hearing your voice later too. The anticipation will carry me through whatever happens today. Bye for now, Kate."

Alonzo did not wait for her goodbye. Instead, as soon as he spoke her name, his heart burst with joy. He was realizing how lucky he was and how thankful he was to have her in his life, to be able to speak her name, Kate. He knew he would never again speak the word *mom* to his beloved mother, and he thanked the God that hated him that he could speak the name Kate as a replacement.

*****

Alonzo spent the next morning thankful that he would see Kate soon and no more couplets of police officers glaring at him antagonistically. He was half right. Kate showed up at his Snell Island home, looking majestic. Her earrings were long black onyx, barely visible beneath her long red hair. On her right wrist, she wore a sterling silver cuff bracelet with a black onyx stone in the middle. On her left hand, she wore a sterling silver ring with a tiny onyx teardrop. How appropriate that was for a day on which copious amounts of liquid sadness would be shed. When Alonzo met Kate at his front door, unexpected emotions propelled him to kiss Kate passionately, as if he never wanted to let her go. She was surprised, but the kiss had felt incredibly loving, and it made her spirit soar. She interpreted the message correctly; this man cared for her intensely, perhaps as much as she cared for him.

Where Alonzo was utterly wrong was his belief that the cops would not dare to pull a stunt at the gravesite. The police did something worse. Fifteen minutes before the eulogy began, officers began walking from the parking area to the grass about seventy-five feet behind the far side of the casket. There were dozens of them, and they seemed to just keep coming. They lined up in ordered rows of ten. Alonzo's stomach dropped and began to churn. Kate, standing beside him, felt a similar bomb go off in her gut. Alonzo did not count them, but by the time they stopped coming, there were exactly one hundred, lined up in ten perfect rows, ten deep. All projected a blank stare toward the casket and not one spoke a word. All this was planned to perfection by Glade and Stone. Each one of the officers wanted to hurt Alonzo for the Fairfax massacre, which they were certain he had orchestrated. Their plan was working. Alonzo's thoughts were racing.

*Did these guys really help to murder my mother?* he wondered a thousand times.

*Are they going to arrest me during my mother's eulogy? How could they begin to think that way? If they arrest me in front of Kate, and she figures out the drug boss side of me, will she leave? Then what will I have?*

The answer to the last question was that he would have millions of dollars, immense power, but no one to love his truly monstrous self.

\*\*\*\*\*

The policemen and policewomen stood erect during the entire eulogy, which extolled the virtues of the beloved Beatrice Johnson. When the casket was lowered, the cops did not salute. They remained motionless at Parade Rest like dead people standing. When the casket was in its final place in the ground, none of the police left politely, as the mourners hoped. They simply outwaited the attendees, depriving them of their last bits of privacy with the deceased. The police waited for Alonzo to leave the cemetery. By that time, Alonzo's stuffed rage had melded with his paranoia. His once-unbreakable psyche had been blown into inconsequential bits by the St. Pete's police department's most recent slap in the face. Kate, though unknowing of the overwhelming depravity of her man, was beginning to see more than a glimpse of it, by seeing how the police were behaving around him. This did not make her happy. Despite this, she could still feel the positive effect of Alonzo's morning kiss on her tender lips.

\*\*\*\*\*

During the funeral and wake, Mace was living his peaceful non-murderous retirement lifestyle on Pass-a-Grille. He took a complete break from stalking and thinking about killing Alonzo until at least two weeks after Beatrice was laid to rest. He wanted Alonzo to feel the loss of a loved one, as he had endured the agony of the deaths of Bobby Banner, Pete Laughlin, and Ellis Wong. He painted extensively, looked at coins, swam, bird-watched, cleaned his guns, worked out hard at the gym, listened to music on the Victrola, and made sure Princess was polished and ready to roll around St. Pete. It was a good life, a little lacking in the companionship area but a good life. Anything of importance that he had to say to anyone, he expressed through his painting. His life was simple and uncomplicated, and he almost liked it.

# CHAPTER 44

The night Beatrice was buried, Alonzo treated Kate to dinner and dessert at Bern's Steakhouse in Tampa. He wanted to impress her and to remind her that he was still the wonderful man she fell in love with a few weeks ago. He succeeded. Kate felt happy and adored. Underneath Alonzo's pleasant facade, his pain and paranoia were festering. Every time he felt himself slipping to the dark side of his emotions, instead of reveling in the splendor of the moment, he thought of Kate. Those thoughts brought him back to the present and away from his fearful thoughts of the future. He thought about her incredible beauty, her soothing voice, her sense of humor, her elegance, her body, and how she treated him and responded to him in the bedroom. These thoughts eased his torments. While with Kate, he wondered in silence why he was a drug dealer, and while he was responsible for the deaths of so many people, Alonzo was finding out that it was impossible to be around Kate and not want to be a better man.

\*\*\*\*\*

The next few days were a blur for Alonzo. He had to get back to work. He had seriously neglected his three businesses for several days. He felt he could ill afford to let any of these enterprises go south, especially the magnificent little drug empire that brought him thousands of dollars a day. That operation was suddenly becoming more difficult to manage. He was uncomfortably alone with over a hundred employees to control, most of them from the bottom of the barrel and rotten to the core. He had a number three and a number four man in the organization, but for the last couple of years, they had dealt primarily with DeMarkus. Alonzo no longer knew them well.

*Oh my god,* he thought. *What if those two guys had something to do with these deaths? Except my mother, of course. The police had to do that. My guys could not get anywhere near that hospital. They could have become friends with somebody there and got in that way. I better do my own investigation.*

Every thought fed his paranoia. The only person he trusted was Kate. Even then, he wondered how long she would remain after she found out what he truly was.

Still, he continued to work. At the restaurant and store, he put on a brave face, if not a very friendly one. There was so much more work, especially accounting since DeMarkus died. With his men in the field, he took a much sterner tack. They might be killing each other, and he needed to know who it was, why, and fast. In the next two days, he asked every one of his men if they were happy with their jobs and if they had any problems with the system or any coworkers. To a man, including numbers three and four, they were content. He even talked with all the scouts, the thirteen-, fourteen-, and fifteen-year-old bike-riding kids. He talked more deeply with the more innocent kids. He asked if they knew any disgruntled coworkers if they heard any untoward talk. He brought himself to their levels. By the time he finished talking with everyone, his status was increased. He had maintained his gentleman persona, though he was fighting a paranoia that was ripping him apart. He did not feel any deception from his men and boys. Therefore, he still felt loyalty within his ranks. This eased his suffering a bit.

For three consecutive evenings after his mother's burial, he saw Kate. They went to dinner two nights at 400 Beach and one night at the Vinoy. The fourth and fifth nights, Kate was in Pittsburg. She would be home the sixth afternoon, and they made plans to share dinner that night at TGI Friday's. On burial day plus six, Kate returned from Pittsburg well-rested, happy to see Alonzo in a few hours, and feeling successful, professionally, after closing a couple of huge business transactions. Her boss gave her the afternoon off, and she headed straight for downtown St. Pete. She had a craving to satisfy. She went directly to Joy's hot dog cart, which was located a hundred feet from the front of the Morean Art Center. Kate thought that Joy's polish sausages were the best in town, and she wanted one with the works.

"You want your usual, right?" Joy asked robustly.

"You got it," Kate said, all smiles.

After she paid for the sausage and diet Coke, Joy threw in a free bag of chips. She took a big bite of the polish sausage right away. "Yum!" she said, feeling on top of the world. "I've been dreaming about this for three days."

"Well, thank you for including me in your dream, Kate," Joy joked.

"Thank you, Joy. Have a great day, girl."

She took another bite, turned and walked a few steps to the front of the Morean, and peered through the windows at the myriad paintings hanging on the walls of the first floor. Students had painted them. Most paintings were appealing. The Center liked to sell them. A sold painting was highly encouraging to a student. Kate was most attracted to an impressionistic painting that featured the aftermath of a sunset. The sky was streaked with dainty red-and-orange cirrus clouds high on the canvas. Hints of purple tickled the golden lower clouds, and the ocean reflected each color that ruled the bright heavens. The water was alive and moving swiftly. Kate felt like the bay in the picture was going to splash over the beach all the way to her toes. The landscape she held in her gaze took her spirit to heights it had not been to in several weeks. Time was short today. She wanted to stop at her office, despite having been given the day off. She would make time in her schedule so that she could buy the painting tomorrow and enjoy it for the rest of her life. She thought it might even be nice to meet the artist one day.

Kate took another bite of her sausage and a swig of her diet Coke and began walking west toward where her car was parked about two hundred feet away. She walked briskly, confidently, and happily, almost as if she were walking on the cirrus clouds of the painting she had just seen. She took another bite of sausage and bun. Yum again. One bite left. When she stopped at the red light at Central and Ninth Street, she chugged the last of her Coke and threw the aluminum into a nearby trash can. She was thinking about how interesting life was, how exciting, how much she loved her new home, St. Petersburg. She was thinking about Alonzo.

The light changed to green. The little white walking man appeared, reminding pedestrians they could cross now. Kate stepped into the crosswalk, her bag of potato chips sticking out of her purse for later. She took the last bite of her polish sausage, thinking, *Yum, yum, yum, that was tasty. Boy, am I having a good day!*

The crash was so brutal it broke her pelvis and bent her body abruptly to the left like a rag doll over the hood of the old white Cadillac. The wrong way drunk driver knew that he had hit something but did not stop, wanting only to get to wherever it was he was going. Millions of blood vessels and several organs exploded inside Kate's body upon impact. The last few seconds of her life were spent in a thoughtless haze of excruciating pain before the drunk driver made a wild left turn onto Third Avenue North, throwing the little rag doll onto a parked car, breaking all the ribs on the opposite side of her body. She bounced off the car and banged into the street, hitting her head twice and ending her earthly existence.

There were several witnesses to the hit-and-run, but no one focused on the driver, the car, or the license plate. The abject brutalization of Kate's body was so horrific that all eyes focused on her and filled with tears. There was no way a human being could survive this kind of trauma. There is no way a human being would want to survive this kind of unwelcomed event. Kate was dead. A few bystanders called 911 and a couple rushed to her crumpled and bleeding body. There was no suggestion of life. When the EMTs arrived, they quickly realized there was nothing they could do for Kate. They covered the body and let the blistered-eyed observers know she was gone.

Police arrived moments after the ambulance. Some of them taped off a large area and called it a crime scene. Some went straight to the body. A couple asked questions of anyone who saw anything at all. After questions had been answered, police knew that the car was one of the millions from its era that looked alike. For the driver, they were left with a nameless, ageless, colorless, faceless ghost who would never be found. The killer was another of Tampa Bay's infamous wrong-way drivers, who destroy life with no regard for anyone.

*****

Alonzo and Kate were supposed to meet at his Snell Island home at 7:00 p.m., then head off to TGI Friday's for some truly fall-off-the-bone ribs. By 7:20 p.m., Alonzo was concerned and called Kate's cell phone. No answer. More worry. At 7:35 p.m., he made a second call. No answer. Intensified worry. She had not called him. Had something happened to her heart, where she did not love him anymore? Did she meet a man in Pittsburg and fall for him? What-ifs and maybes poured down on him like cold rain.

Finally, on his fourth call to Kate's cell phone at 8:15 p.m., a strong male voice answered.

"Who the hell is this?" an angry Alonzo shouted, plummeting further into the dark side.

"This is Detective Morrison of the St. Petersburg Police Department. May I ask who this is?"

"This is Kate Faraday's husband," he lied vehemently. "What's going on?" Alonzo was having an impossible time controlling himself, the killer and misanthrope emerging.

"I'm sorry, Mr. Faraday, but I am charged with being the bearer of some bad news for you."

"What is it, man? Come on, speak up," the angry man with no filter shouted.

"There was a serious accident today at Central and Ninth Street. Unfortunately, your wife was seriously injured, and she succumbed to her injuries. It was a hit-and-run, and we have not yet found the perpetrator."

"A hit-and-run? What do you mean?"

"Sir, your wife was crossing the street and was hit by a wrong-way driver. I am sincerely sorry for your loss. We have some of your wife's things here at the main station, including her cell phone and her purse. If you come down here, ask for me, and I will be glad to help you."

Alonzo calmed down enough to be polite to the detective.

"Thank you, Detective."

"A few of her things may still be at the hospital. Of course, her body is at Bayfront."

He chose not to use the word *morgue*. It was too gruesome.

"Thank you again, Detective."

That was the end of their conversation. Suddenly, Alonzo was alone and left to his own coping devices. Nothing was working.

*Someone killed her*, he thought. *Otherwise, why would Morrison use the word "perpetrator"?* This was a word he had heard many times in relation to his and his cronies' crimes and misdemeanors.

*What else could it mean? The police think someone killed her.*

He was not being logical, but intellectuality and good reasoning skills were not the realm in which he was trapped. He was reeling off-kilter from the gentlemanly dancer and kindly boss that he tried to portray. Four walls of intimidating fear were crushing in on him, and Kate was not there to push them back. No longer could he speak her name to her with love. She was the last person he held that feeling for. At the conclusion of that thought, he saw a quartet of loneliness demons pushing walls upon him. He could no longer say Kate or mom or DeMarkus. He realized these three people were the ones who kept the walls and the demons away, and they were gone forever. As his mind declined into abject disillusionment, the walls and the demons shape-shifted into his enemies. The walls became scores of St. Pete's policemen and women, led by Detectives Glade and Stone, as well as Chief Garrett. Behind the police were his so-called loyal employees from Eldo's and his corner store. Behind them were the soldiers of his drug army. They all looked angry. Behind them were all his waiters and waitresses. At the back and barely visible was that big handsome stud that hung out at the Blue Parrot but never danced. They were all inching forward.

Soon, they would crush and smother him. Breathing became difficult. His mind was filled with fear-based mental illness, paranoia. *One of these people will probably kill me*, he thought. *But which one? There are too many out there. No place to run.* Alonzo reached into the drawer of his bedside table and pulled out his .38 Special, hoping to get some of them before they got him. He fired five shots, four of which passed through the door of his bedroom, one through the white wall next to the wounded door. In his mind, three of those bullets ripped through the torsos of Detectives Glade and Stone. One of them hit Chief Garrett. He no longer realized he was resting on the comfortable mattress of his king-size bed. His mind had cracked into myriad shards of kaleidoscopic glass, blurring all his enemies into brightly colored demons. Suddenly, the frenzy ceased, and Alonzo snapped back to reality. For a moment, he pondered everything in his life, the reality of it. That is all it took. The sixth bullet from Alonzo's gun passed through his neck, straight upright to his brain. It was his final, implicit intent. And he was gone.

# CHAPTER 45

All the way across town from Snell Island, Mace was waking up to his alarm clock on Pass-a-Grille. It had been three and a half days since Alonzo had fired upon himself. Mace was feeling great and looking forward to a good workout, a run on the beach, a cool ocean swim, and maybe a pit stop at David Reynolds Coins. The *Price Is Right* passed quickly as he made a six egg and cheese omelet, then plopped himself onto the couch to watch the second half of his favorite show. He had no idea what he would see when a teaser appeared during a commercial break: "Gruesome discovery made in Snell Island home this morning. Details upcoming on the Noon News." A few minutes later, he was ecstatic to see a tiny Filipino woman win $56,738 in cash and prizes.

When the show was over, Mace decided to sit awhile, sip his giant glass of orange juice, and see what was going on in the news. Comfortable physically and unfettered by any unseemly thoughts during his stalking hiatus, the retired cop listened intently as the bad news story came ahead of the burgeoning Trump news.

"A grisly discovery was made this morning at the Snell Island residence of St. Petersburg's reputed drug lord, Alonzo Johnson.

"What?" the tough vigilante said aloud.

"His body was found a couple of hours ago by St. Petersburg police officers, the apparent victim of a self-inflicted gunshot. The fifty-year-old multimillionaire and bon vivant around town had recently suffered the deaths of his first cousin and his mother. On the same day of his demise, his girlfriend was killed by a wrong-way driver in downtown St. Petersburg."

Mace turned the TV off and sat on the couch for several minutes, stunned. He lifted his eyes above the short concrete wall across the street and focused on the ocean. He was trying to find something to soothe his suddenly agitated spirit.

"Why did this happen?" he asked himself silently. "What am I supposed to do now?"

He wondered what the point of his life was if he no longer had the mission of stalking and finishing off Alonzo. His final satisfaction had not been met. Instead, he felt as if the last viable relationship of his life had been destroyed prematurely.

*How dare he take this final fulfillment away from me?* Mace angrily wondered.

Without a goal or a relationship, he felt a stinging aloneness settle upon him. He felt barren, directionless. Instead of washing his dishes, as he always did after eating, he carried them to the kitchen, tossed them into the sink, and left them. He walked into his mother's and Willie's room, which for many years he had made his own. With no energy whatsoever, he threw himself on top of his pristine white sheets and lay there for hours. When he awoke, darkness had settled on the tiny peninsula. Mace felt exactly as the time of day he was looking at, dark, devoid of light.

*****

Eventually, over the next few days, Mace adjusted his mind somewhat to think of himself as a more normal person. Most importantly, he would not kill anymore. He did not want to kill. His short reign of vigilante serial killing was over. There was no one left to hate that much. His three murders had been logically planned and bracketed. There was no need for any further action. His self-appointed mission was complete. He was not a murder junkie who eighty-sixed people for the thrill of it or for some type of sexual gratification. Even Mace admitted to himself there was a certain amount of joy connected with each execution. The truth about Mace was that he did these things out of a sense of duty. He considered himself a serial killer because it felt so wonderful eradicating evil people from the earth. It also made him feel good because he was helping people who lived near the executed ones live a more normal and safer life.

Mace never shared these thoughts with anyone. They were his private musings. It would never matter to him what any other human being might think of these ideations. He understood them, and that is all that mattered.

*****

The future began to reveal itself slowly, begrudgingly. The passage of time behaved as if it did not want to occur. If it did participate at all, it did so, reluctantly. Mace's likes were still his likes, but his movements around them were happening sluggishly. He was alone and lonely, and that dragged time to a crawl. He was bored, and that reduced life's tempo to a slug's pace. His favorite records played slower. The love songs sounded sadder. Even the birds were cruising at such lesser speeds that they appeared to him to be flying backward.

His workouts were weighted with the additional pounds of his personal oppressions. He was not light on his feet while running. He felt heavy in the water. As life drifted droningly by, he felt his joylessness dominating every intersection of his life. To stave off absolute madness, he found himself every few days at the soup kitchen. There, he decided to contribute money, not to the betterment of the program but to individuals who really needed it. He reduced the plight of many homeless in St. Pete in the winter of 2018. Talking with as many disenfranchised people as possible reduced his suffering. Time returned to normal as he displayed sympathy toward these underprivileged almost friends.

Mace also treated himself to dinner at restaurants all around town so he could at least converse with the myriad waiters and waitresses he knew. He took himself to David Reynolds Coins and Jewelry, the most expensive place to fraternize. In the first three weeks after Alonzo died, Mace had brought over $5,000 worth of gold coins from his favorite store. He did not have a problem spending money for gold. He was merely adding to the $250,000 in gold he already had stashed in his collection.

*****

His annoyances began the moment he left David Reynolds. He did not have anyone to drive with on his way home to Pass-a-Grille. He wanted to talk with someone. He wanted to share Princess with someone. Her seats were so large and luxurious. Her shocks were so top of the line that a bump could hardly be felt. He realized he had never bought a piece of jewelry for a woman at David Reynolds. He wondered if he ever would. He wanted to, but he did not think that his odds were good. Even with a beautiful St. Gaulden's gold coin in his pocket, his ride home to Pass-a-Grille was somber. Loneliness was becoming an irritating itch that slowed time. Not having a dream or goal came in a close second. For the first time in his life, the phrase "share with somebody" kept replaying itself in his troubled mind.

Still, he took himself out to the Blue Parrot on Christmas Eve of 2018. Of course, he went alone, but he saw several familiar faces there. They were faces he had smiled at in the past, faces that had returned his smile. He hoped that these faces and the music would provide him with some holiday magic.

Forty-five minutes into the music, Mace was enjoying a slow, dulcet rendition of Gershwin's 1928 "Embraceable You." He did not mind that time slowed down during this music. That was the way it was supposed to be during this classic.

"Would you like to dance?' he heard someone nearby ask. He did not even turn his head. Five seconds later, he heard the voice say almost the same thing again, this time directly into his left ear.

"Excuse me, sir, but would you like to dance to this beautiful old Gershwin tune?"

He smelled her before he saw her. It was the cologne his psychiatrist, Dr. Rafferty, wore over a quarter of a century ago. It was his mother's only scent. It was Willie's favorite body spray. He liked it. When he focused on the woman behind the voice, she was clothed in a white dress abundant with lace. The color was identical to the pristine sheets he always kept on his bed. The bottom of her dress was fashioned with more lace. It was dainty and lovely.

"I am not much of a dancer," he said, kindly.

He saw her face for the first time. It exceeded his standards for beauty by a wide margin. He was overwhelmingly drawn to her. She was irresistible.

"That's okay," she said through an alluring smile. "I can take the lead if you're willing to follow for a couple of minutes."

Her teeth were perfect, obviously cared for by the most talented orthodontist. Her tight curly hair was cropped so closely to her scalp, that it appeared to be painted there.

"I think I can do that," he said, shyly, totally out of character.

He was simultaneously excited and frightened as he reached out his hand to meet hers. Her skin was smooth, velvety, not a wrinkle anywhere, though she had probably passed her fortieth birthday quite a few years ago. Mace's huge body rose from his chair and moved lithely to the dance floor. The woman was surprised to see how tall and muscular this man she was going to dance with, really was. By the time his arm was around her waist, scores of eyes were upon him. They had seen him fifty times in the past, but they had never seen him stride to the dance floor with a beautiful woman.

His shyness led as he placed his right hand on her back, but by the time he held his left hand for her to take, she was in control. He had never held a woman this way. Her body was close to his but appropriately so. As she whisked across the dance floor, he glided with her. He noticed an elegance about her that no other dancer possessed. He was wondrously attracted to it. He saw the other male dancers smile slyly at her, hoping to receive a smile from the tall beauty. His sensual partner kept her eyes trained on him. That behavior added to the innate classiness he sensed she possessed. His shyness returned occasionally, and he dropped his eyes to the floor. Each time he looked up again, her eyes met his with what looked almost like affection. His eyes fell to her shoes. They were pristine white ribbons that wrapped around her ankles and returned to the front, culminating in a tiny bow. Then he would raise his eyes again to meet her unaltered gaze, which seemed to say, "Welcome back."

After two minutes, Mace finally spoke.

"Do you mind if I ask your name?" he asked, looking suave but with a pounding heart.

"Of course. It's Rana, like rain. I'm Egyptian."

For the first time since she approached his table, he saw how black she was. Her color did not matter at all. Something undeniably magnificent was emanating from her. For this fleeting interlude, he felt like a king, at least on the dance floor. He felt also that she was his queen because that is how she presented herself every second since he first became aware of her. A moment later, when the song ended, Mace did not want to leave the physical contact he had established with Rana. She must have felt the same because her next sentence was superimposed on Mace's thoughts.

"Did you like that?" she asked, looking up at him with a kind smile on her face.

"I did," he responded shyly. Not wanting to act too familiar, he politely released her hand and removed his other hand from her waist.

"I did too," she said, standing upright with perfect posture. "Would you like to wait here and see if the next song is slow and we can share it?"

"I'd love that more than anything." The last half of his sentence slipped out completely beyond his control. His face did not reflect his embarrassment.

"So would I," she said confidently.

It took the piano player less than a minute to make an inane joke that neither Rana nor Mace heard. He also announced the name of the next song. They did not hear that either. They just stood there, waiting, like a couple of eighth graders, hoping the song would be slow so they could feel the warmth of one another as soon as possible.

Fate and chance worked hand in hand for once. When the music started again, it was slow and inviting. As if they had done it a thousand times, the two new acquaintances moved gracefully into each other's arms. It only took a couple of notes for the couple to realize they were dancing to Henry Mancini's "Moon River."

"I love this song," Rana said after a few bars.

"I do too," Mace added.

"You have good taste," Rana said.

"Thank you, Rana. No one has ever said that to me before."

"What did you think of 'Embraceable You,' Mace?"

"I loved it. Music like that reminds me that I grew up listening to Gershwin, Cole Porter, Glen Miller, Count Basie, all those guys, on my father's Victrola."

"Wow! That is cool. Do you still have the Victrola?"

"I do. I keep it in great condition and listen to old-time records on it at least twice a week. Do you want to hear something really cool, Rana?"

"Sure."

"That Victrola is about eighty years old, it's almost in mint condition, and my grandfather passed it on to my father when he died."

"That is something," Rana said excitedly. "And by the way, you are dancing remarkably well. You are a natural. The fact that you are an athlete probably is helping you a great deal."

"How do you know I'm an athlete?"

"Anyone with your build has to be an athlete."

He was surprised at the compliment but appreciated it.

"Thank you," he said shyly again.

"I will bet with a little practice, you could become a great dancer."

"How can you know that after only parts of two dances?"

"I'm using my sixth sense," she said convincingly.

This was not something he had ever considered, but he was interested in her.

"You might be right, Rana, but wouldn't I need a good dance partner to help me along?"

"You are probably right about that, Mace, but there are plenty of good teachers out there and several great venues to dance at that provide a variety of partners."

"I'm not the kind of person who would be happy with multiple partners. I know I would prefer one single partner, someone like you."

It was the bravest comment he ever made to a woman, and he was scared to death speaking it.

"That is the nicest thing anyone has said to me in a long time, Mace. It might be fun to help you learn a new hobby."

Fun? That was a concept he never considered. He had reproached himself many times over the years for not sharing more of it with his Marine and cop buddies. In a split second, in this wonderful present moment, he had a revelation. The most fun he ever had in his long and winding life filled with death was reading bedtime stories to Johnny Paige's children and almost all the time he spent with Willie.

"I'm having fun right now," he said, surprising himself.

"Me too," the ultrarefined woman spoke, surprising herself almost as much as Mace had surprised himself.

The song ended far too quickly. Neither had spoken since Rana said, "Me too." They simply danced and reflected on their comfortability with their partner. Now came another awkward moment. As the dance floor cleared, Mace and Rana were swept from it by a small but powerful people wave. It all happened so fast that an instant later, the two new acquaintances were standing next to Mace's table. So far, they had spent twelve minutes together. When Rana said, "It was a pleasure to meet you, Mace," he did not want to experience the emptiness her leaving would create.

"Rana, would you like to join me for a drink and maybe some chicken wings?"

"I would love that, Mace. The chicken wings sound good. I haven't eaten yet. He pulled a chair out for her, and she seated herself gracefully.

"Would you like dinner? I would be happy to order some for you."

"I really am hungry, Mace. I'll take you up on your offer. Can we get a menu?"

She liked his name. It suited him. It was strong like he was. He enjoyed saying her name, Rana, like the rain. For a few seconds, they did not speak. Mace connected with her eyes, reveling in their deep blueness against her dark skin. A kindness was emanating from them. It was putting him more at ease with her than with any woman he had ever known. Words by the millions, stuffed into the most cavernous recesses of his soul, suddenly wanted to emerge one by one, in simple conversation with her.

"Where are you from, Rana?"

"I'm from Cairo."

"Tell me about your life there."

"It's a bustling metropolis, Mace. Anything a person could ever want can be found in Cairo. My husband came from generations of shipping magnates. We were married when I was only sixteen, an arranged marriage of sorts. I grew to love him though and rather quickly. He was a good man, a hard worker, a tremendous provider, and quite handsome, like you, but in an Egyptian sort of way."

Mace took the compliment silently, as a sincere tiny smile graced his face. Nikki, the waitress, stopped over to check on drinks, and Rana asked her for a menu and a Bud Light. Mace thought there was nothing shy about this erudite beauty.

"Go ahead with your story, Rana, please."

"My husband, Arturo, wanted a big family. Of course, I thought I could oblige him. I was a young, healthy Philly. After three years of making love almost every night, I had not become pregnant. Arturo, who was double my age, grew worried that something might be wrong with one of us that might be able to be fixed.

"First, we checked his sperm count. Normal. Then I had a thorough examination. Unfortunately, the problem was with me. I could not have children. At first, we were heartbroken. Arturo had an outlet for his sorrows. He poured himself into his work. Before we found out the bad news, he would spend ten to eleven hours a day at work. Afterward, he stretched it out to fourteen, sometimes fifteen hours. I, on the other hand, had nothing. I was a less than twenty, modestly educated woman, with no real skills but cooking and cleaning for my husband. Everything began to change one day when my husband told me his secretary was going to leave in two weeks to accompany her husband to Rome where he had taken a great job promotion. I didn't think about it for a second. I just blurted out, "Do you think I could take her place?" A look I had never seen before consumed my husband's face. He was pondering my life's fate without either of us knowing it. He squinched his skin all around his chin, lips, and eyes and held that pose for nearly a minute before he spoke.

'I don't see any reason why we can't give it a try.'

"I threw my arms around Arturo, kissed him, and said, 'Thank you, darling. I love you so much.' Arturo kissed me, then he pushed me away by my shoulders and said, 'Now slow down a little, Rana. The job is hard work. There is so much to learn. My secretary worked ten hours a day.'

"'That's okay, darling. I'm smart,' I said. 'I can learn fast. As far as work hours, I can drive in with you in the morning and drive home with you at night.'

"'Rana, that would be a lot more than ten hours a day.'

"'I can handle it, honey. You watch.'

"That was the start for me, Mace. Arturo was right. There was so much to learn, but I learned that business and business in general. For the next twenty-five years, Arturo and I were inseparable, a real partnership. There were so many different people to communicate with that I learned five languages. In our time off, we traveled the world. Money was abundant, and we enjoyed helping the poor as often as we could."

Mace liked her more when she said that. He had always had a soft spot in his heart for the less fortunate.

"One day, in 2016, Arturo had a job across town. He went alone, as he often did, while I stayed in my office. On the way back from his meeting, less than a mile from our building, a drunk driver crossed the center line and hit Arturo's car head-on. My husband was killed instantly. I was shocked, then heartbroken. I could barely breathe for weeks. Though Arturo had many strong men in positions of power within our company, it felt immediately like they were all jockeying for the position of the head honcho. I stayed in my office, despite my heartache, and ran the company from there. I had to stand up to all those strong men.

"Finally, seventeen days after Arturo died, his will was read in our boardroom. He left me everything, the business, the cars, the houses, his investments, everything. He did leave some cash to some of his long-term loyal employees, even a few of them who were fighting for power. That foolishness ended with the reading of the will. Then my third life, as I like to call it, began. Now what about you?"

"Wait a minute, Rana, that was 2016. What happened since then?" Mace was leaning forward in his chair, his elbows on the table and his chin on his fisted hands. He was absolutely, unpretentiously interested in her story.

"For about two years, I ran the company wholeheartedly. Then earlier this year, I began dreaming about a fourth life. I missed traveling and helping poor people along the way. I worked with my top men and women and restructured the company so that I could get away anytime I wanted and stay away as long as I wanted. I made sure that I would still be the boss, but it would feel to me as though I was more of a daily consultant. I taught my staff to be brief and concise with what they told me was happening each day, and I taught myself to make swift decisions so that phone calls would not last more than an hour a day. When I returned from wherever, I would work in the office if I chose to be there. This is my first trip since I restructured. It is the beginning of my fourth life. By the way, Mace, I am surprised how much poverty there is in Florida. Even here in St. Pete, there are so many homeless."

"I know," Mace said while Rana took a swig of beer. "Could you explain to me what you mean by your four lives?"

"It's simple. My first life was the one I had growing up with my family. My second life was the life of a housewife the first three years of my marriage. My third life was all those years I helped my husband run the business, including the two years after he died. My fourth life is the one I am creating now. I'm traveling, seeing the United States, helping good people who are in need. I am finding my true purpose in life, Mace. I want to create great things, Mace, change lives. My fourth life is not rounded out yet. There are too many holes in it. I have so many things to think through and organize."

Mace was smitten with her, especially the part about helping the poor throughout her travels. Her innate goodness seemed to be flowing out of every pore of her beautiful body. He felt out of control, falling for her wondrously and with unrelenting speed.

"Now how about you?" she said with a smile.

Mace did not panic, but he felt fear. In a moment, he would be talking about himself, something he was not used to doing. He was not fond of sharing his story. There was too much heartache and death in it. To make things worse, he would be telling his story to this strong, angelic woman.

"Rana, I have to admit that I am quite reserved when it comes to talking about my life. I'm kind of shy overall and not much of a talker, but I'll give it a try. I was born on a farm in Illinois. My parents moved our family to Florida when I was a baby. My mother was always cruel. She pushed me to be the best swimmer, wrestler, and I was. Looking back on it now, I realize a lot of what she taught me was illogical, like laughing was a waste of time. I think she was trying to make me look invincible. I believed what she taught me for a long time. She died in a car crash, like Arturo.

"My father was a real sweetheart. He taught me how to work on cars, shoot a gun, how to hunt. He taught me about big band music, coins, gold, and silver. He never raised his voice or hit me. He was always logical and kind, the opposite of my mother. He died of leukemia while I was in the service. He left me his old Victrola, scores of records, his coin collection, old currency, and a beautiful antique gun collection that had been passed to him by his great-grandfather. I almost forgot. He taught me about birds. Now I love them too, and when I watch them, I see incredible beauty, and it relaxes me."

Rana's dinner came, and while she ate, she listened undistractedly to Mace while the sounds of the orchestra provided a pleasant background for their conversation.

"Then I spent nine, almost ten, years in the Marines and twenty-one on the police force right here in St. Pete. That brings me to the present."

He did not tell her about his recent vigilantism or his favorite numbers, especially the killing one, which he hoped would remain at thirty-seven. He mentioned nothing about his heroism, his honors, or his physical or mental wounds. He had never spoken so many uninterrupted words about himself, not even to Dr. Rafferty.

"What about love and marriage, Mace?"

"I've never been married, Rana."

"What about girlfriends? Do you have one now?"

"No girlfriend now. I have never had one. I guess with my careers and my hobbies, I've never had time for one," he lied. He had plenty of time.

"Never? That's a long time."

"Too long."

Rana heard the next song begin. It was a perfectly danceable rendition of "You Made Me Love You." She put a forkful of food immediately on her plate. "Would you like to dance again, Mace?"

"I certainly would, Rana."

Rana, who was closer to the orchestra, stood first. When Mace rose, Rana extended her hand. When Mace saw it, his spirit skyrocketed without any external show of it. It was the first time a woman ever reached out her hand to him warmly.

# CHAPTER 46

They only shared three more dances that night before 9:30 p.m. put an end to their initial tenderness with one another. Neither being the type to sleep with someone after just meeting them, they exchanged honest phone numbers. Mace summoned the courage to tell Rana he looked forward to talking with her again, and he would call her in a couple of days. Rana told Mace that it was a pleasure to meet him. She reached out her right hand. When Mace met it in the air between them, Rana extended her left hand and with it covered the dorsal surface of his large hand. The show of affection touched him emotionally and made him tingle all over physically. When they parted, Mace could not remove her from his head. Twenty minutes later, he was painting outside on his patio. His heart and mind, bursting with a different feeling, transferred all that energy through his arms, hands, and brushes to the canvas. He painted with unrecognizable passion for the next seven hours until exhaustion overcame him. Before he slipped into bed at 5:00 a.m., he opened his mother's perfume bottle that he had never thrown away. He took several whiffs of the musk inside. It made him feel closer to Rana on the first night he ever felt he was too far away from a woman.

*****

Mace kept his promise and called Rana Wednesday afternoon. He asked her to dinner. She accepted, and he treated her to the Don CeSar. She had never been there. They each drove their own car and enjoyed a wonderful meal, followed by two hours of conversation. Though Rana did most of the talking, Mace was engaging and showed genuine interest in her stories. He was calm around her. She liked his listening skills. He did not impose himself upon her, as many men had in recent months. Her tales were exotic and exciting. He was captivated by her and felt like he was listening to Scheherazade.

*****

Wednesday night's dinner was followed by a Thursday night dinner at Cheddars and a Saturday night dinner at TGI Friday. Each time, Mace paid for everything and did not mind a bit. During dessert Saturday, Rana surprised Mace.

"Would you like to go to the Blue Parrot with me Monday night, my treat?"

"I would," Mace answered.

"Good. We can work on our dancing. I'll teach you how to spin me."

"Is it difficult?" Mace asked skeptically.

"It's easy, sweetie. Trust me."

She called him sweetie, the first endearing term she spoke to him. He liked it. He wondered if he could ever speak an endearing term to her.

Two days later, Rana taught Mace how to spin her. It was easy, and she looked stunning while spinning. She was so graceful and athletic it prompted him to ask her a question while they danced.

"Rana, how have you managed to stay in such great shape? You don't have an ounce of fat on you. Do you attribute that to dancing?"

"Partly, Mace," his happy partner answered. "The last ten years of our marriage, we danced twice a week. We learned all kinds of dancing, but I developed myself those almost three decades I've worked for our company."

"How so, Rana?"

"Arturo built a gym, with a variety of weights and cardio machines on our third floor. The area was designed for health and fitness. I could lift weights, walk or run on the treadmill, ride the stationary bike, then shoot baskets in the gym if I wanted. I learned the game of basketball there and became a rather good player. I still am."

"Would you like to work out at the gym with me sometime?"

"I would really like that, Mace."

Mace grew instantly happier, as did Rana.

Monday was their fourth date. Their relationship was moving smoothly toward a good friendship, at the very least. Outside dancing together, there was no physical romance between them, to this point, except for the guarded flirtations that occasionally escaped from their eyes.

Mace, always the lover of numbers, kept track of their dates. At the end of the eighth date, before Mace dropped her off at the Vinoy, Rana asked him a simple question.

"Mace, instead of going straight into the hotel and my room, could you park Princess and take a walk with me?"

"Sure, Rana."

Mace noticed the full moon as he drove across town, and he guesstimated the temperature was a balmy seventy-eight. It was the perfect night for a walk. Mace parked his precious chariot and walked around it to open the door for Rana. She got out, closed the door, and walked with him quietly to the curb. There, she took Mace's left hand into her right. Silently, they crossed the street and turned south toward the unfinished pier. Mace began to feel exquisite sensations coursing through his body. He treasured this simple moment with this exotic woman. The white-hot moon illuminated the boats and the water of the marina with a bright light that reminded Mace of the angelic dress and shoes Rana wore the first time he saw her.

Rana felt something also. This was the first man's hand she held since her husband's. She felt safe. Most couples smiled at them as they passed and smiled. A few looked like troublemakers. She was sure that her tall muscular companion could easily protect her. Her feelings for this quiet, shy man were developing curiously. Though she recognized his glorious structure and his power if needed, she regarded him as a gentle soul.

They walked to the corner, wordlessly, turned in unison, and walked back toward the Vinoy. Rana broke the silence.

"Mace, what number life do you believe you're living right now?"

He knew exactly what she meant. He had listened carefully to the story of her four lives.

"Do you mind if I think about it for a couple of minutes?"

"Not at all. Take your time."

A block later, Mace spoke, "I am definitely on number five." He paused, then picked up again. "Like yours, my first was one was my childhood with my mean mother and my lovable father, but no extended family. My second was about ten years of active duty in the Marines. My third was my twenty-one years as a police officer. My fourth was my first couple of years of retirement. I did not like my life much during that time. I needed and wanted a change. I was not sure what choice I should make. I had no direction. Then fate brought you to me, and now I'm wondering how long I might be able to make this dance last."

Mace made his statement, courageously, having thought about it during his quiet time before speaking. Though it was a bombshell to Rana, she received it with the same finesse that Mace delivered it.

"Mace, those are the kindest words anyone has said to me in a long time. I admit to thinking the same way about you. I have enjoyed every minute I have spent near you, Mace. That makes me wonder about spending a great deal of future minutes with you."

"Thank you for thinking that, Rana."

He retreated into his silent world. The couple turned around and began their final approach to the Vinoy. They walked through the front door together and headed for the elevator. Along the way, they drew both admiring and jealous stares. People saw them as a handsome power couple, hence the range of emotions from strangers.

"Would you like to come upstairs with me?" she asked kindly.

"Not yet, Rana," he said boyishly, trying to hide his lack of experience.

Rana reached both hands to Mace's head, pulled him down to her lips, and kissed him in more than a "just friends" fashion. The kiss took Mace away from every sorrowful place he had ever been. It stopped time, transporting him to a blissful dimension where there was no anger or pain. Even shyness melted away, leaving in its wake the hope of an intriguing fifth life. When their lips finally parted, Rana made a request before saying good night.

"Do you know what I would like to do with you soon, Mace?"

"No, what?"

"I'd like to come out to Pass-a-Grille and see your place, maybe spend a couple of days at the beach."

"We can arrange that," he projected strongly while feeling sheepish.

Then she reached up, kissed him on the cheek, caught the elevator, and disappeared into the belly of the Vinoy.

# CHAPTER 47

From Rana's departure, going forward, Mace knew that the hard work for him to become man enough for her would begin now. Thus far, it had been relatively easy for him to relate to her. It did not take much character for him to be kind, patient, gentlemanly, but soon she would be coming to his home. She wanted to stay with him a couple of days. She had kissed him and asked him to come to her room. She revealed in unspoken, but certain terms, that she was a woman with desires, and she was ready for him to fulfill them.

Mace was completely inexperienced when it came to dealing with a woman's needs. He was a virgin. His shyness extended far beyond his reticence. It permeated his sexuality. *How embarrassing it will be when I reveal I'm a virgin?* he thought. *What if I can't satisfy her?* Though all manner of fears swirled within him, he decided to face them one at a time. He determined that being embarrassed with her in his life was better than a drone existence without her.

The night of the Vinoy kiss, Mace painted for two hours after getting home. Then he put his brushes in a glass of water and began cleaning his house. He vacuumed every room and dusted canvasses and countertops. He dusted the old safe in the guest bedroom and end and coffee tables in the living room. He dusted every surface in his bedroom and dropped into bed at 4:00 a.m. He was making sure that no matter how crowded his little beach house was with his stuff, it would be clean when Rana came to visit.

*****

Four dates and seven days later, it was time for Rana to see how Mace lived. He picked her up at the Vinoy at 10:30 a.m. on a Friday. The plan was to spend the weekend on Pass-a-Grille, then return to the Vinoy sometime Monday. Mace surprised Rana with a dozen red roses when she stepped into Princess. The ride to Pass-a-Grille was quick and quiet. Quiet was something Rana was always comfortable with. She scooted next to him on the seat after she received her flowers. She kissed his right cheek and rested her left hand on his right thigh, feeling his huge muscle. "Oh my!" slipped from her lips. Mace smiled and shifted into second gear using the gas pedal. His slightly flexed muscle was even more impressive.

"Mama Mia, Mace, you've got concrete in your pants."

They both laughed.

He was taking her to a house filled with secrets. How would Rana react as at least some of them were revealed? He parked his beautiful Chrysler on the far south side of the block so the two of them could have a better view of the water. The car would not bother anyone. Long ago, Willie bought the other two lots on the block. Willie and Mace both decided to keep the lots empty. Privacy was imperative to Willie, and Mace was the same. He grabbed Rana's bags as she slid across the seat and put her hands on the enormous steering wheel, moving it back and forth, excitedly, like a small girl.

"Will you teach me how to drive your baby one day, Mace?"

"Of course, I will," he said, once again showing confidence but feeling worried about Princess. He helped Rana out of the car, his heart pounding.

"After you, Rana."

This woman he was loving more deeply each day was about to enter his sanctuary.

Three steps in, Rana could not believe what she saw. On the wall that was immediate to her left hung an almost life-size portrait of her. She stopped to peer, not noticing Mace as he walked in. He carried her things directly to his bedroom. Rana was entranced. She stepped back into the living room to get a better perspective, not noticing Mace sitting on the couch behind her. It was absolutely herself that was staring back at her, correct in every way, down to the most minute details. It was she at the Blue Parrot the night she met Mace. She was wearing her white dress and her white shoes with the pretty straps that tied. Her face was beautiful, with an inviting smile, and he had painted her close-cropped hair exactly the way it was, showing the curl patterns on her scalp.

"How did you do this without me posing?" she asked as she turned and saw Mace.

"I did it by memory. Your face and body were seared into my brain. As I painted, it was like you were standing right beside me. Did you notice I got all the jewelry right?"

"Oh my gosh, you did. You are amazing!" she said after she scanned the jewelry. She also noticed the tiny faces of the band members in the background, their tiny faces, looking exactly like the real musicians she knew so well.

"I'm glad you like the painting."

"Like? I love it with all my heart. It must be worth a fortune!" Mace was in his element now, feeling rather good about himself. "Come on, I'll show you the rest of the house."

Four steps later, they reached the hallway that led to two bedrooms and a bathroom. What caught Rana's eyes first was what was on the floor. There were seven rows of finished paintings against each wall, four or five deep. At first glance, it looked like a hoarder's hallway. Though crowded, however, it was organized. Rana noticed the outer paintings first. Each was a different scene, telling a unique story, expressing distinctive emotions. There was so much to investigate.

It took clear focus to take in the meaning and the artistry of each painting. For the next thirty minutes, she never raised her eye level more than a few inches above the top of the canvasses. She was mesmerized. She squatted to the floor and got as comfortable as she could. There were so many images, so much to absorb. She began looking at the approximately seventy paintings, one by one. The first she inspected depicted eight policemen in vibrant blues, carrying a flag-draped coffin. Each of the officers had tears streaming down his face. Mace was one of them. The next was a picture of a monstrous red devil casting a menacing glare.

Following was a painting of a police car in the middle of a dark street, being riddled with bullets. Multiple shooters were firing from the trees and the street in front of and behind the embattled vehicle. Large trucks blocked the streets' ends so that no escape was possible from the onslaught. It was a heart-wrenching scene. Rana had no idea that this would be one of many of Mace's depictions of the Fairfax massacre.

There were paintings of war battles, of St Pete's homeless, of worn-down men, women, and children with their deeply crusted faces of pain. There were multiple paintings of the Holocaust, of the Hutu's and Tutsis, of Idi Amin's troops terrorizing his people, of Pol Pot's killing fields. There were seascapes and sunsets, paintings of birds, and marinas of bridges and buildings. There were even three paintings of his beloved 1950 Chrysler Imperial, Princess.

Before she looked at every painting, Rana unexpectedly raised from her seated position and kissed Mace squarely on his lips. Mace stood speechless after the kiss, as he did the entire time, she admired his paintings.

"Mace, these are wonderful. There must be a fortune in art here. When did you paint all these?"

"Over the last ten years or so."

"My goodness," she said, feeling stunned, delighted, and deeply moved. "You are prolific as well as a marvelous painter," she said, having no idea what she would soon see.

"Thank you, Rana," Mace said humbly. "Would you like to see the bedrooms at the end of the house?"

"Sure, but I haven't seen all your paintings."

"I know you haven't, but you can always wander back into this hallway and look some more right."

"Right," she said, taking his extended hand and following him down the narrow passage to the bedroom on the left. He opened the door for her.

"Go in."

A light shock wave passed through her. It was like a hoarder's room. Paintings were organized on the floor in multiple rows, facing outward, exactly like in the hallway. They covered almost every inch of the floor, save for enough space to walk around. There was no bed where it should have been. Instead, art supplies were everywhere. Directly across and facing the door was a huge old safe. The antique beauty drew her toward it.

"Would you like to see what's inside?"

Rana stood there a moment looking at the safe's archaic markings.

"I sure would."

Mace saw the little girl in her face again.

"Okay then, here we go!"

He rubbed his hands together several times, trying to make the moment seem more magical. The shy man was being playful in a way he had not been since he hung out with Johnny Paige's children.

"Close your eyes."

Rana complied. She placed her hands over her eyes and turned away.

"Voilà! he said.

Rana opened her eyes and turned to see another stunning sight. Before her were multiple drawers and compartments filled with gold and silver coins. Mace opened another drawer for her to view. It was filled with American currency dating to the 1830s. Rana's face morphed from the face of a child to a serious adult, as she thoroughly inspected his visible treasures. After several minutes, she finally broke the latest silence between them.

"I can't believe we have this in common, Mace."

You collect coins too?"

"It's more than that, Mace. Investing in gold and silver started with Arturo's great-grandfather. When he died, he left everything to his son, Arturo's grandfather. Grandfather passed it to Arturo's father, and Father passed the entire collection to Arturo. When Arturo died, he left everything to me. We have an extremely secure safe in each of our houses, one in Cairo, one in Italy, and one in Greece. We also have safe-deposit boxes in each country. Our collection is voluminous, coins from all over the world and from all periods of history. We collected many of them on our travels together. I must admit, Arturo's forefathers gave us a magnificent start to our collection."

"That is truly cool, Rana. I would love to see that collection someday."

"I hope you can, Mace."

An hour passed before Rana finished looking at scores more coins and dozens more of his paintings. There were so many topics, so much energy emanating from them. One motif was consistent. It was the fact Mace believed that humanity was suffering. For some reason, Mace was especially sensitive to the plight of his abused fellow man. Rana wondered how Mace had suffered, to be able to pour so much emotion into his work.

"Let's go across the hallway Rana," he said when she finished making her way around the room. "I'll show you my old bedroom."

There were paintings everywhere, again. They were piled on the bed in four rows, four feet high. In the far-left corner was Mace's beautiful antique gun cabinet. Rana was immediately attracted to it, wondering again with the little girl's face, what was inside. She asked Mace to open it.

"Everything in here has a name and a story, Rana. Too many to tell you now. You can look more in here anytime. Nothing is loaded, so you will be safe. Voilà!" He unlocked the one lock with a key from his key ring and opened the cabinet. There it was, another magnificent collection, glistening before her. This time, it was forty highly polished antique guns being housed.

"Some of these date back to the wild west. A couple have survived from our Revolutionary War."

"May I touch them?" the youngster inside Rana asked.

"Help yourself," he said to his lovely girlfriend, making the child inside incredibly happy.

"I've never held a gun before," she said with great fascination.

"I've held and used far too many of them in my lifetime," Mace said sadly. Then he changed in an instant and said, "I'll teach you how to shoot one if you would like."

"I would love that," she said, surprising him.

One by one, she handled each weapon, marveling at how polished they were, both metal and wood from stock to barrel. Fifteen minutes into Rana's exploration of this interest in her life, Mace asked if she would like something to drink.

"How does a Michelob Ultra sound?"

"Delightful." She finished with the last gun, then began looking at his paintings.

After Mace returned with her drink, he noticed how much time she was spending on each painting. He grew weary of standing in the same place for so long.

"Rana, do you mind if I take a break on the couch and close my eyes while you look at the paintings?"

"Not at all, Mace. I'll wake you when I finish."

"Take your time, Rana."

She did. She did much more than peeking at pictures. She intensely focused on Mace's artistry, comparing them to some of the masterpieces that she and Arturo owned. Each time she looked at a painting, she felt as if she were opening a book and reading a compelling story. She also felt as if she and her shy boyfriend were having a meaningful conversation. Slowly, he was revealing himself. Before she entered the house, Rana had no idea of the range of emotion Mace possessed that he could inject into his paintings. Now, in this tiny bedroom, she became convinced that Mace had limitless potential to create a prolific amount of truly masterful and evocative art. As she peered at each well-crafted canvas, she created a plan as to how she would discover the being that Mace truly was. She would also learn what type of person he wanted to be in his fifth incarnation. If they were a match, she would open her heart to him completely and share the magnificent life she could enjoy, with him.

An hour and twelve minutes later, Rana finished looking at the scores of paintings that had been placed and hung around the room. As she stepped into the hallway, she carried a three-foot-by-five-foot painting she loved more than the others. It showed a young boy and girl of mixed ethnicity, tucked in their beds, and Mace was sitting on a nearby chair reading to them from a large children's book. Around him was a heavenly canary yellow glow, the same kind of light that surrounded the children. Mace looked saintly, engulfed in his bright cloud.

Rana had also liked a couple of more paintings almost exactly like the one she carried, but the story readers were different. One was a black man. One was a young pretty white woman. Rana wanted to ask Mace if the paintings came from his imagination or if it was a scene that actually happened.

As Rana began to proceed carefully down the narrow hallway, she cast her eyes forward to find Mace. Before she could, something bright caught her eye from the right.

"My god," she said softly, "it's me."

Facing her was another almost full-length portrait of herself. Set again at the Blue Parrot, this time, she was wearing her favorite and most flamboyant red dress. Her outfit was not quite Roaring Twenties, but it was close. Again, Mace had every detail correct down to her red lace shoes and her sea-themed jewelry.

As she viewed Mace's incredible work of art, she began to feel the odd, unrealistic sensation that someone was standing behind her in the crowded hallway. She turned around and gasped, her heart literally skipping a beat. She was staring at a third nearly life-size portrait of herself. Immediately, this became her favorite. She and Mace were at Sunken Gardens. She was wearing a white dress that featured about four dozen watermelon quarters all bright with their green rinds, red fruit, and black seeds. Rana was petting a white parrot. Its head was lowered, and its eyes were closed. There was no doubt the parrot, Roxy, was absorbing all the kindness that Rana was attempting to give. It rested, completely still, relishing the joy of interspecies affection. Ironically, there was a sign on Roxy's cage that read: "Please do not touch Roxy. She may bite."

In the painting, Mace was watching Rana. He was filled with wonder. Rana was smiling lovingly, amid worn brown trees, and exotic and colorful shrubs and flowers. The scenery in the background was beautiful, but bird and human connecting, that was the highlight that made the painting iconic.

Mace had not yet told Rana he loved her, but his feelings were undeniably revealed through the three portraits. Rana walked briskly into the living room and woke Mace with a kiss. A single tear slid from her right eye and landed on Mace's cheek.

"How long was I out?" He yawned.

"A little over an hour."

"Are you hungry?"

"Not right now, Mace. I saw your portraits of me in the hallway. They are gorgeous. You should do portraits and sell them. You could make a fortune, darling."

He heard her last word.

"I'm afraid I wouldn't be able to put the same amount of passion into those paintings, Rana."

"Hogwash, Mace. You can do anything you put your mind to with a paintbrush. No matter what else you do in your fifth life, promise me, painting will be a big part of it."

The room was silent for a few seconds. Mace looked puzzled.

"Promise me, Mace," she said more firmly.

Mace had no idea what he was getting himself into, but he said, "I promise."

"Good, now you can show me the rest of the house."

Mace showed her the kitchen, and she could see the living room already.

"Is that what I think it is?" she asked curiously.

"If you're thinking it's an old Victrola built around 1920, you're absolutely correct."

"That's what I thought."

"The bottom part is filled with old records. So are the cabinets on either side of it. Pretty cool, isn't it!"

"It sure is, Mace."

She walked toward it. The dome was open. She looked inside. On the turntable was an old 78. The label said Vocation, and the song was "Highways Are Happy Ways."

"I love old music too, Mace, but I have never heard of this song or the label or Ray Herbeck and his music with romance."

"There are quite a few songs and labels you've probably never heard of before, Rana. Listening to them together from time to time might be fun."

"I would really enjoy that, Mace."

The next surprises were on the patio. Rana could not help but notice a huge tarp covering something.

"What's under the tarp, Mace?"

"It's my other car."

"May I see it?"

"Sure."

Mace pulled the tarp and began telling Rana about his beautiful white Cadillac Escalade. Before he could finish, Rana's attention waned, and she was now curious about what might be resting beneath any one of four much smaller tarps.

"Mace, what's under those?" She pointed.

"Take a look."

Beneath the tarps were four stacks of twenty paintings, eighty in all. Though fatigued, Rana was compelled to study each painting. There was so much pain and a little joy. There were about fifteen paintings where Mace had painted himself into the scene. Most depicted his Marine buddies and his friends in the police department. They were stories of young men in happier times, with smiles on their faces. Mace's face was neither smiling nor sad. It was neutral. Even when they were partying in the islands, in their shorts and handsome Hawaiian shirts, Mace wore the same look on his face. Rana wondered why he always looked like he was everyone's protector. She would have to find out why, soon. He rarely seemed happy.

Another hour passed, and now Rana was exhausted. She had spent over four hours looking at Mace's paintings, absorbing the wide breadth of emotions they emanated. When the couple returned to the living room, Rana walked straight to the couch and sat. She held the painting she found in his old bedroom.

"Mace, can you tell me the story of this picture? Is it real or a fantasy?"

Mace sat on the opposite end of the couch and reached his hands out to accept the painting from Rana. When he looked at it, the warmest smile she had ever seen on his face appeared.

"This was one of the most real and wonderful moments of my life, Rana. The children belonged to the man who was ultimately my best friend when I was on active duty in the marines. They were super kids. One night while visiting my friend, Johnny Paige told me that he and his wife liked to read bedtime stories to their kids. Everyone enjoyed those moments immensely. Johnny asked me if I wanted to sit and watch a couple of times. I did, and it touched my heart. When the story was finished, Johnny and his wife would kiss the kids on the forehead, tuck them in, and say, 'Good night, precious ones.' The ritual was so tender and beautiful I almost cried. I had never seen anything that loving in real life. Imagine, a big guy like me, almost crying over something so simple."

Rana imagined it and felt her love for the gentle Marine, growing as he spoke.

"Then one night at dinner, the little girl asks her parents if Uncle Mace could read to them that night. Johnny and his wife ask me if I want to do it. I said yes because I didn't want to disappoint the kids. I was scared to death. I didn't have any experience with anything like that. A few hours later, I was in my new role as a storyteller to two very tired little children. I could not believe it, but from the first sentence I read, I became overwhelmingly happy. The children interrupted me constantly, but I didn't mind at all. They were filled with questions about the story. I had to answer them, but all the answers were not in the storybook. I had to create them. From the very first make believe answer I gave them, till the last ones I gave them years later, the kids loved my comments. Over time, I became more creative. I actually liked my ad-libs quite a bit.

"When I painted those pictures a couple of years ago, I painted the halos around the kids because I saw them as angels. I painted the halo around myself because I saw myself as their protector, a guardian angel of sorts. I saw their parents the same way. You may have seen my pictures of them."

"I did, Mace. They are all beautiful and heartwarming. Now can I see the rest of the house?"

"There's only one room left, Rana, my bedroom.

She did not say a word. She merely followed him to the last room.

"Here it is," he said matter-of-factly. "Nothing much to see."

Rana disagreed, though she remained silent. Every piece of furniture was an antique. All the woods were polished. The sheets were lacey and pristine white. The room was spotless, not a painting on the floor or walls. Five pillows were propped up at the head of the bed, three in the back and two in front of those.

There was a serenity to the space, and Rana correctly but silently guessed that Mace left the visible part of the room exactly as his mother kept it.

"Mace, would you mind if I took a nap?" she asked, still holding her favorite painting.

"Not at all," he said shyly, feeling both excited and terrified. "Would you like me to make some dinner while you rest?"

"No thank you. I was hoping that you would join me."

Mace was in shock. Her request came out of nowhere. He was not prepared for it. He was gearing up for the much later night when they would sleep together, and God knows what else for the first time. He forced himself to go with the flow, though he suddenly became shaky on his feet.

"Okay. That sounds like a great idea," he said strongly, concealing the fact he felt like a sixteen-year-old boy.

"Great. When we wake up, I would like to eat dinner at the Hurricane. How does that sound to you?"

"Sounds like a good plan to me."

"Excellent. Now let me put this picture back in your bedroom, use the bathroom, then join you in a few minutes."

"Okay, Rana," he said gently, complying with everything she was suggesting. While Rana was gone, Mace took off his shoes and stretched himself out on the old bed on top of the finest mattress and box springs money could buy. Rana walked to the back bedroom and placed the painting on top of the stack from which she had removed it. Before she left the room, her curiosity piqued. Behind her was an end table with one small drawer. Rana was not a snoop, but it had been years since she had looked inside a man's drawer, and she simply wanted to peek, one quick little peek. She was not looking for anything specific. She just wanted to see what things looked like, even if it was a cluttered mess. She opened the drawer. Inside was a bountiful assortment of military ribbons and medals. She had no idea what any of them meant, but she was correct in assuming that Mace had to have done something extremely brave to have earned them. Before her were Mace's Purple Heart, Navy Cross, and both a Silver and a Bronze Star. She closed the drawer after only eight seconds. She had seen enough to be fortified as to how masculine her man was.

Rana walked back to the main bedroom, seeing Mace already comfortable. She walked to the other side of the bed, sat down, and removed her shoes. She stretched out her body and lay quietly for a moment, thinking what the right thing was to say before she spoke.

"Mace, would you like to hold hands while we nap?"

"That would be special, Rana," he said, his eyes closed.

They felt for each other's hand, found them, then grasped each other lightly. The rest of their bodies were more than a foot apart. The electricity between them was arching, and the connection between them was strong and enjoyable. Each person fell asleep, dreaming about taking their relationship to the next level. For now, they fell asleep, holding hands and nothing more.

# CHAPTER 48

Darkness engulfed the small peninsula by the time they both awoke. Rested, in good moods, still holding hands and hungry, they dressed handsomely and walked a couple of blocks to the Hurricane restaurant. People who knew him, some for most of his life, were shocked to see him there, holding hands with such a stunning woman—and she was black.

Dinner was lengthy and romantic. Rana took the lead, sending deep messages of love whenever she made eye contact. Mace could not keep up with her. Repeatedly, he would drop his eyes in boyish embarrassment. In those moments, he wondered exactly what she was trying to say to him through her exotic gazes. If this is what love looked like, it sure was powerful. He would raise his eyes again and meet hers shyly but trying to project to her the good feelings he had inside. Rana knew exactly what Mace was thinking. She knew what his fears were in relation to this moment. She was positive she could assuage those fears, and she unselfishly looked forward to the day they would become equal partners in the expression of their physical love for one another. She knew instinctively that Mace was a virgin. She also knew that Mace's development as a lover would be, in part, her sacred responsibility. She would approach it with wisdom and tenderness she had never expressed.

"Would you like to watch some TV before bed, Rana?"

"Thank you for asking, Mace, but I think I'd rather go to bed soon so we can get up early and share sort of a sports day together. But I would love if you joined me in bed."

Mace was already living a new lifestyle, and he did not want to disappoint Rana. "Honey, I will take a shower, put on my pajamas, and join you in twenty minutes, okay?"

She smiled.

Now he had twenty fleeting minutes to get his act together, to project strength and confidence where there was none. He had more fear in his heart about going to bed with Rana than he ever had about going into battle during war. He pondered how strange he was. How did he ever get to be over fifty years old and never be with a woman the right way? He remembered, in perfect detail, the day his mother sat on his back to rub lotion on his body. Her strong fingers pressed the lotion onto his back and his body into the sand. She stretched out her body to rub his arms that were extended above his head. Her firm, beautiful breasts slid back and forth on top of him. In an instant, he orgasmed without warning, feeling like a young wild stallion. How wrong he thought that it was his mother, who mistreated him most of his life, who initiated him to the wonder of orgasming with a woman. Even if it was not intercourse, it sure felt amazing. Then he remembered how Elise began moving her hips forth and back, back and forth on his buttocks. He remembered her moving slowly, then picking up speed until she began to quiver in complete ecstasy. She moaned and panted while her body quivered, not caring who heard or witnessed her behavior. Mace did not know it, but that was the first time Elise had an orgasm since Willie died, and she felt no guilt. The feelings were too delirious, taking her by surprise. She concluded that what happened between them was her right. Nature had put her son there for a reason. It was for her animalistic pleasure, and she enjoyed every instant, without regret.

When his shower was over, he dressed in his rarely worn but most expensive sleepwear. They were a pair of Derek Rose of London, pure satin, black pajamas. He bought them online for $400. Before Rana returned from her shower, Mace slid under the lacey top sheet and waited. A few minutes later, Rana entered the room like a movie star in a romantic film. She moved naturally like a welcomed zephyr on a hot Pass-a-Grille night. She was wearing a full-length ivory gown from Bergdorf Goodman. It was a bijoux lace inset silk evening dress / nightdress. Its lovely plunging neckline barely hinted at the firmness of her natural breasts. She bought it to wear for her husband because an advertisement said it was the latest in luxury fashion. She wore it for him only one time, shortly before he died.

Mace's heart beat unmercifully when he saw her. She was a vision from another dimension he dreamed about his entire life. She walked almost weightlessly, not an acting icon at all but a real-life night exquisiteness. Her feet were shoeless, pretty, and as appealing as the rest of her. She strolled to the opposite side of the bed moving lithely, with a look he recognized as love. He wondered how that unusually soul-lifting look could cause so much fright in the being of the recipient. After stretching out fully, she reached for Mace's hand and held it. For a moment, she did not move, nor did Mace, except for his heart, which was beating like the stallion he truly was. Suddenly, and with undeniable force, she began pulling him toward her. Mace did more than not resist. He utilized his free hand to scoot his Samson-like body beside hers. Then to Rana's surprise, he let go of her hand and put both of his hands on the mattress. He pushed, made a little twist, and placed his torso gently upon hers while holding himself up on his elbows slightly so she did not feel the brunt of his weight.

"Is this what you wanted, Rana?" he asked unsurely.

"Not exactly, Mace, but soon." She chuckled. "I must admit, you're a big boy, Mace. I think I am going to have to get used to you little by little in more than one way. I have some ideas that will help us move right along."

"I'm not sure exactly what that means, but it sounds good," he said as he slid to her right side. In his second courageous gesture of the last minute, he positioned his right arm across her chest, barely, but noticeably touching the underside of her breasts.

"Since you were honest with me a minute ago, I'll be honest with you now," he said, his heart thumping unceasingly. He took over a full minute to swallow hard and think how to express his third courageous act in three minutes.

"Rana, I don't know what to do in situations like this."

"That's okay, Mace. It's perfectly normal. Even older people than us, who have been married for decades, sometimes don't know what to do in these situations." Her first thought lessened his anxiety. Her second comment confused him. She saw it.

"Whatever you need to feel comfortable with me, I will help you with, Mace. And we can learn together what makes us happy."

"I may not know exactly what to expect right now, Rana, but I know one thing. Everything I share with you makes me happy."

"Thank you, Mace. That means a great deal to me. From my point of view, the start of sex begins with tenderness and patience, two qualities you have shown me you have in abundance. Each woman's body is a complex vessel. Each requires a different approach from a man. The best way to learn about a woman is to ask her. Talk with her, find out what she likes and does not like. If a woman is fair, she will ask you what you like. Then each partner should try to give their partner what they enjoy. Feel free with me to be creative with your touch. Nothing on my body is out of bounds to you, Mace. My body is yours entirely. I don't know what to expect from you, but I know that anything you share with me will be beautiful because I know you love me."

Mace did not speak, but his stallion heart slowed to a trot.

"If something doesn't work the way we would like, that's okay. There are dozens of ways we can help each other. And there is always the next time and the time after that and so on. There are limitless opportunities to improve physical intimacies between partners, Mace, and I cannot wait to start our journey tonight."

Mace remained speechless, overwhelmed with her thoughtfulness. Instead of responding verbally, he began lightly stroking her breasts, instinctively believing this was a good place to start. A moment later, Rana began to moan softly. Mace interpreted that as "Thank you for making me feel so good." He slid his hand under the fabric of her nightgown, and for the first time in his life, he began to soothingly massage the flesh of a highly appreciative woman. He continued for a couple of minutes, before taking his hand away, propping himself up, and straddling her. Rana's eyes remained closed as Mace slipped his hand under her Bergdorf Goodman and began stroking her right breast. A minute later, Rana opened her eyes. Mace caught them. Through his eyes, he sent her a sensitivity he had never experienced. Through her eyes, she projected that message of love to him in its exactness. Their gaze was rare, the kind that makes a receiver feel they are directly peering into the sender's soul, somehow seeing the other person's best self. Their gaze connected them before the pinnacle of sharing united them more deeply. Mace bent down and kissed her gently, one after another. He kissed her cheeks, her eyelids, her forehead, and her other cheek before returning his lips to hers. This time, she offered her tongue to him. The sensual gesture sent signals from his brain to the lower part of his body. He was becoming firm.

Rana continued her playfulness with her tongue, and Mace willingly shared his. It was a fun and easy game to play. Suddenly, Rana summoned a great deal of strength, flipped Mace onto his back, and straddled him. She bent down and kissed him like a butterfly wing, then backed off and began undoing his pajama top until it was gone. She began kissing his lightly haired chest like that same butterfly, familiarizing herself with his body one precious inch at a time. She marveled at the size and hardness of his muscles and wondered how much tension was locked inside them. When she was finished with his chest, she scooted down his legs, got a good grip on his pants, and with the strength of two average men, pulled them off in one forceful tug. Knowing full well how to pleasure a male, Rana began bestowing affections upon Mace that propelled him into physical rapture. He was receiving the kind of attention that most men dream of but rarely receive from a woman as sultry as Rana.

Before taking Mace to the end, Rana raised and removed her nightgown. Mace felt blessed to be viewing a Venus Di Milo with arms. She let him look at her for a moment and let him feel how close his hardness was to her softness. Without warning, she slid off Mace and onto her back.

"Your turn," she said jovially to her quiet lover.

Mace knew exactly what she wanted. It was his turn to reciprocate her thoroughly tender touches. His actions were easy to perform. He copied most of what she had bestowed on him. There was not a single spot on her muscular but sinewy body that was not a joy to peer at, touch, or kiss. When he nibbled her neck and behind her ears, the scent of musk permeated his nostrils. His mind clicked open to memories of Elise and Dr. Rafferty. He dismissed the thoughts immediately and began kissing Rana below her waist. As tenderly as a hummingbird with a human voice, she began instructing Mace on the most exquisite ways to please a woman. Mace, a pliant beginner, gave what she asked for without hesitation. After a few minutes of Mace's newest learned affection, Rana's body began to quake and quiver, as if she were having a life-threatening seizure. She gasped for breath and sounds escaped from her throat that Mace had never heard. He was worried. He paused a moment and watched her until the spasming stopped with an enormous gulp of air.

"Are you okay, Rana? I didn't hurt you, did I?"

"You didn't hurt me, Mace. On the contrary, you made me feel ecstatic."

She giggled. So did he. He felt a twinge of embarrassment, understanding now what Rana experienced. On a night filled with tenderness mingled with quick moves, Mace flipped his beauty onto her stomach. She said, "Oh," but immediately relaxed into a different form of ecstasy, as Mace began rubbing her back with the perfect amount of pressure. He did not miss a spot from the top of her shoulders to the bottom of her feet. Rana was paralyzed with pleasure beneath an avalanche of strong hand presses and kisses as delicate as a warm zephyr.

Everything Mace was doing in this sacred moment was far more than sex to him. He was entering into an extensity into which he had never delved. He was learning rapidly, how giving attention to this dynamic woman brought him to an emotional and physical high he never experienced. His passion for her grew as his emotions for her burgeoned. He wanted to thank her for her kindness, fairness, her beauty, elegance, for all the profound gifts she was giving him in this tiny bedroom near the tip of Pass-a-Grille.

He was almost dainty when he turned her over again. He wanted to see her eyes. He missed them.

When eyes met, energy traversed between them that was wholesome and revealing. Rana understood Mace's wordless conveyings. Adoration was easily readable. In the next few moments, Mace and Rana moved equally toward each other with an almost perfect blend of tenderness and passion.

Then came a joining that was as powerful and wonderful as a sunrise breaking through a long night of darkness. Once intertwined, a bond between them was sealed. It was ethereal and therefore unbreakable.

# CHAPTER 49

To say that Mace was a changed man the next morning would be a slight stretch. To say that he was a changing man would be more accurate. Unlike the unstoppable river of negativity that had raged through his mind prior to this day, a new tributary of positive thoughts splashed off and headed into its own undeniable direction. No longer did he doubt that he could satisfy a woman. Between one Florida sunset and sunrise, he had proven to himself beyond any doubt that he could more than satisfy a woman. He had satisfied the refined and exquisite woman that he loved. No longer did he doubt whether he could have a lasting relationship. As morning sunlight streamed through the slats, Mace knew he would never leave Rana and that she would never desert him. On this gorgeous morning, he wanted to combine his fifth life with Rana's fourth life.

As the tributaries crashed through new territory, he wanted to find out everything Rana wanted to do in her current incarnation. After he discovered what that was, he would deduce how much interest he had in it and how he wanted to participate. Though it was just past seven, Mace got out of bed and made himself and Rana a hearty breakfast of eggs filled with tomatoes, cheese, and freshly cut strawberries.

While he cooked, he considered multiple questions he wanted to ask Rana, questions he wanted to ask her since he painted her first portrait on his wall from memory.

Rana woke to the smell of breakfast. She had just enough time to wash her face and brush her teeth before she emerged into the small dining room between the living room and the kitchen. As Mace was beginning to serve the hot food, Rana gave him a strong hug. Mace set the food down and kissed her. He broke it off gently, led her to a chair, and helped seat her.

"Do you like to talk deeply in the morning, Rana?"

"With you, Mace, I would like to talk deeply anytime. What is on your mind, Mace?"

"My curiosity is skyrocketing, Rana. I want to know everything about you, what you think about God, people, death, your business, the people who work for you, your challenges, fears, everything. I want to be there for you. I love you, Rana."

"Are you sure, Mace?"

"I have never been surer of anything in my life."

"It's not just because of last night, is it?"

"No, Rana. It did make me want to share more with you. I don't want to waste any more time keeping my feelings to myself, especially when I care about someone. In the past, I was too shy to open things up between myself and anybody, including friends. I never shared enough of myself with anyone. It was because of my mother's meanness. It kept me bottled up. She took my voice away before I had one. But you have made me want to talk, to listen, to learn, to share. You've popped the cap off the bottle."

"You know, it works both ways, Mace. I would like to learn as much as possible about you. I think I can help you with your life voice too. I think you might benefit from some good old-fashioned moral support and day-to-day love. There is also something I thought up when I entered my fourth life. I call it my behavioral voice. What kind of activities do I want to participate in day to day?"

"Before you, Rana, I thought I would paint my life away. I would look at my collections, listen to my records, work out, look at birds, everything by myself. I did not care whether I sold any paintings. I did not care if I laughed or had fun. Before you, I was a living dud, except for my trips to the food kitchen."

"Not only did those people need you, Mace. There is a whole world of hurt out there. I do not want to waste my life, Mace. I want to give as much as I can to others, but I want to have fun living. Have you ever thought that you could combine fun things with meaningful activities, Mace?"

"I'm not sure I understand, Rana."

"My husband, Arturo, always gave a great deal of money to charities. I admired him even though I knew that some of it were for tax purposes. I knew he cared for the poor and underprivileged, but I really started to see his true feelings when we began to travel from our homes in Egypt, Italy, and Greece. I was turning forty, and Arturo said, 'How would you like to see more of the world for your fortieth birthday?' I was all in. We had worked so hard, for so long. Vacations were rare. Responsibilities were high. Even when we went to our vacation homes, we worked hard.

"Suddenly we were traveling. We were finally spending some of our fortunes. Along the way, we saw so much poverty and despair. It broke my heart. I did not handle it well at first because I was merely an observer. One early morning in India, I saw a frail and filthy family of four living in an enormous cardboard box. There was no front, so you could look right into the box and their dismal lives. There was no heat or electricity. There was a pile of dirty clothes on one side of the box and a pile of cleaner clothes on the other side. There was not much else in that box.

"It broke my heart to see it, Mace. I had my own money, and I wanted to give the family a bunch of it. Arturo always carried a great deal more money than I did. I asked him if he would do something magnanimous for the young family. He surprised me. After talking to the father for a few minutes, he decided to help the family find an apartment in a much nicer part of town. He paid for the deposit and the first month's rent. Then he drew up an agreement with a bank to draw the next five months of rent from his personal account. He also authorized the bank to give the family an allowance once a month for living expenses. He even told the bank an amount to give the family for fun activities once a month for six months.

"While I watched him pour his heart into his giving, my heart was bursting with pride for my husband. After we moved the stuff they had into the empty apartment, we asked them to take a shower and get dressed in their cleanest clothing. Their best clothes were ratty, worn, and wrinkled. Arturo drove the six of us to the nearest clothing district. He bought enough clothes to last for years. By late afternoon, Arturo had procured a job for the father on a construction site near his new residence. You can probably imagine that Arturo greased that boss's hand extremely seriously. We spent the rest of the day shopping for groceries and furniture for them. Then we said our goodbyes and disappeared from their lives forever.

"Arturo must have spent $10,000 on that family. That was the happiest day of my life to that point. I had never seen Arturo have more fun. Arturo and I and that family laughed and giggled all day after we got some food into them. We talked a great deal about that day until Arturo died. The result was that everywhere we traveled from that day forward, we would always find people to help. We never helped anybody as much as we did that first family, but we often impacted people's lives. It never ceased to be fun and heart-warming. Even in St. Pete, I've made a splash with the homeless, thanks to the soup kitchen. I know a few names down there, Mace."

"Do you mean the soup kitchen on Fourth and Fourteenth North?"

"I do."

"I love that place, Rana."

"Do you know the boss there?"

"Walk! He is a super person. He genuinely cares about his clients."

"I could not agree more."

"How do you know about the kitchen, Mace?"

"I have always had a place in my heart for the homeless, Rana. I'm not sure where those feelings came from, but I always thought that people in those situations had two strikes against them, maybe three. They were in those spots through no fault of their own in most cases. I always felt I had at least two strikes against me because of my mother's cruelty toward me when I was young. I felt there was something wrong with me that I could never figure out. I never fit in with normal people. If it had not been for my father's love, I would have probably been in jail now. My father's love was gentle, soft, mellow, and fun. My mother's cruelty was wild, powerful, like a raging river of ice. That's why I feel like I have so much in common with the homeless and poor. I feel like they have struck out, and I almost did. I know what it's like to be a displaced person. I think we have something in common, don't you?"

"Not only do we have something in common, but we also have something we can share as a tandem."

"What do you mean, Rana?"

"Since we're talking deeply, I want to ask you a couple of personal questions. Please don't take these questions wrong. I promise to explain in a moment, okay, Mace?"

"Okay, Rana," he said, feeling extremely curious.

"Mace, do you have a good pension?"

"I think so, Rana. It's a little under $60,000 a year. I can live very well on that."

"Any debt?"

"None."

"What do the rest of your finances look like?"

"I've been a lucky man, Rana. Unlike your husband's family, my recent ancestors were Illinois farmers. They worked hard and saved every penny they could. My father's memory went all the way back to his great-grandfather, who lived to be 102. When he died, he left his farm and wealth to his only child, his son, my dad's grandfather. Now my grandfather had two farms. He worked them both till he died. He left them to my grandmother. Two farms were too much for her and her only child, my father, so she sold one. She died four months later, of what people used to call 'a broken heart.' Now it's called clinical depression. When she died, she left all her inherited wealth, and the farm, to her wonderful son, Willie. Dad was a masterful carpenter and a savvy farmer.

"Willie was not only a hard worker, but he was also a rich young man. He saved as much as he could. His dad, grandpa, and great-grandpa taught him how to invest in gold and silver, in the stock market, municipal bonds, collectibles, you name it. The reason we moved to Florida was because my mother fell on the ice twice while she was carrying me. Both times, she was hurt badly. The years passed quickly, too quickly for my father. He died at forty-three while I was in the service. He left everything he owned to my mother and me equally. When Elise was killed in a car crash, I was shocked that she even had a will, much less leave everything she had to me. I thought she would give everything to an animal shelter or that crabby old monsignor confessor she liked.

"All my life, I was a saver, Rana. I have built quite a collection of coins, currency, municipal bonds, and stock shares. Since I have always loved numbers, all that was interesting and exciting. I took what I inherited, and I built on it. Honestly, Rana, I don't have a single money worry."

"Are you ready for my idea now?"

"I sure am. Don't you think I've talked enough?"

"All right, Mace, my boy, get ready for some fun." She looked like that six-year-old girl again.

Mace was percolating with anticipation while wondering if he could ever cut completely loose and share true fun and laughter with Rana.

"I don't have any worries about money either, Mace. My house in Cairo is almost a castle. My houses in Italy and Greece face the ocean. You will fall in love with each home as soon as you see it. My idea comes from the fact that you have such a good heart."

Mace shivered, knowing full well that there was another part of his heart that he would never reveal to her.

"What would you think of accompanying me to various countries and helping the underprivileged and suffering?"

Her idea was outrageous but interesting.

"What would I do, Rana, just give money to people?"

"No, Mace. You have so many talents you can share with people. Think of how many people you could influence if you carried your paints, brushes, canvasses, and some paper with you. You're strong. You know how to exercise. You can teach people how to lift weights, work out, build their confidence, be stronger, and live longer. With all your bravery, you could help people who are abused to better face their abusers when we are gone."

"What makes you think I have enough bravery for that life?"

"I think I know you, Mace. You are a good man, the strong, silent type. Your thoughts and feelings run deep. You sincerely care about people who are suffering. With me, you can expand your kindness, by helping people in a variety of ways as we travel the world. Do you know how everyone talks about their bucket list? Well, helping people on an ongoing basis is on my bucket list. I want to help fill their buckets. I think it would be special to share that with you. Can you imagine the experiences we will have, the friends we will make?"

"Won't our money run out at some point?"

"Absolutely not, Mace. We will work together to make sure that never happens. We will give modestly and smartly. In some cases, we can help people to buy what they need to make money. Because of you, I will never sell my shipping company. I make a tremendous amount of money, Mace. We will never have a problem in that area. I guarantee it. Maybe you will want to learn the shipping business. It is interesting and thrilling at times. I would love to teach you, Mace. You could learn at a slow, comfortable pace. Lots of vacations, learning while traveling, and on beaches on beautiful islands. I could sure use a man like you. Can you imagine if we could only do some of those things together? It could be quite a fulfilling life."

Mace was speechless. They had only begun talking deeply and his head was already swirling a slew of ideas for a way of life that was totally different from anything he could ever imagine. Rana saw the confused look on his face.

"I know I probably overwhelmed you, Mace. Arturo used to tell me that I tended to behave that way. I would get excited about something, and I wouldn't let it go until we followed it through all the way to whatever the end of it turned out to be."

"That's one of the qualities I like about you, Rana. I'm not used to it. I have never seen a woman with your vivaciousness and spirit before. I would be a fool not to join you on your bucket trek. You used a word I'm not used to, Rana, fun. I've always held back in that area. I've always wanted to be the toughest in a group, the strongest, not the joker or a laughing clown. With your wisdom, I believe you could teach me the concept, and then we could share it."

"I'm not so wise, am I, Mace?"

"You are the most elegant, poised, refined, sophisticated, and cultured woman I have ever known. After you told me what you would like to share with me, I am adding Mother Theresa-type generosity to my short list of your attributes. You may also be one of the greatest adventurers the world has ever known. You're not a great mountain climber or cave diver or a famous ultralight pilot. You're an adventurer because you go right to the dregs of the earth and help pull them up by their own bootstraps."

"Your compliments make me want to share those adventures even more with you, Mace. Talk about fun, can you imagine the smiles we can put on the faces of so many people we meet?"

"I can imagine all of it, Rana. The thought of it is wildly entertaining and heartwarming. Your ideas help me feel a sense of purpose the likes of which I've never had. Most of my life has been about eradicating bad guys from the earth. I have also loved to rescue people from the jaws of death. But you come along and make me feel like I can do what I love best, most of the time, and that's saving people, if not from death, from pain. Around you, I don't have to be angry and frustrated all the time, like I was before I met you."

"There are always going to be bad people who need to be taken out, Mace, but as we grow older, it might be wiser to contribute our energies to good people who have never had a break in life."

Mace's mind was deep in thought, wondering if he could pull off living Rana's proposed lifestyle day to day, year after year. Rana's mind was filled with hope that Mace would accept her proposition.

"Rana, I don't know if I could pull it off. A great part of me wants to, but another part of me thinks that your ideas are all too fantastic, unreachable dreams like Don Quixote's. Everything you speak is idealism at its highest level. Can two people really live like that for twenty or thirty years? And besides that, I'm wrestling with self-doubts as to what I can offer you on a continual basis when your goals of sharing with the destitute are so lofty."

"Mace, I can easily understand your concerns," she said, looking sadder than he had ever seen her. "But what is wrong with dreaming? Do you know what the opposite of dreaming is? Not dreaming. If you don't dream big, you flatten yourself out like a pancake. What do those kinds of people have to live for, quiet lives of desperation? Is that what you want for yourself, for me? I certainly don't want it for myself. As for what you could offer me over time, it is just yourself, the man that you have been these weeks since I have known you. You do not have to change a thing about yourself, nothing."

She was almost crying, fighting for her dream.

"Mace, I did not ask for this life. It was given to me, thrust upon me without any of my say in the matter. As I grew up, I began to see the injustices in the world and the poverty, especially in comparison to what I had acquired merely through marriage. What I chose to share with humanity after the age of forty was one of my destinies. I would like the sharing of it to be one of your destinies. You said something about ideals. Sure, I have them, and so do you, but I'll tell you, Mace, I've had to go through some harsh experiences just to be able to help some people. I have been spat on, kicked, shoved, called a bitch in five languages, and stabbed once in my own hometown of Cairo for trying to help a poor woman on the street. And it was her husband who stabbed me. You try to give a dollar to someone, and people nearby think that for some strange reason, they are entitled to two dollars. Even people with real money look at you either like you are a fool or like they want some of that free money you're passing around. Sometimes, I have been truly afraid out there trying to be kind. I would not be afraid if you were there, Mace."

"Stabbed?"

"Yes, stabbed. And it almost cost me my life."

"What happened to the guy?"

"Some of the locals saw what was going on, and they pulled him away from me. He was arrested and went to prison for a long time."

"I didn't notice the stab wound."

"It was on my back, Mace. Money paid for some good plastic surgery. Arturo made sure of that. So, you see, Mace, giving is not all fun and games. It is not always pleasurable even though it is always righteous."

"I had no idea."

"How could you, Mace?"

There was silence for the next several minutes. Then like a young innocent, Mace asked a question.

"Rana, in your concept of our future lives together, how long could we live in Pass-a-Grille?"

"Three or four months a year."

That seemed fair to Mace. He merely wanted to be able to maintain and drive Princess around town, like he had for over thirty years. Right on cue, knowing how Mace's brain worked, she surprised him with her next comment.

"If you are worried about missing Princess, we can have her shipped to Cairo, and you can drive her around town there. I can easily make all the shipping arrangements."

They both laughed, as Rana's eyes brightened.

"I was just thinking about missing Princess the instant you said that."

"I know, Mace," she said, her eyes still twinkling."

Eventually, the conversation turned to God. Mace thought he would have nothing in common with her in this area. Again, he was proven wrong. Neither of them had an ounce of dogma in them. They both believed that God was a spirit. After that, things were wide open. Rana asked Mace what he thought the second most powerful thing in the universe was after love. Mace answered, "Creativity."

"That's what I believe," she agreed. "If the universe is expanding, isn't that God's creative spirit at work? Every planet is different, every moon, every sun. I think that's why God makes everything different because he wants intelligent beings to learn about them."

Mace had never thought about God's creativity that way, but it was easy to agree with her. Mace also did not believe in hell, nor did Rana. If hell did exist, he did not believe he was going there. Though he considered himself a serial killer because he enjoyed destroying evil men, his reasoning for not going to hell was extremely plausible—at least to him. If a singular judge in an American courtroom could decide what killers would be allowed to live or be executed, so could he. He was equally as fair and as rational as any judge. Would all the judges who ever condemned someone to be executed be condemned to eternal hell? He thought not. When he was a vigilante, wasn't that simply another name for a judge but wearing a different robe? By that logic, his conscience was clear.

The more Rana spoke, the more Mace respected and loved her. She was a woman of great moral values, someone to admire. This was the highlight of the day, listening to her above all else. Both would always remember this day. Breakfast lasted an hour and a half, conversation about their deepest personal realities flowing fluidly between them. Rana spoke with complete honesty. Mace spoke guardedly, protecting the facts of his ten most recent killings. He would never speak of them, no matter how long he and Rana stayed together or how well they grew to know one another. Mace would remember the day because it was the one on which he spoke the most about himself. It was also the day on which he listened to someone's life story and deepest beliefs more than he ever had.

By the end of the sports and good home cooking day, Mace was convinced he would have no problem following Rana around doing the things she wanted to do. Each time she suggested an activity they might share one day, he liked it. Several of her ideas he thought might be fun, that word again, that his mother hated. Elise was the antithesis of Rana, who talked about creating fun in almost everything she dreamed of sharing with him.

There was another reason Mace would never forget this wonderful day. It was on this day he determined that he would never love another woman. If something happened to Rana, he would not even try to love a woman again. Instead, he would travel the States, then farther away places loving the helpless, homeless and innocent children. He was not only stuck on Rana, but on the way she thought, her deepest beliefs. He had always wanted to be a hero, not only for his country but for needy people everywhere. It was Rana whose encouragement would take him to a grander stage than St. Pete's soup kitchen. She knocked him off his self-centered, selfish ass. He would not be marching into battle against evil men, directly, but against poverty and despair. He would not be carrying an automatic weapon but bread and vegetables and clean water.

How could he know all this so soon after Rana suggested it? He believed in her and her ideas. When he believed in something, Mace Madison Stutzman approached it without reservation, the same way he did while preparing for battle as a marine or a cop or as a vigilante. Now he would prepare as a man who cared. He knew that he and Rana would not double-handedly win the war on poverty. He also knew that the two of them would win countless battles in this grossly unfair conflict.

As for learning about the shipping business, he figured, what did he have to lose? He could only gain. He had nothing invested in the business, except his love for Rana. The only problem he would have to deal with would be the strong men he would have to deal with in a male-dominated business. He did not have a problem with men, except criminals. He had dealt with thousands of strong men during his thirty-plus years as an active marine and police officer. He liked them. It was women with whom he had far less experience.

By the end of this wonderful day they were sharing, Mace was ready to share his most important thoughts with his one true love. In bed, it was the quiet ex-cop who started the conversation.

"Rana, I have some interesting news to share with you," he said with a comforting smile.

"Oh yeah, what is it?" she asked, happily playing along.

"Do you remember telling me this morning all those ideas about how we could live our lives in the future?"

"Of course," she said, still playfully.

"I know you're real excited right now because I can see a smile on your face, but I've made an important decision today that will affect our lives in ways you've probably never truly expected possible." He was setting her up for a good chuckle as the smile slipped from her face.

"What is it, Mace?" she said worriedly.

"I have concluded that all the ways you suggested we could live are adventures that I could not possibly live without. I am all in, Rana."

His woman was beaming.

That night, their lovemaking proved they were two people in new and blissful love. This time, Mace looked more at what he was touching. He focused on every part of her body, finding incredible beauty in each anatomical element. He also found a small scar to the left of her lumbar spine. A fast learner, to both his and Rana's surprise, he was able to bring his woman to idyllic physical places she had never been. The new and mutual fascination they had in each other's lovemaking would be the lock that kept them in the same bedroom till the end of life.

*****

During their remaining weeks in St. Petersburg, Mace and Rana were together all the time, talking, planning specifics, fantasizing about what countries they would travel to, what kind of people they would help. In the service, Mace would move at a moment's notice. Now the couple decided they would leave for Cairo in four weeks. That was more than enough time for Mace to organize his affairs. He was as focused and dedicated to this, as he was when he was on active duty as a Marine or for all those years as a cop. He did not have to take an oath, like he did when he became a cop or a Marine. This time, the oath was silent and remained unspoken in sacred compartments in his heart and mind. Once a commitment made its way into these chambers, it was irrevocable.

Mace's heart now belonged to Rana. Her fantasies had become his. She was easy to follow, and like a strong magnet pulling a piece of metal, she pulled him into her glorious life without resistance. The true death of Mace Stutzman's fourth life was coinciding with the birthing of his fifth life. For a man who never had much, his present happiness was immeasurable. He could not wait to start a new favorite number. It would be how many people he helped while he was with Rana. Then he laughed at himself for thinking the thought. After all, that number would probably spring into the thousands. How could he ever keep track of it? Why should he waste time even thinking about it? Why not simply go out and do for people? Why not just grow up and let loose of all those clingy numbers that were never fulfilling anyway?

Three days before leaving for their trip, Rana made arrangements for Princess to be shipped to her home in Cairo. Within a few weeks, Mace would be driving her and Rana around on new turf. He packed a couple of guns, just in case, and a variety of art supplies. Like guns, those could be bought almost anywhere.

Before Mace left Pass-a-Grille, he bought the most secure shutters he could find for his windows. He boarded up the sliding glass back door to the patio. He triple-checked his top-of-the-line security system, making sure it was functioning at maximum efficiency. Then he knew he was ready to leave for Cairo.

Mace felt lighter, physically than he had in his entire lifetime. Shedding his negativity and his focus on making the world a better place through killing were the reasons for his new sense of buoyancy. He would also be traveling light. Rana had convinced him to take only a few items with him.

"The less we travel with, the less chance for luggage loss," she told him one night over dinner. "Besides, I can't wait to take you shopping in beautiful Downtown Cairo."

Mace was more than cool with her thinking. In fact, he looked forward to shopping with her. He was not merely thinking about developing a more Egyptian flair; he was fantasizing about surprising her with clothes and jewelry in which she might express an interest.

Rana was ready to leave for Cairo a week after she moved in with Mace. Her company was clipping along nicely without her direct presence. That was the way she designed it, to run smoothly though she would be away most of the time. The hours she spent on her laptop almost every day kept her linked with her staff. Rana was certain she could share a thrilling life with Mace, without injuring her massive company.

Once, days crawled by for Mace. Since Rana's entrance into his life, the days were flying past. Filled with love, their unusual speed of passing became the norm. The fact that Mace could converse with Rana about such a multitude of topics, not only added to his sense of lightness but to the flight of days.

Departure day was ushered in by dozens of enormous lightning bolts and thunderclaps, though the sun revealed itself brilliantly. After a soft kiss upon waking, Mace and Rana behaved like two happy worker bees, flitting around the hive, getting the last-minute jobs of predeparture completed. Plastic bottles of unopened water, small snacks, and sandwiches carefully placed inside their carry-ons. Mace checked the shutters and the back door board-up. Everything looked good. The gas was off, and the electricity would be shut off later in the day. The garbage had been thrown away and the refrigerator was empty and clean.

At 9:55 a.m., the pre-ordered Bat's Taxi van arrived precisely on time. The driver exited his vehicle, walked to the open front door, and greeted Mace and Rana.

"Good morning. Can I help you with that luggage?"

"Sure," Mace answered. "There's a ton of it."

The driver smiled warmly when he saw Rana carrying two large suitcases.

"Leave those there, ma'am. I'll get them." He carried her bags to the van first. It took him two trips.

By that time, Mace had carried most of his luggage to the van and had returned to lock the three strong locks on the shuttered front door. The van driver carried the last of Mace's bags to his van while Mace took one more walk around the house, checking every detail. Things looked good. It was time to go. The last item the driver packed into the van was Mace's big black artist satchel.

The ride to TIA was quiet. Rana and Mace were already exhausted, brought on by a relatively sleepless night due to thunderstorms and restless nerves. They were thankful they could doze for about thirty minutes. They woke at the terminal when the van stopped. The driver helped the handsome couple place their luggage onto the baggage cart. Mace paid him and tipped him 40 percent. The driver was appreciative and thanked Mace profusely.

A few minutes later, Mace and Rana's bags had been checked. All they had to do was go through the personal security checkpoint, wait a while, and fly away to their next destination. They passed through the scanners successfully after removing their wearable jewelry and placing it in a small plastic container.

They moved out of the area of the scanner, then picked their carry-ons off the end of the conveyor belt. After walking a few steps from the conveyor belt, Rana asked Mace a question. "Mace, do you mind if we stop somewhere for a minute so I can put my jewelry back on?"

"Not at all, Rana. How 'bout by the wall?"

They moved out of the way of the main flow of pedestrians, feeling an odd sense of privacy against the wall. Mace finished putting his jewelry back on first, then waited for Rana to return the rest of hers to their proper places. When she finished, Mace made the strongest and most dynamic move he ever made toward his sweetheart. He took a step toward Rana, picked her up from the ground, and held her seven inches above it. When she looked down at him with wildly excited eyes, he kissed her with intense passion and bit her lovely lips lightly. When he put her down and backed away, she came to him and kissed and bit his lips harder than he had done to her.

"You are the thunder I heard last night, Rana, and the lightning that ushered in this morning's sunrise. You are the reason my fear of not living life fully is gone."

They put on their backpacks, grabbed the carry-ons, and headed for their gate. A minute later, they disappeared among the throng of travelers that were pursuing their next adventures.

# ABOUT THE AUTHOR

Jeff Lombardo, originally from Chicago, left Illinois in 1968 to attend Pepperdine College. He graduated in 1971 from what had become Pepperdine University. His BA was in theatre arts, with a minor in physical education. He graduated again in 1973 with a master's degree in education, specializing in what was then referred to as working with educable mentally retarded children. Jeff's working career spanned forty years and included acting in a variety of venues, writing educational theater, and working with all ages of children with a wide spectrum of physical and emotional problems. Jeff assures you that *The Making of Mace Stutzman* will tug at your heartstrings as well as take you through a multitude of Mace's heart-throbbing adventures.

CPSIA information can be obtained
at www.ICGtesting.com
Printed in the USA
LVHW031943110223
739160LV00001B/7